First World War
and Army of Occupation
War Diary
France, Belgium and Germany

3 DIVISION
Divisional Troops
Royal Army Medical Corps
8 Field Ambulance
5 August 1914 - 28 May 1919

WO95/1407/2

The Naval & Military Press Ltd
www.nmarchive.com
Published in association with The National Archives

Published by

The Naval & Military Press Ltd

Unit 10 Ridgewood Industrial Park,

Uckfield, East Sussex,

TN22 5QE England

Tel: +44 (0) 1825 749494

www.naval-military-press.com

www.nmarchive.com

This diary has been reprinted in facsimile from the original. Any imperfections are inevitably reproduced and the quality may fall short of modern type and cartographic standards.

© Crown Copyright
Images reproduced by permission of The National Archives, London, England, 2015.

Contents

Document type	Place/Title	Date From	Date To
Heading	WO95/1407-1		
Heading	3rd Division Medical No.8 Field Ambulance Aug-Dec 1914		
Heading	War Diary of No.8 Field Ambulance From 5th August 1914 To Volume I		
War Diary	Devonport	05/08/1914	17/08/1914
War Diary	Troisville	26/08/1914	26/08/1914
Heading	No.8 F.A Sep 14		
War Diary	Vancourtois	04/09/1914	04/09/1914
War Diary	Lesches	03/09/1914	03/09/1914
War Diary	Vancourtois	03/09/1914	04/09/1914
War Diary	Retal	05/09/1914	06/09/1914
War Diary	Hautefeville	07/09/1914	07/09/1914
War Diary	Les Corvelles	08/09/1914	08/09/1914
War Diary	Bezu	10/09/1914	10/09/1914
War Diary	Chezy	10/09/1914	10/09/1914
War Diary	Oulchy	11/09/1914	12/09/1914
War Diary	Braine	12/09/1914	13/09/1914
War Diary	Chassemey	14/09/1914	14/09/1914
War Diary	Braine	15/09/1914	28/09/1914
War Diary	Oulchy Le Chateau	01/10/1914	01/10/1914
War Diary	Troesnes	02/10/1914	02/10/1914
War Diary	Crepy En Valois	03/10/1914	03/10/1914
War Diary	Roberval	04/10/1914	04/10/1914
War Diary	St Maxence	05/10/1914	06/10/1914
Heading	No.8 F.A Oct 14		
War Diary	Hautvillier	07/10/1914	10/10/1914
War Diary	Sains Les Pernes	10/10/1914	11/10/1914
War Diary	Hinges	11/10/1914	12/10/1914
War Diary	Leslobes	12/10/1914	16/10/1914
War Diary	Le Croix Barbee	16/10/1914	18/10/1914
War Diary	T Of Baquerot	18/10/1914	22/10/1914
War Diary	Le Croix Barbee	22/10/1914	27/10/1914
War Diary	Le Croix Marmuse	27/10/1914	03/11/1914
Heading	No 8 FA Nov 14		
War Diary	Bailleul	04/11/1914	25/11/1914
Heading	No 8 F.A Dec 14		
War Diary	Bailleul	26/11/1914	02/01/1915
Heading	3rd Division Medical No.8 Field Ambulance Jan-Dec 1915		
Heading	No.8 Field Ambulance Vol I Jan-Feb 1915		
War Diary	Bailleul	03/01/1915	27/02/1915
Heading	No.8 Field Ambulance March 1915 Vol II		
War Diary	Bailleul	02/03/1915	13/03/1915
War Diary	La Clytte	13/03/1915	17/03/1915
War Diary	Bailleul	18/03/1915	24/03/1915
War Diary	Dickebush	24/03/1915	30/03/1915
War Diary	La Clytte	30/03/1915	30/03/1915
War Diary	Dickebush	30/03/1915	31/03/1915
Heading	No.8 Field Ambulance Vol III April 1915		

War Diary	Dickebush	01/04/1915	24/04/1915
War Diary	La Clytte	24/04/1915	27/04/1915
War Diary	Dickebusch	27/04/1915	27/04/1915
War Diary	La Clytte	28/04/1915	30/04/1915
Heading	3rd Division 8th Field Ambulance Vol IV May 1915		
War Diary	Dickebusch	01/05/1915	01/05/1915
War Diary	La Clytte	01/05/1915	31/05/1915
Heading	3rd Division 8th Field Ambulance Vol V June 1915		
War Diary	Farm Rene De Baene	01/06/1915	03/06/1915
War Diary	Farm Charles De Kervel L 22a.	04/06/1915	14/06/1915
War Diary	Farm De Kervel L22a.	15/06/1915	16/06/1915
War Diary	Farm Charles De Kervel L 22.a	16/05/1915	30/06/1915
Heading	3rd Division 8th Field Ambulance Vol VI		
War Diary	Farm Charles De Kervel L 21d	01/07/1915	22/07/1915
War Diary	Hoograaf G 26 (c)	23/07/1915	31/07/1915
Heading	3rd Division 8th Field Ambulance Vol VII From 01-31.8.15		
War Diary	Hoograaf G 26c	01/08/1915	31/08/1915
Heading	3rd Division 8th Field Ambulance Vol VIII Sept 15		
War Diary	Hoograf G 26c	01/09/1915	03/09/1915
War Diary	Hoograaf	03/09/1915	07/09/1915
War Diary	Hoograaf G 26c	07/09/1915	14/09/1915
War Diary	Poperinghe	15/09/1915	24/09/1915
War Diary	D Station Brandhoek	25/09/1915	25/09/1915
War Diary	Brandhoek	25/09/1915	28/09/1915
War Diary	Poperinghe	28/09/1915	30/09/1915
Heading	3rd Division 8th Field Ambulance Oct 1915 Vol IX		
War Diary	Branhoek	01/10/1915	01/10/1915
War Diary	Poperinghe	01/10/1915	22/10/1915
War Diary	Steenvoorde	23/10/1915	01/11/1915
Heading	3rd Division 8th Field Ambulance Nov Vol X		
War Diary	Steenvoorde	03/11/1915	23/11/1915
War Diary	Boeschepe	30/11/1915	30/11/1915
Heading	3rd Div No.8 Fd. Amb. Dec Vol XI		
War Diary	Boeschepe	03/12/1915	31/12/1915
Heading	3rd Division Medical No.8 Field Ambulance Jan-Dec 1916		
Heading	8 Fd. Amb Jan Vol XII		
War Diary	Boeschepe	26/01/1916	26/01/1916
Heading	No.8 Field Ambulance Feb 1916		
Heading	War Diary of No.8 Field Ambulance For Month Of February 1916		
War Diary	Boeschepe	01/02/1916	06/02/1916
War Diary	Octazeele	07/02/1916	07/02/1916
War Diary	Nordausques	07/02/1916	28/02/1916
War Diary	Boeschepe	02/02/1916	06/02/1916
War Diary	Ochtezeele	07/02/1916	07/02/1916
War Diary	Nordausques	10/02/1916	29/02/1916
Heading	3rd Div 8th Fld Ambulance March 1916		
Heading	8 Fd Amb Vol Xiv		
War Diary	Nordausques	06/03/1916	07/03/1916
War Diary	Ochtezeele	07/03/1916	08/03/1916
War Diary	Reninghelst	08/03/1916	31/03/1916
Heading	3rd Div No.8 F. Amb April 1916		
Heading	8 Fd. Amb Vol XX		
War Diary	Reninghelst	01/04/1916	03/04/1916

War Diary	Meteren	08/04/1916	22/04/1916
War Diary	Westoutre	26/04/1916	26/04/1916
Heading	3rd Division No. 8 Field Ambulance June 1916		
War Diary	West Outre	13/05/1916	27/05/1916
Heading	3rd Div No.8 F. Amb May 1916		
War Diary	Meteren	01/06/1916	18/06/1916
War Diary	Wemmars Cappel	18/06/1916	19/06/1916
War Diary	Broxelle	20/06/1916	20/06/1916
War Diary	Cormette	26/06/1916	26/06/1916
Heading	3rd Division No. 8 Field Ambulance July 1916		
War Diary	Cormette	01/07/1916	01/07/1916
War Diary	Wizernes	02/07/1916	02/07/1916
War Diary	Candas	02/07/1916	02/07/1916
War Diary	St Hilaire	03/07/1916	03/07/1916
War Diary	Flesselles	03/07/1916	04/07/1916
War Diary	Cardonette	05/07/1916	05/07/1916
War Diary	Corbie	06/07/1916	06/07/1916
War Diary	Bois Les Celestins	07/07/1916	08/07/1916
War Diary	Near Morlancourt	09/07/1916	20/07/1916
War Diary	XIII Corps Main Dressing Stn	20/07/1916	31/07/1916
Heading	War Diary of O.6. 8. Field Ambulance For The Month Of August 1916 Vol 19		
War Diary	XIIIth Corps Main Dressing Stn.	01/08/1916	19/08/1916
War Diary	Main Dressing Station	19/08/1916	23/08/1916
War Diary	Main Dressing Station XIV Corps	24/08/1916	24/08/1916
War Diary	Vacquierie	25/08/1916	25/08/1916
War Diary	Beauvoir	26/08/1916	26/08/1916
War Diary	Blangerval	27/08/1916	27/08/1916
War Diary	Huiclier	28/08/1916	28/08/1916
War Diary	Ruitz	29/08/1916	29/08/1916
War Diary	Noeux	30/08/1916	31/08/1916
Heading	War Diary of No.8 Field Ambulance From 1st Sept 16 To 30th Sept 16		
War Diary	Noeux Les Mines	01/09/1916	22/09/1916
War Diary	Allouagne	23/09/1916	23/09/1916
War Diary	Radinghem	24/09/1916	30/09/1916
Heading	No.8 F.A. 3rd Division Oct 1916		
Heading	War Diary No.8 Field Ambulance From 1/10/16 To 31/10/16 Vol 21		
War Diary	Radinghem	01/10/1916	05/10/1916
War Diary	Ambricourt	06/10/1916	07/10/1916
War Diary	St. Pol	07/10/1916	07/10/1916
War Diary	Belle Eglise	08/10/1916	08/10/1916
War Diary	Lealvillers	08/10/1916	08/10/1916
War Diary	Mailly Maillet	09/10/1916	13/10/1916
War Diary	Forceville	14/10/1916	31/10/1916
Heading	3rd Div No.8 Field Ambulance Nov 1916		
Heading	War Diary O.C 8 Field Ambulance November 1916 Vol 22		
War Diary	Forceville	04/11/1916	23/11/1916
War Diary	Vauchelles	25/11/1916	29/11/1916
Heading	War Diary of 8 Fa Ambulance From 1 Dec 16 To 31 Dec 16		
War Diary	Vauchelles	01/12/1916	31/12/1916
Heading	3rd Division Medical No.8 Field Ambulance 1917		

Type	Location/Description	From	To
Heading	3rd Division War Diary of O C No.8 Field Ambulance for Month of January 1917		
War Diary	Vauchelles	03/01/1917	07/01/1917
War Diary	Beuval	08/01/1917	09/01/1917
War Diary	Canaples	11/01/1917	12/01/1917
War Diary	St Ouen	13/01/1917	28/01/1917
War Diary	Beuval	29/01/1917	29/01/1917
War Diary	Beavoir	30/01/1917	30/01/1917
War Diary	Blangerval	31/01/1917	31/01/1917
Heading	War Diary of O.6 No.8 Field Ambulance From Febry 1st 1917 To Febry 28th 1917 Vol 25		
War Diary	Marquay	01/02/1917	08/02/1917
War Diary	Wanquetin	09/02/1917	09/02/1917
War Diary	Hauteville	12/02/1917	28/02/1917
Heading	3rd Field Ambulance No.8 Field Ambulance Mar 1917		
Heading	War Diary of O.C 8 Fd Ambulance March 1917 Vol 26		
War Diary	Hauteville	01/03/1917	31/03/1917
Heading	No.8 F.A. April 1917		
War Diary	Wanquetin	01/04/1917	11/04/1917
War Diary	Arras	11/04/1917	30/04/1917
Miscellaneous	Summary Of Medical War Diaries Of No.8 F.A. 3rd Div 6th Corps 3rd Army		
Miscellaneous	8th F.A. 3rd Div. 6th Corps 3rd Army		
Heading	War Diary of No.8 Field Ambulance From 1-5-17 To 31-5-17 Vol 28		
Miscellaneous	8th F.A. 3rd Div 6th Corps 3rd Army		
War Diary	Arras	02/05/1917	15/05/1917
War Diary	Berneville	16/05/1917	18/05/1917
War Diary	Gouy En Artois	19/05/1917	19/05/1917
War Diary	Lignereuil	20/05/1917	31/05/1917
Miscellaneous	Summary Of Medical War Diaries Of No.8 F.A 3rd Div 6th Corps 3rd Army		
Miscellaneous	8th F.A. 3rd Div 6th Corps 3rd Army		
Heading	War Diary of No.8 Field Ambulance From 1/6/17 To 1/6/17		
War Diary	Lignereuil	01/06/1917	01/06/1917
War Diary	Arras	02/06/1917	17/06/1917
War Diary	Noyelette	18/06/1917	18/06/1917
War Diary	Liencourt	20/06/1917	28/06/1917
War Diary	Beurepaire	28/06/1917	29/06/1917
War Diary	Gomiecourt	29/06/1917	30/06/1917
Heading	War Diary of No.8 Field Ambulance From 1st July 1917 To 31st July 1917 Vol 30		
War Diary	Beugny	01/07/1917	31/07/1917
Heading	War Diary of No.8 Field Ambu From 1 August-To 31 August 1917 Vol 31		
War Diary	Beugny	03/08/1917	30/08/1917
Heading	War Diary of No.8 Field Ambulance From 1.9.17 To 30.9.17 Vol 32		
War Diary	Beugny	04/09/1917	04/09/1917
War Diary	Barastre	08/09/1917	16/09/1917
War Diary	Watou	19/09/1917	19/09/1917
War Diary	Poperinghe	19/09/1917	30/09/1917
Heading	No.8 F.A. Oct 1917		
War Diary	Brandhoek	01/10/1917	02/10/1917
War Diary	Winnezeele	03/10/1917	03/10/1917

Type	Location	Start	End
War Diary	Renescure	04/10/1917	04/10/1917
War Diary	Berlencourt	05/10/1917	11/10/1917
War Diary	Bihucourt	12/10/1917	31/10/1917
Heading	No.8 F.A. Nov 1917		
War Diary	Bihucourt	04/11/1917	30/11/1917
Heading	No.8 F.A. Dec 1917		
War Diary	Behagnies	15/12/1917	31/12/1917
War Diary	Bihucourt	06/12/1917	06/12/1917
War Diary	VI Corps R.S. South	07/12/1917	14/12/1917
Heading	3rd Division Medical No.8 Field Ambulance 1918		
Heading	No.8 F.A. Jan 1918		
War Diary	Boisleux-Au-Mont	04/01/1918	31/01/1918
Heading	War Diary of No.8 Field Ambulance From 1/2/18 To 28/2/18 Vol 37		
War Diary	Boisleux Au Mont	04/02/1918	28/02/1918
Heading	No.8 F.A. Mar 1918		
War Diary	Boisleux Au Mont	01/03/1918	23/03/1918
War Diary	Near Mercatel	27/03/1918	28/03/1918
War Diary	Wailly	30/03/1918	31/03/1918
Heading	8th Field Ambulance Apr 1918		
Heading	War Diary of O.C No.8 Field Ambulance From 1st April To 30th April 1918		
War Diary	Leger	01/04/1918	01/04/1918
War Diary	Anchel	04/04/1918	04/04/1918
War Diary	Annezin	05/04/1918	10/04/1918
War Diary	W.20.b.8.8	12/04/1918	12/04/1918
War Diary	W.20.b.8.8 Bethume Combined Sheet 1/40000	14/04/1918	14/04/1918
War Diary	W.20.a	15/04/1915	15/04/1915
War Diary	Annezin	18/04/1918	22/04/1918
War Diary	L'abbaye	25/04/1918	29/04/1918
War Diary	Labeuvriere	30/04/1918	30/04/1918
Heading	No.8 Field Amb May 1918		
Heading	War Diary of O.6. 8 Field Ambu From 1/5/18 To 31/5/18		
War Diary	Bois Des Dames	01/05/1918	31/05/1918
Heading	War Diary of O.6 8 Field Ambulance June 1918		
War Diary	Bois Des Dames	02/06/1918	30/06/1918
Heading	No.8 F.a. July 1918		
Heading	War Diary of No.8 Field Ambu From 1/7/18 To 31/7/18		
War Diary	Bois Des Dames	04/07/1918	26/07/1918
Heading	War Diary of 8th Field Ambulance August 1918 Vol 43		
War Diary	Bois Des Dames	01/08/1918	07/08/1918
War Diary	Gricourt	08/08/1918	08/08/1918
War Diary	Warluzel	13/08/1918	13/08/1918
War Diary	Saulty	15/08/1918	23/08/1918
War Diary	Hamelincourt	28/08/1918	31/08/1918
Operation(al) Order(s)	3rd Division R.A.M.C. Operation Order No.111	30/08/1918	30/08/1918
Heading	No.8 Field Amb Sept 1918		
War Diary	Hamelincourt	01/09/1918	03/09/1918
War Diary	Ransart	06/09/1918	10/09/1918
War Diary	Gomiecourt	11/09/1918	16/09/1918
War Diary	Beumetz	16/09/1918	30/09/1918
Heading	No.8 F.A. Oct 1918		
War Diary	Ribecourt	01/10/1918	09/10/1918
War Diary	Beaumetz	11/10/1918	12/10/1918
War Diary	Ribecourt	15/10/1918	22/10/1918

War Diary	Solesmes	23/10/1918	31/10/1918
Heading	No.8 F.A. Nov 1918		
War Diary	Bevillers	01/11/1918	03/11/1918
War Diary	Solesmes	04/11/1918	08/11/1918
War Diary	Romeries	10/11/1918	15/11/1918
War Diary	Frasnoy	15/11/1918	18/11/1918
War Diary	Neuf Mesnil	18/11/1918	18/11/1918
War Diary	Ferriere Le Grand	20/11/1918	23/11/1918
War Diary	Bousignies	24/11/1918	24/11/1918
War Diary	Thuin	25/11/1918	25/11/1918
War Diary	Somzee	26/11/1918	26/11/1918
War Diary	Furnaux	28/11/1918	28/11/1918
War Diary	Yvoir	29/11/1918	29/11/1918
Heading	No.8 F.A. Dec 1918		
War Diary	Awagne	01/12/1918	01/12/1918
War Diary	Girbels Rath	01/12/1918	31/12/1918
Heading	No.8 F.A. Jan 1919		
War Diary	Girbels Rath	02/01/1919	30/01/1919
Heading	No.8 F.A. Feb 1919		
War Diary	Girbels Rath	03/02/1919	28/02/1919
Heading	No.8 F.A. Mar 1919		
War Diary	Girbels Rath	04/03/1919	05/03/1919
War Diary	Efferen	06/03/1919	29/03/1919
Heading	No.8 F.A. Apr 1919		
War Diary	Efferen	04/04/1919	28/05/1919
Miscellaneous	Lt. Robinson's Narrative of experiences when with No.8 Field Ambulance during the Retreat and subsequent Months		
Miscellaneous	No.8 Field Ambulance Narrative of Lt. H. Robinson, R.A.M.C.		
Miscellaneous	The Advance To The Marne, And The Battle Of The Aisne		

WO 95 14071/1

3RD DIVISION
MEDICAL

NO. 8 FIELD AMBULANCE
AUG - DEC 1914

Confidential

War Diary
of N° 6 Field Ambulance
from 5th August 1914
to
Volume I

On Pages 94
Aug 1914
5

Folio 1

Army Form C. 2118.

WAR DIARY
or
~~INTELLIGENCE SUMMARY.~~
(Erase heading not required.)

No 8 Field Ambulance

Hour, Date, Place	Summary of Events and Information	Remarks and references to Appendices
DEVENPORT 5th August 1914 4 p.m.	1st Day of Mobilization — No 8 Fd Am commenced to mobilize — Lt.Col. C.A.STONE. R.A.M.C. arrived and assumed Command and the following joined:— Major A.G. THOMPSON RAMC and 23 N.C.O. and men R.A.M.C. from No 7 Coy. Billets (1) ST DUNSTANS ABBEY SCHOOL for 10 officers (2) WOLSDON ST SCHOOL for 95 men (3) TRAVELLERS REST for 14 men (4) ST PETERS SCHOOL for 133 men These billets are in PLYMOUTH — in the vicinity of VICTORIA PARK in which the Transport of the unit is to be parked. The Accommodation and Sanitary arrangements of the billets is satisfactory. Blankets, paillasses, and barrack stores were issued.	C.A.Stone Lt Col R.A.M.C.
6th August 1914 DEVENPORT	2nd day of Mobilization 10 am opened Orderly Room at ST DUNSTANS ABBEY SCHOOL	

Folio 1

Army Form C. 2118

No 8 Field Ambulance

WAR DIARY
or
~~INTELLIGENCE SUMMARY.~~
(Erase heading not required.)

Instructions regarding War Diaries and Intelligence Summaries are contained in F.S. Regs., Part II. and the Staff Manual respectively. Title pages will be prepared in manuscript.

Hour, Date, Place	Summary of Events and Information	Remarks and references to Appendices
DEVENPORT 5th August 1914 4 p.m.	1st Day of Mobilization - No 8 F.d Am. commenced to mobilize. Lt. Col. C.A. STONE. RAMC arrived and assumed Command and the following joined :- Major A.G. THOMPSON RAMC from No 7 Coy. and 23 NCOs. and men RAMC from No 7 Coy. Billets (1) ST DUNSTANS ABBEY SCHOOL for 10 officers (2) WOLSDON ST SCHOOL for 95 men (3) TRAVELLERS REST for 14 men (4) ST PETERS SCHOOL for 133 men These billets are in PLYMOUTH - in the vicinity of VICTORIA PARK in which the transport of the unit is to be parked. The accommodation and Sanitary arrangements of the billets is satisfactory. ~~Our~~ blankets, palliasses, and barrack stores were issued	CAStone Lt Col R.A.M.C.
6th August 1914 DEVENPORT 10 am	2nd day of Mobilization opened Orderly Room at St DUNSTANS ABBEY SCHOOL	

folio 2

Army Form C. 2118

WAR DIARY
or
INTELLIGENCE SUMMARY.
(Erase heading not required.)

Instructions regarding War Diaries and Intelligence Summaries are contained in F.S. Regs., Part II. and the Staff Manual respectively. Title pages will be prepared in manuscript.

Hour, Date, Place	Summary of Events and Information	Remarks and references to Appendices
DEVONPORT 6th August 1914	The following joined the unit:— ⊞ · RAMC Reservists } 81 ✠ Infantry Reservists	CRE
	from	

7th August	3rd Day of Mobilization
	The following joined the unit:—
	10 { RAMC Reservists
	    Infantry and RGA Reservists
	    RAMC Special Reserve
		CRE

8th August 7.45 am	4th Day of Mobilization 98 prs boots 133 trousers 126 jackets (Service Suits) were drawn from the NCOs and men, being second article of clothing in their possession, and sent to the A.O.D. DEVONPORT in accordance with Telegraphic Instructions	

folio 2

Army Form C. 2118

WAR DIARY
or
~~INTELLIGENCE SUMMARY.~~
(Erase heading not required.)

Instructions regarding War Diaries and Intelligence Summaries are contained in F.S. Regs., Part II. and the Staff Manual respectively. Title pages will be prepared in manuscript.

Hour, Date, Place	Summary of Events and Information	Remarks and references to Appendices
DEVENPORT 6th August 1914	The following joined the unit :— RAMC Reservists } 81 ☓ Infantry Reservists	CRE
7th August 1914	3rd Day of Mobilization The following joined the unit:— 10 { RAMC Reservists Infantry and RGA Reservists RAMC Special Reserve	CRE
8th August 1914 7.45 am	4th Day of Mobilization 98 prs boots 133 trousers 126 jackets (service suit) withdrawn from its NCOs and Men; being second article of clothing in their possession, and all to AOD DEVENPORT in accordance with Telegraphic instructions	

Folio 3

Army Form C. 2118

WAR DIARY
or
~~INTELLIGENCE SUMMARY~~

(Erase heading not required.)

Instructions regarding War Diaries and Intelligence Summaries are contained in F.S. Regs., Part II. and the Staff Manual respectively. Title pages will be prepared in manuscript.

Hour, Date, Place	Summary of Events and Information	Remarks and references to Appendices
5th August 1914 DEVONPORT	The following joined the unit :-	C.P.S.
10 a.m.	Capt. B. CONNELL RAMC	
12 noon	Capt. W.M. DARLING RAMC Special Reserve	
7.40 p.m.	Capt. C.H. DENYER RAMC	
	5 { Inf. + RGA. RAMC Reservists / Reservists / Special Reservists	
	25 Drivers ASC	
	1 L. Corpl. ASC.	
9th August 1914	5th day of Mobilization.	
	The following joined the unit :-	
6 p.m.	Major W.H. STEELE RAMC Special Reserve	
1 p.m.	Major H.E. DALBY RAMC	" "
3.30 p.m.	Major R.L.V. FOSTER RAMC	" "
	1 Infantry Reservist	
	6 RAMC. Reservists	
	2 Buglers RAMC	
7.10 a.m.	22 RAMC from No 7 Coy	
	14 ASC drivers	

Folio 3

Army Form C. 2118.

WAR DIARY
or
INTELLIGENCE SUMMARY.

(Erase heading not required.)

Hour, Date, Place	Summary of Events and Information	Remarks and references to Appendices
5th August 1914 DEVONPORT	The following joined the unit :-	
10 am	Capt. B. CONNELL RAMC	
12 noon	Capt. W. M. DARLING RAMC Special Reserve	
7.40 pm	Capt. C. H. DENYER RAMC	C.P.S.
	5 { Inf. RAMC Reservists	
	{ Inf + RGA Reservists	
	Special Reservists	
	25 Drivers ASC	
	1 2d Corpl ASC	
9th August 1914	5th day of Mobilization.	
	The following joined the unit:-	
6 pm	Major W. H. STEELE RAMC Special Reserve	
1 pm	Major H. E. DALBY RAMC " "	
2.30 pm	Major R. L. V. FOSTER RAMC " "	
10, 11, ?	1 Infantry Reservist	
	6 RAMC Reservists	
	2 Buglers RAMC	
7.10 am	22 RAMC from No 7 Coy	
	14 ASC drivers	

Army Form C. 2118.

WAR DIARY
or
INTELLIGENCE SUMMARY.
(Erase heading not required.)

Hour, Date, Place	Summary of Events and Information	Remarks and references to Appendices
9th August 1914 DEVONPORT	Major W. H. STEELE RAMC Special Reserve medically examined and found unfit for service abroad.	WS
10th August 1914 4.30 pm 8 pm 7.30 am	6th Day of Mobilization The following joined the unit. Lieut. & Q. M. E. J. TILBURY RAMC diew J. G. GREENFIELD. Civil Surgeon Specially engaged 1 Sgt. ASC Harness, saddlery, 1 bicycle and Reft Vehicles drawn from A.O.D Store Bunward DEVONPORT	WS

folio 4

Army Form C. 2118

WAR DIARY
or
INTELLIGENCE SUMMARY.
(Erase heading not required.)

Instructions regarding War Diaries and Intelligence Summaries are contained in F.S. Regs., Part II. and the Staff Manual respectively. Title pages will be prepared in manuscript.

Hour, Date, Place	Summary of Events and Information	Remarks and references to Appendices
9th August 1914 DEVONPORT	Major W.H. STEELE RAMC Special Reserve medically examined and found unfit for service abroad.	WS
10th August 1914	6th Day of Mobilization The following joined the unit.	
4.30 pm	Lieut Q.M. E.J. TILBURY RAMC	
8 pm	Lieut J.S. GREENFIELD - Civil Surgeon Specially engaged	
	1 Sgt: ASC	WS
7.30 am	Harness, saddlery, 1 Bicycle and 24 Vehicles drawn from A.O.D Store Bull Point DEVONPORT	

folio 5

Army Form C. 2118.

WAR DIARY
or
INTELLIGENCE SUMMARY.
(Erase heading not required.)

Instructions regarding War Diaries and Intelligence Summaries are contained in F.S. Regs., Part II. and the Staff Manual respectively. Title pages will be prepared in manuscript.

Hour, Date, Place	Summary of Events and Information	Remarks and references to Appendices
DEVONPORT 11th August 1914. 12.25 a.m. 11th August 1914	7th Day of Mobilization 68 Horses arrived at DEVONPORT Passenger Railway Station – detrained in to be and led and picketed in VICTORIA PARK (West End) and watered in wooden Troughs erected near the children's Swings – then fed. Medical Equipment drawn from the Military Hospital DEVONPORT 8th day of Mobilization Shoeing of Horses commenced – as the Contract not be carried out by the ct 21 Coy A.S.C. Civil labour was utilized. Fitting of harness commenced 1 Corpl A.S.C. joined.	C.P.S.

folio 5

Army Form C. 2118.

WAR DIARY
or
INTELLIGENCE SUMMARY.
(Erase heading not required.)

Instructions regarding War Diaries and Intelligence Summaries are contained in F.S. Regs., Part II. and the Staff Manual respectively. Title pages will be prepared in manuscript.

Hour, Date, Place	Summary of Events and Information	Remarks and references to Appendices
DEVONPORT 11th August 1914 12.25 am	7th Day of Mobilization. 68 Horses arrived at DEVONPORT Passenger Railway Station - detrained in 2 hrs and led and picketted in VICTORIA PARK (West End) and watered in horselines troughs erected near the Childrens Swingin - them fed. Medical Equipment drawn from the Military Hospital DEVONPORT	
12th August 1914	8th day of Mobilization. Shoeing of Horses Commenced - as this could not be carried out by the unit 21 Coy A.S.C. Civil labour was utilized. Fitting of harness commenced. 1 Corpl A.S.C. joined.	CB

Fol 6

Army Form C. 2118.

WAR DIARY
or
INTELLIGENCE SUMMARY.
(Erase heading not required.)

Instructions regarding War Diaries and Intelligence Summaries are contained in F.S. Regs., Part II. and the Staff Manual respectively. Title pages will be prepared in manuscript.

Hour, Date, Place	Summary of Events and Information	Remarks and references to Appendices
DEVONPORT 12th August 1914	8th day of Mobilization Medical Comfort Pannier drawn Shoeing of horses, fitting of harness continued One horse injured	US.
13th August 2.15 pm 3.30 pm	9th day of Mobilization Shoeing of horses, fitting of harness continued Veterinary Inspection of horses held — all passed fit for service Marching order parade of the unit held — Inspection of horses.	CRS

Army Form C. 2118.

WAR DIARY
or
~~INTELLIGENCE SUMMARY.~~
(Erase heading not required.)

Instructions regarding War Diaries and Intelligence Summaries are contained in F. S. Regs., Part II. and the Staff Manual respectively. Title pages will be prepared in manuscript.

Hour, Date, Place	Summary of Events and Information	Remarks and references to Appendices
DEVONPORT 12th August 1914	8th day of Mobilization Medical Comfort Panniers drawn Shoeing of horses, fitting of harness continued the horses in pound	C.S.
13th August	9th day of Mobilization Shoeing of horses, fitting of harness continued	
2.15 pm	Veterinary Inspection of horses held — all passed fit for service	
3.30 pm	Marching order parade of the unit held. Inspection of officers horses.	CAF

Army Form C. 2118.

WAR DIARY
or
INTELLIGENCE SUMMARY
(Erase heading not required.)

Instructions regarding War Diaries and Intelligence Summaries are contained in F.S. Regs., Part II. and the Staff Manual respectively. Title pages will be prepared in manuscript.

Hour, Date, Place	Summary of Events and Information	Remarks and references to Appendices
DEVENPORT 14th August 1914	10th day of Mobilization	
11.30 am	Telegram sent to G.O.C. Southern Command that the mobilization of No 8 Field Ambulance is complete except for one officer under orders to replace one in guard. Strength and war horses required to proceed to War Station. No 8 Fd Amb awaiting orders to proceed to War Station	C.F.
15th August	Awaiting orders to proceed to War Station	as

Army Form C. 2118.

WAR DIARY
or
INTELLIGENCE SUMMARY.
(Erase heading not required.)

Instructions regarding War Diaries and Intelligence Summaries are contained in F. S. Regs., Part II. and the Staff Manual respectively. Title pages will be prepared in manuscript.

Hour, Date, Place	Summary of Events and Information	Remarks and references to Appendices
DEVONPORT 14th August 1914 11.30 am	10th day of Mobilization. Telegram sent to G.O.C. Southern Command that the mobilization of No 5 Field Ambulance is complete except for one officer under strength and two horse required to replace two injured. No 5 F.d Amb awaiting orders to proceed to War Station	CJF
15th August	Awaiting orders to proceed to War Station	CJF

fol 6

Army Form C. 2118.

Instructions regarding War Diaries and Intelligence
Summaries are contained in F.S. Regs., Part II.
and the Staff Manual respectively. Title pages
will be prepared in manuscript.

WAR DIARY
or
INTELLIGENCE SUMMARY.
(Erase heading not required.)

Hour, Date, Place	Summary of Events and Information	Remarks and references to Appendices
DEVENPORT 16 August 1914	Awaiting orders to proceed to War Station.	
17th August 1914	Awaiting orders to proceed to War Station.	
1 pm	Lieut H. ROBINSON. RAMC. Civil Surgeon Specially Employed joined the unit vice Major W.H. STEELE RAMC Special Reserve - posted to Tent Subdiv^n C Section	C.B.
3 pm	Chaplain to the Forces Rev. H.C. MEEKE joined the Unit and is posted to C Section	

fol 6

Army Form C. 2118.

WAR DIARY
or
INTELLIGENCE SUMMARY.
(Erase heading not required.)

Hour, Date, Place	Summary of Events and Information	Remarks and references to Appendices
DEVENPORT 16 August 1914	Awaiting orders to proceed to War Station.	W
17th August 1914	Awaiting orders to proceed to War Station	
1 pm	Lieut H. ROBINSON. RAMC. Civil Surgeon Specially Engaged joined the unit vice Major W.H. STEELE RAMC Special Reserve : posted to Tent Subsec' C section	Cpl.
3 pm	Chaplain to the Forces Rev. H.C. MEEKE joined the unit and is posted to C section	

Army Form C. 2118

July 9

WAR DIARY
or
INTELLIGENCE SUMMARY.
(Erase heading not required.)

Hour, Date, Place	Summary of Events and Information	Remarks and references to Appendices
DEVONPORT 17th August	Major W M STEELE RAMC Special Reserve is struck off the strength of the unit this day.	W
5.30 pm	Chaplain to the Forces Rev. E S F MACPHERSON joined and is taken on the strength.	
6.15 pm	Inspected the Billets - no complaints from the Caretaker except grease stains on the Seaside flooring - have arranged to have these scrubbed tomorrow morning.	
10 pm	Paid Billeting accounts by cheques obtained from OC No 7 Coy RAMC.	

Army Form C. 2118.

WAR DIARY
or
INTELLIGENCE SUMMARY.
(Erase heading not required.)

Hour, Date, Place	Summary of Events and Information	Remarks and references to Appendices
DEVONPORT 17th August	Major W R STEELE RAMC Special Reserve is struck off the strength of the unit this day	
5.30 pm	Chaplain to the Forces Rev. E S F MACPHERSON joined and is taken on the strength	
6.15 pm	Inspected the billets - no complaint from the Contingent except green stains on the flooring - have arranged to have these scrubbed tomorrow morning.	
10 pm	Paid Billeting accounts by cheques obtained from OC No 7 Coy RAMC.	

Army Form C. 2118.

WAR DIARY
or
INTELLIGENCE SUMMARY.
(Erase heading not required.)

Instructions regarding War Diaries and Intelligence Summaries are contained in F.S. Regs., Part II. and the Staff Manual respectively. Title pages will be prepared in manuscript.

Hour, Date, Place	Summary of Events and Information	Remarks and references to Appendices
TROISVILLE 26 August 1914	Nos 7 and 8 Fd Amb in billets – ADMS present – operation order No 2, by Lt Col G. JONES O.C. R.A.M.C. 3rd Div issued and explained verbally to all concerned. Nos 7 & 8 Fd Amb moved to MONTIGNY where B. Section No 6 Fd Amb. opened a dressing station in the parish church, and in 2 sheds, and in the Protestant Church, for the action of MONTIGNY in rear of the position of 3rd Bde in CAUDRY – ADENCOURT – TROUVILLE. The Bearer Subdivisions operated:– A area CAUDRY – ADENCOURT – MONTIGNY, B area between ADENCOURT and MONTIGNY C an ADENCOURT – TROISVILLE – MONTIGNY. The church rapidly received Casualties, and operations were performed in the neighbouring school. Orders received for a General Retirement – left dressing Station in charge of Major A.S. THOMPSON R.A.M.C. with personnel of the R.A.M.C. ( ) and the remainder of No 6 Fd Amb (less Ambulance Wagons with Casualties and marched via CIARY - ELINCOURT to BEAUVOIR)	OPS

Army Form C. 2118.

WAR DIARY
or
INTELLIGENCE SUMMARY.
(Erase heading not required.)

Place	Summary of Events and Information	Remarks and references to Appendices

August 14th   No 8 Field Ambulance sent 6 Ambulance wagons
12.5 am   to ST QUENTIN
              2 Officers and 32 men Sick and wounded loaded
              on a clearing Hospital Railway Train
              No 5 1st Amb. marched with 3rd Divs to HAM

Nº 8. 7 A.

Army Form C. 2118.

WAR DIARY
or
INTELLIGENCE SUMMARY.
(*Erase heading not required.*)

Hour, Date, Place	Summary of Events and Information	Remarks and references to Appendices
VANCOURTOIS 4th Sept 1914	6 am. No 8 Fd Amb. in bivouac on the hill. Place for meeting Train 5 sent up SANCY - as Train is unable to be kept intact the Cooks wagon with Sick for Evacuation was sent to the Train.	
	1 Ambulance wagon still absent -	
	10.55 am. 1 Ambulance wagon arrived with 1 Case of Shrapnel wound (not in knee joint — about a week old)	

Army Form C. 2118.

WAR DIARY
or
INTELLIGENCE SUMMARY.
(Erase heading not required.)

Instructions regarding War Diaries and Intelligence Summaries are contained in F.S. Regs., Part II. and the Staff Manual respectively. Title pages will be prepared in manuscript.

Hour, Date, Place	Summary of Events and Information	Remarks and references to Appendices
LESCHES. 3rd Sept. 1914	Nos 8, 7, +9 3rd Amb in bivouac awaiting orders – orders received to proceed to PIERRE LAVÉE – No 7, 8, +9 Fd Amb, marched via COUPVRAY – COUILLY – CRECY to the Road N of LA CHAPELLE where they halted for further orders on the arrival of a Staff Officer of HQrs Quarters Major RAWTON –	
5 p.m.	Received orders verbally to proceed to Bivouac Bleeding Areas COULOMMES – VANCOURTOIS – SANCY – 7. 8. +9 Fd Amb marched and bivouacked :– No 7 at SANCY, No 8 at VANCOURTOIS, No 9 at COULOMMES	
VANCOURTOIS 7 p.m.	No 9 Fd Ambulance bivouacked – Capt DARLING reported 2 Ambulance Wagons present and 1 absent that had been sent back to MEAUX to load a casualty – MAJOR DALBY placed on the sick list –	
9.55 p.m.	1 Ambulance Wagon arrived with 1 injured man	
VANCOURTOIS 4th Sept 1914	In bivouac during the day	
5.45 p.m.	No 9 Fd Amb marches as head of 3rd Div to LA CHAPELLE thence towards RETAL	
RETAL 5th Sept 1914 6 a.m.	No 9 Fd Amb arrived and bivouacked with its 5th Company Poles – One draught horse was left on the road unable to proceed further	

Map 66 PROVINS

4

WAR DIARY
or
INTELLIGENCE SUMMARY.
(Erase heading not required.)

Army Form C. 2118.

Place		Summary of Events and Information	Remarks and references to Appendices
Sept		Water procured in billets, and scanty - wells down peeled with Pr. Pennons. by Capt DENYER. RAMC	
	3.35 pm	Court of Inquiry held on loss of G.S. Wagon at HAM on 30th Aug. Major FOSTER President - Capt CONNELL and CAPT DENYER members - proceedings forwarded to A.D.M.S. 3rd Div.	
		Recommendation in writing sent to 8th Bde to have water for troops boiled and that as far as possible the water bottles be filled with tea.	
		Sent list of deficiencies Medical Equipment of 8th Inf. Bde and No 8 Fd Amb. to A.D.M.S. 3rd Div.	
Sept		No 8 Fd Amb. marched, and joined No 7 Fd Amb. at LA MOTTE Fm	
	3.40 am		
	9.10 am	Herded - watered horses Major DALBY. RAMC Res. taken off the sick list	
	11.15 am	Still halted	
	6 pm	Halted in a field at CREVECOEUR	
	6.45 pm	Marched in rear of Divisional Ammun. Col through FORET DE CRECY to a field ½ mile W of HAUTEFUILLE	

WAR DIARY or INTELLIGENCE SUMMARY

Army Form C. 2118.

Hour, Date, Place	Summary of Events and Information	Remarks and references to Appendices

HAUTEFEUILLE 7th Sept 1914
7.15 am

No 8 Fd Amb bivouacked in field W of HAUTEFEUILLE. Major DALBY RAMC sent with 3 Amb waggons loaded with sick and wounded, 3 officers and 9 men to transfer to M.T. at LUMIGNY and to conduct them to Railhead. — The waggons to return with 8th Bde train.

Marched to FARÉMOUTIERS where the 7th Bde were halted. No 7 Fd Am. had formed a dressing Station in the village, and had received wounded from an action in the morning.

Marched to LES CORVELLES W of CHAUFFEY. Hn 8th Inf Bde Area arrival 12.15 am 8th Sept.

LES CORVELLES 8th Sept 1 am

CAPT. CONNELL detailed to medical charge Royal Irish Regt. and gordon Highrs 8th Inf Bde. Detached Capt. DARLING RAMC to march with advance.

Received operation orders.
Ran with One Bearer Subdivision. Found same at hy Post.
Morning - 3 Amb waggons that were detached on 7th Sept. to take sick to M.T. at LUMIGNY

Army Form C. 2118.

WAR DIARY
or
INTELLIGENCE SUMMARY.
(Erase heading not required.)

Instructions regarding War Diaries and Intelligence Summaries are contained in F. S. Regs., Part II. and the Staff Manual respectively. Title pages will be prepared in manuscript.

Hour, Date, Place	Summary of Events and Information	Remarks and references to Appendices
7.30 a.m. 10-9-14 BEZU	We reluctantly handed over our 10th our charge of No 8 & 9 Ambulances & one of G.O.C. III Div Orders to cir parc	
CHEZY 10-9-14 10 p.m.	1.24 Marches 17-9 parc. 9 marched to 9 Ambulance the way to CHEZY. Found the horse had hit sore very bad. 13 horses were foin without any shoes. I see our artillery Officer & told him to somme and to some strong arms in the implements. I found some farmers there were a field and ordered two of them. There should be a farrier with every field ambulance. Corporal is a certified Smith. Give an order for the horses.	

WAR DIARY
INTELLIGENCE SUMMARY

Sept 11, 1914
OULCHY

Marched from CHEZY to OULCHY. Trail left by A.S.C. driven for six reasons to any one abounded the road and most I clear they more & lean is strain. Found a man of 7 A.M.C. the acting on what rep to an N.C.O. that have tried to a lard. Very wet day.

Left a large convoy of stock & wounded in the hope & with return for some of them here. Picked a severely wounded German officer on the line of march.

So in honoring turn to OULCHY. No killed or wounded. Till to count in a not field – 177 men complement there they had no had a clean for 10 days.

WAR DIARY
or
INTELLIGENCE SUMMARY.
(Erase heading not required.)

Army Form C. 2118.

Instructions regarding War Diaries and Intelligence Summaries are contained in F.S. Regs., Part II. and the Staff Manual respectively. Title pages will be prepared in manuscript.

Hour, Date, Place	Summary of Events and Information	Remarks and references to Appendices

Found everybody else had left. Went out saw the General + Brigade Major + Blessing Officer. Who told them were in billets. Divisional details near la Somal. Saw a steward how was busy to steamer then stole some + very very pleased that Smith with a lot of Summers who have come to live a bunker hut by troop train. Put it in under arrest. Sin for them their Toll him of the cheese an to be looked my new move to in on they would get the ground and his men took he had seen them leave to live it. So it went to see the Officer turning Officer and my men for them things of the repulsion.

Army Form C. 2118.

WAR DIARY
or
INTELLIGENCE SUMMARY.
(Erase heading not required.)

Hour, Date, Place	Summary of Events and Information	Remarks and references to Appendices
Feb 12. 1916. 5 p.m. OULCHY.	In connection with the forward area with his above Dept. at by Tanks behind in charge of Lt Stevens - And Duques started Sidecars for transport & Ordnance. We have been most. Trucks and Lorries now there. Be might have as too heavy for the horses to draw to Oulchy. Left the received Sidecars & stored truck with the Lorry there. Took on 3 civil Inspector from No 7 & 8 Ad. to circulate through the 8th Brigade.	
En of march BRAINE. 8.30 p.m.	Marched into BRAINE. Front & rear close there by motor in the Town. No Trans- engine.	

WAR DIARY
or
INTELLIGENCE SUMMARY.
(Erase heading not required.)

Army Form C. 2118.

Hour, Date, Place	Summary of Events and Information	Remarks and references to Appendices

Nov 13 & 15/14
BRAINE
	Show at moment the field ambulance to
	be thus constituted.
	A section Major G.T.K. MAURICE RAMC
	    Capt W. DARLING RAMC. D.S.O
	    Lt — ROBINSON Stan. Res.
	    Lt + Q.M. TILBURY — R.A.M.C.
	B. section Captain CONNELL RAMC
	    Capt DENYER — RAMC
	    Lt BASSETT. aud
	C. section Major FOSTER — RAMC
	    Lt GREENFIELD Can Ar
	    Lt DAVIDSON Cav Bdg	

WAR DIARY
or
INTELLIGENCE SUMMARY.
(Erase heading not required.)

Army Form C. 2118.

Hour, Date, Place	Summary of Events and Information	Remarks and references to Appendices
Sept 13 1914	Heavy firing at CHASSEMY and at VAILLY. Took my troop to cross the AISNE. Found enemy shelter half way between BRAINE & CHASSEMY. with C. Section. Pushed forward 2 Bearer sub divisions to rear of MIDDLESEX ½ mile beyond Cable Saving + 2 went forward to reconnoitre with a few stretcher bearers behind as the ½ squadron advanced. Got under my heavy rifle fire. Took cover for 3 hours. Formed a few wounded. Crept in on in a battery waggon into Alma 350 yards where Field amb. was.	

WAR DIARY
or
INTELLIGENCE SUMMARY.
(Erase heading not required.)

Army Form C. 2118.

Instructions regarding War Diaries and Intelligence Summaries are contained in F. S. Regs., Part II. and the Staff Manual respectively.   Title pages will be prepared in manuscript.

Hour, Date, Place	Summary of Events and Information	Remarks and references to Appendices
BRAINE Sept 13 1914 6.30 p.m.	When shell fire grew too heavy took to and which was tucked just N. of BRAINE. Advanced toward CHASSEMY after a conversation with General HAMILTON who assured me it was safe to go on and told me to do so. Parked under cover of a wood by the road just S. of CHASSEMY.	
CHASSEMY Sept 14 1914	Saw shell fire commenced on to the station and the road about 10 a.m. I left the wagons parked, drew the men and horses about 200 yards away. Made the men lie down under shelter of a bank and the edge of a wood. Distributed the horses as widely as possible. Men lay down holding them. Shell fire very hot all day. 7" shell and an occasional shrapnel burst all around about 4,000 ... from us. I had 2 horses slightly wounded and ...	

(9 26 6) W 257—976 100,000 4/12 H W V $\frac{79}{3298}$

Place	Summary of Events and Information	Remarks and references to Appendices
11/4	The Officer Comdg. the Regiment - C.S. slightly wounded. Men behaved really splendidly & the enemy that they began to wonder at first the troops and then whilst they pressed the N.C.O.s and 2nd Lieuts at NCOs we had Sergts. & - What amounts for not having troops here I have Cpls. to Comm. Platoons & he formed into troops N.C.O. wanted. Such a lot formed in tents N.E. I & Platoon tents opened (though the battn has no cmnd the tents though the tents are no cmnd.	
12/4	Returned to Billets – to BRAINE & the Bruce Smith Tr. Tr. Dickens Lieuts also – They have had Major FOSTER Capt CONNELL Lt ROBINSON Lt GREENFIELD	

WAR DIARY
or
INTELLIGENCE SUMMARY.
(Erase heading not required.)

Army Form C. 2118.

Hour, Date, Place	Summary of Events and Information	Remarks and references to Appendices
Sept 15, 1914. BRAINE —	Inspector LEE and oth. the forwards I could push [illegible] across the RIVER AISNE this night. Sept 14 + 15 also 2 J.K. [illegible] are very state I told the gun. of the Field Artillery back to BRAINE further in have the battery station and [illegible] evening station there to [illegible] movement.	
6:30 a.m.	I took the day at BRAINE and with the [illegible] troops at 6:30 to the C.O. DARLING went into a dressing room and the address began to hear	
8:30 a.m.	a moment. He from came down to [illegible] me home I have burner here to lodge and together to see [illegible]. May be to the other side. It will sent out that	
Sept 16, 1914. 6 J.K.	to the [illegible] of the D.E., [illegible] in [illegible] of [illegible]. Addresses began fall of [illegible] pm at 6 J.K.	

WAR DIARY
or
INTELLIGENCE SUMMARY.
(Erase heading not required.)

Army Form C. 2118.

Instructions regarding War Diaries and Intelligence Summaries are contained in F.S. Regs, Part II. and the Staff Manual respectively. Title pages will be prepared in manuscript.

Hour, Date, Place	Summary of Events and Information	Remarks and references to Appendices
July 16. 1914 BRAINE	Route march to BRAINE Pte No. 18290 Saml Peake a JC transferred and report him as still under med treatment ? S catarrh. Strength of Battn Officers up to war estt Other ranks by 16/7/17 - O ranks on 40 Sgts transf 18 Sgts & other ranks in Bn 6 & 63 ? Officers. Jas. Muir disc whilst on command - may not have held my list -	
6.30 h		
July 17 1914 BRAINE	Capt DENYER Lee & Lecture on Cath KEMPTHORNE transfd. Capt DARLING won and K ? ? & Brown Partition	

WAR DIARY
or
INTELLIGENCE SUMMARY.
(Erase heading not required.)

Army Form C. 2118.

Hour, Date, Place	Summary of Events and Information	Remarks and references to Appendices
17-5-14	Went to meet Colonel CONNELL Lt ROBINSON Lt BATTERFIELD Lt BASSETT 2nd in command Mm—— Lt DAVIDSON Lt BASSET I took in return Major FOSTER I send Major FOSTER in early this at night come back She also went out with the troops round to from VAILLY and to spread relief. Had to let two horses Mr. Todd to work.	
18-5-14 B PAINE	Lt ROBINSON went out & arms would at the river. Extended us day —	

WAR DIARY
or
INTELLIGENCE SUMMARY.
(Erase heading not required.)

Army Form C. 2118.

Hour, Date, Place	Summary of Events and Information	Remarks and references to Appendices
BRAINE. Sept 15 1914	Extremely wet day. Managed to obtain some of the supplies. Short time but I the day hurting wounded and others. All my stronger horses are now dead. Everything wanted at night as a rest. Pte. Mathewson very slight but our only steward. 3 M[…] and B Tait stalwarts answered well in the heavy rain all the morning. The ambulance wagon were hopeless. Couple broken. Lt Colonel Mac McLOUGHLIN. I was on duty. Every man was held to the very last we knew. The O which a bit annoyance. It however gotten unknown for the horses and for the wounded. I always send off and wagon as soon as it is loaded. 2nd & 3rd the have possible unknown to the motor for my men & horses and also for the tea for the wounded in 3 or 4 hours earlier than they'd be on the morning.	H.Q. … 8am O.C. 8.30am Brunes of R. DDMS 2 Letts Anxious is it to evacuate the VALLEY tonight until known heavy sniper for Ambulance. A Cutting. Brune n.y. 9am 15 pm SAS 1.45.
BRAINE. Sept 20 1914		

WAR DIARY
or
INTELLIGENCE SUMMARY.
(Erase heading not required.)

Army Form C. 2118.

Hour, Date, Place	Summary of Events and Information	Remarks and references to Appendices
BRAINE Sept 20	I crossed the river myself to VAILLY and relieved Major FOSTER with Col. CORNWELL and Lt. DAVIDSON with Capt. DARLING. Village very much knocked about by the fire. It only takes a shell or 2 down & street to be very damaging. Major FOSTER has now had most Therese and I have at his billets. No 8 & 9 sections Three horses killed to Vet. officer's visit. Horses employed 60.	
BRAINE Sept 21	Quiet day. Went by self is down to Brigade antennae Bryan took oh the horned B No 6. I went to No 9 D and returned me – Still billets at BRAINE. Put in two returns, reports & today received 4 new draughtsmen.	
BRAINE Sept 22	1st Reinforcement Today I thought I should start D to the Officer-beat - time arranged strenues recense Tired to he for chosen with me how 3 ? from 3 D Pm. No 7	
Sept 23	at 1 then 25 drevers 20 D drawghts hour retinal fun No 1.	

Army Form C. 2118.

WAR DIARY
or
INTELLIGENCE SUMMARY.
(Erase heading not required.)

Instructions regarding War Diaries and Intelligence Summaries are contained in F. S. Regs., Part II. and the Staff Manual respectively. Title pages will be prepared in manuscript.

Hour, Date, Place	Summary of Events and Information	Remarks and references to Appendices
BRAINE Sept 24 - 27th	Halted at BRAINE Std. Few casualties every day with very little.	
BRAINE Sept 28 9 a.m.	On 26th 2 drought horses recd 6 sick officers + sick J.K. killed. Today 28th one rider returned to No 7 Field Amb	
OULCHY-LE-CHATEAU Oct 1st	Left BRAISNE about 6.30am. Marched by CUIRRY HOUSE r BEUGNEUX to OULCHY-LE-CHATEAU. Arrived 3am Oct 2. wagons hidden in farm Lieuts + personnel confined to billets The machine phoned our billet.	
Oct 2	Marched at 6pm via OULCHY-LE-VILLE, CHOUY to TROESNES arrived 4am Oct 3. Lieuts ROBINSON + DAVIDSON were sent with 3 wagon loads of sick to NEUILLY Stn. wagons + men hidden as last night	
TROESNES Oct 3	Marched at 6pm via LA FERTE MILON, COYOLLES, VAUVUOIS CREPY-EN-VALOIS - arrived 4am Oct 4. wagons + personnel again hidden.	
CREPY-EN-VALOIS Oct 4	Marched at 7pm via DUVY, RULLY, to ROBERVAL	
ROBERVAL Oct 5	Marched in the afternoon of Oct 5 & 6 between at St MAXENCE. arrived at 8pm. the mens bivouac into a field until 3am	
St MAXENCE Oct 6	Sept - loaded the wagons - the ambulance wagons were an NC and party of RAMC were left behind because there was no room for the wagons on the train	

Nº 87A

Oct/4
5

Army Form C. 2118.

WAR DIARY
or
INTELLIGENCE SUMMARY.
(Erase heading not required.)

Instructions regarding War Diaries and Intelligence Summaries are contained in F.S. Regs., Part II. and the Staff Manual respectively. Title pages will be prepared in manuscript.

Hour, Date, Place	Summary of Events and Information	Remarks and references to Appendices
Oct 4th HAUTVILLIER	After we detrained at NOYELLES-SUR-MER the strength was resumed. In afternoon of 8th/9th marched to HAUTVILLIER. Major FOSTER & Lieut ROBINSON were detailed with drivers & horses to bring forward the ambulance wagons which arrived by train.	
Oct 9	Marched at 2 am via CRECY & DOMPIERRE to RAYE. At 6 am all the vehicles and horses proceeded to SAINS LES PERNES. Hy arrived 9 am Oct 10th. The horses had done 40 miles in 31 hours.	6 am
Oct 10	The bells out of RAYE and into SAINS-LES-PERNES necessitated double-teaming. At Raye I brought horse rumpled — "Rupture"	
SAINS-LES-PERNES	from RAYE the remainder of the Division marched to REGNOUVILLE and thence to near HESDIN. Motor transport joined them at there and carried them to near SAINS-LES-PERNES	
Oct 11	at 9 am marched via PERNES, FLORINGHEM, LOZINGHEM to HINGES. "C" section marched with the advance guard.	
HINGES Oct 12	Marched via LA TOMBE, WILLOT to LESLOBES "C" section established a dressing station at VIELLE CHAPELLE Reported at 14 h. 2. III Div at ZELOBES and saw General HAMILTON who ordered me to take a section forth by a horsed wheeled convey to VIELLE CHAPELLE. The dressing station	
LESLOBES — Oct 13	away to VIELLE CHAPELLE was evacuated by ammunition Night of our surgeons.	

WAR DIARY
or
INTELLIGENCE SUMMARY.
(Erase heading not required.)

Army Form C. 2118.

Hour, Date, Place	Summary of Events and Information	Remarks and references to Appendices
LES LOBES Oct 13	"B" section relieved "C" section in VIELLE CHAPELLE	
Oct 14	General HAMILTON killed. — went to fenerine.	
Oct 15	"C" section relieved "B" section at VIELLE CHAPELLE	
Oct 16 LE CROIX BARBEÉ	On 17 received 1 draught horse. Moved to LE CROIX BARBEÉ.	
Oct 18 "T" of BAQUEROT	Moved to "T" of BAQUEROT about 1½ miles E. N. of LA CROIX ROUGE. Reported to General DORAN in AUBERS — one draught horse shot by rifle near "B" section went to AUBERS. They formed an advanced dressing station at LE PLOUCK. Received two draught horses	
Oct 19		
Oct 20	LE PLOUCK was reported to be under plus fire. I went with 3 wagons and evacuated the wounded there. One draught horse abruptly returned. Royal IRISH returned to the Batty and at	
Oct 21		
Oct 22 LE CROIX BARBEÉ Oct 23	Ordered to move to CROIX BARBEÉ. Dressing station drawn in during night. Ordered to move to FOSSE. A dressing station was formed at BOUT DEVILLE with an advanced party at FLINQUÉ	

Army Form C. 2118.

WAR DIARY
or
INTELLIGENCE SUMMARY.
(Erase heading not required.)

Hour, Date, Place	Summary of Events and Information	Remarks and references to Appendices
Oct 24-25	During the night the Gordons were driven from their trenches and our Bearers retired behind them.	
Oct 27	A French regiment of dismounted cavalry advanced our lines. I commenced with A.D. of M.S. We were ordered to LE CROIX MARMUSE	
LE CROIX MARMUSE Oct 28, 29, 30	The dressing stations remain as before	
Oct 31	Lieut BAZETT and I went to NEUVE CHAPELLE to order by the General Thinning D.D. of M.S. A report of our efforts was asked for by, and sent to, the G.O.C. III DIV.	LAHORE DIV.
Nov 1	The 8 Languages to today attacked to the Lauffenfeld. Driver SHERYER med - inhumation - Lauffenfeld.	
Nov 2	Lieut ROBINSON was pulled out of the dressing station near FLINQUE. Driver GILLING galloped in well. The news on an artillery horse. He had lost his horses. He and another driver Lieut BAZETT and I went drag to investigate. VAUGHAN went out to investigate. A pair of horses was sent out to bring in the abandoned wagon. What he damaged by shell fire	Attendant
Nov 3	The horses lost yesterday were found by the advanced dressing station party. They were but slightly wounded	

Nº 87A

Army Form C. 2118.

WAR DIARY
or
INTELLIGENCE SUMMARY.
(Erase heading not required.)

Instructions regarding War Diaries and Intelligence Summaries are contained in F.S. Regs., Part II. and the Staff Manual respectively. Title pages will be prepared in manuscript.

Hour, Date, Place	Summary of Events and Information	Remarks and references to Appendices
Nov 4	Ordered to concentrate field ambulance and await orders. One transport lorry and 1 motor received and 1 man + 2 weapons + 2 dinghys received.	
Nov 8	9th I thought thought Informed by the LAHORE DIV. that we are no longer attached to them.	BOWES
Nov 9	I went and reported to General Bowes. There are 67 horses on strength today.	
Nov 15	Shell exploded here. Beechin today sent out to relieve Indian dressing station and others back at night. One NCO and 18 other ranks joined from base.	+ BOUT DEVILLE
Nov 16 BAILLEUL	Marched to BAILLEUL via MERVILLE. Beechin was sent out to NEUF EGLISE at night to relieve 2 cavalry field ambulance. A draft of 25 men joined from base.	
Nov 18	Rev. Macpherson left unit.	
Nov 19	C Section relieves Beechin.	
Nov 20	Colonel Matheson here + proceeds to Headquarters.	
Nov 21	One N.C.O. posted to III Supply column. Two NCO's transferred pick to base. One horse shot last night because of injury to off hind.	
Nov 22		
Nov 23	Beechin relieves C section.	
Nov 25	Rev H Marshall joined unit. A heavy draught horse fell, broke its leg, and was shot. Three officers depart on leave.	

Nº 8 A.

WAR DIARY
or
INTELLIGENCE SUMMARY.
(Erase heading not required.)

Army Form C. 2118.

Instructions regarding War Diaries and Intelligence Summaries are contained in F. S. Regs., Part II. and the Staff Manual respectively. Title pages will be prepared in manuscript.

Hour, Date, Place	Summary of Events and Information	Remarks and references to Appendices
(BAILLEUL)		
Nov 26	Received 1 ordered (filled) 1 received plow cart, 4 lightdraught horses and 2 drivers A.S.C.	
Nov 28	Bovison is released by XV Field Ambulance and reforms headquarters. A section forms an advanced dressing station at LOCRE	
Dec 3	Three officers return from leave	
Dec 4	Two officers go on leave	
Dec 7	A section composed - All sections now together	
Dec 9	One NCO and 2 men (R.A.M.C.) released (1 NCO and 2 men (RAMC) from the Godowa	
Dec 10	Two officers return from leave. Lieut Steward joined the Godowa	
Dec 13	Capt Connell returns. Capt E.H Denyer goes on	
Dec 16	Lieut J.M. Maurice arrives duty with 40th Brigade R.F.A. Lieut Greenfield goes to Honourable Artillery Company.	
Dec 14	Received one fallen white cart, 2 draught horses and one A.S.C driver.	
Dec 18	Major Rawden forms. Lieut Robinson with A section leaves goes to LOCRE	

Army Form C. 2118.

WAR DIARY
or
INTELLIGENCE SUMMARY.
(Erase heading not required.)

Instructions regarding War Diaries and Intelligence Summaries are contained in F.S. Regs., Part II. and the Staff Manual respectively. Title pages will be prepared in manuscript.

Hour, Date, Place	Summary of Events and Information	Remarks and references to Appendices
BAILLEUL		
Dec 19	Major Forber left and for HAVRE - as presiding officer Corporal Richard, French interpreter joined unit.	
Dec 20	Capt E.P. Edwards arrived from No 4 Section. Lieut Maurice went to 23rd Brigade R.F.A. Two officers go on leave and one N.C.O	
	A draft of 113 men arrive from Base.	
Dec 25	Rev Father O'Shay Lynessy arrives and one NCO	
Dec 28	Two officers return from leave and two officers go on leave. Lieut Maurice got from 23 Brigade RFA to 40th Brigade R.F.A. Lieut Heaton goes to Forget Scot on temporary duty. Major Lawder attached to 9th isolation Hospital in BAILLEUL. Lieut Maurice on leave.	
Dec 29	Lieut Steward proceeds on leave Lieut Maurice reports from 40 Brigade R.F.A.	
Dec 30	Lieut Maurice and fever pulverisers of Bacher go to LOCRE in relief of A section Lewis.	
1915 Jan 1		
Jan 2	A section and B sent pulverisers go to WESTOUTRE in relief of No 9 Field Ambulance. Lieut pulverisers of A section from a dressing station at WESTOUTRE	

3RD DIVISION
MEDICAL

NO. 8 FIELD AMBULANCE
JAN-DEC 1915

No. 8 Field Ambulance

Vol I.

Army Form C. 2118.

WAR DIARY
or
INTELLIGENCE SUMMARY.
(Erase heading not required.)

BAILLEUL

Hour, Date, Place	Summary of Events and Information	Remarks and references to Appendices
Jan 3	Two officers return from leave. One officer & B bearers return from LOCRE. Three officers Lieut Weston reports from leave.	
	Go to WESTOUTRE	
	2 me Royce sick. The officers return from leave	
Jan 5	A section tent subdivision form a dressing station at ST JANS CAPPEL	Capt Hore to BAILLEUL and retires
Jan 6	Reconnoiter St end at WESTOUTRE proceed to LOCRE. Draft of 6 A.S.C. drivers arrive from base. One driver transferred to base park.	
Jan 11	B section at LOCRE relieved by C section	
Jan 13	Fourteen men of R.A.M.C transferred to base park.	
Jan 20	Lieut Bazett took over temporary medical charge of all H.A.C at Locre. Lieut Wrangel Kerr dead.	
Jan 25	Fewer subdivision of B section and bearers of C section relieve C section at LOCRE	
Jan 26	A section transferred to base-park	
Jan 28	One man R.A.M.C transferred to base-park	
Feb 2	Twenty one details R.A.M.C arrived from HAVRE Lieut Robinson takes temporary medical charge of 48th Battery R.G.A	

Army Form C. 2118.

WAR DIARY
or
INTELLIGENCE SUMMARY.
(Erase heading not required.)

Instructions regarding War Diaries and Intelligence Summaries are contained in F. S. Regs., Part II. and the Staff Manual respectively. Title pages will be prepared in manuscript.

Hour, Date, Place	Summary of Events and Information	Remarks and references to Appendices
BAILLEUL		
Feb 2	5822 Pte Taylor RAMC admitted to hospital suffering from trench fever.	
Feb 3	One horse strangled transferred to BETHUNE sick marge. S/Sgt Coffey promoted 2nd Sergt. Acting Single Cpl Pitman promoted Single Corporal Gerard promoted Sergt. Acting Cpl Clerk been promoted corporal.	
Feb 5	Heavy reinforcements of A+B sections report headquarters from LOCRE	
Feb 6	Forty nine Heavy draft units to ST OMER	
Feb 8	Forty four sick at ST OMER handed over to Vet officer	
Feb 10	One heavy draught horse transferred to unit for work. Temporarily Lieut H Robinson reports from temporary duty with R.G.A. Six men transferred to unit.	
Feb 11	Two men transferred pub to casualty clearing station	
Feb 12	Temp Lieut H Robinson proceeded to HAVRE for duty.	
Feb 14	Lieut Trigwell reports from temporary duty with C.H.A.C.	
Feb 15	Two riders, two bridle draught and one heavy draught re- III Div. Two riders, two ammunition coleman, coal from ammunition temporary duty with 1st W. Ries.	
Feb 17	Lieut Weston takes over temporary duty with the very reported for duty from XIV General	
Feb 19	One NCO posted to HAVRE for duty	
Feb 20	One army proceeded to BOULOGNE for duty	
Feb 21	One NCO proceeded to ST OMER for duty and Rehsevas. NCO reported for duty from HAVRE	

Army Form C. 2118.

WAR DIARY
or
INTELLIGENCE SUMMARY.
(Erase heading not required.)

Hour, Date, Place	Summary of Events and Information	Remarks and references to Appendices
BAILLEUL		
Feb 22	O.C. proceeded to England on leave of absence.	
Feb 23	Lieut May notified that he is to proceed. Lieut + 2 Tucker	
Feb 24	went the return for ALDERSHOT	
Feb 25	Lieut Maguire proceeds on leave to England	
Feb 26	Capt Edwards takes temporary medical charge of 4/2nd Brigade R.F.A. Major Saunders takes command of 8 L/Field ambulance temporarily & Represent charge goes from Filhet to do leave in England. Lieut Greenfield proceeds on leave to England. Regl.	M.D.
Feb 27	Smith and others 21 S Field ambulance and other to follow. Lieut 7/2 M Elbury proceeds to England on leave.	

29

Co. 8. Field Ambulance

Vol II

WAR DIARY
or
INTELLIGENCE SUMMARY.
(Erase heading not required.)

Army Form C. 2118.

Instructions regarding War Diaries and Intelligence Summaries are contained in F.S. Regs., Part II. and the Staff Manual respectively. Title pages will be prepared in manuscript.

Hour, Date, Place	Summary of Events and Information	Remarks and references to Appendices
BAILLEUL		
March 2	O.C. returns from leave.	W Wheeler Rifleman
March 4	Lieut Maurice returns from leave.	WW. Glass Ambulance
March 5	Lieut Greenfield returns from leave. Serj't Mays would join for duty from No 9 Field Ambulance.	WW
March 6	Lieut & Q.M. Tillberg returns from leave.	WW
March 9	Lieut Weedon reports from temporary duty with E. Kent. Col. Maurice O.C. No 8 Field Ambulance admitted to hospital and further of Capt Allen.	WW
March 10	At 11.30 A.M. received wire from D.M.S. 2nd Corps. "Lieut Col. Huddlestone will temporarily assume command of No 8 Field ambulance." A.D.M.S. arrived noon conferring wire. Lent me car to proceed to BAILLEUL arrived BAILLEUL 2 p.m. Ordered checking of medical equipment by persons. All deficiencies to be re-ported to 2. M. by morning. Proceeded with Capt Edwards & Capt Darling to LA CLYTE to find out site of proposed dressing station & required. Saw Maj. FIELDING at LOCRE on return journey. The removal of ambulance wagons and extra horses if necessary.	WW

WAR DIARY
or
INTELLIGENCE SUMMARY.
(Erase heading not required.)

Army Form C. 2118.

Hour, Date, Place	Summary of Events and Information	Remarks and references to Appendices

BAILLEUL
March 10 (cont)
	Ascertained location of unit as follows
	Personnel at Dressing Station, St JANS CAPPEL
	    LT. GREENFIELD
	    TENT SUB. DIV. A. Section
	    1 AMB. WAGON
	
	Personnel at LOCRE
	    LT. MAURICE
	    CPL. JIPSON
	    5 AMB. WAGONS with drivers + orderlies
	    10 pairs H.D. horses with 5 drivers for the
	    spare H.D. horses
	
	Personnel at BAILLEUL.
	    CAPTs. EDWARDS + DARLING
	    LTs. BAZETT, WESTON, STEWART
	    LT. Y Q.M. TILBURY
	    BEARER SUB. DIVS. A.B.C.
	    TENT SUB. DIVS. B + C less 3 nursing orderlies
	    B Section
	Personnel at ISOLATION HOSPITAL
	    BAILLEUL
	    MAJOR LAUDER 8 bearers of B section
	    3 nursing orderlies B.
		W Wheeler
		Lt Colonel

Army Form C. 2118.

WAR DIARY
or
INTELLIGENCE SUMMARY.
(Erase heading not required.)

Hour, Date, Place	Summary of Events and Information	Remarks and references to Appendices

BAILLEUL
10 March (Cont)
	Location of wagons
	
	           BAILLEUL LOBRE ST JANS CAPPEL
	Amb. wagons 4 5 1
	G.S. wagon 7 1 1
	Forage cart 3 1 1
	Water cart 3 1 1
	
	Horses with unit
	  L.D. 16
	  H.D. 34 } In good condition
	RIDERS 18
	
	Officers posted to sections as follows
	  A section LT.COL. HUDLESTON
	                    LT. WESTON
	  B section CAPT. EDWARDS
	                    LT. BAZETT
	                    LT. MAURICE
	  C section CAPT. DARLING
	                    LT. GREENFIELD
	                    LT. STEWART
		M. Hudleston
		Lt. Col.
		R.a.m.c.

Army Form C. 2118.

WAR DIARY
or
INTELLIGENCE SUMMARY.
(Erase heading not required.)

Hour, Date, Place	Summary of Events and Information	Remarks and references to Appendices
BAILLEUL 11 March	Deficiency tent in Medical equipment allotted by 2nd in and some of deficiencies drawn at once from M.O.'s Medical place A.D. DEPOT. Remainder of Ordnance equipment indents for various articles of ordnance equipment deficient. Infact account inspected therein details not understood. Letter to Lt Col MAURICE from Capt DARLING A.D.M.S. arrived and ordered our section to be held in readiness to move our photo lorries. Bmston delivered and equipment packed and increases by such articles as blankets + stretchers We received 8 am. "Be with your party at LA CLYTTE at 7.30 am tomorrow, acknowledge. From ADMS 3rd DIV." B section ordered to parade at 4.30 am. The following additions to tentment + equipment LT WESTON added. LT STEWART relieved LT MAURICE 1 Amb. wagon of A section 25 Extra blankets 18 stretchers	W Mulholm Lt Col RAMC

WAR DIARY or INTELLIGENCE SUMMARY

Army Form C. 2118.

Hour, Date, Place	Summary of Events and Information	Remarks and references to Appendices
BAILLEUL 11 March (Cont)	9 pm. Having the day drawn Francs 6000 I pay for all men of B section freed in Bailleul paid out.	M. Malcolm Lt Col RAMC
12 March	Accompanied Party above noted - Marched for LA CLYTTE 4.30 a.m. - Arrived 9 a.m. Found the place cleared for us - also a promise of the back house for extra accommodation if required - and billets for men and house opposite school for officers. Received every assistance from staff of 8th Brigade and interviewed aid advanced Pala who would at arrangements made by Capt EDWARDS.	M St
	10 am ADMS & DADMS inspected. Report to be handed to A.D.M.S. when 20 casualties have been received. Line motor ambulance under Lt FRIAR placed at my disposal. Cases to be transferred rapidly to C.C.S. BAILLEUL. Dressing station have fully equipped & ready. Back house to be equipped if necessary tomorrow morning.	
	7.30 p.m. A.D.M.S. wire "Rates of pay required and motor ambulances to No 7 F.Amb. Have returned to 8.15 pm NOIR Bazett & Weston started to collect wounded	

WAR DIARY
or
INTELLIGENCE SUMMARY.
(Erase heading not required.)

Army Form C. 2118.

Hour, Date, Place	Summary of Events and Information	Remarks and references to Appendices
BAILLEUL 13 March	12.5 a.m. First field of sick & wounded arrived. Following were received "2 or 3 Field Amb. Attend 40 stretcher cases collected at wood 1 mile NE of SCOTCH HOUSE: Stretcher & bearers deficient. Cannot execute any further." from M.O., WILTS, WORCESTERS & SURREYS. No reference to map given SCOTCH HOUSE not marked in Belgium sheet 26 – 1:40000. All bearers lorries sent out and sent in 5 motor ambulances under command of Lt BAZETT to Hd Qrs KEMMEL to ascertain location and evacuate. Extra stretchers carried. Lt WESTON follow with 3 AMB wagons, and will receive a message from Lt BAZETT as to where to proceed on reaching KEMMEL. Wounded collected in forced transport & trans to KEMMEL by the means only, were the wounded collected by dawn. The wounded collected – 1 officer & 58 other ranks. First convoyment of wounded were left at 9.30 a.m. for C.C.S. – Second at 12.30 p.m.	W Audleyson L/Col Baur

WAR DIARY or **INTELLIGENCE SUMMARY.**
(Erase heading not required.)

Army Form C. 2118.

Hour, Date, Place	Summary of Events and Information	Remarks and references to Appendices
LA CLYTTE 13 March (Cont)	A.D.M.S. instructed 12·30 pm and gave following orders. 1 Dressing station in the field to be maintained and went for treatment of all sick R.O. 8 Brigade. Arrangements to be made for treating cases up to 3 days, with a view to checking wastage. 2 ST JANS CAPELLE to remain as before 3 A detachment to be billeted in tenements to open at WESTOUTRE in place of detachment of 7 no 9 F.Amb A.D.M.S. again inspected new A.Q.M.C. 2 3rd Divn to decide whether School Building already standing be retained as dressing station. Matter of providing hut accommodation for Laundry and drying room to be put to G.O.C. 69rd Divn this evening. Proceeded to BAILLEUL via LOCRE. Ordered D. MAURICE to return to BAILLEUL with light ambulance wagon and 10 hrs horses. He will have charge of all transport Horses at BAILLEUL	W. Shapter Lt/Col RAMC W.S.A
14 March	Following arrangements to return. Daily that A/did towounded for LACLYTTE to be sent over to ficial BAILLEUL by 11·30am. This awaits attg to the place for STJANS CAPELLE the ambulance whole well be said to ADMS Notification of transfers to O.C. Stations to reach BAILLEUL	

WAR DIARY
or
INTELLIGENCE SUMMARY.
(Erase heading not required.)

Army Form C. 2118.

Hour, Date, Place	Summary of Events and Information	Remarks and references to Appendices

LA CLYTTE
14 March (cont)
	Left 11.30 am daily and to be distributed by cycle orderly at Div H.Qrs as before.
	Capt DARLING to detrain detachment from G Rection to proceed to WESTOUTRE if ordered. Lt GREENFIELD ordered to proceed to WESTOUTRE and ascertain the duties & report
	Lt. TILBURY to meet for following articles of use at dress -ing station at LA CLYTTE
	  Shifting frame 30 large 10 x 11
	  smaller pairs 50
	  Pyjama suits 30
	  Plates 3 doz
	  Knives, forks, spoons 30 each
	  Cups & Saucers 3
	  Tumblers 3 doz
	  Towels Bath 50
	    " hand 50
	  Drawers 50
	Three ambulance wagons sent out to collect at 8.30 pm as there has been a considerable attack on our left in the region of ST ELOI
		McCullock S/Sgt
		Driver.

WAR DIARY
or
INTELLIGENCE SUMMARY.
(Erase heading not required.)

Army Form C. 2118.

Hour, Date, Place	Summary of Events and Information	Remarks and references to Appendices
LA CLYTTE 14th March	Reports in Dressing Station at WESTOUTRE received. Party detailed from R. Section to proceed to westward of present to WESTOUTRE at short notice. Three motor ambulance wagons arrived and lay at 10 AM at this Dressing Station for evacuation of sick & wounded.	McCulloch W.S.H.
15th March	Report called for on mobility of transport of unit with explanation of any - Report rendered that following - war deficiency of 4 horses H.D. (3) Ambulance wagon partially unserviceable being stored on 1 tent subdivision, also deficiencies: extra ? to S.I. Westgarten infantry required. (3) Liability to carry the extra equipment authorized under Contingent Order No 19 dated 22 Feb. inspected depot with lorry K. to tender for the purpose. (a) Suggested substitution of G.S.W. motor ambulance wagon for two of the horsed wagons (b) Suggested that the 3 spare F.O. horses allowed by War Estab. be replaced by 3 MD's. The two MS now Dressing Station and escorts to bikes at WESTOUTRE to have inspection the Brigades ... to obtain still further accommodation as to exit of wounded as the number of troops in this Bde area had now increased.	W.S.H
16th March		W.S.H
17th March	Returned to my HQ Drs at BAILLEUL.	W.S.H

Army Form C. 2118.

WAR DIARY
or
INTELLIGENCE SUMMARY.
(Erase heading not required.)

Instructions regarding War Diaries and Intelligence Summaries are contained in F.S. Regs., Part II. and the Staff Manual respectively. Title pages will be prepared in manuscript.

Hour, Date, Place	Summary of Events and Information	Remarks and references to Appendices
BAILLEUL. 18 March	Inspected dressing Station at ST JANS CAPEL, found all correct.	RE Nedlich Lt/Col Rawle
19 March	Orderd "GREENFIELD" to have Motor telegram prepared for personnel return to command.	MSH
	Return to command. Left Hosp. during Stines duty for hours. Inspected isolation Hosp. where Major LAUDER kept breeches, rifles and equipt in disinfecting house, orderd these disposed of to Ordnance.	
20 March	Received 4 HD under LD here.	MSH
	This morning about 11.30 am went to aerodrome of No MALCOLM RFA attached. No 5 Squadron RFA who fell in a monoplane in a firm plans whilst took him away in a motor wagon, bearers in route to hospital by Capt RITCHIE Rawle. Inspected out Rawle men of the Field Ambulance now in BAILLEUL.	MSH
22 March 10.30 am	Met ADMS 3rd Division at LA CLYTTE this morning by appointment. Orderd to proceed on 11 March with the Field Ambulance less "B" Section and detachments to ST JAN CAPEL and Jedalin Hop. to DICKEBUSH 83rd FAMB. Our bearer to collect on being a dressing Station, reliving 83rd FAMB. Our bearer to collect on night 24/25. "B" Section to remain at LA CLYTTE and other detachments to stand fast till relieved.	MSH
23 March	Late to DICKEBUSH with Lt WESTON and went round with Lt Col EDGAR to see all medical sanitary and billeting arrangements. Billetting certificates in accordance with Local and Rendezv Orders made out and signed by Local Civil Authority. One copy left with Local authority and one sent to Dep. Base of Re quartering office at Rouen.	MSH
24 March	Field Amb marched as follows to DICKEBUSH. Advance party - 1 NCO 1 Omen each from A.B.C Sections with cart & motor wagon marched at 7 am to Report HQ to Capt F. WESTON at LA CLYTTE who will take them on.	

Army Form C. 2118.

WAR DIARY
or
INTELLIGENCE SUMMARY.
(Erase heading not required.)

Hour, Date, Place	Summary of Events and Information	Remarks and references to Appendices
BAILLEUL 24.3.15	Tpr Grey mounted at 10 AM. Turned back by RAMC Officer who informed me that 13 F Amb had orders to stand fast. Returned to LA CLYTTE and was A.D.M.S.'s instructions.	W.E. Malcolm Halleure
12.30 PM	Saw ADMS and was instructed to proceed now to DICKEBUSCH. Arrived and took over from 83rd F.A.M.B. - Column marched in two sections. Skilled in the area between LA CLYTTE & DICKEBUSCH in ambulance waggons.	
DICKEBUSCH 3 PM	The whole town is liable to be shelled at any time. The Dressing Station and Convent House, School buildings and wooden huts close to the Church. The top of the Church tower has been destroyed by Shell fire. "C" Section under Capt DARLING opened, and took over the following: 1 Officer 1st Canadian Rifles dead, 1 man of the same Regiment wounded on admission (kidney injury), 1 man 1st East Kents ? Sunstroke. 16 men H.Q. who sick and on the Major in Yesterday. Took over billets lately occupied by 83 F Amb Tours the Captain of the yeoman about ½ mile West of the town. At this Farm the out- buildings & Barn has commenced to be used into a visit to Jacqueminet. The whole Farm and the scavenowaies on account of the liability of the present-building to shell fire.	
5 PM.	The A.D.M.S. having orders me to his Sanitary Officer. I had a look round part of the Town and find that the back latrine system have from in large for water interested on the street level - These foully have all been withdrawn by the outgoing Division. Wired to A.D.M.S. These throne and boxes are wanted in that Town these. The outgoing troops have been using latrine buckets buckets in general. Sent Cpl L. & orwait to product about sent to reports.	

WAR DIARY
or
INTELLIGENCE SUMMARY.
(Erase heading not required.)

Army Form C. 2118.

Hour, Date, Place	Summary of Events and Information	Remarks and references to Appendices
DICKEBUSH 7.30 PM 24.3.15	Reply from ADMS. Latrine trenches must be dug pending the move of Division.	W.E. Skellington Lt/Col Comme.
25-3-15	Informed Sanitary Officer 27th Division and ascertained the following sanitary details:— Here is a hand standpipe by Inlay at the Granary. In the loft there is a tank of 50 gallons capacity which is filled by means of a small oil burner or a wind force pump. Steam pipes leading from a boiler with movement from a trough lay tank, by means of these the water in the tank is raised to boiling point and kept so for 10 minutes. The boiled water is then led off in pipes, and through covered troughs into storage tanks from which the water can be filled at a raised platform outside the building. The maximum daily output is 2000 gallons. The supply is from a shallow well about 30 yds outside the building. This well after been a shell dampout is treated to lime every. Another well was trunk sunk in the immediate proximity but had not yet reached water. The [?] and required amount to be had for 7 men. The water from the boiler is also utilized for boiling & washing / clothing and a fan is run from the oil engine to dry articles after sterilization. The engineman is trained intern[?] pending this 25 placement by a man of the Division.	

Army Form C. 2118.

WAR DIARY
or
INTELLIGENCE SUMMARY.
(Erase heading not required.)

Hour, Date, Place	Summary of Events and Information	Remarks and references to Appendices
25.3.15 DICKEBUSH	There has been a considerable outbreak of Enteric fever in this town, amounting to 35 cases during March since the 22nd Jan. The worst area being hung LA RUE STREET. Such cases can be transferred to the SACRE COEUR hospital YPRES or the CHATEAU ST ELIZABETH hospital at POPERINGHE. The latter institution is run by the BRITISH SOCIETY of FRIENDS, and the MO ye will on receipt of a message send a motor ambulance for the cases. His MO is also in possession of cards bearing the names of houses to house contacts recently cleared out. A map showing the houses in the DICKEBUSH area is in the possession of the SMO of the Sanitary detachment of the 3rd Division now working here. The personnel of this detachment consists of an N CO & his men of the Divisional Sanitary detachment, and a fatigue party of 20 men of the R.I.R. Regt. Three [underlined] NCO who appears to be thoroughly reliable & competent. There is a field kitchen in a neighbouring brewery but it is at present closed on account of a defect in the plant and also because the huts have been removed by the Dl of gang [?] Division	Mr. Malcolm I Myt R. Dav

79
3298

WAR DIARY
or
INTELLIGENCE SUMMARY.
(Erase heading not required.)

Army Form C. 2118.

Hour, Date, Place	Summary of Events and Information	Remarks and references to Appendices
DICKEBUSH 25-3-15	The DADMS 3rd Division visited the place this morning. I pointed out to him several encroaching earthwire, especially the importance of finding enough unsoiled ground to build the three fillers for latrine trenches. He informed me that the pails have been sent for but may be some time in arriving — I also pointed out the logality of the Dressing Station of A to Shelled, and suggested the advisability of moving the hut in course of construction at the farm some little further — He agreed and said the matter would be brought to the notice of the G.O.C. at the conference this evening — I also interviewed Capt SPRAWSON the normal Sanitary Officer with a view to getting from him they defects respited — The farrier is still in charge of men with the result that regiments of both Divisions as in this area return which makes all medical sanitary arrangements difficult — Major LAUDER and the detachment from the Lancashire Fusiliers BAILLEUL joined today on being relieved — Issued written order to Division Medicine to O's C sections re appx.	M.E. Myddelton Lt. Col. RAMC
26·3·15	Made sanitary inspection of hut encampment in the copse. The huts consist of large tarpaulins hung over large poles fixed to trees. The tarpaulins hang to felt under sides at the front from a floor. The huts are dirty and the wholeearing is found to be foggy and has been condemned by Revenue.	NSH

Army Form C. 2118.

WAR DIARY
or
INTELLIGENCE SUMMARY.
(Erase heading not required.)

Hour, Date, Place	Summary of Events and Information	Remarks and references to Appendices
DICKEBUSH 26.3.15	There is ample cover in the surrounding fields for later in the war owing to the frequent changes in units occupying this encampment. The problem of sanitation will be an acute one. The 2nd Lancashire Regiment are vacating tonight and the 1st Wilts coming in.	W.E. Nudsh T/Cpl Reut.
At 3.0 PM	Received message from A.D.M.S. that the real detachment at BOESCHEPE is now open and cases are to be evacuated there by utilising cars of No 8 M.A.C. Sic R.S. cases at LA CLYTTE not sick.	
27.3.15	There will in future be arranged this morning to try use Horse transport independent of the M.T. convoy for R Detachment sorties. Transferred as cases to BOESCHEPE this afternoon. Sent L/Maurice with a horse wagon to bring in a wounded man of 19th R.F.A. from VYVERHOEK. Wounded by a shell from one of our own Airplane guns which failed to capture in the air and fell as a dud out. Message from A.D.M.S. Keep in sick in DICKEBUSH make them use of R Detachment. Evacuation detachment is doing good work. Inspected the bath house in the brewery VYVERHOEK, both it and the laundry seem in order.	MsH.
5.30 PM		
28.3.15	Visited by A.D.M.S. who saw the bath house and a type here with small cistern and fed pipes for three water carts. These are at present useless owing to a fault in the water laid off the enclosure. Recommended that there should be a total fully strength of so many made up from sections available for each of the Field Ambulance and attached permanently to the sanitary sections, these places being freed by in their battalions. Also suggested that the Regal Engineers arrive at the Brewery & a couple of haratte.	M.H.

WAR DIARY
or
INTELLIGENCE SUMMARY.
(Erase heading not required.)

Army Form C. 2118.

Instructions regarding War Diaries and Intelligence Summaries are contained in F. S. Regs., Part II. and the Staff Manual respectively. Title pages will be prepared in manuscript.

Hour, Date, Place	Summary of Events and Information	Remarks and references to Appendices
DICKEBUSH 26.3.15	Interview to new Camp Commandant, who will arrange for coal supply for laundry and Creamery and water for bathing —	W.E. Hulluh-Lt Col also
" 29.3.15"	Shells dropped 100 yards behind and 20 yards in front of Orange Stables at Rt CLYTTE.	
" 31.3.15"	Took O.C 7.9 Avd asking to Cancel 1st half duty to be claimed by my rules. Gave him as far as knew the position of the 2nd Div ambulance stations together. 8th Inf Bde at KRUISTRAAT. Informed him how the Indian ambulance manages.	
LA CLYTTE 8.45 AM	Reported to G.O.C 8th Inf Bde at KRUISTRAAT. Informed him the work being done by ½ of the 8 Fd Amb on trenches, and the work being done. The most being done by ½ of the 3rd Div Sanitary Section. His own special attention to the sanitary condition at WERSTRAAT, the Lain inspected. But that where keemen are confined in the trench, no Buckets kept or used. Here and sanitary arrangements for the men only for Coward only at night, as the lines are continually under rifle fire. Arranged of G.O.C. Sand Corporal Memorandum to all Regts.	
	Notes regarding Regt Sanitary duties. Reynolds Capt S Runn. Staff to Plan 8th Inf Bde to have all S.A. Memorandum numps from entrance of R.D. Stations.	
DICKEBUSH 10 A.M	Saw G.O.C 7th Inf Bde Arranged that both ambulances should send down the further Stone Church Door, as beyond this this road is visible from WYTSCHAETE Rige —	
	Arranged for Capt Chapllain to hold Early Services in Dickebush and Stay with my unit from 1st April & 3rd April Easter Sunday.	
	Arrangements to deliver to all Officers and the 5 Wltyhr. in the event of this place being Shelled —	
31.3.15	Arranged for the being filled with day sack to be placed between The trench to use to come by fire.	
	Bath house to men from in use.	WH.

12/5/94

1/11/94
April 2, 1915
Summarised but not copied.

60. Field Ambulance

Vol III

S/

WAR DIARY
or
INTELLIGENCE SUMMARY.
(Erase heading not required.)

Army Form C. 2118.

Hour, Date, Place	Summary of Events and Information	Remarks and references to Appendices
DICKEBUSH 1.4.15	The following cases of Infectious disease reported and were sent to Dublin Hosp.:- S/James Lt COLLINGWOOD. C. Meads. B/Lt HECTOR GOUDERIS ~ DICKINSON A-Pte 1/WILTS REGT. Scarlatina. ~ but in every Encampment. The billet in each case was disinfected by the Sanitary Section. The M.O. 1/WILTS Regt informed necessary segregation of contact. In the billet occupied by the officer the Q'Mr Stores in men H/S Lance are billetted and the men from time to time and the occupants kept. The house is placarded under isolation. The H/S Lance detachment will be removed to a hut on RE Sheet as soon as it is available. Pte DOYLE forwarded with cable from DUBLIN reply "Mother dying" need to ADMS to have Reply The GOC will not Entertain Pt DOYLE'S application unless confirmed by letter " Pte DOYLE informed of reply and sure home to this effect from 2nd Corps HQn BAILLEUL. WOLSELEY motor Ambulance broken down sent to OC No 1 MAC. for new Spring clip for front wheel. Orders for MAJOR LAUDER to proceed England and Report War Office received ADMS for warrant. L/Col HULKE & 2 E NFMTS sent to C.C. Station Locrinnine. B/S Latimer briefs sent for from Ord Depot WESTOUTRE by C. Commdt. Arrangements to be made with major to have mended. Also 85 13th HQ supplies. Increased ration for horses. Shoes 1 Clydesdaler 19lbs only. G.O.6+R. D 12 lbs only. Report from St. B. Sicklier 2e No 2468. Pte Hemmings a "C" Coy 4th Lancs. who was wounded today with a wound what he stated was self inflicted, ADMS wires reference to RAMC.	Sanitation. Forage. Administrative Orders 669.

WAR DIARY
or
INTELLIGENCE SUMMARY.
(Erase heading not required.)

Army Form C. 2118.

Hour, Date, Place	Summary of Events and Information	Remarks and references to Appendices
DICKEBUSH 1.4.15 2.30 PM	Inspected all billets on East of main Street from house No 104 to 144 A, with the Camp Commandant. Instruction to hand any bedding etc. The following needs to be supplied were arranged with by the man in 113 & 6A. 144 A – A damp latrine needs to be dug in field immediately N of billet 144 A and billets in R.E. Street. Sent GS wagon to draw 138 latrine pails from Ord Depôt WESTOUTRE these to be handed over to Camp Commandant.	N.E. Shudicahr 1/1st L. Rami
6 PM.	Major LAUDER left en route for England to report to W.O.	
2-4-15	Report re vaccination turning brightly about midnight last night. Staff Officer went round to Hospitalivain in which was damped down for the nite – Sgt Richards made report. Wire to ADMS re disposal of cases of Scabies. Received Laveracks and Lewis Jr. Lhuford to Regtl Trans of 7th 8th + 9th Rangers. Two lowes of Shell dressings & bottles of Iodine one Issued to each Regt.	
10.30 A.M.	Messenger arrived from O.C. No. 1 MAC with new Spring Clip to WOLSELEY Cart.	
11.30 AM	Visited Sth Avenue which is there now there is a reconnaissance post. Man who took along K.Ty Corps. The road from the latter is damaged to the edge of the DICKEBUSH – VOORMEZEELE road, and curved into a lane in the burning yard. Sty enemy of a wooden carved from the hill it is occupied with fire by means of a steam engine – the water to the Lothar is heated by running steam into it. The trough would show that side is from field.	Sunday

WAR DIARY or INTELLIGENCE SUMMARY

Army Form C. 2118

Hour, Date, Place	Summary of Events and Information	Remarks and references to Appendices
DICKEBUSH 11.30 AM	Inspected the brewery — 23 Bn is billeted in Brewery. Saw the Bn MO & decided a half latrine trench to be dug to replace the pail system in front of the brewery. Advised also to dig in field N Eg# + A billet, by sanitary section. — M.A.C. complain there is no water for washing purposes in their encampment. On investigation found there was no reason for it. A Kly, a shallow well and a pond.	W.E. Hadlock L/Cpl RAMC Sanitary
" 3.H.15	Visited area occupied by 7th Bn Pioneers at N E angle of square H.33.(1) Two cases of Scarlet Fever occurred in the billet on 19th inst. Bn Hd has been occupied by pioneers of 55th Inf Bde. Conf overcrowded. Two men these women and tuitchelbren. Saw all except the two women, 10 officers & 135 other ranks. The pioneer number 155 of whom 110 are usually billeted here and 25 at YPRES H.22.E.8. There are canteen tents for on annexed to the Right occupying the trenches. The billet & Br officered by present occupants who will be inspected daily by AMO No walk to be brought of the farm — Recommendation to be about effect sent to Bn Maj Q & Capt A. No 13416 GEORGE R 3rd MIDDX under observation since Jan 29 51/15 to 9 p/a. A full character sent with a certificate for L. Knights R Inniskilling Canteen sercet. Capt DARLING R. J commanding these too physically & mentally fit for duties as a soldier. Taken back to his regiment.	BELGIUM Sheet 28 1/40,000
	12.67.15.19 Injected futols or M Sly M from Sheet 5 — Orderly lorry Cullum (Marine School trees occupied by 57 By R.B.	Sanitary

Army Form C. 2118.

WAR DIARY
or
INTELLIGENCE SUMMARY.
(Erase heading not required.)

Instructions regarding War Diaries and Intelligence Summaries are contained in F. S. Regs., Part II. and the Staff Manual respectively. Title pages will be prepared in manuscript.

Hour, Date, Place	Summary of Events and Information	Remarks and references to Appendices
DICKEBUSCH 3.4.15	and much Eft to be turned, also deep latrine trench & 9 & dug in sanitary area behind three feet. Sanitary conditions in Dickebusch of this area fairly good.	W. Nesbitt Lt.Col.Comdt
4.4.15 1.45AM	Wrote OC 3.1 Lances asking for Car to bring Lt COWAN 3/Lancer shot in stomach from BRASSERIE. Motor ambulance sent to Capt EDWARDS at D Station LA CLYTTE for this purpose. The officer was brought in and treated at dressing station. Transport about 2 hr 2 hr Detachment BOESCHEPE. Interviewed them & officer at BAILLEUL.	NSH
5.4.15	Compiled sanitary returns. 11.30 am & S Buffs 5 J POPERINGHE. Running again. VLAMERTINGHE good. Fairly good. The HA Company Infantry have a large number of minor cases of Influenza which under treatment left to trench duty. Capt PHILLIPS (Munster Fus:) attended last night multiple steel wounds Officer bullet wound to head arm shield and sole.	NSH
6.4.15	The ADMS. 3rd Division Col WHITE inspected the Dressing Station here and at LA CLYTTE No. 1572 Pte DUNN 3/Lancer admitted a circular wound 500 yards S of the LA CLYTTE - DICKEBUSCH VIERSTRAAT - OUDERDOM cross roads. The bullet was recovered.	NSH
7.4.15	Visited the billet from which the Outbreak was having occurred. It is a left about a cattle shed, the floors & tiles about filthy covered by about bucket of dirty straw and filth. Recommended to Owner and MO that all their shd be turned out and burnt.	On

WAR DIARY or INTELLIGENCE SUMMARY

Army Form C. 2118.

Hour, Date, Place	Summary of Events and Information	Remarks and references to Appendices
DICKEBOSH 7.4.15	The Men then took thoroughly disinfected with Creol by the Sanitary Section - The Camp Commandant was then informed and promised to rid the area any Sanitary fatigue - The billets may then be re-occupied. The Regt. will for the present night was well to retaliate by the gas Standards - Instructions re chlorinating water used for drinking purposes. Wire from ADMS stating that 1 F Detachment BOESCHEPE Cloak only accommodation available for use for officers at 5 Cl. # HAZEBROUCK - Farm hulet near OUDERDOM - YERSTRAAT, DICKEBUSH - ACLYTTE area were shelled. One shell entered at about 2 PM and killed one man and wounded another - LT MAURICE and Stretcher Bearers took four Stretcher Bearers were sent forth to the billets to render aid, and a Ambulance wagon was sent down the road. The farm was empty and the dead and wounded were found in another farmhouse They had been removed by the Regt farmers, and the Regt M.O. - Six cars and a motor bicycle with bayonets arrived, and under-	W.Hinkston M/Sgt Rawe
7.4.15	Serial number Make/ChassisNo Letter/Bonnet No Driver NOT NAMED 1 AUSTIN 7432 A 9886 2 " 7427 A 9885 3 7440 A 9882 4 " 7428 A 9883 " 7435 A 9746 6 FORD 650015 A 9750	DOUGLAS CYCLE 3203 C {033020 P'te GRANT {050361 P'te ROCK {050069 P'te DENYER {049862 P'te MINNEY {050393 P'te HERNAN {050382 P'te COVERDAHA {049904 P'te COOPER 20499 36 P'te LISBITER 049948 P'te FORBES 052596 P'te SLOANE 050050 P'te ROSS 052799 P'te BRUNTON

WAR DIARY
or
INTELLIGENCE SUMMARY.
(Erase heading not required.)

Army Form C. 2118

Hour, Date, Place	Summary of Events and Information	Remarks and references to Appendices
DICKEBUSH 7.4.15	Each car is fitted with two acetylene and two oil lamps, a spare wheel complete and a spare inner tube and inner tubes. There is one man on each car viz:- 7. TA/ROTS 812 A 9887 050 HOG. Cpl. FELLOWES / 04 6656 Pte. REARDSLEY NCO with body 04 5694 S/Sgt BANGE Detailed arrangements for disposal of wounded abdomen cases at Capes area funnels now allotted to C gr. Brigade. Also reconnoitered use of bucket latrines instead of trenches. The Brigade are erecting hoop-board huts which will be a great improvement. The Capes still get very boggy after a little rain. Cars No 1 proceed to RACKLYTTE from SCB of "B" Section.	M.C. Haslechi / Maj.
8.4.15	Summoned to attend slight cases of sickness to 5 and 10 Cav Stations HAZEBROUCK, ambulance keys. Shelly Cases sent today by means of No 3 M.A.C.	NCH
9.4.15	Motor used for first time collecting, not a very dark night, drivers not used to driving without lights, but did fairly well.	
3.30 PM	Wire from A.D.M.S. Withdraw detachment from ST JANS CAPPEL today No idea even to be sent to C.C Station HAZEBROUCK. Accommodation up to duty at and detachment WESTOUTRE. Transfer patients at ST JANS CAPPEL to WESTOUTRE. Communicated by messenger in Car (R Lt G Pte ENFIELD) Cases all transferred by 5 P.M. but detachment unable to move on account of insufficient transport.	NCH

WAR DIARY
or
INTELLIGENCE SUMMARY.
(Erase heading not required.)

Army Form C. 2118

Instructions regarding War Diaries and Intelligence Summaries are contained in F. S. Regs., Part II. and the Staff Manual respectively. Title pages will be prepared in manuscript.

Hour, Date, Place	Summary of Events and Information	Remarks and references to Appendices
DICKEBUSH 9.4.15	Refilled Ambulances with horses and drawn comforts, blankets &c to O.C. 3rd Divl. Train — Letter to A.D.M.S. 3rd Division :— Reference your D.697 dated 8th April, I am anxiously for heard ambulance wagons for O.C. 3rd Divn Train this day, and wishing the other for the following reasons 1. Seven of the Motor ambulances deficient 2. The substitution of 7 motor ambulances for a similar number of horsed wagons diminishes my carrying capacity to a very poor extent as shown in the attached table. This in view of the increased number of Battalions in Inf. Bde. would appear to be very undesirable. 3. It is the common experience of all officers who have commanded and served with Field Ambulances that three horsed ambulance wagons would not be sufficient. 9.4.15 In table of Carrying Capacity see table overleaf.	McKestoli Lt Col Rance Comdl 8 F.A.

WAR DIARY or INTELLIGENCE SUMMARY.

(Erase heading not required.)

Army Form C. 2118

Instructions regarding War Diaries and Intelligence Summaries are contained in F. S. Regs., Part II. and the Staff Manual respectively. Title pages will be prepared in manuscript.

Hour, Date, Place	Summary of Events and Information	Remarks and references to Appendices
DICKEBUSH 9.4.15	Carrying Capacity of Vehicles for Wounded	

Motors	Sitting	Lying	Ambulance Wagons, horsed Sitting Lying	Ambulance Wagons Sitting Lying	Space for Accommodation Sitting Lying
5 Ambulances	40	20	4 Ambulance Wagons	84 28	2
X 1 Talbot car	8	4			
1 Ford car	3	2			
	51	26		84 28	33 2
					Some Sitting Lying
Seats (Vehicles wounded)			Old Scale		
5 Ambulances	40	20	10 Ambulance Wagons	120 40	9 6
X 1 Talbot car	8	4			
1 Ford car	3	2			
5 Horsed Wagons	60	20			
	111	46		120 40	9 6

X Ambulance car not yet arrived

… Army Form C. 2118.

WAR DIARY
or
INTELLIGENCE SUMMARY.
(Erase heading not required.)

Instructions regarding War Diaries and Intelligence Summaries are contained in F.S. Regs., Part II. and the Staff Manual respectively. Title pages will be prepared in manuscript.

Hour, Date, Place	Summary of Events and Information	Remarks and references to Appendices
DICKEBUSH 10.4.15	Visited ADMS at Divl HQ, REMINGHELST, discussed question of moving Dressing Station for further forward OUDERDOM – VLAMERTINGHE road. This appears to be inadvisable since within the divisional area which only embraces Nº of DICKEBUSH village an average depth of 10-20 yards. Pointed out necessity the danger of parking with 6 convoy of 7 Ambulances. Nº 7 Ambl. has opened a Divl RS at WESTOUTRE. Vacancies therein to be notified immediately by ADMS. Coach to return by Cars of Nº 7 FA. Supplies of petrol, lubricants, oil and carbide to be obtained through Supply Officer.	
4 PM	DADMS. to have question with Senior Supply Officer re 19 lb food ration for Swine his horse, this having been refused by SM Pakn. S.O.B. Lt GREENFIELD and detachment from ST JANS CAPEL have rejoined. Another men wounded with shrapnel in neighbourhood of farm we lived in 9th April. Swine Commanded, junction the high.	
11.4.15	Searched whole area for unsuitable place for the Dressing Station. The school being technically shrapnel fire at this morning the only possible place is "the hut encampment" on the HALLEBAST – OUDERDOM road.	

Army Form C. 2118.

WAR DIARY
or
INTELLIGENCE SUMMARY.
(Erase heading not required.)

Instructions regarding War Diaries and Intelligence Summaries are contained in F. S. Regs., Part II. and the Staff Manual respectively. Title pages will be prepared in manuscript.

Hour, Date, Place	Summary of Events and Information	Remarks and references to Appendices
DICKEBUSCH #1. 12.4.15.	Memo to O.C. 7th D. Wors recommending me to see a list of number of huts required. 4O.C. 7th Inf.Bde willing to allot number of huts required.	M/Malcolm McRae
2.30 PM	Arrived & inspected D. Station, Convent huts, and the lake.	
13.4.15 9-30 AM	Met Staff Capt.n 7th Inf Bde and pointed out huts repaired, and houses in which billets would be required for officers.	M/4
	The O.C. 56 Bay R.E. arranged for repair of certain huts, erection of works shelters also fitting up of steam pipe to disinfector van and repair of pump at the Creamery.	
10.15	Sent off fatigue party to clean huts and encampment.	
10-30	Wrote for return "No men of No8 F Ambulance to be arranged for in full uniform in readiness by 9 pm."	M/4
3.PM	Visit by MOMS and DADMS II Corps to whom valuable particulars of Dressing Station was demonstrated. Also arrangements carrying over ... wounded by substitution of stretchers from pool seats.	
	A Zeppelin passed over last night about 11.30 PM, shedding a shell from over the house and then proceeding in direction of BAILLEUL. Orders received motor ambulances based with the convoy to be carried except under very urgent circumstances, and no written instruction for an officer.	
14 AP. 15	O.C. 56 Bay R.E. informed me that he is intend transport sheeter of earth house shelter at Convent huts arranged for yesterday.	
9-15 PM	Arrival N?65. 14. Inv reckons 8th F. Amb heas advance dressing Station detached will run from DICKEBUSH to KACLYTTE... morning and been RAMC Arrangement Staff Captain 8th Inf Bde in use morning, and take over full transcribed Bn 8th Bn 8th Lancing LACLYTTE.	

WAR DIARY or INTELLIGENCE SUMMARY.

Army Form C. 2118.

(Erase heading not required.)

Hour, Date, Place	Summary of Events and Information	Remarks and references to Appendices
DICKEBUSH 14.4.15	From LA CLYTTE School occupied by guard. 5th Bat B its element to be taken over for main dressing station. Arrangements for B'tn dug-outs must be provided from billets taken over by same. Advanced dressing station to be opened DICKEBUSH. Report of reconnaissance by senior staff of 14th Div. Exchange.	H Chadwick / Lt Col Roome.
15.4.15 9.30 am	Met Staff Captain 5th Bat B. at LA CLYTTE. The extra accommodation for sick & wounded is inadequate. The billets for personnel suggested are extremely V. Reported same to A.D.M.S personally at D.H.Q.	
10.30 am	A.D.M.S personally inspected accommodation at LA CLYTTE and some farms on DICKEBUSH – KEMMERTINGHE road, with me.	
9.50 pm	Message April 1787-15th. Referring my N.787-comped instructions from A.D.M.S. Yares Island School will be vacated by the A.D.A. Have arranged for section of S huts and an ambulance coverage with 5th Fd Ambulance for accommodation required ready A.D.A. No further accommodation in School available at present A.D.A. Ackn. Roy 2.	
	Last night an unusually large number of casualties, a result of shelling at Ypres & urful cottage over	
16.4.15	"Aitcheson" Lance Sergt. Rifleman, H Ryan & Dpten. proceeds to LA CLYTTE late. R.O. DRISCOLL	Total Casualties 1 Officer 1 R.A.M.C. N.C.O. 5 N. Other ranks/others 3 N. Other Nil run

WAR DIARY
or
INTELLIGENCE SUMMARY.
(Erase heading not required.)

Army Form C. 2118

Hour, Date, Place	Summary of Events and Information	Remarks and references to Appendices
DICKEBUSH 16.4.15	On arrival of the party at LACLYTTE, the 3 Medical Reg.t were discovered to be still in possession of the former Infirmerie, the School. Sent A&MS Telegram over to Staff Captain who arranged to have their billets elsewhere. On my return here Capt DARLING informed me that the MOH's had visited this A.D.Station and given him verbal instructions that no cases of sickness or wounds were to be or anywhere near kept here — That the wounded and collected tonight were to be taken direct to LA CLYTTE loc Capt DARLING pointed out that no extra accommodation for sick or wounded had been provided at LACLYTTE AAMS Telegram N°81 of 15/4/15 quoted above) I proceeded out to the hound when we inspected the accommodation at LACLYTTE on 15/4/15, that 40 was the extreme limit of the travel accommodation at that evening stations, and that the number of beds was the average regained by the 8th Brigade above, and that the average accommodation required for sick in the 7th 8th & 9th Brigade areas was 70.	M.E.Shopkin Lt Col R.AMC
17.4.15.	The usual collection parades carried out tonight, and those from the 7th 9th & 8th Trenches carried in the School. Arrangement with OC B Section to transfer all sick rounded collected tonight up to 15 cases direct to him.	
18.4.15	There were only 3 cases in spite of the fact that a very heavy attack was carried out on our left, a shell by by the F.A. Division in which our troops co-operated & Commenced at 9 P.M. Fighting proceeding never left all day.	

WAR DIARY
or
INTELLIGENCE SUMMARY.
(Erase heading not required.)

Army Form C. 2118

Hour, Date, Place	Summary of Events and Information	Remarks and references to Appendices
DICKEBUSCH 19.4.15 1 PM	That night the sick & wounded were again transferred direct to LA CLYTTE. Some shelling occurred in the neighbourhood of two farms on the DICKEBUSCH - VIERSTRAAT road, and finally two shells were put into the town, one knocked a large eelm(?) in the main Street about 100 yards direct from the D. Station, and the other fell near the Steep nearly opposite this billet. Meantime all the sick were got away in Motors and me wounded away from the billet in to Horse wagons — fighting still proceeding on our left. As President of the Local Sanitary Committee — I met the Burgermaster and 9 Town Commandant at 11 A.M. an interpreter being present. The Burgomaster agreed that the civil authority should be responsible for the following 1. Emptying and disposal of contents of all privies & pits under cow byres drains 2. Burying and keeping clean all the main storm water drains. 3. Removal of stable litter in country carts, and its disposal by digging into the fields. The Burgomaster further proposed that the Sanitary contractor shall sell him sacks for the Horse manure for removal of which in carts at rate mentioned to Pet — He offers 25 francs a hundred kilos. This offer to be put up by me to the Military authorities — It was also decided at this week's Local Ptte The Sanitary Attachment shall construct incinerators for garnts of forces an infected, also dig pits for disposal	WSWindham Lt Col

WAR DIARY
or
INTELLIGENCE SUMMARY.
(Erase heading not required.)

Army Form C. 2118

Place	Summary of Events and Information	Remarks and references to Appendices
BUSCH	If the contest of latrine pails - treats it the ulmost care for the Emptying of these pails and covering the filth with a layer of Earth - where trenches are used the want of it impossible for digging true and keeping them in a proper sanitary state — All any kitchen refuse and everything to be disposed of to be incinerated by units — We are more than risks round the main dressing and sounded out three sewing "incinerate cleaning". The whole of the personnel and equipment of Mr. I. sent to LA CLYTTE, but a small detachment of "C" section under CAPT DARLING which opened a dressing station in the Brewery (2 NCOs and 10 men). The shrapnel building is entirely intended as a dressing station, as they are too exposed to shell fire, and the coal are as such. Sick to be transferred to LA CLYTTE when they require treatment at ADS station, and direct to WESTOUTRE otherwise. Daily Convoy of 2 cars from No. 2 MO Ambulance at LA CLYTTE and not later the fore- afternoon or evening as required.	
12 Mon	Proceeded to LA CLYTTE and inspected the fore- front where unit first took over the premises of "C" section — On return met Stevens and informed him of any move of personnel, and general arrangements.	

WAR DIARY
or
INTELLIGENCE SUMMARY.
(Erase heading not required.)

Army Form C. 2118

Hour, Date, Place	Summary of Events and Information	Remarks and references to Appendices
DICKEBUSCH 21.4.15	Sanitary inspection of tour of the billets of M4T5, 2 S. LANCS, WORCESTERS, H.H.C. and H2. SIEGE COY RE:— Memorandum to Staff Captain 7th & 9th Brigades:— 1. Recommended that the use of straw for field bivouac shelters and straw at present in use to unused and burnt. 2. That all alternative arrangements for purposes of latrines should. Whenever a source of water is the only one available, it should be replaced or removed of available supply. So that workers can be stopped and attention paid to them. I'm made sure 10 or so men from the barracks and polishing for disposal of extra twenty-five. I find the following had bt. SCHERPENBERG SEEN M7g 160 Camera not to being badly guilt by men washing in it. 3. Recommended that bed g. General Fisk's relative condition in the trenches should always compare the same killed or other will may need the tolets sanitary arrangements in the line of precaution and work also. He withed in the condition of their toilets. ~ I have to have been attached to the troops of Sich W.R.M. CRYTE First head to near more for however mud cases of troubles to the DCMS troops here and Capt 4 the D.DO. WESTOUTRE. present sending all such. Capt EDWARDS reports that these toilets are now cleaned and are ready for use. LT JACOBS sister to duty work this morn. arrived yesterday. LT MARTIN returned to tomorrow's Service assistance.	Reference Map BELGIUM Sheet 28 1/40,000
6.PM		
22.4.-15	Names of one officers and two sergts. sent to MOMed for members. that a LACKITT & three. with me, necessary personnel obtained from A Section. LT STEWART in medical charge. Sanitary inspecting of billets in old school occupied by me and six officers at RDa and 4th Coy 2/S.Lancs- Baths and Cook house of brass dirty and latrine arrangements for this billet insufficient to be largest unit but of employ.	MC Mulhohun R.C.al. Rams

WAR DIARY
or
INTELLIGENCE SUMMARY.
(Erase heading not required.)

Army Form C. 2118

Hour, Date, Place	Summary of Events and Information	Remarks and references to Appendices
DICKEBUSCH 22.4.15	Routine fatigues, and the construction of our urinals ordered. Tonight LT. MAURICE will take 5 men out to the aid posts by following route LACKYTIE - DICKEBUSCH - VOORMEZEELE - PLAS EEZENVAAR - Cross road S.E of IM de MADELING. - W border of wood N.5.6. KEMMEL - LACKYTIE. The men cleaning the three aid posts at VOORMEZEELE will return via DICKEBUSCH. He will make the circular tour. If this proves successful it will save sending out an officer each night to clean up.	Belgium Sheet 28 ⊥ moors
23.4.15	Transport lines as shewn sketch marked. Our intercepts work for groups 1.2.3 and N.5. 4th continued, also proper latrine trenches. The new system of collecting wounded worked well last night. LT. J.A.C.O.B, accompanied LT. MAURICE in order to learn this work and position of aid posts.	Map shewing transport lines 1 Wilts Regt. 2 R.Scots Fusiliers 3 Worcesters Regt. 4 S.Jaunes. 5 2 S.Jaunes. 6 Liverpool Scottish. From V.Lamertinghe Mad Plantation 15cm. Belgian Oats To YPRES Creamery To Vierstraat DICKEBUSH From La Clyte
2.9.M	Proceeded to KA CLYTE and paid out "A" & C" sections. Found billets and huts for sick, all satisfactory. Seen informed by Capt EDWARDS that the A.D.M.S thought that the LINCOLN Regt had proceeded that night to trenches in the S. & D in area, and to rather their carriers to be collected by us. - Wired to 9th Brigade asking when & A collected their wounded last night, and position of aid post. Reply Airport at CHATEAU LAMKHOF Squant T.26.d.7 Wounded to be evacuated last night by 14 F.A. Wired O.C. 14 F.A. Can you arrange to collect casualties LINCOLN REGT. AID POST CHATEAU LAM KHOF Squant T.26.d.. Reply from O.C 14 F.A. 14 F.A. will collect.	
11.20 PM	On arrival of ems near LT O'DRISCOLL at rendezvous DICKEBUSH reported that wund road blocked by a fallen tree. Came out via DICKEBUSH church. - VIERSTRAAT road.	

H. Kinchant Capt.

WAR DIARY or INTELLIGENCE SUMMARY

Army Form C. 2118.

Hour, Date, Place	Summary of Events and Information	Remarks and references to Appendices
DICKEBUSCH 24.4.15	Moved Bgde HQrs to LACLYTTE by order of ADMS.	
	Sent Lt. Col. A.W. HASTED 1/Wilts to Bailleul. Sent out two cars to 27th Bde RFA HQrs	
LACLYTTE 3 PM	to collect 8 all ranks of Canadian Division who had arrived there via YPRES	
25.4.15	ADMS orders that all cars for 3RD WESTOUTRE shall in future be collected at LACLYTTE	
	and then handed on cars of No.7 D.A. arrangements made with Captain DARLING at	
26.4.15	DICKEBUSCH, and O.C. 7th 3 and at WESTOUTRE.	
	Sgt Shelley detailed to duty of handing over discharges from hospital to R.C. NCO	
	who will attend at D. Station en at 10 am daily.	
	Report to Staff Captain 8th Bde that have put horses of 1/Borders in trenched Sanitary	
	in the stream by LACLYTTE Rails.	
	Severely four admissions today, including 15 civilians, 18 R.I. Rifles wounded in	
	Canada huts by aeroplane bombs and 18 RFC wounded behind their billets	
	in DICKEBUSCH. Will Sharpnel. Evacuated by convoy from BAILLEUL during the	
	night 26/27.	
27.4.15	Aster's Inspected receiving post at DICKEBUSCH and Canada Rails, also D.Station	
	at LACLYTTE.	
2.30 PM	Report from Captain DARLING again under Sharpnel fire very few casualties	
6.30 PM	Report from (?) Lt/Col DARKING that DICKEBUSCH under shell fire again, two lines	Belgian Sheet 28.
DICKEBUSCH 7 PM	of horsing pedestrians about 12 Casualties.	
	Proceeded to DICKEBUSCH in Ford car on arrival the shelling had	
	ceased but shells had struck the stables behind and also a road a few	
	yards in front of my Advanced Dressing Station.	
	Found no decomposition the Salve road about ½ a mile	
	further west at a farm in N.M. corner Square H. 26.6. Ordered the	
	Dressing Station to be moved there and arranged for remove of the	
	Casualties. Returned to LACLYTTE.	
LACLYTTE 9 AM 28.4.15	Proceeded to mis D. Station at DICKEBUSCH. Officer in Charge in gaol.	N.E. Kruistom Left
	The 9.0.C 9th Lof Bde has suggested that the billet vacated by one last	Reams
	night should be reoccupied for use of the Infantry	

WAR DIARY or INTELLIGENCE SUMMARY.

Army Form C. 2118.

Hour, Date, Place	Summary of Events and Information	Remarks and references to Appendices
LA CLYTTE 28/4/15	The A.P.M. arrived about 10 a.m. and I accompanied him in search of another available building for the advanced dressing station. Failing to find one before we verbally then 'known' in learnt that which he would then allotted to us.— Lt. JACOBS, and the interpreter VEERHOUSTAETEN and some of the R.A.M.C. personnel, with all the horses, and kit to LA CLYTTE. Returned to DICKEBUSCH.	
2.30—3.30 pm	Showered again over DICKEBUSCH. The Talbot car arrived and goes for food for tonight.	
2g or 15 10 A.M.	Proceeded to DICKEBUSCH. Received from Jones (Commandant, to transport location of the units of 15th & 19th Bgd Rd.) and arranged for extra latrine accommodation when required. Investigated case of Dekene, woman LIEVENS, reported by priest as suffering from Typhoid fever. Report to DDMS as follows:— To DDMS 3rd Division. I have investigated the case of alleged Typhus and report as follows:— Name Mme LIEVENS. Age 30. Address MULLENAEREN Farm, Square W. 30.c. Alsace Entrée Farm (probably). Duration of illness 5–7 weeks. Husband said to have died of same illness 4 weeks ago. She was immediately outside the farm has been recently in the back yard by the A.P.M. and six men of the 19th Rd. Bgon. This detachment was brewing up the preliminary arrangements to blindfold the civvies of my short occurrence of the woman. She was admitted to the civil hospital there.	Sanitary Belgium Belgian Zehulde moore.
2 PM	by order of the Staff Captain 9th Div. I am advising with Bn Nhoo to the farm is apparently infected in the 5th Divisional area. There is fresh Hercine to the above at present up abode that milk has been obtained from this farm by troops in neighbouring billets. Sa H. Curtiscelle Lt Col R.A.M.C.	A. Churlescr Lt Col R.A.M.C.

WAR DIARY
or
INTELLIGENCE SUMMARY.
(Erase heading not required.)

Army Form C. 2118.

Hour, Date, Place	Summary of Events and Information	Remarks and references to Appendices
LA CLYTTE 29.4.15		
30..4.15	The interpreter was sent with a letter to the Mayor of BAILLEUL and obtained permission for the women to remain in the Hospital Providence.	Sunday
11 am	Sent into Hulles with infection ambulance wagon and removed the women's linen to this place.	
	Made the halts in cart pulvitation and neighbouring fields. Went round with LIEUTs of SCOT FUSRs and provided and secured for a bullion water — 90 wounds recovered about 10 Staff Captain Q.R.	
	[See App. X 1. wall empty.]	App!
7 pm	Arranged for removal of Officers and Dressing Station DICK=BUSCH to farm in square H 31.B. This form allotted by Staff Captain 7th Div. Move of Adv. Dressing Station completed.	N.E. Shadlow 2nd Rance

12/5573

12/5572

3rd Division

8th Field Ambulance

Vol IV

May 1915

Army Form C. 2118

8th F.A. Ambulance

WAR DIARY
or
INTELLIGENCE SUMMARY.
(Erase heading not required.)

Hour, Date, Place	Summary of Events and Information	Remarks and references to Appendices
DICKEBUSCH 1.5.15. LA CLYTTE. 2.5.15	Report to A.D.M.S. Advanced Dressing Station was at Barn H 31 b. Inspected course of SCHERPENBERG — RENINGHELST — OUDERDOM road to DICKEBUSCH huts. Reported to O.C. 2nd N. Midland Field Amb. and O.C. 14th F.Amb. was found fitting this Scheme. Went to O.C. 2 L.G.J. making appointment for Col. Sir A.Bowlby tomorrow. Captain BLAIR-CUNYNHAME consultation at 2 Batt. E. Surrey Regiment. Last reconnoitred L.G.S.	Belgium Sheet 28 1/40000
8 P.M.	Wire from M.O. R.I.Rifles 15 dying and 8 sitting cases. Car out off at once.	
8.15 P.M.	Message from O.C. 27th Bde R.F.A. through O.C. 25th Bde R.F.A. asking for ambulance. If 26 sitting and 1 lying case from HALZEBROUCK RD. Car leaving. This message was noted to O.C. 15 F.A. S.A.H. who asked him if he could send ears. He replied "regret no cars available." Wired O.C. 9th F.A. for loan of cars, which on arrival were taken over by Lt. MAURICE and twenty cases for present brought in this transport. The total number of the S.A. in this division exceeds the knowledge of the number of the R.F.A. appears to have no procedure to be adopted when he requires cars. to be evacuated.	
3.5.15	The cases of the foregoing all sent to C.C.S. except seven of the more severe ones. These all have all the physical agent sent. Carefully bandaged and are slightly exposed about the tf. bd. and face generally. Three washouts for sick trying completed are taken over for use today. They five accommodation for 175 cases. They are high, light, airy and will constructed.	
4.5.15	Visited advanced dressing station — A.D.M.S. also arrived this morning. Authority for moving Civilians from their homes to Hospital DMS. 2nd Army. applications to wind to Sanctuary F.P. Zone.	W. E. Kinglake Col. R.A.M.C.

WAR DIARY
or
INTELLIGENCE SUMMARY.
(Erase heading not required.)

Army Form C. 2118.

Instructions regarding War Diaries and Intelligence Summaries are contained in F.S. Regs., Part II. and the Staff Manual respectively. Title pages will be prepared in manuscript.

Hour, Date, Place	Summary of Events and Information	Remarks and references to Appendices
LA CLYTTE 4-5-15 5-5-15	Reported to Staff Captain 8th Inf Bde huts on KEMMEL-RENINGHELST road, no longer required for sick. Went round DICKEBUSCH huts area, found occupants + Rmen, sanitary condition not satisfactory, arranged chiefly to removal of billets of Sanitary Section and fatigue to LA CLYTTE. Discussed situation with Town Commandant, and despatched the following urgent message to Sanitary Officer 3rd Division:- "I have been round the huts at present occupied by troops of the 9th 9th Inf Bde and recommend the following permanent daily Sanitary fatigues as shewn below; each fatigue in charge of a man of the Sanitary Section. 1. DICKEBUSCH huts (1500) men, 15 men; 2. Canadahuts (1500) men, 15 men; 3. Halter fatigue ordinary, 4 men; 4. DICKEBUSCH town 16 men.. Please let me know if this can be arranged.	Sanitary
9 p.m	Received correspondence re case of ? Cerebrospinal Meningitis in 3 Worcester Regiment, which recurred in Canada huts, arranged for disinfection of hut.	
14-45 9/4	Note from MO of 3 Worcester Regiment that he is sending 9 Contacts in connection with above case of Cerebro-Spinal meningitis to Observation - Lodock aggregated to the right wing of 165 men huts.	

W S Hurghata
LtCol RAMC

WAR DIARY
or
INTELLIGENCE SUMMARY.
(Erase heading not required.)

Army Form C. 2118.

Instructions regarding War Diaries and Intelligence Summaries are contained in F.S. Regs., Part II. and the Staff Manual respectively. Title pages will be prepared in manuscript.

Hour, Date, Place	Summary of Events and Information	Remarks and references to Appendices
LA CLYTTE 6.5.15	The following cases suspected of Cerebro-Spinal Meningitis have occurred during the last 48 hours.	
	No 5379 Pte BRIGGS R/ RIFLES	
	No 9181 Pte HART 3/ WORCESTERS — "B" Coy } Sent to Isolation	
	7257 Pte WOOD — "C" Coy } Hosp^l BAILLEUL	
	13443 L/Cpl WINSTONE — "D" Coy } this morning	
	6525 Pte BENNETT — "A" Coy } except 2 final yesterday	
	18928 Pte ROSENBERG — "D" Coy	
	5380 Pte WHITMORE — "B" Coy } Sent to No 7 F Amb	Sanitary
	7920 Pte NORMAN — "B" Coy } WESTOUTRE for	
	14535 Pte ARMSTRONG — "B" Coy } observation	
	19766 Pte WRIGHT — "B" Coy	
	14629 Pte LUXMORE — "B" Coy	
10-10 AM	Wire to A.D.M.S. 3rd Division. Five probable cases C.S. Meningitis	
	Sent to Isolation. Five more contacts suspicious. Where shall	
	latter be sent for observation. All cases 3rd Worcesters.	
	Saw D.A.D.M.S. later, who informs me that arrangements were	
	made for contacts & cases if C.S.M. to be kept under observation	
	at No 7 F.A. and I & sent there direct in future.	
11 AM	Rode round front of 7th & 9th Bde area.	
2.30 PM	Took (Capt) FRASER round DICKEBUSCH area, and to the Toron Observation — Capt F was appointed in place of Capt SPRAWSTON who has been sent to L of C Sick.	M. Muirhead Lt Col R.A.M.C.

WAR DIARY or INTELLIGENCE SUMMARY

Army Form C. 2118.

Hour, Date, Place	Summary of Events and Information	Remarks and references to Appendices
LA CLYTTE 7.5.15.	In accordance with an arrangement made with Divn Commander yesterday have fixed a town in DICKEBUSCH as allotted to unit of Sanitary Section as a permanent Sanitary latrine. Rode round some of 7th Bde area. Took Col Jenkins to new billet and arranged for accommodation of the whole of 7th Bde billets to stand with 7th Bde field Service Sanitary Section and Fatigue work & new billet	Sanitary
5 P.M.	Very heavy attack starting about 4 P.M. in neighbourhood of Y Mitsenbeeke MT. YPRES - MENIN road, later in day 28 T Division involved in this attack - a Arranged with L OWEN that the Cav Fd Amb Bn stand by for cleaning and overhaul, Fd Amb Bn struck off for cleaning and overhaul Cav Fd Amb Bn this bivouacs at WISTOUTRE.	
8-5-15	That g.A.D.M.S. following orders 1. Cases under treatment not to be detained more than 4 days, after that to be transferred either to A.D.O. Woolwork or C.Cd 2. To arrange with D.S.G. 7 K. Fg 2 DA for lorries of words, autos or wagons in case of emergency. 3. I am no not by S.D.M.S. 2nd Corps in case of urgent need for ambulances. The accommodation for sitting cases in Dickbn can reduced by order to Six.	M.S. [signature illegible]

WAR DIARY or INTELLIGENCE SUMMARY

Army Form C. 2118.

(Erase heading not required.)

Hour, Date, Place	Summary of Events and Information	Remarks and references to Appendices
LA CLYTTE 9-5-15	Visit of A.D.M.S. to see the new found outfit & services within a few days removal of the Bngde. 1 Brigade M.M.H. Ladies Division to distress poor women of the regiment by 6th R.B. tonight.	
10-5-15	Visited Canada huts and sanitary arrangements. Arranged with Staff Sergt of sanitary section to supply disinfectants etc to trenches tonight & is working tomorrow.	
11-5-15	Notification of a new method of aggregating cases to the Dressing in BAILLEUL. Motor orderlies from DMS 2nd Army's, and if sent called the Regulating M.O. will be kept informed of the arrival in No 2-3 H.S. C.C.S. Station, & will be responsible for telling them & man is [fit?] night & day at the [-----] Bn in Mr. [-----]-BAILLEUL road, and will stop all motor ambulances & [wagons?], and direct them where to go. This will [-----] us improved [---] for O.S.C. Ambulances to for information as to disposal of cases [----] from their limits, and as this information is constantly being demanded, I have written to MMHS. providing this [----]	
12-5-15	The sick rate amongst officers is rising considerably, especially within the last 6 weeks or so. The 1st & 4th GORDONS and 2/ R SCOTS left about 2 PM for duty in 3rd Div Area. The sanitary fatigue men of 8th Brigade have been all withdrawn.	

M. Studholm
R C Davis

WAR DIARY
or
INTELLIGENCE SUMMARY.
(Erase heading not required.)

Army Form C. 2118.

Instructions regarding War Diaries and Intelligence Summaries are contained in F.S. Regs., Part II. and the Staff Manual respectively. Title pages will be prepared in manuscript.

Hour, Date, Place	Summary of Events and Information	Remarks and references to Appendices
LA CLYTTE 12.5.15	Went to L.C. San. Feb. 3rd Division asking for an NCO and one man of our section to be spared to look after the third echelon and the divers' packs that gather here in our in the gale area	
13.5.15	Saw LT. NASH R.A.M.C. who was concerned in the investigation he had managed to have than all line and to demand helpers from the various regiments who had been detailed for this 8450. Enquiry in to loss of Kit of Rev. B.H.M##H C.F. Kit and ammunition to await Head Quarters from DICKEBUSCH on their arrival on 28th inst. S/Sergt. HIRST admonished, in respect of duty in connection with the case of this and other officers kit rental the same time—	Consequential kit of two other officers
14.5.15	D.G. No 26/2 circular memorandum dated 10 May 15— Received last evening and distributed to day the whole of the station Corps picks kept in the field under the arches one of them was cracked & broken across Those and part of them and to be forwarded to DOMS and be F.A.M.hut Subsidy broken—Waller reported to DOMS and be F.A.M.hut 3rd Brigade	
2 PM	Circular Memorandum DG also noted read out and circulated in my presence. I handed out to all ranks that its clauses applied equally to the personal belongings of NCOs & Men & also their	
15.5.15	PICK a Wounded Lt. GREENFIELD returned ad advanced dressing station, by Lt. O'DRISCOLL—	
	Two civilians (puls aged 13 & 12) wounded by shrapnel in DICKEBUSCH yesterday. Tried to bury in accordance with instructions to Sunday op zone. Squadron as On Br.	

W Mueblehm

WAR DIARY or INTELLIGENCE SUMMARY.

(Erase heading not required.)

Army Form C. 2118.

Hour, Date, Place	Summary of Events and Information	Remarks and references to Appendices
LA CLYTTE 15-5-15	Returned wire, unable to find any such Telegraphic Order — Sent Telegrams to ADMS & AG reminiscent of their admission to Hospital Furneaux, and received permission for same. Cases were not sent in the usual categories of Patients treated by Surgeons. Saw ADMS and informed him re/Scrue the dispatching of the Red Cross considerable differently in ammunitions by war from HR. In accordance with Telegram from ADMS arrived for 150 marks and 5 gallons of anti—for solution. Solution as follows: Mercurithiol Soda 10lb / Washing Soda 2lb / Glycerine ½ ctr / water 1 gallon. The following efficient for first dress disinfection for Second oil antiseptic dips — Lt. Surgery on injury to No. 35744 Ptc Blanchford RAMC who flees of Sergeant + the Mwd of the left knee with detonator in a gl granade. On duty. to blame, and responsible alone for the injury he sustained. Agreed upon on 6589 Pte FORSYTH W 1st SCOTS FUSRS Medical Board on 6589 Pte FORSYTH W 1st SCOTS FUSRS as to gunshot wound to his medical condition. Interviewed Lt GLYNN R.O. N. FUSRS re the above forwards to A.D.M.S 3rd Div not yet up today for Extraction of teeth, as a rise for a.	W.Shephard R.Cockram
16.5.15		

WAR DIARY or INTELLIGENCE SUMMARY

Army Form C. 2118.

Hour, Date, Place	Summary of Events and Information	Remarks and references to Appendices
LA CLYTTE 16.5.15	Ambulance wagon sent here instead of a message to Advanced dressing station. This officer is guilty of a great deal of unnecessary traffic. Staff Capt. King deceived by certain information in DICKEBUSCH area, but such information is very hard to obtain owing to the enemies never being far off the apathetic skill by which the enemy Rev. MEEK C.F. Presbyterian left for HAVRE on the way by Rev. MUIR. W.S. —	
17.5.15	Wire from N-Land asking for Dr BLANNING R.A.M.C. for him evacuated — reply "not evacuated." Letter fm. O.C. 2nd N.W. 3rd Division suggesting that stretcher to be used in carrying of damaged types. Reply that chance for me bring up right collection absolutely essential, otherwise considerable broken up in ditches. Letter to Staff Captain 9th Div. Lys. N.E. asking for transfer of Sgt. Scotton appointed by him to in charge N. Infirmary. of 9th R.E. This is carrying fiction and saving no useful purpose. Copt Co.N.NELL reported unwell yesterday returned to	
18.5.15		Sanitation
19.5.15	Board on	
20.5.15	Sgt FERGUSON 1/ Royal Scots two or years proceed for duty with 1/North-umber Fusiliers an 21/5/15 — Board on. The mental condition when he recovered, self as present. The reviewer Capt EDWARDS R.A.M.C. 1st GREENFIELD R.A.M.C. Finding PTE FERGUSON is at present same. He is not responsible for the care in which he is charged N.B. Descriptum when in active service	

Army Form C.2148.

WAR DIARY
or
INTELLIGENCE SUMMARY.
(Erase heading not required.)

Instructions regarding War Diaries and Intelligence Summaries are contained in F.S. Regs., Part II. and the Staff Manual respectively. Title pages will be prepared in manuscript.

Hour, Date, Place	Summary of Events and Information	Remarks and references to Appendices
LA CLYTTE 21.5.15	The R.A.M.S. reached the Dressing Station at 10.30 P.M. with reference to the room which is occupied by Stretcher Bearers, this room opens directly out of the Dressing Station, and is reserved for an officers' ward. The Brigade was refused to put it up on its plea that it was absolutely necessary to have the Brigade Maker in their room, which is opposite the office used by the Staff Captain. Capt. CONNELL assumes the 4/Northumberland Fusiliers for duty in relief of Lt. GLYNN.	
10.30 P.M.	Message from Staff Captain asking if Orders authentic of Formation sets had been issued from the Brigade office by the troops under my command.	
22.5.15	Full enquiry when in the if formation above asked was fully investigated. Reveals nothing known except one broken chair which was found by a Sgt. of one men when clearing the best yard a week which he turned to his Quarters. Subsequently find destroyed by another fires men was punished. Reply sent to Staff Captain.	
9 P.M.	News from R.A.M.S. to send two for Railway duty with 4 th S. Inn R., Sick; Lt. Jacobs sent.	
23.5.15	Received my inspection of head of 7 th & 9 th Brigades Areas.	
24.5.15	Very severe bombardment from N.F. YPRES commencing at 3 A.M., about the same hour north of the DICKEBUSCH, RESKOWIKZ WESTOUTRE areas were also shelled indirectly affected by	M. Murdoch Lt. Col.

WAR DIARY
or
INTELLIGENCE SUMMARY.
(Erase heading not required.)

Army Form C. 2118.

Instructions regarding War Diaries and Intelligence Summaries are contained in F.S. Regs., Part II. and the Staff Manual respectively. Title pages will be prepared in manuscript.

Hour, Date, Place	Summary of Events and Information	Remarks and references to Appendices
LA CLYTTE 24.5.15	My few lines. Trip in LACLYTTE was only slightly affected. The wind during the night 23/24 was in the North and was only a gentle breeze at 3 AM but soon increased in velocity. The R. I. Rifles were billeted in a farm billet in the neighbourhood of HALLEBAST. This billet was received by two gas-powders, and whilst crossing the men were playing football outside the billet when at least two German aeroplanes passed over. The billet has been shelled before, about 12 men were wounded and one killed on this occasion.	
2 P.M.	The 8th Inf. Brigade left LA CLYTTE for an unknown destination. A convoy of 3 carts was used for a demand about 6 R.H. from BIKSCHOTE to bring in the wounded collected this morning.	
25.5.15	Inspection from the 7th M.S. Capt. DENYER, G.A.'s mission the [illeg] and Lt. [illeg] Army Pay, June the R.E. Officer (50) reported this morning.	& L. O'DRISCOLL
	(Capt. HOLMES & Dr COVERDALE both made remittance... being reported by the Chief Bowen an C.O.'s advice of the [illeg] envelope for [illeg] and family of [illeg]. the RAMC men's informed and that Drink [illeg] Days	
26.5.15	7. P.M.! Visit from GOC's 13 Inf Bde belong to Inf. Bde tonight. 8th Irish to collect for 13th Inf. Bde. duck forwarded from this Bde to Relief route as follows. Cross fm C.C. Station to be used as now to BIXSCHOOTE, and from there to No 15 "JR" at REININGHELST.	

M Sheehan Lt. Col.

WAR DIARY or INTELLIGENCE SUMMARY

Army Form C. 2118.

Hour, Date, Place	Summary of Events and Information	Remarks and references to Appendices
LT CLYFFE 2 AM 2.7.5.15	Wire received thro' gr 3rd Div HQ from 13th Inf Bde asking if 2 cases can be evacuated from BEDFORD HOUSE, no reference to any map. Sent 1 car to HQ 13th Inf Bde as to whose BEDFORD HOUSE. Stable. Reply BEDFORD HOUSE whereabouts by enquiry Regt. This being an area collected for that purpose by 8 F.A. Unit, and I am trying through staff get nothing further been done.	
10 AM	Wire from Div HQ to the effect that 13 Aug M.O. does not understand our scheme of evacuation, and asking me to send representative of scheme. Also stating two cases to be evacuated from KOSB at BEDFORD HOUSE as he has been specially summoned, for evacuation from 8 F. A. in reference to any such p.m. Sent Capt EDWARDS to arrange with 13 F.A. to evacuate any cases of 13th Inf Bde in hand, spare animals. Captain EDWARDS sent first to HQ 15 F Amb to arrange for continuance of evacuation of this area by them, and secondly to HQ 13th Inf Bde.	
10.30 AM	Doctors & Officers arrived and I proceeded to brief the foreman of the ord[?] Eng's on the scene. Was taken over by the Bdy C[?] Bde also took the opportunity of mentioning the necessity of C[?] rest night and assuring my thanks.	
7.30 PM	Spoke to the 7 O.C. Cos tonight. Read out in funds' speech to 27th & 28th Divisions, delivered by Gen C, also instructions regarding the use of means and how they are to be carried, also notes regarding name of 3rd Division to YPRES Salient, issued by Gen O 3rd Division.	

M Hughesly[?]
Lt Col R.A.M.C.

Army Form C. 2118.

WAR DIARY
or
INTELLIGENCE SUMMARY.
(Erase heading not required.)

Instructions regarding War Diaries and Intelligence Summaries are contained in F.S. Regs., Part II. and the Staff Manual respectively. Title pages will be prepared in manuscript.

Hour, Date, Place	Summary of Events and Information	Remarks and references to Appendices
LA CLYTTE 27.5.15	This afternoon reached part of the 27th Divisional area, in company with Capt DARLING & Lieut MAURICE, and examined the following facts. The main evacuating route, is in several divisions, viz 27.K 28.K & the 1st Cavalry Division is the YPRES — POPERINGHE road. Consequently there are Dressing Stations of various Ambulances of these units at about the road L.8.9 to M.2.K.F. Ambulances, and 3rd is Cavalry F. Ambulances on the main road in the vicinity of VLAMERTINGHE another. Both had a Dressing Station in the cellars of the Civilian Asylum in squares H.12.d. The Headquarters of the 27th Division are at BUSSEBOOM Square G.15.d. 22.a — The 81st F.Amb is at a farm in Square G.15a. This is approached during bright sun in a School where food Class wounds are available, and tested for transit further than tramway Ambulances in the vicinity, back there hitherto were worked, and the School could then be used by the outgoing F.Amb. Similar arrangements for use as an advanced dressing station were considered. The evacuating arrangements are as follows. The wounded & sick from the trenches are collected in the cellars of the Refectory School East of YPRES Square I.9.c. A small detachment one officer & 2 or 3 nursing orderlies and the same number of stretchers are posted here in the cellars. The motor ambulances can proceed as far as the entrance to this School by night, and several horsed formed and Car cars proceed from the trenches which are situated roughly along the POTIJZE — ZILLEBEKE road. Wheeled stretchers carriages are useful here. The whole of the YPRES — HOODGE — MENIN road from its emergence on the moat to the trenches is under rifle & machine gun fire, and points along this road are carefully registered here, and Artillery fire by the enemy. Collection by day is therefore barely practicable, both on account of visibility	Reference Belgian sheet 28 1/40,000 ✱ ※ G.12.b

W. Finchlen?
Lt. Col R.amc.

Army Form C. 2118.

WAR DIARY
or
INTELLIGENCE SUMMARY.
(Erase heading not required.)

Instructions regarding War Diaries and Intelligence Summaries are contained in F.S. Regs., Part II. and the Staff Manual respectively. Title pages will be prepared in manuscript.

Hour, Date, Place	Summary of Events and Information	Remarks and references to Appendices
LA CLYTTE 27.5.15	to overalls, ammunition, personnel and wounded there in and increase the friction of this Shelter which seems also for Brigade Staffs and other mounted officers revealed to the enemy. The D.A.H.S 27th Division had first all the 7 Ambulance Cars (two numbers), and on receiving a message each evening as to numbers requiring evacuation be detailed the required number of cars in the ones to the Regimental Schools and Carry over back to the Cure to the Regimental Schools and Carry over back in the cars to the Loft Hucks — The cars when emptied proceed back to de BRANDHOEK and on return much rock to the Ammunition West of YPRES square #12 c, where they are met by horse wagons which bring them into Ypres 7 Rudhleury. The Field Ambulance had formed a R.R.O N.W. of POPERINGHE and one is in reserve the troops of the 27th Division when not in trenches are stationed chiefly in the neighbourhood of BUSSEBOOM, and the daily exch. or really by the Regimental M.O.S of BRANDHOEK, and disposed of to C.C.S at BAILLEUL, or A.D.S as necessary. The M.A. (many evacuating to hops under Major L'ESTRANGE) and the necessary numbers of cars are obtained by application to D.D.M.S 5th Corps. It is to be noted that POPERINGHE, VLAMERTINGHE, YPRES are areas very subjected to severe shelling by enemy guns, and the road between these towns is practically swept with shrapnel fire. An officer from No 17 F.A was taken on a car to-night to the fair back in was a VOORMEZEELE, by L'SEMPET.	Ref Belgium Sheet 28 1 100000

Hugh Rowe
M. Stewart

WAR DIARY
or
INTELLIGENCE SUMMARY.
(Erase heading not required.)

Army Form C. 2118.

Hour, Date, Place	Summary of Events and Information	Remarks and references to Appendices
LA CLYTTE. 28.5.15	Pte TUCHER 2/East Kents 05/0 attached coy of Arrct discharged from hospital and sent to No 8th 25th Division. Attached by A.P.M. of that Division.	
	Revd Marshall left for AIREEUL on 2'/5 No 6 General Hospital Rouen. Revd CRISFORD arrived from rly at B.ef Chatham and has taken on the strength.	
29.5.15	2nd Army Routine Orders No 85. RE officers kits not all trunks to be carried on pl & pl2 trv, transports of future. Unjustice together with instructions as to disposal of surplus articles.	
30.5.15 10 AM	143rd Bde 1st R.E Brigade arrived with Company consisting to take over nos of huts LA CLYTTE. Moist information to TOMS, and received orders to rem. aux. here till afternoon 31st when moved. Signed time and place to be notified later.	
	Received the following orders: "The Bde will march tomorrow afternoon also leave to be notified later. MOs and men will use their baths and be ready on wagons by 10 am. Fires extinguished and picketed by 12 noon.	
	Equipment will be packed and loaded by 12 noon. The detachment at DICKEBUSCH will join this Bde at DICKEBUSCH.	
12 noon	Handed over to O.C. 4378 (Wood Brig.) at OUTTERSCH LACLYTTE, and got my DICKEBUSCH tent, handed over to this Bde 28th F.A. Assumed charge 75 Inf Bde. afternoon of 31st also charge of No 6 Fd & 1st RE at 6:30 Bde RE also 127/54 RFA - Arrt ground had 3 new 3rd Divl Area with Capt EDWARDS in can, and I trench and broken to be inspected by this Bde.	*signed*: H.T. Anglesea Lt Colonel

WAR DIARY
or
INTELLIGENCE SUMMARY.
(Erase heading not required.)

Army Form C. 2118.

Instructions regarding War Diaries and Intelligence Summaries are contained in F.S. Regs., Part II. and the Staff Manual respectively. Title pages will be prepared in manuscript.

Hour, Date, Place	Summary of Events and Information	Remarks and references to Appendices
31.5.15 LA CLYTTE	Completed knocking out Dressing Station, and sent to G. H.Q. #3 Z. Ambulance. Captain Edwards Rad. on with advanced party in 5 cars at 8 P.M. Marched at 12.noon in accordance with Divisional Orders, to form a point 1/4 mile due south of pt 41, also Section I, via SCHAERENBERG - WESTOUTRE - HESKEN.	Ref HAZEBROUCK 5A
7.30 P.M	Three Cars Read. out under Lt BAZETT to rendezvous at Lunatic Asylum on POPERINGHE - YPRES Road #12 d.	Belgium Sheet 28 <u>access</u>.

W S Anderson
Lt Col R.A.M.C
O.C. 5th Cav Amb.

121/5992

aust.

3rd Division

8th Field Ambulance

Vol X

June 1925

Army Form C. 2118.

WAR DIARY
or
INTELLIGENCE SUMMARY.

(Erase heading not required.)

8th Field Ambulance

Instructions regarding War Diaries and Intelligence Summaries are contained in F.S. Regs., Part II. and the Staff Manual respectively. Title pages will be prepared in manuscript.

Hour, Date, Place	Summary of Events and Information	Remarks and references to Appendices
Farm RENE de BAENE* 9 A.M. 1/6/15	Sent spare kit of 8th Inf Brigade 6th Division round claim this Unit. Sent strgent, messages to ADMS to lich reply received 9.30 A.M. "3rd Division inform me yours form is in 3rd Division Filled gaps in A.M. Detachments. A.H.T. ran garants, L.O. and Staff &c. for New curtain pattern of gas mask to ADMS replied up field at 2 noon — Our share of the clearing work last for tiffs carried out yesterday. The feul trips and field long time car, 28 or so, were owing to careless driving. At Staden was paralled in not keeping together the ford car. One 9 through YPRES is difficult & away partly to ANNZ Officers and partly to 8 Inf Bde trans surrendering train up. The necessity to act not obvious to his out fuel of other it very important. O.C's from 3 that many drivers had other they rules of ADMS. Fact M.T. drivers is carry a spare wheel twice now would today Intended sent to Divine for Auxtofe up to full Ordnance send also for Anoto 2 church Lieu. Dufforum & Sther sorts	* Total unit to make due entry of Arks of LeH? 00 Section I HAZEBROUCK St
7.30 AM	Thro' E Corn. Order Lt. GREENFIELD dept arst Colonel, no telegram at Lunat the trageles "Signed H. L. S."	Belgian Band 28 niens
2.6.15 4 AM	Motor car sent out to advise undergone to march to No 7 I ambulance which at 3 A.M. to G.26.C.	

A. Middleton
Lt. Col. R.A.M.C.

WAR DIARY
or
INTELLIGENCE SUMMARY.
(Erase heading not required.)

Army Form C. 2118.

Hour, Date, Place	Summary of Events and Information	Remarks and references to Appendices
Farm Rue de BACRE 2.6.15 6 PM	The M.O. on 16 Inf Bde left. Divn sent an advance guard under 2/Lieut Bates about 8 P.M. received astonished no other available away for men were sent.	
3-6-15	Officers, horses and transport re-inforcement. A B Capt Denner Capt Edwards Capt Darling 2/Lt Bazett 2/Lt Greenfield 2/Lt Jacobs 2/Lt Stewart	
	Daily guard consisting of 1 NCO 4 men Daily Orderly Officer as pr. kept.	
Furnes CHARRES de KERVL 1.22pm 4.6.15 7.30am	Received orders to move at 9am to Spring Lane. Sent 2/Lt Maurice to ? . No farm in this Square which will hold a complete Bttn [unclear] had to divide unit up between two [unclear] farms villas 1L22 & - kept men to ? bearing out that no suitable billeting available. Squad Lot C. About rested 1st & later & Offirs & & others Billeted another site, a farm in L.22.a.	Belgium & France Sheet 27 north
7-3. P.M.	Found to him bullet which was at the same time wounded by a Battery of the Northumbrian Division. Whole Unit accommodated in bivouacs.	
5-6-15	Job, piece cleaning up lines, a large quantity of manure requires carting away from the horse lines. Incinerate filled and drains cleared. The works empty & kennels of the VLEETER BEEK which is a fine stream the course of this stream from 1/4 of a mile East West of the street were investigated - St's probably being considerably fouled both by troops bathing in it and washing clothes in it. At a point about 1/4 mile west of my billet a Piengsh here actually been constructed.	

M.E. [unclear]
Lt Col ? .

WAR DIARY
or
INTELLIGENCE SUMMARY.
(Erase heading not required.)

Army Form C. 2118.

Hour, Date, Place	Summary of Events and Information	Remarks and references to Appendices
From CHARLES H. KERVEL L 32 a 1. 6.6.15	A finishing touch constructed on the banks of the VIERTSTRAAT. The funeral of the Sheriff reported to A.D.M.S. No 150-61 S/Sgt HURST. W transferred to No 9 F. Amb. was relieved by No 3088 H. Sgt LEWIN Rewie. The above exchange in conformance with an order from A.D.M.S. to send a N.C.O., a reliable clerk to 9th A.	
	Lt C. JACOB Rewie SR. joins 2/15 R.I. Rifles in relief of Lt CARBRY who joins the unit.	
	Motor driver MT. Short R.S. Glen originally deficient in total personnel auxilis for sick with measles.	
	Auspice lengthy from A.D.M.S. regarding haulage — by water for full scale of Fontage VS B. Opinolly and 13 Ancient tubes, but to draw in 1st June and not yet overplied with.	
7.6.15.	The O R.O. HS. 3rd Division visited the Field in Connection with my report regarding fouling of the water supply.	Similar plan.
	The unit which has constructed the Plunge Bath is 112 Coy R.E. — Recent stand order from G.O.C. 3rd Division making 20 yd Pail mud to be provided for some prevention of pollution of water supplies in these areas. The A.D.M.S. by telephone paid a visit this afternoon and I should have the plunge Bath, as the 112 Coy R.E. want a 30 set brand.	
	An inspection of all equipment of the 3 sections made, with a view to dispose of all surplus material.	

W. Kutherford
W. McRavie

Army Form C. 2118.

WAR DIARY
or
INTELLIGENCE SUMMARY.
(Erase heading not required.)

Instructions regarding War Diaries and Intelligence Summaries are contained in F.S. Regs., Part II. and the Staff Manual respectively. Title pages will be prepared in manuscript.

Hour, Date, Place	Summary of Events and Information	Remarks and references to Appendices
Farm Charles de Nord 8/6/15	Orders issued Conveying of 1400 Horses detailed to duty daily from 5 am to 7 pm. Horses at a time to patrol the stream and pass through the ADS ambulance area, and prevent all bathing in the stream or other fouling thereof.	
9.6.15	Heavy thunderstorm in early afternoon, extremely hot previous to it. Orderly Bathing parade for all available men daily. Was ordered that the kits the sent to ADMS. Transfer it to worn each day at the Field Parade for 10-15 minutes under supervision of orderly officer.	
10.6.15	Severe Rain & Dust never prevents arms rusting if known. Very heavy thunderstorm again in the early hours of this morning. Nor Australia has been the crack in the chassis which necessitated its being sent down to OC for repair. Visit from two officers of a neighbouring French medical unit adjacent to the railway.	
11.6.15	Car sent off in charge of Dr Sloan to Rock to St OMER, the necessary description of car and repairs required being furnished. Lt book Lt Rogers Ravne sent to hospital – NOT certain denied	
13.6.15	Wine from Divvm as a rep't from rations complete. Reply "Complete." Deficiencies were so all who could to made up from Reserves. Others SWR – No HIS2. Gr WILDE transferred to duty & troop raising Gun Battery. Armd-Wardle billet seen the water supply and filter cleaned.	
14.6.15	Lt GREENFIELD proceeds to duty to 3rd Armoured Supply (a) as a temporary measure.	

M Shedlock
M C Paul.

WAR DIARY
or
INTELLIGENCE SUMMARY.
(Erase heading not required.)

Army Form C. 2118.

Hour, Date, Place	Summary of Events and Information	Remarks and references to Appendices
Farm de Kervel L.22.a.	Auxiliary Lorries Nos (9745) sent to O.C. A.S.C. M.T. Repair Workshop, ROUEN to refit. Sent via GODESWAERSVELDE. Sent RTO personally yesterday and the former it should be sent by No. A. Be Pull train. Ordered to take over 180 patients in N.T.S. Issues of No.7 Field Amb, and Lieuts Henn in Japan. Square 28d3 - Capt. EDWARDS & L. CARBERY with necessary personnel sent to perform this duty. Visited the farm this morning. The ground is not sufficiently large to accommodate the [?], 10 picketing lines and 8 [?] to be pitched in addition.	Belgium and France Sheet 27 1/40,000
1.30 P.M. 15.6.15	Baggage wagon of "A" Column formed to harness extinction arrests in fire [?]. Wagon sent to O.C. No.5 Company 3rd Divl Supply Train for refund. All Brances and form officers reported for duty logged at OXR N Gate No.9 P.O. at Lunatic Asylum YPRES at 8.45 P.M. Also all cars and the Douglas bicycle. Brances and personnel march as follows:- Party A 1 Officer 38 Rank & file b.S.U. in Lunatic wagons to school of E. VLAMERTINGHE Party B 1 Officer 34 " " " 6 R & F in 5 Cars " " " " Party C 2 Officer 20 " " " " 7.45 P.M. " to Asylum Lorries N.T.B. march from VLAMERTINGHE to destination. Ford car with orderlies on balls party for 24 hrs to accompany each party. Lt BAZETT and STEWART to assist in collecting. Capt. DOMELING to carry out all intelligence reporting Capt. DENYER to assist in D Station.	

M. Shadbolt
Lt. Col. R.A.M.C.

WAR DIARY
or
INTELLIGENCE SUMMARY.
(Erase heading not required.)

Army Form C. 2118.

Hour, Date, Place	Summary of Events and Information	Remarks and references to Appendices
Ferme Krules de KERNEL 16.5.15	All available cars sent to Ypres at 11 am by rats of 14 M.T.S. These cars were working all the afternoon between the Asylum and the Ecole de Bienfaisance Road at Ypres. M.6 Bell Sight ambulance sent by S/Sgt BLISS & convoy from nr. Asylum. The final party under Capt DARLING to march from VLAMERTINGHE. Twenty two stretcher sent with 2nd party. Visited Capt EDWARDS who now has three med convalescents to look after for No7 2 ambulances, the fourth he has been forced into to take the place of the 2 Army Portage who are demanding first. Lt MAURICE sent 16 from overseas by M IRISH HORSE to hand 50 German prisoners and report on their state of health. Report that all in front teeth except two suffering from chapped hands from all means, and one with tender feet, no signs of infections diseases. Prisoners not known to any marker extent. This report signed and R.D.M.8.M.G 3rd Division at 6.30 P.M.	Belgium France Sheet 7 1/100,000
17.6.15	No 2841. S/a Stacey J. wounded during circulation night of 16/17. Report from Capt DARLING all correct with ambulances at 4 asylum. Total casualties in attack 16th about 2500.	
4 P.M.	Capt General SLOGGETT visited any S/Bn on which time were 303 S wait wearing about 40 slightly wounded Germans. Shortly afterwards these wounded were removed in the cars of No7 2 ambulance ... Lieut No7 943 ambulance Captain E. BRULEN	
6 P.M.	Rev O'SHAUGHNESSY joined from "C" Motor ambulance	
18.6.15	Four officers and horses returned to duty at Asylum for duty. For AA Capt EDWARDS	M Whytehele Lieutenant.

WAR DIARY
or
INTELLIGENCE SUMMARY.
(Erase heading not required.)

Army Form C. 2118.

Hour, Date, Place	Summary of Events and Information	Remarks and references to Appendices
From Charles de KEREL L22.a.4.	above detachment handed back to No 7 F. Aml. by order of A.D.M.S. Capt DENYER & 28 reinforcements arrived in camp at 3 A.M.	Belgium Sheet 27 noon.
19.6.15		
1.30 P.M.	The Capt and the MT drivers returned off duty from Isolation Hospital. One Off. from D.R.S. BAILFUL	
20.6.15	All officers, horses returned from Asylum. B'Alion had an American Drill at town Square 23 A Inspection of A.D.M.S. Capt EDWARDS and took out division of B'Alion required headquarters. Lieut J.G.GREENFIELD rejoined from temporary duty with 3rd Dri Supply Column. Lt A.L.Y. de WESSELOW joined from No 7 Stationary hospital	
21.6.15	Self and Capt EDWARDS attended at HQrs 1. R Scots Fus.Rs for evidence re L.F.A. Confidential in Sgt FORSYTH of that regiment presumably examined by us as to his responsibility for act of desertion and cowardice Lt MAURICE proceeded to HQ. 3rd Dri Ammunition Column and exchanged four horses & one off. with that unit. This afternoon. Lt J.L. STEWART proceeded for temporary duty with R. Scots Fus.Rs and Lt. A.O. CARBERRY for temporary duty with 1st GORDON HIGHRS.— Application for leave of absence for the following officers and men and it A.D.M.S Capt EDWARDS, Capt DENTER, Sgt MEAD, D'LONE R, Pt PITTS, Bly DOYLE + SHEARS.	
22.6.15	Sent in by ADMS this morning and then to schools at G.12.6. at travel occupied by an division of 2nd Northumbrian F. Amb.	Belgium Sheet 28 noon.

R.W.Nothcliffe
Lt. for A.Amb.

Army Form C. 2118.

WAR DIARY
or
INTELLIGENCE SUMMARY.
(Erase heading not required.)

Instructions regarding War Diaries and Intelligence Summaries are contained in F.S. Regs., Part II. and the Staff Manual respectively. Title pages will be prepared in manuscript.

Hour, Date, Place	Summary of Events and Information	Remarks and references to Appendices
Farm CHARLES de KERVEL L 22 a. 22.6.15	Under orders from A.9.H.S., sent one officer and an advance party with the equipment of our section to Adm: Schools to take over buildings as soon as evacuated. Three Sergeants and 88 Other ranks under Lt. BAZETT & Lieut. Bayliss YPRES for duty tonight. Lt. de WESSELOW sent to dining station to await.	Belgium 1/nel M France Sheet 27 1/10000.
23.6.15	All ranks and both officers returned early this morning. Message from Capt. DARLING to effect that Schools at RANDHOEK would not be evacuated by NORTHUMBRIAN ?. And Hill communication sent to A.D.M.S. at 9.30 a.m.	
24.6.15	Capt EDWARDS proceeded on leave. Capt DARLING with Lt. de WESSELOW and Lt Smith went entertaining after a dining station at Schools ARMDHOEK, at 12 noon. Austin Car. No. A 9883, chassis No 7428 dispatched from Raithwaite 3rd division by 4-30 a.m to train to ROUEN to repaired & see Mt Sharp CHANTIER de NORMANDIE. This car like the one sent on 14th has a cracked axle member which requires welding. The crack in both cases is the width of a bolt head near the edge of the plate to carry a feed pipe. The car. No 9743 to chassis 107935 has not yet returned, and is probably en route.	
25 "	Information that 9TH S. arranged that Schools at BRANDHOEK should be taken over. Tel from division to Lieut under Capt DHARING sent to army giving Lt. Q & J Lane to take over the evacuated station at the Barleuc YPRES Ready 22 The 7th J. Quant and him arranged with him that he should continue to provide the bungee party at BRANDHOEK	Belgium sheet 28 1/20000 W.Widdelm.

Army Form C. 2118.

WAR DIARY
or
INTELLIGENCE SUMMARY.
(Erase heading not required.)

Hour, Date, Place	Summary of Events and Information	Remarks and references to Appendices
From Chateau de KERVER 4.2 a 25.6.15	Saw D.A.D.M.S. Matthews Q.H.Q. who informs me that my 2 ambulances should all be sent to Ambulance D.S.D. for repair and want to CHARTIER at NORMANDIE, as and them as directed from certain orders. Informed him of my difficulty in filling car warrant, and asked instruction from him, met number 3 & 4 at the Camp here at L. ROWEN.	Belgium / France Sheet 27 Hoven [?] Belgium Sheet 28 ½ [?]
26.6.15	Last night met Lt. Col E. BLISS at Bailleul YPRES and noted the general position at the Dressing Station HERE and arrangements as to personnel etc. Very heavy thunderstorm yesterday afternoon and evening which was badly wanted to augment water supplies. Went again to Asylum at YPRES with Lt MAURICE and saw the arrangements, accommodation, and amount of extra labour, dress up etc there. Sent in brief instructions for Ralls arranged that all lying down cases should be sent direct to my Dressing Station at BRANDHOEK tonight and onwards. Also visited May H.Qr. and made following arrangements:	
27.6.15	1. All cases from Asylum up to maximum of 50 should proceed to BRANDHOEK School as sufficiently arranged the with OC of Field. 2. The taking over of the Dressing Station at Asylum is postponed as the officers I now have doing Right duty are still required for their purpose. 3. The arrangements for evacuation of wounded that continue as heretofore, and the accidentally shell cases to number at BRANDHOEK and at Asylum. Consequently Capt DARLING I informed him of these arrangements.	M. Anderson L.H. McRae

Army Form C. 2118.

WAR DIARY
or
INTELLIGENCE SUMMARY.
(Erase heading not required.)

Hour, Date, Place	Summary of Events and Information	Remarks and references to Appendices
Forw Carlo de KEMMEL L 2 2 a. 28.6.15.	Captain EDWARDS returned from leave. Capt HURLSTON proceeded on leave. Arrangements for collection and disposal of wounded of the Division now as follows. No 7 Ambulance will clear all wounded and attend the sleight cases at the Asylum, showing their brother three will be evacuated to No 9 stationed in the wood in rear of No 9 Amb & dealt with all save for the trenches and transf. them to MRS. No 7 Amb. Stretcher cases will be sent to my Advanced Station at BRANDHOEK and trained to No M.C. Station. sick from Divisional Rest Station area will be treated also by my 7 Amb, and transferred to No 7 Amb. Injured will proceed at Asylum Each night for collection. Reinforced at Asylum Each night at 8 P.M. No 9 Amb to relieve the transit. Empty ambulance wagons should ??? be ??? ??? sent.	Belgium + France Sheet 27 town
29.6.15.	Application to base 1 N.C.O. 12 men forwarded ??? and officer for leave forwarded to ADMS.	
30.6.15.	Understanding from Col BLISS asking Amb. coming station at BRANDHOEK on forward to take all such wounded of Division. Asylum Amy handed over to No 3 & 7 Amb in Division. No 9 Amb returning to M.R.S. Amb G.S. Escten stated at BRANDHOEK, 1 throad wagon (ambulance) 1 G.S. Wagon, 1 cook as cart, 4 N.C.Os, ambulance & sgrms.	

W.Shuckligh
Lt/Col RAMC

WAR DIARY
or
INTELLIGENCE SUMMARY.
(Erase heading not required.)

Army Form C. 2118.

Hour, Date, Place	Summary of Events and Information	Remarks and references to Appendices
Farm Ouest de KEMMEL I.22.a.	Lieut. Col. REISS arranged to go with the Ambulance Wagons from No. 7 Amb. and 2 from No. 7 and should report nightly at BRANDHOEK at 10 P.M. for vehicle duty under him as per orders by Lt. Col. Seelie. Capt. DARLING informed personally of these new arrangements. The extreme capacity for receiving & evacuating sick & wounded at BRANDHOEK with tents will be 200. The site for placing tents is a good one. Seven wheeled stretchers are broken & taken over to No. 9 Amb. Capt EDWARDS reports to the Brown at YPRES as to its unsuitability as an Advanced Dressing Station, in case of heavy casualties. The town is at hand and used as a billet for the KING'S LIVERPOOL Regiment. There are good cellars and a good yard. The P.O. states that there cellars would be available in case of emergency and agreed to the storage there (of Stretchers) which are real and mighty at present. The Salvage Corps at the Infantry Brown was under orders to write in for chances in case of need, but as they are mostly men aged & up from physique they are not likely to be of much value. Lt. BAZETT proceeded to duty to BRANDHOEK, also Lt. HOGG Lent by No. 7 Ambulance.	Belgium Sheet 27 moves — Belgium Sheet 28 11 N.W. W Shepherd Lieut. & Adj. R. Amc.

Army Form C. 2118.

WAR DIARY
or
INTELLIGENCE SUMMARY.
(Erase heading not required.)

Instructions regarding War Diaries and Intelligence Summaries are contained in F. S. Regs., Part II. and the Staff Manual respectively. Title pages will be prepared in manuscript.

Hour, Date, Place	Summary of Events and Information	Remarks and references to Appendices
From Photo Ho de KERVER 22 a	The collection arrangements are as follows. The collecting officers and stretcher is 6 carry leave BRANDHOEK at 8 A.M., when loaded with casualties the trip car returns to A.D.M.S. office & then a bearer car is assumed for return to I.M.H. Collection. If there is born 15 bearer return in cars a foot return journey, and uses cars if available. All cars and lorries to bristly who are empty out the I.M.H. Collection. Received the quartermaster. Stretcher arrangements in pairs. Six had of casualties are requested and the evacues on return of the troops	Belgium: France Sheets 27 & 28 Belgium Sheet 28 10000 M Spelate Lt Col R.A.M.C.

121/6243

3/5 15 Interior

121/6243

8th Field Ambulance

Vol VI

WAR DIARY
or
INTELLIGENCE SUMMARY.

Army Form C. 2118.

8th Fld Ambulance

Hour, Date, Place	Summary of Events and Information	Remarks and references to Appendices
Farm (North de M) FRWK L.21.d. 1.7.15.	The daily state to be forwarded direct to A.D.M.S. from Div. Hdqrs of station BRANDHOEK.	Belgium. Sheet Kortryk Belgian field 28
3.7.15	Three suspicious cases of death from typhoid. One to go pro-forma copy forwarded to Capt DARLING. Instructions issued to all nursing orderlies. Helmets themselves placed in a room spray with Permang: Potass: lightly turn on & they the other side. Helmets then fielded as follows. Place take side under fold over the sides backwards & inset in circle, then this top is forced down over the side flaps, finally the follows is forced on in line forced to meet the lower edge of the top — The solution for spray is Hypo 6 lbs [diagram of 5 helmet shapes] for 500 helmets. Glycerine 2 lbs Water 3 gallons Helmets require spraying when the crystals show on the surface.	
No 9.U. 4.7.15	Orders to march from Divn. Wheeled. Resumed drawing station BRANDHOEK. Personnel were doing duty there as follows:- Capt. DARLING, Lt BARRETT, Lt de WESSELOW, Lt HOGG, and named out by No 9 F. Amb. Bearer out divisions of M.C. and tent out divisions of 'C' Section.	W Shudlock Lt Col RAMC

Army Form C. 2118.

WAR DIARY
or
INTELLIGENCE SUMMARY.
(Erase heading not required.)

Hour, Date, Place	Summary of Events and Information	Remarks and references to Appendices
Farm Churches RESERVE L 24 d 4.7.15	The accommodation for personnel is reported today all round good in tiers as except that officers who have not beds have a accommodation for patients in the school huts urgs is about 80, but Capt Booking thinks this could be expanded to 150 sitting cases, in annex near by. We is to undertake the probability of using the building now in use as a Divisional Laundry. The personnel is constructing a dug out for use in case of emergency, the material being provided by the R.E. Report on practicabilities of tunnel build as a M.R.S. in own hrs, and to A.D.M.S. should the authorities prove such a purpose.- All men of and who have previously experienced one dose of asphyxiated vaccine are being re-inoculated with fresh doses commencing today.	Belgium / France Sheet 27 & Belgium Sheet 28 4000.
5.7.15	Arrangement found an ambulance wagon every other day to recover for BRANDHOEK to No 7 P. Amb.? Then sport the horses kept turn are by at BRANDHOEK Reported the serious amount of drunkenness which is occurring in the neighbourhood of BRANDHOEK, there are six estaminets in close proximity and many other cottages are evidently public houses	A.S. Ryalock R. H. for R. and

WAR DIARY
or
INTELLIGENCE SUMMARY.
(Erase heading not required.)

Army Form C. 2118.

Hour, Date, Place	Summary of Events and Information	Remarks and references to Appendices
Farm Charles de RENINGHE L2 d. 5.7.15	Ptes TURNER & CHASE took horses today in absence from Bearer parade last evening and drunkenness. Report to A.D.M.S. re horse return. Grey two nos. in Ambulance wagon & sent to repair to CHARTIER de NORDANDIE on 14th & 25th June respectively.	Belgium & France Sheet 27 40000 Belgium Sheet 28 40000
6.7.15	LT STEWART returned from required hospital duty with many supplies & LT CARBERY returned to duty with 30 Bde R.F.A. Both these officers returned last night. The medical charge of 3rd Div. Supply Column was undertaken by No. 9 & No. 2 Amb Talbot. & Lieut. in charge. J. MOGGE return to HQ. 9. Aug. in July. Visited Dressing Station at BRANDHOEK. The work is light but slow, and that for the money made by the return of R. HOGGE to this unit will not be filled up for the present. The sanitary arrangements are bad, chiefly owing to the overcrowding of the neighbouring houses by refugees, who foul the yards and fields extensively. The dug outs which we twenty constructed by our personnel are excessive protection & surface water between depth of between 25–3 feet depth.	

W.C. Nicholson
Col RAMC

WAR DIARY
or
INTELLIGENCE SUMMARY.

(Erase heading not required.)

Army Form C. 2118.

Hour, Date, Place	Summary of Events and Information	Remarks and references to Appendices
Laurice Charles du KERVER L.2.1 (d) 6.7.15	Lance Bugler L SNELL MFD transferred to duty 6.30 on 8am. No NCO or private come in his place. The following reinforcements found on duty for L of C. No (12457) Bugler WYNESS. - 30508 Pte DOUGLAS. 30376 Pte FURNEAUX.	Belgians/French Shis 27 10000 Belgians Shis 28 "
"	Aviation. MO No A9888 has a cracked chassis in the same position as the other two previously noted. The car was sent to the P.A. W-W, and the Opt proceeded to STOKER there the MO DENT Thompsons for instructions as to repair – the instructions of the D were to transport, dated 2.7.15 are as follows. Cars requiring repair outside the scope of the mobile Workshop Unit are to be sent to ROUEN on SPRIS (according to the type of car) and are to be re-covered hence to the I Aust from which they were sent –	
7.7.15	I am now in receipt of Mess Cars out 7 seater al Leucolair, and all unserviceable through the same defect broken axle pluck, due to having a hole near the edge to carry a clip for a feed pipe. Saw RTO GODEWAERSVELDE and arranged for dispatch of Aust. Opr MO A9888. in charge of drivers FORBES & GRANT. In view of possibility of gassing recurring again in a large scale – Supt hour is to train 5 of Aspni Lieuk on Resp.	

W Shepherd
A/Collaire

WAR DIARY
or
INTELLIGENCE SUMMARY.
(Erase heading not required.)

Army Form C. 2118.

Hour, Date, Place	Summary of Events and Information	Remarks and references to Appendices
Farm Charlesto NERVEL L21.2 9.7.15	in large quantities as available from the Adv. Depôt. WOULVERGHEM. The re-inoculation of all personnel who have not formerly had their two doses of anti-typhoid vaccine is being carried out.	Belgium & France Sheet 27 & Belgium Sheet 28 1/40000
8.7.15	ADSENYR proceeded on leave yesterday afternoon. Visited D Station at BRANDHOEK, met A.D.M.S. MORRIS, who inspected. Gave instructions to Capt. DARLING to make me off the dugouts in R.E. reserve trenches about 1/4 mile on the BIRRINGHE side of his dressing station, in case of need. Lt. BAZETT proceeded on leave by 7.36 P.M. train from BAILLEUL. Lt. CARBERY returned from temporary duty with 30 RIFLES. The arrangement by which cases requiring specialists examination should be sent to Bed. for transfer to No. 10 Stationary Hospital POPERINGHE, requires readjustment. See A.D.M.S. on the subject.	
10.7.15	Visited main station BRANDHOEK. Inoculation of personnel proceeding, also large numbers of the combatant units. Discussed the shewing of the feet to be carried out in soon as solution is ready. Saw ADMS on form on which formerly, and reported that new arrangements regarding dewards forces terminates to 10 Cas approx. 1/2 pt my feet as yet no apparent advisable. Has yet received one.	W.F.Macleod Lieut. Col. R.A.M.C.

WAR DIARY
or
INTELLIGENCE SUMMARY.
(Erase heading not required.)

Army Form C. 2118.

Instructions regarding War Diaries and Intelligence Summaries are contained in F.S. Regs., Part II. and the Staff Manual respectively. Title pages will be prepared in manuscript.

Hour, Date, Place	Summary of Events and Information	Remarks and references to Appendices
Farm East of MERCKE 2 p.m. Oct. 10/15	Saw O.C. 10 C.C.S. who informed me that never in King's Road that only lying down cases, sick & wounded, of a serious nature are to be sent to 10 C.C. Station; all other cases to be transferred to one of the C.C. Stations at HAZEBROUCK. Arranged with Capt. DARLING at BRANDHOEK as follows:— "In future only lying down cases are to be sent off on account of a train and be transferred to 10 C.C.S.; all others will be transferred to a C.C. at HAZEBROUCK. You should therefore arrange for Capt. of No. 5 M.A.C. to evacuate all cases coming under the latter category". Until further orders the eye cases will be transferred to 10 C.C. Station. Pte AVERY has been detained at 10 C.C.S. for the next three days for examination as a possible typhoid carrier — all stool tests proved negative, and he returns to duty today. 7 P.M. Three Ford cars and six drivers arrived without previous intimation or any instructions as to whether they are on loan or a permanent issue. Details of cars returned as:— Drivers: Galloway, S. Chassis Index Number Ford 703105 - A 14737 Ford 671748 - A 14575 Ford 654472 - A 14580 M2 101185 Pte POTTER M2 101791 Dr. ARMSTRONG M2 078919 Dr. BINGHAM M2 099250 Dr. GOODALL M2 099727 Dr. CRAMPTON. E.R. M2 099726 Dr. CRAMPTON. G.	Belgium Honour sheet 27 woo to Belgium Hr. 1. 28 Honor W S Shurbeshi Lt. McLaine

WAR DIARY
or
INTELLIGENCE SUMMARY.
(Erase heading not required.)

Army Form C. 2118.

Hour, Date, Place	Summary of Events and Information	Remarks and references to Appendices
Farm Charles de KERVEL L2f.d. 10.7.15	Letter to A.D.M.S. on the subject:— "This afternoon R.S.M. Parker has consulted with six drivers from ST. OMER. No correspondence has as far reached me, and the drivers appear to have only received verbal orders from Sergeant, to report to regiment. His pronounced that these cars are sent on loan, until my further cars are returned from ROUEN. I should be glad of information in this respect, as the carrying capacity of these Cars is only half that of the Austin Cars, and they are in every way a real and indifferent substitute". I am not enter satisfied re shortage of carrying smoke helmets and masks.	Belgium & France Nov 27 + 00.00 Belgium Sheet 28 +00.00
11.7.15	Wire to O.C. M.T. Workshops. CHANTIER de NORMANDIE ROUEN no 97. 11.7.15. AAA. Tide instructions dispatch transport noted 2.7.15 AAA. Please state where AUSTIN Cars A9745, A9863, A9868 will be reclaimed from. D.C.O. S. & T. Amb. X897. Reply. O.C. S&T Amb. X897. W.K. your telegram 97 all their cars on licences ready in me week. AD.Dapper unit ROUEN. Corpl DENYE Rn returned from Leave. Pre O'SHAUGHNESSY and Pte FERGUSON proceed on leave via N.T. Depot, Ino of the FORSCAM sent for duty to "C" Section BEACHHEAD as detailed here.	

N.R. Nuttoh
J. MacRae

WAR DIARY
or
INTELLIGENCE SUMMARY.
(Erase heading not required.)

Army Form C. 2118.

Hour, Date, Place	Summary of Events and Information	Remarks and references to Appendices
From Charles McKeever L.R.L. 12.7.15	Received information of death of No 998 Pte William J. RAWLINGS RAMC from recent failure following Enteric fever. This was first reported sick on 28 June, but was sent to CCS on 1-7-15 as a typhoid case of Enteric fever. He died at No 1 B.R.C. Hospital on 9 July 15. No Bors Pte MIDDLEDITCH F.W. of the same section reported sick on 5 July and was kept under observation being to use and transferred to CCSlah HAZEBROUCK as a probable case of Enteric fever. A specimen of blood for culture was taken for examination by Fuller & Rowlands who on reaching the lab to great to ascertaining Fuller & Rowlands had stopped investigation of these cases reveal that these men both stayed to a party of 8 billet who went to Poperinghe to a regimental funeral on the period 15-19 June. and the rest [illeg?]. Subsequently it was ascertained that three civilians were suffering from Enteric fever in the next town, and one of these died from the disease. This information was little not being from the brickmaker who also is attacked. The two CCS and who examined these cases. The O.D.H. was informed of above facts. Precautionary action hitherto follows. A wooden wall of the penty of "B" [illeg] billet a tarpaulin was made. Tea.C. was picket and the fully infected their an separate latrine & urinal was provided. The intr were kept under daily observation. The men N.C. and R and civils mark by the occupants of the billets reinforced and PR BRAYSHON and disinfected kept in the throph. Steam disinfector.	Belgium. James Ward 27/woo & Belgium. Sheet 28.
13.7.15	No 35713 Gr BOFFIN S.C was transferred to CCSlah at HAZEBROUCK as a probable case of Enteric fever, he reported sick about the same from as MIDDLEDITCH. These two men have been inoculated against Enteric fever as follows: MIDDLEDITCH 1CC on 15/1/15, 1/2CC 5/7/15 BOFFIN. 1/2 CC and 1 CC on 14 1CC entry on Jan 15. The blood examined for the fourth in the case of MIDDLEDITCH	

N.C. McMullan Maj. RAMC

WAR DIARY
or
INTELLIGENCE SUMMARY.
(Erase heading not required.)

Army Form C. 2118.

Hour, Date, Place	Summary of Events and Information	Remarks and references to Appendices
Dr m Charles de KERVEL L 2 A d 13.7.15	Visited D.Station BRANDHOEK. met Captain BRYDEN RAMC came to report his impending transfer to my unit.	Belgium 1 France Sheet 27 NW.00.00 ½ Belgium Sheet 28 NW.00.00 ½
14.7.15	Following orders received last night W/I OC No 8 Fd Amb. I have detail Capt G.B EDWARDS to take over permanent medical charge of 2 R Irish Rifles from Lt C JACOBS. He will act as senior Med Officer. I h/of B/n. This will be in event out when Capt. R.A BRYDEN RAMC reports to you for duty. Sgnd Col AMS This move deprives me of my second in command and at the same time of my 3rd senior RAMC Officer. I saw the A.D.M.S. personally and also protested in writing offering the services of another Regular RAMC Officer of nearly the same years service. My protest was of no avail. Bringing the total to 6 warps I have available under the following reliefs for other units. 1. a NCO clerk for No 9 F. Ambulance. 2. a corporal to the Division Ammunition Column. Neither a cpl who was then posted to No 7 F. Amb. 3. A mp 2nd in command who is relieved by an officer who had never done duty with a Field Ambulance in service.	
15.7.15	The above changes are so obviously to the disadvantage of my unit that I think it right to record them.	
16.7.15	Visited the Dressing Station at BRANDHOEK, the following have been reported to the ADMS by Capt DARLING. Three cases of measles have occurred in the BERMUDA volunteers attached to 1st Lincoln Regt. 79 Natives of BERMUDA are notoriously prone to measles.	

Army Form C. 2118.

WAR DIARY
or
INTELLIGENCE SUMMARY.
(Erase heading not required.)

Instructions regarding War Diaries and Intelligence Summaries are contained in F.S. Regs., Part II. and the Staff Manual respectively. Title pages will be prepared in manuscript.

Hour, Date, Place	Summary of Events and Information	Remarks and references to Appendices
Transferred to HERMES 21.d. 15.7.15	It will probably be desirable to divide the Unit detachment at once. The A.D.M.S. Guards having no preference of this information seems rather any step to obtain advisable. Some Interior rich of the 5th Mountain Battery having been detached at the Dressing Station, application to the A.D.M.S. for instructions as to final disposal of these if recovery toward them down safe. 7/ A.D. CARBERY proceeded on leave. Capt. G.A. EDWARDS left for duty with 2 Irish Rifles. Capt. R.A. BRYDEN reported bad evening for duty with this unit. Visited Station BRANDHOEK. The work is proceeding satisfactorily. Large numbers of re-inoculations are being performed daily. This has been necessary as when the troops were first inoculated against Enteric Fever last Autumn tourist in a large number only received a single dose ICC. There were now all receiving the two doses 1/2cc + 1cc with 10 day interval. In this work my officers are assisting the Regimental Medical Officers, and the necessary vaccine, and equipment is provided at my dressing station — The 9th Light Battery was now in action in another portion of the line held by the 5th Division a Mej I Lee broker a bone of his ... A Dressing Station at H 31 (d) 4.9. and all these sick and 16.7. Wounded are transferred to my dressing station at.	Belgium & France Shed 2000 & Belgium. Shed 28

M.C. Anderson
Lt Col R.A.M.C.

WAR DIARY or INTELLIGENCE SUMMARY

Army Form C. 2118.

Hour, Date, Place	Summary of Events and Information	Remarks and references to Appendices
Ferme Charles de Kerret L. 21.d. 16.7.15.	BRANDHOEK, and from there an addition to W.C. Station the CCStation HAZEBROUCK or DRStation & Ambulances as required as required cases against treatment at CCStations, under arrangements made by HQ 2nd Army, they are distributed in flavors. All equipment cases sick and wounded to No 10 CCStation by means of cars of the F. Ambulances. All other cases to CCStations at HAZEBROUCK by means of cars of No.5 M.A. Convoy. — The CCStations at HAZEBROUCK take in cases in rotation as follows: Mondays & Thursdays No.5 C.C.S. Tuesdays & Fridays S. Midlands C.C.S. Wednesdays & Saturdays No.2. C.C. Station It is then possible for declination of all cases passing to L of C. through my unit to be made in the A&D Room and AF.A.36, an important point in view of the frequent unquired cases from OTE. 3rd Echelon and regarding distribution of patients.— No. 7 23032. a/SM CHANTER.R.R.O.C. joined for duty in relief of a/SM HEAD who proceeds to No.3 Div.Amm.Train. The weather has been extremely wet and somewhat cold of late, and in consequence the amount of sickness	Belgium (France Sheet 27A 1/40,000) & Belgium Sheet 28

Army Form C. 2118.

WAR DIARY
or
INTELLIGENCE SUMMARY.
(Erase heading not required.)

Instructions regarding War Diaries and Intelligence Summaries are contained in F.S. Regs., Part II. and the Staff Manual respectively. Title pages will be prepared in manuscript.

Hour, Date, Place	Summary of Events and Information	Remarks and references to Appendices
Farm Charles de KERVEL L21.d. 16.7.15 17.7.15	Ration increased. — Decline to all officers found at NQ in General Organization of the army in the Field and its administrative services. Wanted 10 Station at BRANDHOEK gave instruction that the destination of all cases sent to C.C. Station shall be noted in A.B. Book. Instruction from N/N that as there is no accommodation at DRS or 10 C.C. Station for sick officers other than lying down cases I am to make arrangements to transfer them if from Adv.D Station preferring men's tents. 1. may please be informed if these cases are to be sent to C.C. Station at HAZEBROUCK 2. If so am I to apply for own forms 5 M.A.C. through your office. 3. These could not supply I.A. burial parties and require only about 7 days rest, they could be at all times of the day 10 hours no facilities at BRANDHOEK for their rest and feeding. These officers while waiting for the Cars the routine Daily evacuation by 16 or N.A.t. takes place at 6 A.M. —	Belgium & France Sheet 27 20000 or Belgium Sheet 28..
18.7.15	Re question of accommodation of sick officers Q.O has agreed recognition "Place rule for hire" at BRAN BACK. Interview with O.C 112 Coy R.E. who at my suggestion will arrange an alteration bench, and such for washing clothes on S. bank of YPERBEEK.	
19.7.15	Saw MO and arranged to find known officers to transfer to C.C Station at YPEROUCK, and reported that they Should be at as practicable soon after their evacuation. — Localized attack planned for full bright, details communicated 3208 to me at 12 noon; natural arrangements as follows :—	M.E. Michelot Lt Col RAMC

(9 26 6) W 257—976 100,000 4/12 H WV

Army Form C. 2118.

WAR DIARY
or
INTELLIGENCE SUMMARY.
(Erase heading not required.)

Instructions regarding War Diaries and Intelligence Summaries are contained in F.S. Regs., Part II. and the Staff Manual respectively. Title pages will be prepared in manuscript.

Hour, Date, Place	Summary of Events and Information	Remarks and references to Appendices
Ferme Charles de NERVEL L.21.d. 19.7.15.	A post for lightly wounded is to be established in a house near ramparts in vicinity of the LILLE gate. A post to stretcher cases at Culvert beneath YPRES-HOOGE-MENIN road. Square I.18.a. The aid post in Sanctuary wood T.18.c.(6) and 24.(6). The attack consists of the blowing up of a mine under a redoubt formed by the remnant of the HOOGE CHATEAU, subsequent attack by two mines (front party) of 1st GORDONS and two companies of 4 MIDDX Regt. Orders issued as follows. Collecting Arrangements for night 19.20. 1 Lt WESSELOW and RAMC detachment as shewn will report at Hqrs 8 INF Bde at 6 PM today to take over depot for walking cases detailed by DADMS this morning. Those cases will be evacuated by motor ambulance wagons during the night. Reinf detachment 1 Sept 2 N. Orderlies & Bearers. 2. Lt STEWART RAMC will collect wounded from Culvert on YPRES-HOOGE MENIN road and neighbourhood square I.18.a. These wounded will be in charge of F.T. PHELAN. He will proceed from BRANDHOEK at 6.15 PM with the following cars, bearers and personnel. 2 TALBOT Cars. 16 Bearers 2 Trailers 3. AUSTIN Cars 21 Bearers 3 Trailers 3. FORD Cars 9 Bearers B. Trailers. The wounded will be evacuated direct to advance dressing Station BRANDHOEK 3 Lt BAZETT RAMC will collect from aid posts SANCTUARY WOOD Squares I.18.C(6) and 24 (6). Aid posts will be in charge of MO. 4 K MIDDX & 1st GORDONS. He will proceed from BRANDHOEK at 8.15 PM with his following car bearers and personnel. The wounded to be evacuated direct BRANDHOEK to A & D Station BRANDHOEK. 4 AUSTIN Cars 26 Bearers 14 Trailers 1 motor cycle with S.TS.T BARGE	Belgium 1 France Sheet 17 10000 Belgium Sheet 28

W. Fincham
Lt. Col. RAMC

WAR DIARY
or
INTELLIGENCE SUMMARY.
(Erase heading not required.)

Army Form C. 2118.

Hour, Date, Place	Summary of Events and Information	Remarks and references to Appendices
Farm Railes de KEMEL L 21 (d). 19.7.15	Proceeded myself to the Dressing Station, taking Capt DARLING & Lieut MAURICE to assist in dressings. — Everything worked except City front detachment of wounded arrived.	Belgium & France Sheet 27 west. Belgium Sheet 28.
	10.40 A.M. and the whole line dried up, preceded by H.A.C. by 5.30 A.M. Total casualties 5 Officers (5 us Bouverie) aid of wounds. LT BARRIE ERSKINE 4th A/yle Sutherlands Hyrs attached to (Gordon—118 Rank & file. 1 Died of wounds Sgt LAW 4th HIGHR REGT.	
20.7.15	Extra personnel all returned to H.Qr. by 7 A.M. — Capt DENYER R.A.M.C in charge of Dressing Station did well this, being his first experience of a heavy day's work in a Dressing Station. Subsequently Seven more slightly wounded arrived at post in Sandbags all of were evacuated during the morning hingry. The total sick & fit up to 125. Notified to H.Q. 3rd Division that six wounded German prisoners were awaiting examination by Intelligence Officers. —	
7 P.M.	Major SIMPSON saw me and & stated information as regards the cleaning arrangements in our present zone, & his officer will proceed with my attending officers & went to inspect aid posts dwelt etc.	
	D.A.D.M.S. reports probability of extra activity our front tonight. I therefore made the following arrangements. Detailed on NO. 7 Amb for six cars — LT. MAURICE proceed with M/C FORD and 1 N.C.O. to proceed to bal in rear parts, he will report to H.Q. 9th Bde.	M S. Buchan 9. YouRene

WAR DIARY
or
INTELLIGENCE SUMMARY.
(Erase heading not required.)

Army Form C. 2118.

Instructions regarding War Diaries and Intelligence Summaries are contained in F. S. Regs., Part II. and the Staff Manual respectively. Title pages will be prepared in manuscript.

Hour, Date, Place	Summary of Events and Information	Remarks and references to Appendices
Farm C 20 b. de 14-NWR L21.d. 28.7.15	and will send truck except as they come in with the Car at midnight.	Belgium / France Sheet 27 & Belgium Sheet 28 1/40000
8 PM	Capt BRYDEN with 2 NCOS & D Brown, proceed in six cars to BRAYDINGEN. These cars and extra bearer will proceed to collect wounded, Lt STEWART in the same area as last night, Lt B & 21 ST had already started with the usual nightly collecting party. Capt BRYDEN to await at R. Station.	
10 PM	I went to R. Station. Inf all collected 6 officers & 2 O.Ranks wounded and 26 sick. The wounded were about all shell wounds and 87 of them were severe & generally multiple. The collection was much slower than on night 19/20 as owing to the requests not being warned, the collect post was not used, one Lt STEWART's lorry and cars were to a large extent idle. In addition to this the road from the entrance to ECOLE BIENFAISANCE to culvert about very severely shelled up to midnight - Pte CONNOR R.M.C. was killed. Several cars were struck, and one AUSTIN had to be towed back owing to a hole in the petrol tank. In spite of this Lt STEWART, & his bearers kept up to the culvert displaying great coolness and courage.	

A.R.Malcolm
Lt Col RAMC

Army Form C. 2118.

WAR DIARY
or
INTELLIGENCE SUMMARY.
(Erase heading not required.)

Hour, Date, Place	Summary of Events and Information	Remarks and references to Appendices
Farm E. belo de WERVEL L 21 d 21.7.15	All quiet, except three German wounded were evacuated by 6.A.M.	Belgian Prince Shell 27 to Belgian Reel 28 40000
10 A.M.	Received following:- Two officers and some NCOs should proceed to ADrsg Station 5th Division. Sg 27. c. 6.7. Grounds Hey. and they should learn ground east of YPRES canal, and arrangements for collecting that further 5th Div front. can to hed done thy day equivalent 5th Div AD SA will furnish guides and BRANDHOEK will probably close morning 22nd and re-open at Farm #36 a. 86. Same morning. new operation orders will be issued later. — In accordance with above Capt BRYDEN ordered to be ready to open with 'B' Section on morning 22nd July. LT TILBURY to make an inventory of extra equipment now at BRANDHOEK.	
2 P.M.	Saw Capt BEDDOES RAMC in charge of ADStation which is in Square #27 (6), obtained outline of collecting arrangements, and arranged for 2 officers & 2 NCOs to meet further there at 3 P.M. and go over area. LT BAZETT, LT de WESSELOW, Sgt BARTON & Cpl FERGUSON, left in party above noted. Received verbal notice now that time to 1st hour.	

M.Mulholm Lt Col RAMC

Army Form C. 2118.

WAR DIARY
or
INTELLIGENCE SUMMARY.
(Erase heading not required.)

Instructions regarding War Diaries and Intelligence Summaries are contained in F. S. Regs., Part II. and the Staff Manual respectively. Title pages will be prepared in manuscript.

Hour, Date, Place	Summary of Events and Information	Remarks and references to Appendices
Farm to East of KEMMEL L.21.d 21.7.15 6 P.M.	Received orders cancelling above, and ordering me to close retained D Station at BRANDHOEK on morning of 22nd July, and withdraw the section.	Belgium 1 inch Sheet 29. Belgium Sheet 28 20000
22.7.15	Reconnoitred from 7 to line selected at BRANDHOEK on 23rd. HOOGRAAF G.26.(c) Sheet 28. Arranged time of open with OC 9.A gr.6 Bn at present in occupation. OC outgoing 9.A. promised to clear by 2 P.M., assuming renewals done accordingly. Issued instructions to close D station BRANDHOEK at 12 noon on 23rd, but to leave one gun for three men of 6th Bn here till the 1st Middelburg? arr., probably about 1.5 P.M. Collection from D Station carried out by one Tcar pel 22/23 and after by 44th D.A. in person.	
HOOGRAAF G.26.(c) 23.7.15	The Field Ambulance lend "C" Section and Rover field division "A" Section at BRANDHOEK went to school at HOOGRAAF G.26 c Sheet 28. It was arranged in conjunction with OC 1st 9.A.N. Midlands Division, who arranged to relieve officer by 2 P.M.	
7 P.M.	The NGH. The NG.M.S. respectfully certain difficulties were truly inland at local accommodation. Buildings difficulty of placing tub use for the patients. The small field of the School C. Arrachep here was totally wanting though this school would turn from our Excellent gift to Pat Yr kindness to Fail Cabinet offered to the only attempt, situated in large fields, fair, not available, as according to Statts	

M. Anderson Tyler Aane

WAR DIARY
or
INTELLIGENCE SUMMARY.
(Erase heading not required.)

Army Form C. 2118.

Hour, Date, Place	Summary of Events and Information	Remarks and references to Appendices
HOOGE 1st.F. G.26.c 24.7.15	The rest of July 7 and 8 left with us observing the following dead not wounded - In Leicesters 3598 Pte MARRIOTT. R.G. QSW Abdomen Adm 10 PM 23/7/15 died 5:30 am 24/7.15. Buried in cemetery at back of Chapel. 1 Pte 4th Leicesters, 1 Pte 1 Bugler of 1st Staffords, 1 Cpl 3 Staff 1 Pte 1 D.of B. Coldst 1 D.S.G. —Tomorrow sick round this morning 2 D. of B. Coldst 1 D.S.G. Irish Derbys, 1 A.S.C.T. are the entire Strength of "b" Division - At 10-30 AM sent note to HQ 118 46 Brown. The Pte M.H. Brown Gd. Ambulance and yesterday. Sick of the 46 "b" Brown are coming here buried the remains of the division and 6th Field Ambulance to informed where these dead should be sent. At 3 P.M. as no reply was received learnt there 8 cases at 11:20 of 146 Brown near by, and arranged for burial of the cases above named - Notification of the death was sent to the man's record, and kits from all effects. Two men on an a rice not planned from the Regiment. Went to DICKEBUSCH and saw Brethren some of the 3rd and Latrine said, which were left there about the end of May when the Brethren moved. Only one messing tin filled back. Some tins were frightfully, and a length of hose — 7.30 Lt. EXPLAYER and BRANDMARK Party went to the urgent post of Central ave dragon trench 1st BA 25.77 arrived 81 M.O.R.	Belgium & France Sheet 57 & Belgium — Sheet 28 North

W. Nicholson
Lt. McLaurin

Army Form C. 2118.

WAR DIARY
or
INTELLIGENCE SUMMARY.
(Erase heading not required.)

Instructions regarding War Diaries and Intelligence Summaries are contained in F.S. Regs., Part II. and the Staff Manual respectively. Title pages will be prepared in manuscript.

Hour, Date, Place	Summary of Events and Information	Remarks and references to Appendices
HOOGRAAF G 26 (C) 24.7.15 - 7PM 28.7.15	Lt BIZET with motor ambulances are gone to join from BRANDHOEK. Kash Insp. also having left the building area. Made tour of Artillery area and decided on necessary sanitary details. — Pick still being transferred from No. 9 7 Amb, reconstruction as yet on 6 dispersal received from A.D.M.S. — D.O. No. 3 & 21st July para 3 have 20 & 7 July inclusive all sick from 3rd Division will be sent to Hop. Hund. in fit for further duties. Report of Cars sent night of Hosse Komstein, description sent for to flick horse in Bart Ordered, sent to A.D.M.S. Following journies in reply to move sent to A.D.M.S. were repeated that relieves of motor ambulances from G.H.Q may be essential before D.C. 5 to 9 Aug. A.C. 1190's 20th Ambulances A9883, A9888 sent to G.H.Q by orders A.D.T. labelled to your unit are despatched from June 22 inst. Consig. 37609 A.S.C. Abbville".	Belgian Sheet 28 worn.
2 P.M.	Twenty seven sick also had food to 18 Fd Ambulance 6 men having been in my Camp. Report sent to A.D.M.S 3rd Division. Showing numbers and units:— 4) Gordon Highrs, All came from Regtl transport. 2) Royal Scots 2. 1) RIR Scots 2. 1) Royal Fusiliers 14. Issue to A.D.M.S Reference Q.O. No 3 paras 3 & 7 asking for instructions a following parade:— Are we weed of to detain if the thing doesn't work at no 7 Fd. Amb. transports to my unit. Are Refugees cases to take any referring treatment at QCU prior to evacuation to HAZEBROUCK.	

M Shirley Calvin
Lt Col R AMC

Army Form C. 2118.

WAR DIARY
or
INTELLIGENCE SUMMARY.
(Erase heading not required.)

Instructions regarding War Diaries and Intelligence Summaries are contained in F. S. Regs., Part II. and the Staff Manual respectively. Title pages will be prepared in manuscript.

Place	Date	Hour	Summary of Events and Information	Remarks and references to Appendices
HdQrs RAMC F.26.C.	25/7/15	—	Officer Key to be evacuated by the M.T.C from here or not they to be transferred to No 7. Field Ambulance. In the event of my having no accommodation here may I send cas to No 7 F.A? How are officers to be dealt with? Sent J. Ambulry to Argues & Funk all day. An extensive power of fly breeding found in horse lines 3rd Field Ambulance of Midland Division. Manure to O.C. horse lines to deal with enigo O.C. emerged came up in the afternoon and promised to do necessary comp.— O.C Chapini's Troop R.E. came in answer to a written request and agreed to fit. had advice for 6 pails 2 horse trane shelter for tents, 8 bookhouse shelter for personnel, to boost house shelter for officers mess, & have all main trenches for personnel etc. Issued me all supplies equipmt & surgical & med on supplies to O.C. 9th S. Ambulance. Sewed a 9th S. Section with all Equipt, inspection, and examination of NCOs and nursing orderlies.	B/Spencer that 28 4000
	26/7/15		Austin car No.1 9883, & 9858 arrived back. They were sent for repair to the shops at CHATIER de NORMANDIE, ROUEN on 14th and 21st June respectively. The required report as to repairs required signed by the O.C. 7th A.M. Unit GRONAUM was sent with each car in each case. Here was a crack in the chassis in which repair welding or plating. After a vast amount of the graphing and writing I eventually succeeded in getting the cars back. We have despatched from the above shops on 20 July no less that 18 M.T. and GHQ, taking nearly 6 days to cover a journey of a few hours. The cars No 4 had been plated and on arrival the bolts were several mut. signatures

Army Form C. 2118.

WAR DIARY
or
INTELLIGENCE SUMMARY.
(Erase heading not required.)

Place	Date	Hour	Summary of Events and Information	Remarks and references to Appendices
HOOGRAAF G26(c)	26/9/15	—	Orders from D.D.M.S. to take in ordinary sick and lightly wounded transferred from No 9 Amb & also accessory D.R.S. Pointed out that I was less fit & short of a Field Ambulance's extra equipment and unless small & required note that as far as equipment concerned I might have to obtain some amount of equipment from No 7 & 9 Ambulances.	Belgium 28 1/100000
	27/9/15		Arranged with O.C. No 7 Ambulance to send men discharged to duty from their unit and mine on alternate days, under charge of an N.C.O. These men moved off at 7 A.M. to the Brigade Supply Dump, where they are handed over.	
			The horse ambulance wagon sent in accordance with orders from D.M.S. to G.30.c 4.9. to run local work. No Mot MT Amb went to front there to relieve wagon proceeded to AUBREUX MAISON DICKEBUSCH, and returned not more	
			Lieut L/pl BLISS Corp? Sing Mag 3 Reed also informed me that the outbreak of a lot and three men who had the sick as turn up into the DUGOUDON & HILLHURST having fell called for.	
			Inspected "C" section and then equipments. The men are kept in the lines but expected by the time leaving No 7 Sheet. All clothed & overcoats have been collected and turned to a certain extent. But the lines are still very foul. Sent the Subaltern to see the cooks of the field with a view to getting it altogether, but without success.	
			Having cars and lorries returned to No 1 MFC STOMER	

Army Form C. 2118.

WAR DIARY
or
INTELLIGENCE SUMMARY.
(Erase heading not required.)

Place	Date	Hour	Summary of Events and Information	Remarks and references to Appendices
HOOGERAAF- G 26 c	27/7/15		Sent the following Dental Surgeons NCOs &Men in accordance with that [received] from DGMS in the field. 1. RSur. Price N. 18231 3rd British R. & Gnsn. Hosp. 2746 Pte. Wilkersley J. & Sgt. Thompson S.F. per bus. The [latter] two were deemed to travel to Base for dental treatment. The last [remaining] fit for duty.	Return 28 40000
	28/7/15		In accordance with Depo[...] all [Dental] [Schools] were this day inspected by Col C. [...] [motor] transport [of] [...] personnel, the duty of [same] vs NCOs being [marked] on each [school]. Any differences due to orders experienced being enough [...] The [two] [copies] of the two Ind. cases on [...] from No. 1 Mal. GHQ on arriving [...] [same] [schools], and as they were probably [...] get [...] [...] [...] few [...] with them. — PO W's [...] the [Dressing] [Station], and asked for an officer to attend. [...] Lt. GLYNN 1st Northumberland Fusiliers on night of 30/31 July. Lt. Carling [...] — Being [military] [...] this day [...] the copies of two [...] a [...] [...] [...] [...] were [...] [...] with by [...] of [...] with R. alt. of [...] and [the] use of [...] [...] the Local inhabitants to state that 17 horses are buried there —	
	29/7/15		Completed [survey] of [...] held up with a view to filling up [...] [...] and during [...] in the top of [...] [...] to [...]. [...] accommodation available in vicinity (all except) [...] [...] of this section. Appears that a full R. [...] for [...] [...] [...] a will [...] a marked [...] in [...] [...] [...] [...] sickness — Correspondence from this Source.	[signatures]

Army Form C. 2118.

WAR DIARY
or
INTELLIGENCE SUMMARY.
(Erase heading not required.)

Instructions regarding War Diaries and Intelligence Summaries are contained in F. S. Regs., Part II. and the Staff Manual respectively. Title pages will be prepared in manuscript.

Place	Date	Hour	Summary of Events and Information	Remarks and references to Appendices
HOOGRAFF G.2.6.c.	29/7/15		Water carts inspected with a view to ascertaining efficacy of the chloride of lime being used for sterilization — those in use by the cavalry the for containing the powder were found much rusted, and the powder called moral mustard. Water cart also been arranged that this powder must be replaced and the boxes these from rust.	Belgium Sheet 28 / 40005
	30/7/15		LtCorporal Hospital for Inspection Lt Stewart RAMC & Rev Muir returned from leave. The O.C. Cheshire 9th Bay R.E. came to put up the necessary shelter and latrines that from the recent runs attack of machine gun fire & corrugated iron. The newly appointed officer in the will and found correctly diminishing.	
	31/7/15		Horse shoe in connection with no. 7 & 8 Fd F.A. held at billet of Lt. Moore Ammo Column & open to Field Ambulances of the Division, the runners won: 1st prize Sergt. Snape R.A.M.C Lorie. 1st Pte ... B. Real Spiers in ambulance company. The victor had assisted on the A.D. Lt. personnel & my transport officer	

Lt G.N. MAURICE

121/6650

ams

3rd 5 Division

8th Field Ambulance

Vol VII

From 1 - 31 . 8 . 15

August 1915

WAR DIARY or INTELLIGENCE SUMMARY

Army Form C. 2118.

8th Field Ambulance

Place	Date	Hour	Summary of Events and Information	Remarks and references to Appendices
HOOGGRAAF 28c	1/8/15		The watersupply to drinking troops was insufficient, arrangements made in reconnaissance supply of water was found in BOESCHEPE Sheet 28c N.35.c. Sheet 27. Also the steam ran through wired and a reservoir made to enable a small watercart to be filled. The 3rd Brunival Division is taking over. This is a suitable platform behind the fourgon which will enable water to be pumped out & taken on in pails for water carts etc which cannot come up nearer front lines. Sgt RICHARDS detailed to make this water carts to be pulled than lorries.	Belgium France Sheet 27 Belgium Sheet 28
	2/8/15		Two infantry brigades of 3rd Brunival to relieve two of the 6th Division on night 2/3rd August respectively. They will, to take over Brown's stationary VLAMERTINGHE H.3.c and after on 3rd August. On and after the 4th August the sick of these two Brigades will be collected and dealt with by my unit. Sailed O.C. 16 F. Amb and accompanied him to Adv. D. Station M16A + 18th Ambs and ascertained all necessary details. Capt DARLING & Capt BAZETT accompanied me. On Tue night 2/3 August Capt BAZETT will accompany Collecting party in A29 C28 K. 1570 that area will be collected from by us on Aug 3/4.	
	3/8/15		Lt JACOBS attached for fatigue duty from No 7 F. Amb. Capt DARLING, Capt BAZETT, Lt STEWART and Lt JACOBS with Ranse Personnel conveying Field and division of C. and after France (33rd inf). Six motor ambulance wagons with 2 drivers and 1 orderly each will work together for duty with this detachment. These motor ambulance wagons lend by No 7 F.Amb will be available for use in addition. They will be started at my HQN. Letter to Nor B Aug re fixing that between the 2 Chaplains a record of Jews & RC. Aug on each upon RAC personnel.	W Shephen Lt Col Comdg 8 F.Amb

Army Form C. 2118.

WAR DIARY
or
INTELLIGENCE SUMMARY.
(Erase heading not required.)

Instructions regarding War Diaries and Intelligence Summaries are contained in F. S. Regs., Part II. and the Staff Manual respectively. Title pages will be prepared in manuscript.

Place	Date	Hour	Summary of Events and Information	Remarks and references to Appendices
HOOGRAAF G26.C.	3/8/15	4 P.M.	Started the advanced dressing station at PAMERTINGHE H3(c) which was open and ready for work. Lt. NEWSTEAD visited my D.Q. and seemed satisfied that the steps taken to reduce the breeding of flies were adequate except that the flys in neighbouring farm were a trouble, found which required attention — the chief amongst these flies breeding in Horse Manure STOMYXYS that previously been ascertained that Anopheles mosquitos were breeding in the ponds in this neighbourhood, and in fact in all ephem. collection of water for miles round.	Belgian + French Relief 27 Belgian Relief 28 *neuro*
	4/8/15		Arranged to provide M.O.S. for M.M. Train in charge of Lt. CHERBERT to work. Latter leaving to England 12/8/15 also (2) 3rd WORCESTER Regt. on 6th August in relief of Lt. HARLEY MASON proceeding to England. Made to h. and to A.D.M.S. at noon as possible. Thence passed for M. LT. STEWART 32 and 21 LT de WESSELOW O.S.H. Two R.A.M.C. re-inforcements arrived this day transd with 65th F. Ambulance twee Lt. Gen.l at EASTBOURNE. Proceeded at 1-30 P.M. to Advanced Dressing Station and thence with Lt BAZETT to found dug outs in SQNRS C 25(d). M.O's arranged with equipment there for Removal of daily sick between 2+3 P.M. His state of Chateau REIGERSBURG in indifly collecting sick — Visited H.Qrs. Ambulance post at CHATEAU REIGERSBURG, saw officers of 21st + 22nd B.R.F.A. and arranged for this Car to be used in case of emergency in removal of sick wounded from any unit in vicinity. Sonnel 1 Ofr 2 Ges Divine 2 driver MT.A.S.C. next one Ford car. Visited Camps of H.Q B.A & Sqn.s B 5(a) occupied by regiments of 22nd B4 R.F.A. + Batteries of 32 Bde R.F.A. The sick from the batteries are now obviously seen. Received from here but no many cases without any eases by the MO of 32 Ok. Reconnaissance Arm sent to the Officer asking that in future the sick from the Brigade may be ready for medical daily between 2 + 3 P.M. with the same urgent sick reports.	

Sgd. [signatures]

WAR DIARY
or
INTELLIGENCE SUMMARY.
(Erase heading not required.)

Army Form C. 2118.

Instructions regarding War Diaries and Intelligence Summaries are contained in F. S. Regs., Part II. and the Staff Manual respectively. Title pages will be prepared in manuscript.

Place	Date	Hour	Summary of Events and Information	Remarks and references to Appendices
H.Q.9th F.F. G.26.c	4/8/15		The total force of March Hospital were in all four units of front & back and Camp No 4 F.A. In addition there were of the 3rd Division who had been attached to 16th F. Aurt, during the change of transfer that night, were evacuated. Lt Stewart attached Lt Cresson in charge of Northumb: Field Ambulance. Lt W.P. Pritchard R.A.M.C. T.C. + Lt G. Thom R.A.M.C. T.C. + Lt Jan No 3 C.C.S. joined for temporary duty.	Belgium & France 27 — Assigned Mid 28 — total
	5/8/15		Lt G. Thom sent to duty to aux to Railway station. Re-organization and increase of accommodation under orders of R.A.M.S. Arrangements as follows:— A. Ward 12 men B. Ward 28 — 62 In School buildings C. Ward 26 — D. Ward O.P. Tent 13 E. Ward 0.R. Tent 13 58 In Tents F. Ward 4 Bell Tent 16 G. Ward 4 Bell Tents 16 Grand Total 120	

New organization of A.S.C. personnel & vehicles

	Drivers Mtd	Drivers ASC	Vehicles	Horses Draught	Horses Riding	
Bicycles		1				
Cars large motor Chevrolet B1	6	6	1	12		
Cars B world (two section)	3	3	1	6		
Cars F.75	1	1	1	2		
Wagon G.S. Covered		1	1	2		
Wagons Ambulance	3	3	2	6		
Wagons GS Maltese Baggage	6	2		12		
Horses for Spare Loss				3	3	
Horses Spare		3				
Horses riding					78	
Spare mt. Ambulance K	7	14	2			
Spare mt. Spare K	2					
	28	41	18	22	23	

A.S.C. Personnel

Drivers 5
Farriers 2
Batmen 10
— 40
Drivers Vehicle 25

N.C.O. Sergt 1
Shoe. Vehicle 14
Drivers Spare 2
— 17

X Motorcycle 1

WAR DIARY
or
INTELLIGENCE SUMMARY.
(Erase heading not required.)

Army Form C. 2118.

Place	Date	Hour	Summary of Events and Information	Remarks and references to Appendices
HOOGRAAF G.26.c	6/5/15		LT. C. WESSELOW. O.C. Y Coy 3rd WORCESTER Regt. for duty in relief of LT. HARVEY MASON. Capt. DENYER relieves Capt. DARLING R.A.M.C. at advanced dressing station. Capt. DARLING returns, and reports considerable shelling at wherewhile night and day to rail lines in the neighbourhood of the A.D. Dressing Station — On afternoon of 5th the injured hutment at VLAMERTINGHE and Y press were shelled resulting in 30 wounded 1 Stretcher died, and a certain number of Refugees, most of them women belonged to 4th and 6th Cavalry Brigades. Memo to A.D.M.S. stating that arrangement was made to increase our woolen blanket to 150/- The following articles of equipment which is required in excess of that in my possession :- Ambulance 20. Water Proof Sheets 50. Stretchers 40. Gutter Splints 90. Jacconet Muslin 20. Knives 20. Forks 20. Spoons Table No. Plates Enamel 20. Kettles Camp 6. Ladles cook 2. Stoves cookers 2. Urinals 4. Machine Mincing 1.	Belgium France Sheet 27. Belgium Sheet 28 1/40,000

Dr Beckett also requires. In view of increased numbers required permission to use V Corps Reserve Works Supply.

Army Form C. 21N.

WAR DIARY
or
INTELLIGENCE SUMMARY.
(Erase heading not required.)

Instructions regarding War Diaries and Intelligence Summaries are contained in F.S. Regs., Part II. and the Staff Manual respectively. Title pages will be prepared in manuscript.

Place	Date	Hour	Summary of Events and Information	Remarks and references to Appendices
HOOGRAAF G2 & C.	7/8/15		Visit from A.D.M.S with whom I discussed the requirements in equipment which I would call for in my memo yesterday. None of these are apparently available from No 7 B.A. One operating tent obtained from No 9 F. Ambulance. Visited Adv Dressing Station at VLAMERTINGHE, some French Artillery were occupying the schools which formed the hub of my visit and are some 30 yards from the main building. In these schools a considerable quantity of shells were being fired by them — saw the A.D.M.S. 6th Division at once and reported the matter and took action at once by informing the Q branch. On my return I reported the matter to A.D.M.S 3rd Division stating the shell [?] fallen. These schools have been shelled and are close to batteries which are frequently shelled at the present time. — Capt DARLING proceeded on short leave. Inspected the waterworks now in use. These are the VLAMERTINGHE at a point served by a bridge where a pump has been erected, as a convenient & with supply back in G.7 & Sheet 28. Received from O.C. 7 Fd Amb Notes Sheets Zone 175 pillow husks with tops for nose storage.	Belgium France Sheet 7 & Belgium Sheet 28 1/40,000
	8/8/15		Very heavy engagement lasted night apparently in areas occupied by 14th to 4th & 6th Division. Visited Dressing Station VLAMERTINGHE. The French shells are still stored in the schools, no special in/[?] found and wounded last night.	
	9/8/15		Lieut D.F. FINLAY R.A.M.C. TC joined from LE TREPORT at 9 P.M. O.C. R.F. Ambulance 6th Division acts of avoidance 9.15–20 French Sixteen horses and down in the care of 9 Fd. Ambulance Reporton work done by these horses. Called for form L/1 BAZETT Three horse carts returned to 3rd Brit Train en route Advanced Depot R.T.	

[signatures]

Army Form C. 2118.

WAR DIARY
or
INTELLIGENCE SUMMARY.
(Erase heading not required.)

Instructions regarding War Diaries and Intelligence Summaries are contained in F. S. Regs., Part II. and the Staff Manual respectively. Title pages will be prepared in manuscript.

Place	Date	Hour	Summary of Events and Information	Remarks and references to Appendices
HOOGRAAF 926 C	10/8/15		M*CKBERY returned to H.Q. L*T THOM H*T PRITCHARD to report their writ turnover order from D.O.M.S. L*T FINLAY sent to A.D.D. Station Furlers.	Belgium Itinerary Sheet 27. to Reel 28.
		7.30 PM	Received order to send M.O. for duty with N. Lancashire Regt. as L*T NASH wounded. L*T JACOBS sent. He belongs to No. 7 F. Amb. but I had no other officer available. This leaves me with the following officers acting in B Section with an average daily sick rate of 120. Capt BRYDEN, L*T MAURICE, Capt DENYER, Capt BAZETT and L*T FINLAY at reduced dressing station collecting and disposing of sick and wounded of 9th, 19th Rifle Brigades and 1st Battery of 16th Division. Capt DARLING in town, and myself. L*T CARBERY home on sick furlough.	
	11/8/15		Visited Gen. B. Nation, and proceeding on half felicity L*T THOM H*T PRITCHARD rejoined their unit.	
	12/8/15		Recommendation for gallantry in collecting water during shellfire on 9th/10th Aug sent to O.D.M.S. Maines as follows: Capt H.C. BAZETT RAMC (SR), No.2791 S/Cpl. J. SYKES RMC(SR), No.730 Pte J. NEELY RAMC, No.4889 Pte W.O. BROWNE RAMC.— No. 57, Pte H. HARDY, 1 NORTHUMBERLAND FUSRS: a prisoner awaiting C. Martial for desertion has been detained under observation since afternoon of 10th August. He is in my opinion sane, and is feigning loss of memory and dementia. He was examined by a Medical Board assembled on 11th July last at 17th F. Amb. for the purpose of enquiring into his state of mind.	

M. Shedlock
Lt Col R.A.M.C.

Army Form C. 2118.

WAR DIARY
or
INTELLIGENCE SUMMARY.
(Erase heading not required.)

Instructions regarding War Diaries and Intelligence Summaries are contained in F. S. Regs., Part II. and the Staff Manual respectively. Title pages will be prepared in manuscript.

Place	Date	Hour	Summary of Events and Information	Remarks and references to Appendices
HdQrs RAMC G.26.C.0	12/8/15		The Board consisted of the following members. Major T.F. FIELDING D.S.O. RAMC Capt. C. McQUEEN RAMC and T.E.L. RFD. RAMC. The findings of the Board were as follows. "The Board having met pursuant to order, proceed to examine the above named man. They find no evidence of a depressed fracture of the Skull (under attached medical certificate) Although it is possible that this man may be subject to periodic losses of memory of short duration they find no evidence of any physical disability which would or affect his statements. They find no evidence of delusions of sight, hearing or of the other special senses and can discover no derangement of his mind. They consider that this man is not insane at the present time, and that he was not insane at the time he committed the offence. Signed in the field 11 day July 1915." Major RAMC President Captain Raunt J McQueen Lt Rawe I also obtained the opinion of Lt L.H. RAMC who has had 9 years experience of Asylum work. He also is of opinion that the man is sane. It was decided that this is a suggestion that this diary with a recommendation that the Medical Board be held as soon as possible.	Belgium + France Sheet 29 to Belgium Sheet 28 $\frac{1}{40,000}$

WAR DIARY
or
INTELLIGENCE SUMMARY
(Erase heading not required.)

Army Form C. 2118.

Place	Date	Hour	Summary of Events and Information	Remarks and references to Appendices
H.Q.GR.M.R. G.O.C. 13/5/15	13/5/15		Visited Cdr. A. Stabin. Returned from this section here from conclusively prepared of Col. E. the Leap Camp inspected & exercised men's Cates. Obtained a shipwreck from some of men and told Charles de Kunz a carpenter that no damage was done to their property during the stay they were there. Surrounded accommodation to Captain BAZETT, H/Col SYKES, PICKELL and BROWN no special fare supplied for Dist. H.Q. Investigated several cases of refugees reminding us a refugee family living in the Hotel forse. Brazilla and missing refuge of Camp people there.	Belgian Race Sheet 27 and Belgian Sheet 28 1/40000
	14/5/15		This morning Capt DENYER from my reports Sassing with heavy high explosive within 150 yards of the running station. The M.O.W visited my Headquarters and could for me no information of the patrols through going of my section at WATHERMTINGHE. This morning at about 7 S.M. I visited the Advanced dressing station, and during my visit high explosives bursting within 40 or 50 yards of the track of the house. I remained in a similarly from other buildings of the tower and eventually found a suitable Supply house in God. This is approaching to a Dir area. I saw the April 3rd Brain personally and obtained promise to move the section tonight. He would arrange for my occupation of the Pullstout building. Returned to Cdr A. Stabin and arranged the most ideal should be completed this morning after the evacuation of the sector.	Belgian Sheet 28

W.S. Stubbs Lt. Col. R. Mc. Connell

Army Form C. 2118.

WAR DIARY
or
INTELLIGENCE SUMMARY.
(Erase heading not required.)

Instructions regarding War Diaries and Intelligence Summaries are contained in F. S. Regs. Part II. and the Staff Manual respectively. Title pages will be prepared in manuscript.

Place	Date	Hour	Summary of Events and Information	Remarks and references to Appendices
HOOGRAAF G.26.c	15/8/15	2 AM	Returned from new Advanced Dressing Station, the men will be complete by 6 am, most of the material having already been moved. Capt DARLING WIMS from camp.	Belgium & France Sheet 27
			The Daily State and other returns from O.C."Section" extremely badly prepared. Lately Sgt HOWES relieved of his clerical duties and brought back to H.Q'rs	Belgium Sheet 28 10000
		11.30 AM	Revised the Dressing Station, and sent all motor cars except two back to H.Qrs. In the afternoon and night collections two cars on each occasion will be sent up from H.Qrs. Returned the three cars on loan from No.7 F. Ambulance. Letter to A.D.M.S. acting for arrangements to be made to permanently allotting the new billet for my Adv. D. Station.	
		4 PM	In accordance with telegraphic instructions from Chief Chaplain Revd. W.S. MUIR left for duty with No.8 C.C. Station. His successor Rev. MCLEAN appears to have arranged with the A.O.C. 3rd Divn to live with the 1st GORDON HIGHRS. I have written to A.D.M.S. to ask if this is to be considered official, so that I may fill in my returns A9, B213 and 251.	
	16/8/15		Complaint from O.C. 11 GORDON HIGHRS that No. 2/Cpl WITHERS discharged from my F.Amb on 10/8/15 rejoined deficient of rifle, web equipment, cap etc etc. This O.C. states that men of this regiment sent to 7 Ad Ambulance fully clothed and equipped and seldom return without deficiencies. Report called for by A.D.M.S. for information of D.A.A.A.D.Q. On investigation it was found that this man was a transfer from the 3rd Gordons to 9 F. Ambulance. The nature of his injury was shown as N.Y.D. effects of burial. His diagnosis in my records is shown as "Strain of back." From the I. infer that this man was turned in a trench totally on the wall & ... ... [illegible]	

Army Form C. 2118.

WAR DIARY
or
INTELLIGENCE SUMMARY.
(Erase heading not required.)

Instructions regarding War Diaries and Intelligence Summaries are contained in F. S. Regs., Part II. and the Staff Manual respectively. Title pages will be prepared in manuscript.

Place	Date	Hour	Summary of Events and Information	Remarks and references to Appendices
HOOGE MAP G.26.c	16/8/15		That he did not bring any equipment with him. This statement is contradicted by the fact that L/Cpl MCKENZIE of the same Regiment who came in at the same time had his rifle and equipment. I have overruled entered in the Sick Slip Book. L/Cpl WITHERS rejoined his regiment on 10th August and made no complaint of having lost his rifle and equipment whilst receiving treatment of Ambulance. I have asked to be informed whether L/Cpl WITHERS has stated that he lost his equipment whilst in my F. Amb. — My experience extending over one year with a Field Ambulance, in the field, is that patients seldom arrive with complete kits. — Orders issued that in future men bringing in kits will have them examined again the Sick List Book of A. and B. Co. Any man coming in without kit will sign in Book kept for the purpose that he arrived without kit. The day after admission each patient who is able will clean his rifle and equipment and those who are unable to do this will have their rifle + equipment cleaned by a S.S. fatigue party.	is Belgium [struck] France Sheet 27 & Belgium Sheet 28 — HOOGE
	17/8/15	5 PM	Visited Adv. D station at G.sq Shu 128. Capt DENYER informs me that he should rather take the place yesterday. I am still without any reply. Every means possible had arranged to carry is made with 30" 14 Div" for the permanent relievement of this field for my unit. POPERINGHE should be between 7.30 and 8.30 Sel.	
	18/8/15		Capt DENYER proceeded to take HMH F Amb 14th Division by order of ADMS M6/39/15 dated 14/15/15 — Capt DARLING assumes command of detachment at O'Glencorse + Capt D Station — Orders from ADMS to make arrangements for collection of sick and wounded of 9th Bat Rifle Bde will relieve the 2nd - J 18c. and night fo as usual.	(signatures)

1577 Wt. W10791/1273 500,000 1/15 D. D. & L. A.D.S.S./Forms/C. 2118.

WAR DIARY or INTELLIGENCE SUMMARY

(Erase heading not required.)

Army Form C. 2118

Instructions regarding War Diaries and Intelligence Summaries are contained in F.S. Regs., Part II. and the Staff Manual respectively. Title pages will be prepared in manuscript.

Place	Date	Hour	Summary of Events and Information	Remarks and references to Appendices
HOOGGRAAF G.2.b.c.	18/8/15		extend right to I.30.d. the night of 19/20. First collection by the unit there tonight 20. This will be in addition to the collection now being made from 7th Suff Rs at St Jean Sc. Notification from Capt DARLING that the H.Q. M.G. 14th Divn had previous notice to—	Belgium, France Sheet 27 and Belgium Sheet 28 xxxx
		2 P.M.	Visit our friend Adv Dressing Station at G.5.c.d. Sheet 28 by 10am tomorrow. Immediately communicated personally with the 7th D 7 S and evening 7 Suff received wire the Schools BRANDHOEK G.9.2.d would be handed over to us at 8 AM tomorrow morning. 7— copy forme sent to Capt. D H D. M/ S and Corres and extra transport sent to Cooker Convoy out the more—	
	19/8/15	11 AM	Visited advance dressing station at BRANDHOEK and found the detachment settled in and ready for reception of sick & wounded. Visited I.C. detachment of 18th F Ambulance and arranged for a detachment consisting of 1 SPt and 8 ghl men to share the dug outs and shelters at MAPLE COPSE for 15 Ghl. this bunch leave us the 18th F Amb detachment is withdrawn. The 18 F Amb will collect tonight 19/20.— Sent up front wheeled stretchers and the detachment 1st BRANDHOEK. Capt BAZETT with take them on at the usual collecting place tonight: found out the dug outs and shelters and explain tonight's duties to them—	
		6 P.M.	Proceeded with Lt STEWART and car to KRUITSTRAAT and worked from thence via Bridge 14 — ZILLEBEEK LAKE — ZILLEBEEK VILLAGE — MAPLE COPSE, reaching there at about 7.30 P.M. This is the route by which sick and wounded have been evacuated by day and night by the 18th F Ambulance, a as being permanently stationed at bridge 14, carrying them thence through to in square H.24.a. This made the conduct of a mule road about as far as the cube of square I.22.a and from there to a crossing over trench Sterling. The horse abs stream	W Shudbek K. W Nove

Army Form C. 2118

WAR DIARY
or
INTELLIGENCE SUMMARY.
(Erase heading not required.)

Instructions regarding War Diaries and Intelligence Summaries are contained in F.S. Regs., Part II. and the Staff Manual respectively. Title pages will be prepared in manuscript.

Place	Date	Hour	Summary of Events and Information	Remarks and references to Appendices
HOOGE RAMP. G 26 e 28	19/8		The road is a very bad one. It would be practically impossible in wet weather for wheels. Sketches made judging by the number of shell holes & all says it is subject to severe shell fire. The communication trench is fairly good. Defences in ZILLEBEKE village after the front it is much narrower and thinner. Separate points of junction I 25 6 & I 23 c is under regular rifle fire. The whole distance is about 8½ kilos. In my opinion and that of 1/L STEWART & Capt BAZETT the route is most unsuitable and in wet weather impossible. The collection will therefore be done as formerly when the 3rd Division reached this front, by cars proceeding via JAMMERTJ to the YPRES - MENIN road & down the railway crossing and thence down the ZILLEBEKE road to a building in Square I 19 d. The lying cases being brought by means of wheeled stretchers from MAPLE COPSE along the track around Square I 24 a, 23 H and I 17 b.	Belgium Sheet 28 1/40,000
	20/8/15	11AM	The A.D.M.S. visited my H.Qrs and informed me of arrangement made	
		12 Noon	Worked. advanced Dressing Station Capt BAZETT reports detachment duly posted in MAPLE COPSE last night	
		3 PM	Message sent to Brigade Major 9th Inf. Bde: "Following arrangements for collection and wounded and RAMC detachment in MAPLE COPSE are working well. Shall meet Stone by 9-15 PM. Lying cases taken, first 10-15 DM. are being collection in cars wounded after first collection will be made at I am and Stone inform all Regimental M.O.S. and Stone acknowledge and Received remarks of Lieut. Burton and Sent sub division forward at HAZEBROUCK"	

Remarks...

WAR DIARY or INTELLIGENCE SUMMARY

Army Form C. 2118.

(Erase heading not required.)

Instructions regarding War Diaries and Intelligence Summaries are contained in F. S. Regs., Part II. and the Staff Manual respectively. Title pages will be prepared in manuscript.

Place	Date	Hour	Summary of Events and Information	Remarks and references to Appendices
#10 G.R.M.F. G.2.b.c.	20/8/15		Lt B H BARTON R.A.M.C. joined the Field Ambulance in place of Capt DENYER R.A.M.C.	Belgium Sheet 28 1/40,000
	21/8/15		Last night LT STEWART took 17 FIN A.T. round the wards collecting glass for instruction. Heavy rain again this morning which makes it very uncomfortable for our patients in tents.	
	22/8/15		Posted advanced D. Station. Collecting working party — LT STEWART to take his work in hand. Collection — 71B H. BARTON taken to inspection of equipment of A Section, and given instruction. Shelling of HAMMERTINGHE and POPERINGHE at intervals between 6 am and 12 noon. Enemy aeroplanes active during afternoon —	
	23/8/15		Captain L. BUCKLEY R.A.M.C. joined for duty.	
	24/8/15		Visited dugouts at HQ etc. These are at present occupied by 1 officer and a detachment of No 3 FA. & Swans - they are useless for housing wounded, but might serve as a bathing quarters in without cases. Coming back during a heavy engagement by the communication trench from MILL COPSE to KILLEEN LAKE, and the wind rising the bridge into MR UTS FARM from where they could be taken in horsed wagons to the adv D. Station DICKEBUSCH huts. The 142 F Ambulance commanded by Major WYLIE R.A.M.C. arrived and bivouacked in the next farm to ours.	
	25/8/15	12 noon	Visited Adv Dressing Station and inspected the smoke helmets of the whole detachment 79 strong. The old helmets are all log clay and each man will be issued with his 2nd make helmet today's. The old smoke helmets will be stowed, a record kept and the necessary reduced for in abstracting were provided.	
		2 pm	The remainder of the men at H.Q. were served out with the 2nd smoke helmet. So far the satchels for carrying the smoke helmet are not available at Ordnance.	

Army Form C. 2118.

WAR DIARY
or
INTELLIGENCE SUMMARY.
(Erase heading not required.)

Instructions regarding War Diaries and Intelligence Summaries are contained in F.S. Regs., Part II. and the Staff Manual respectively. Title pages will be prepared in manuscript.

Place	Date	Hour	Summary of Events and Information	Remarks and references to Appendices
HOOGRAFF G 26 c	25/8/15	7 P.M.	Wire from MO WILTS Timed 5.30 P.M. asking when Collection unit to meet Brigade and giving numbers. Sergt Small King at Brigade meeting. Reply collected wire to made at 9.30 P.M. Sgts Arrived from line at 8.30 P.M. Capt BAZETT arranged for collection of R.I.R. wounded in ramparts YPRES	Belgium Ref 28 1/40000
	26/8/15		Ascertained by wire the whereabouts of WORCESTER Regt who could not be located by Capt BAZETT since the 7th Brigade went to reserve. H 22 (C). Verbal O.R.d and discussed arrangements in case of attack. Wire will form the subject of a scheme to be published soon — One officer 1 NCO. and 6 bearers when K.h. attached from N2 F. Ambulance to my detachment at BRANDHOEK for instruction in collecting duties.	
			Lt C.G. DOUGLAS RAMC attached for duty in connection with investigation on poisonous gases, he will be supernumerary to establishment.	
	27/8/15		All the 1st issue of Smoke helmets of 'C' Section have been sprayed. The issue of Smoke helmets of 'A' Section were re-sprayed. I took the opportunity of taking the enfilade issue of Lt C.G. DOUGLAS who formed the mail yesterday. — The following A/Corporals were promoted acting Cpls w.e.f. 25 August 1915. Authority A.B.55 Office of the base A.D.G. Section letter No. ADG/5912 dated 25 Aug 1915 No T24022 A/Cpl MILLS S.F. A.S.C. No T26260 A/Cpl ADLEY F. A.S.C. —	
	28/8/15		Indented for 60 more stretchers and four more wheeled stretchers for use in emergency. Sgt BARTON and Cpl FERGUSON on a short reconnaissance party to Coorn en route to MAPLE COPSE via KRUITSTRAAT June 15 —	

M White toher
Lt Col RAMC

WAR DIARY
or
INTELLIGENCE SUMMARY.
(Erase heading not required.)

Army Form C. 2118.

Place	Date	Hour	Summary of Events and Information	Remarks and references to Appendices
HOOGRAAF- Poperinghe	28/8/15		Visited D Station BRANDHOEK, investigated damage to two types of motor ambulances, which suggested in appearance wilful cutting, the damage was not actually explained.	Belgium Sheet 28 1/40,000
	29/8/15		The following detachments joined for instruction yesterday. At No.1 2 NCOs 16 men, at No.2 1 Officer 2 NCOs and 6 men and from 142nd F. Ambulance.	
	30/8/15		No 1537 Sgt WARD RAMC left for duty with 142 Bde RFA in relief of Pte CLARK RAMC by order of ADMS 3rd Div. OC 46th Bde RFA reports that there is no Sgt instructing with the Bde but their RAMC personnel as one should owing to the loss of Pte NELL saw BRANDHOEK and requested that the strain of this Sheet holes in bottom of STRETCHERS more was trying carry to carried out as soon as possible. Also that Regt MOs be again informed of procedure for disposal of such when in bullet as stretchers are still missing. Sgt Stephens MT O.I.C. proceeds to Rouen for duty at MT Repair Depot.	
	31/8/15		The H/Q Ivor and Lincoln Regt relieved tonight by 10 Sherwood Foresters and Riding Regt Lt DOUGLAS collecting tonight established truck watchers and ascertained that Things are arranged with the collecting arrangements. All the first name female helmets have been now re-sprayed	

W.G. Anderson
Lt Colonel
OC 5 F Amb

3rd Division

unnumbered

121/6973

8th Field Ambulance

Lt Vull

Sept. 15

Sept 1915

S/

WAR DIARY
or
INTELLIGENCE SUMMARY

Army Form C. 2118.

8th I/D Ambulance

Place	Date	Hour	Summary of Events and Information	Remarks and references to Appendices
HOOGRAAF G.26.c	1/9/15		Visited Advanced Dressing Station. Informed Capt DARLING of names of two horses in BRANDHOEK pronounced by hounds to be infectious disease.	Belgium Sheet 28 H.00.02
	2/9/15		Received from 142nd F. A. 50 Stretchers and 3 wheeled stretcher carriers — from Advance B.S Stretcher LISTERAMS proceeded to 4/Middx regt for temporary duty. The 86 stretchers and 3 wheeled carriers sent to Adv: D. Station as an emergency store. Fifty blankets sent to Divl Sanitary Section for steam disinfection, these were retained in the course of the day. Forty tube lanterns sent the helmets forwarded to "C" Section to replace a similar number of the old pattern helmets. These are issued only to Officers and Bearers whose duties take them into or near the firing line. The detachments of Officers and men of the 142nd F Ambulance attempting for instruction still continue at 7a and Adv: D Station. 30 to 40 to 140 plays a considerable number of wounded have been treated at the Advanced Dressing Station with and among go wounded in EVSOL, all such cases have their injuries marked to indicate this fact. EVSOL is made up according to the following formula. Bleaching soda 12.5 grams added to 1 litre / water / shake & grind by hand, then add 12.5 grams of Boric powder and shake again. Allow to stand for 12 hours, then filter off, and the clear solution is ready for use. Solution contains Hypochlorous Acid .54% Calcium Hydrate 1.29%, Calcium Chloride .19 %.	
	3/9/15		Very heavy rain during the night which still continues. This makes the treatment of wounded tents very difficult. Paths between tents and up the Field have been constructed of slate. Site for winter horse lines chosen, and work commenced. Considerable trouble over some sand bags which are said to have been looted over.	W.Maddock M.C.? Lieut.

Army Form C. 2118.

WAR DIARY
or
INTELLIGENCE SUMMARY.
(Erase heading not required.)

Instructions regarding War Diaries and Intelligence Summaries are contained in F. S. Regs., Part II. and the Staff Manual respectively. Title pages will be prepared in manuscript.

Place	Date	Hour	Summary of Events and Information	Remarks and references to Appendices
MORGRAFF	3/9/15		to the M.O.D. at my dug out in Maple Copse and a note regarding Pte McSWEENEY suffering from self inflicted wound. There were typical evidence in Court Martial trying this man. They cannot be found and after extensive enquiry it cannot be established that these articles were handed over with the prisoner.	
	4/9/15	11 AM	Visited Advanced D. Station during my visit to O.DMS. 5th Corps paid a visit and saw the arrangements. I took the opportunity of impressing on him the necessity of a constant evacuation during any period of activity resulting in large number of Casualties.	
	5/9/15		Lt FINLAY proceeded on leave. The V1th Corps DDMS visited the HQs and seemed satisfied with arrangements.	
	6/9/15		Visited ADMS and revised the question of returns which have multiplied to a great extent. Pointed out that the information given in the 8am to 8am returns of admissions and evacuations was equally given in the 12 noon to 12 noon returns and asked that this might be thought of notice at the next Corps Conference. Arrangements for collection and evacuation on a large scale, in conjunction with 142nd I.A. discussed.	
	7/9/15		Lt MAURICE proceeded to transports to find a suitable place for a collecting point for walking cases. The place selected consists of two small copses of trees of knowing some so sitting cases, under the E. follow of Hill Gate. This was referred to ADMS with a request that the place be allocated for the purpose by the Div. Staff	

WAR DIARY
or
INTELLIGENCE SUMMARY.
(Erase heading not required.)

Army Form C. 2118.

Place	Date	Hour	Summary of Events and Information	Remarks and references to Appendices
HOOGRAAF G.2.6.	7/9/15		Lt BAZETT and Lt DOUGLAS have reconnoitred the whole position the spirit of many of collecting & locating wounded in the shelters at present occupied by our No 10 offs 3rd Division. They have constructed a large scale map of the area, and now all the tracks and communication trenches thoroughly.	Belgium Sheet 28 1/40000
	8/9/15		Conference at ADMS office with regard to arrangements for collection on a large scale in forced area. The DMS 2nd Army visited my HQs and made a complete inspection. He noted that the padlocks cases were in some cases insufficiently stuffed and failure to boots were dirty. These points were noted for nearby action.	
	9/9/15		Lt BAZETT, Lt DOUGLAS & Lt SCOTT made a very complete daylight reconnaissance of all approaches to the fire & communicating trenches. They also found unfortunately that away to reach a stretcher case up to about 100 in the ZONNE BEEK ROUTE which is of extreme value as the place could be evacuated in the daytime. Capt BRYDEN left to assume command of S.2. F Ambulance. Capt A.H. Halyard joined from No 7 F.A.	
	10/9/15		Saw Captain FERGUSON & Major WYKIE and explained all arrangements. Lt BAZETT proceeded this morning with an NCO and Orderly to channel our prepare the FCORR but found that the place itself has been damaged by shell fire since yesterday and the approach so undergrown that cases could not be carried thence. So it fails. This place was again shelled while the party was there, it is therefore useless.	M. M. Mitchell Lt Col Comm

WAR DIARY or INTELLIGENCE SUMMARY

Army Form C. 2118.

Place	Date	Hour	Summary of Events and Information	Remarks and references to Appendices
HOOGRAAF G.26.c.	10/9/15		The A.D.M.S. Corps again wrote my N.C.O. and gave verbal orders from the D.M.S. 2nd Army that no more than 100 cases were to be kept under treatment here and no case for more than 4 days. He was on his way to Div. H.Q.rs. to see the A.D.M.S. on this point. Having received no instruction regarding number of sick & wounded we continue to work to A.D.M.S.'s instructions that a great amount of recent sick cases should be gradually evacuated either to C.C.S. or D.R.S. in Division.	Belgrave See /28 40,000
	11/9/15		Last night one of my best L/O Ross [...] some time and fell in a disstench. Now typed out with great difficulty and the least trouble delay entirely prolonged convalescence. Probably fracture of femur. Sent for Lt. SPENCER R.A.M.C. who examined him and that [...] about midnight. All S.M.O.s passed today and [...] that their work late but own [...] and satisfactory. The night is [...] to be long [...] orders and I [...] will visit the [...] under them a [...] interview. The G.O.C. 46th Division Rev Claude L. [...] which he expects to [...] The matter was referred to the Corps and apparently my [...] Meantime Learn an acting order. Under orders from D.D.M.S. 2nd Army Lt. BARTON to report to A.F.A. to-day for duty & in replaced by an officer of that J Staff. This officer only joined me on 21st August as relief of Capt DENYER. He has just settled down to work [...] at the A.D.[...] and our [...] collecting area. These continual changes of personnel are extremely detrimental to the organization & administration of the unit. —	M.C. McRedden D. McClaud

Place	Date	Hour	Summary of Events and Information	Remarks and references to Appendices
HOOGRAAF (Sh 6 (c))	12/9/15		In reply to my memorandum FRMS of yesterday's date the rest of cards to be disposed of, was fixed — Lt FINLAY returned from leave and proceeded to 8th FA in relief of Lt BARTON. Lt BARTON proceeded to 4th R.F.A. to be clerk on temp relieved by Lt C.D. ROBERTS R.A.M.C. (T.C.) Rev CRISFORD left the unit to be attached to SUFFOLK Regt yesterday Rev PRESCOTT arrived for duty in relief of Rev O'SHAUGHNESSY Chaplain R.C. yesterday. Lt SCOTT returned to duty with 142nd F.A. Rev O'SHAUGHNESSY left for duty with at ETHELES Rev PRESCOTT left to be attached for duty with ROYAL SCOTS — Sealed Orders Station yesterday arranged for NCO and bearer to "A" section to return the attack west of "A" section at MAPLE COPSE. The Remainder of the	Belgium Sheet 28
	13/15		Bearers of "A" section (16) to return to HQ ae to found in the cars for night collection cars from HQ each night. In accordance with Div arrangements, all dead during normal hours are to be brought to Cemetery BRANDHOEK to burial. Note of NCO'S regarding that the R.S. to assist to construct or reentany capable working to Bodies. It was also found out that a new site for a cemetery would be opened shortly, and Rest of men Conveyed of it were broken with the freezing area of	

Col of the Infantry Brigades

M.E. Wilcox Lt. Col R.A.M.C.

WAR DIARY or INTELLIGENCE SUMMARY

Army Form C. 2118.

Place	Date	Hour	Summary of Events and Information	Remarks and references to Appendices
BRANDHOEK HQ G.26.c.	13/9/15		The R.E. 46th Division have commenced to construct huts etc. by Nutschook. Laga Staff reported orders as to my new post distribution although same informed that I should take and if my present tent by the 16th. Gave orders to B.C. O'Keefe to transfer all cases to No. 7 F.A. Hitherto other	
	14/9/15		M.A.D.M.S. 5th Corps called & enquired about some cases of "Trench feet". Six was absent on 7th. On 9th enquired for, I returned to duty on 10th, 11th, 12th and I am to returning back on 13th. I have another 2th received instructions to inspect a farm in some way to be suitable for 40th officer ambulance. Reported that it would be suitable with certain additions and equipments etc. It was in occupation by B.C. O'Shea 46th Division and his 3rd Bn'l Area. This invitation to B.C. O'Shea threatening of Insult and 1½ different another 3rd Bn'l had him therefore instructed to inspect billets in "Rue de Brockepe, Poperinghe Nos. 63, 65 and 1. Reported these as not suitable, in account of above if any place within reasonable distance of firing lines, also heard that of these billets had actually been struck by a shell and the Street generally had been shelled, from these it would be impossible to sensors pass and mount it.	
POPERINGHE	15/9/15		My objection to the billets in POPERINGHE have been overruled, and I was ordered to take over the house & School 63,185 Rue de Brocterpe afford same 6 mile as we were allotted to Poperinghe. Moved in this afternoon. Sanitation extremely difficult this evening	

WAR DIARY or INTELLIGENCE SUMMARY

Army Form C. 2118.

Place	Date	Hour	Summary of Events and Information	Remarks and references to Appendices
POP-RINGHE	15/9/15		Clerks were instructed as were Coy and Sanit: H'rns. Sleeping 5 funds in a small hard facing, which can be filled with a pit a large vegetable garden behind the Schools. Part of the accommodation is taken up by personal. The place is most unsuitable situated in a Town where discipline is most difficult to maintain.	Belgium Sheet 28
	16/9/15		The A.D.M.S. Bde Div. has this afternoon. I discussed the situation with him and came to the following arrangements. 1. I should find a suitable farm in the Bon Area. I might move my H.Q. over there, and keep only a section of my section to attend sick at the Schools 85 RUE de BESCHER. 2. The divisional Sanitary section will provide an incinerate and two men to burn all excreta during the winter months. 3. The maximum accommodation for sick and wounded to be required here in the event of this complete action being broad here would be 60–70. 4. Stores that would be taken over at intervals by personnel. 5. The 142 F. Ambulance will house in the freshly billed about boxes accommodated and would chiefly collect all the daily sick from Bon Area. This will leave my section at BRANDHOEK which at present deals with all the daily sick in addition to treating and evacuating all the divisional wounded every night. 6. I again raised the question of the forming of a working by BRANDHOEK there are I thought time to burial at all times of the night and day. 7. I suggested that in normal times we should be informed at once when a new unit is to spend by a Royal H.Q. Lately difficulty in collecting has arisen owing to their being left unknown by the transport Control.	

WAR DIARY
or
INTELLIGENCE SUMMARY.
(Erase heading not required.)

Army Form C. 2118.

Place	Date	Hour	Summary of Events and Information	Remarks and references to Appendices
POPERINGHE	16 9/15		The area in neighbourhood carefully searched for a suitable SAA Farm but none were found. Spent remaining part of day at work cleaning up surroundings. Attention Bearers erected own sandbagged shelters and the truck garden. Also fair latrines and incinerators.	BEKERMM Sheet 28
	17 9/15		Checked T. Coy RE ready to erect cook shelters — Advance asked if latrine buckets for H.Q. of our Bn. could be sent up — Application made to Lt Col SINNOTT SK 1st Corps A.R.E.F. to state if any Royal Engineers etc. — Lt MAURICE returned will inform us that no more shall was available. MC Smith injection again & allot a day for bathing of personnel in Poperinghe also for patients.	
			Eleven men and steeds removed from school and placed in custody of the man in the tavern at No 10 Rue de BOESCHEPE.	
			Applied to 5 MO.S for latrine buckets for H.Q. if authorized establishment supply has not yet arrived MC.	
			Lt DOWLING R.A.M.C. attached for temporary duty from 142 F. Amb. Visited Adv. D. Station. Present arrangements to Divisional burials at H.Q. Its Cavalry Hurs are unsuitable, no mortuary, cemetery full. A considerable stock of material, medical, surgical and comforts have been accumulated for emergencies. Sand to HS who has reported that Div. Cemetery BRANDHOEK is full and reported that a new plot be chosen in the Infantry field trng area and this site be administered and controlled by a special burial squad of old soldiers under an M.O. (2) He has written to ascertain if the motor cyclist authorized to F. Ambulances (Y/S 3 per F.A.) cannot be issued at once. (3) Reported that 2 scavenging infection carts to Isolation Hospl BMAKOK and Mary Ray Corps from there by wire.	W.E. Nicholson Lt Col R.A.M.C.

| 18 9/15 | | |

1577 Wt. W10791/1773 500,000 1/15 D. D. & L. A.D.S.S./Forms/C. 2118.

WAR DIARY
or
INTELLIGENCE SUMMARY.

Army Form C. 2118.

Place	Date	Hour	Summary of Events and Information	Remarks and references to Appendices
POPERINGHE	18/9/15		I am to maintain here 60 beds into 4 day cases, instead of 120 as at HOOGRAAF. The A.D.M.S. 5th Corps visited my Dressing Station during my absence. Capt BUCKLEY took him round, from the comments. The A.D.S. 2nd Army visited the Dressing Station, did not inspect merely asked if Q.M.S. COTTEY could be recommended to Sgt Major a Cleaning Sergt. An officer of the Cheshires of Coy R.E. visited our D. Station and took measurements for the erection of Cook Shelters and drainage works in the front yard, also latrine seats for 6 men &c.	
	19/9/15		Arrangements for care of patients at D. Station POPERINGHE:- Bath Can for patients for 1st two of 10 or patients any morning, there parties will take out down water a M.O. and will be provided with a change of under clothing. Two lorries will be here in Field Ambulance wagons for the supply dumps, at 7am daily and handed over by N.C.O. Cases will be daily kept for 4 days and then evacuated either to C.C.S. by car of N.5.TTAC or K.15.R.S. and be seen by our own cases. Orders for Dressing Station Personnel. The house at the back of the school as used if pointers to all men except Sunday. In case of fire a shelling of the town the following steps will be taken. Men and Cooks going there on duty to dispose of refuse. 1. The whole personnel will fall in at once in the front yard. 2. The A.S.C. on duty will with the necessary personnel being all helpless cases to the stretcher cart and lines for them on the motor ambulance wagon.	M.E.Watson

1577 Wt.W10791/1773 500,000 1/15 D. D. & L. A.D.S.S./Forms/C. 2118.

WAR DIARY or INTELLIGENCE SUMMARY

Army Form C. 2118.

Place	Date	Hour	Summary of Events and Information	Remarks and references to Appendices
POPERINGHE	19/9/15		The remainder of the Bn. tents will be paraded in the yard	
			3. The Coys will nail wooden blocks lined up on the right of the road, in the direction of the march.	
			4. All officers will fall in in the alarm parade. The Second-in-Command and Sgt-Major will check parades.	
			The first Band to which personal and patients able to work, will proceed will be the horse lines.	
			Self-inflicted cases as soon as looked will be ranged at H.Q. F.A., the Cov returning immediately.	
	6-30 pm		Trailed Adm Battalion at BRANDHOEK all covered. Capt STARLING reports that if not sooner have been called for early to H.Q. in Ambulances at 7 P.M. for serious cases in horse. The Cases would start promptly Ame thirty if left till the normal hour at the dug-outs.	
	8 P.M.		150 Stretcher cases from Observance.	
			56 Stretcher on hour from 7 F.A. were returned.	
			94 Stretchers sent for use at Adv. Dn Station.	
			New ambulance work. The original meeting consumed in being one day's ration by order 17 DSD 3rd Division.	
			Water cart scrubbed out, chlorinated for 2 hours in accordance with instructions from dtchment in de Vos in Rue de BOESCHEPE	
			New drinking and cooking water supply taken into use. A well in the house of ___	
	20/9/15		Bn. BARTS following new collection arrangements. Arrangements for special car for urgent cases will be issued by NCO Passcar at MAPLE COPSE answered as follows: - 1 #2 F.A. KRUISTRAAT	
			The DC detachment 142 F.A. at KRUISTRAAT will then send the necessary car. He has been given to understand that although one case only may be urgent, if there are other available cases	

Mr. Middleton
W. McRae

1577 Wt.W10791/1773 500,000 1/15 D.D. & L. A.D.S.S./Forms/C.2118.

WAR DIARY
or
INTELLIGENCE SUMMARY.

(Erase heading not required.)

Army Form C. 2118.

Instructions regarding War Diaries and Intelligence Summaries are contained in F. S. Regs., Part II. and the Staff Manual respectively. Title pages will be prepared in manuscript.

Place	Date	Hour	Summary of Events and Information	Remarks and references to Appendices
POPERINGHE	20/7/15		All sick cases will be dealt with and evacuated by 142 F.A. In addition the 142nd F.A. will make a collection with 3 carts an balances amongst the car ridge-yard at 7 PM each night. The above arrangement to communicated to the NCO i/c 7 F.A. Hosp & pre is a standing order as follows:- In event required for urgent cases between 7 PM & 11 PM or after the final collection by S49A. Cars will be demanded as follows:- 142 F.Amb. REGISTRAR Sections (on tel) Capt Surgent St Sgt — St 7.A. 2. These cars of 142 F.A. will arrive at usual headquarters at 7 PM nightly. 3. The usual collections will continue to be made The above was communicated by me to B.C. No. 2. F.A. who verified the details by a visit to the O.R.M.S.	
		3.15 PM	About 1/2 Shell put into the town at 1/2 to 1 minute intervals a large number fails to explode. The fistles and the whole personnel less self Capt BRATT MAURICE and three NCOs went to the Horse line. Bars closed. Carrying one case inside to U R—	
		4.15 PM	In hands of personnel brought back on shelling had ceased. No real damage, signs of life as far as I can ascertain. The horse about 300 yd behind the school was wrecked. Lt Col Collins R.A.+ Amb visited my H.Qr. Then from A.D.M.S. Capt 27H F.Amb. Rankine posted to 58th F. Ambulance. This officer arrived from	Signatures

1577 Wt.W10791/1773 500,000 1/15 D. D. & L.   A.D.S.S./Forms/C. 2118.

WAR DIARY or INTELLIGENCE SUMMARY

Army Form C. 2118.

Instructions regarding War Diaries and Intelligence Summaries are contained in F. S. Regs., Part II. and the Staff Manual respectively. Title pages will be prepared in manuscript.

(Erase heading not required.)

Place	Date	Hour	Summary of Events and Information	Remarks and references to Appendices
PLOEGSTEERT	20/4/15		No 15 C.C.C. HAZEBROUCK. The brigade was visited this afternoon from A.D.M.S. 2nd Army, for being shewn 1st Wiltsh. Regt. in charge of R.A.M.C. WESTON R.A.M.C. who would from 15 C.C.C. for duty.	
	21/4/15		Capt HOVELL sent to report to A.D.M.S. for orders. Returned with verbal orders to remain with us and for the present.	
			Conference at Bns. H.Qrs. this afternoon in which arrangements for collection & evacuation of sick & wounded were made. Arrangements communicated to O.C. 142 F.A. and O.C. 17th F.A.	
			Cpl. BARTON sent to report for duty at H.Q. 2nd Army under the A.D.M.S. 2nd Army. He was to be relieved by Cpl. ROGERS.	
			Dr. MAURICE passed Captain & Adjutant, dated 1st April 1915.	
	22/4/15		The arrangements for bathing of personnel and palliasses running satisfactorily. Patients to down in small numbers 10-12 daily. So that every patient gets a hot bath during his four days stay here. Blankets have been again put through the thresh disinfector which is now erected at the Divisional baths. Arrangements also made by which the palliasses can be scrubbed by my personnel at the Divl. Baths.	
	23/4/15		Lambage for extra personnel at BRANDHOEK arranged. Visited BRANDHOEK C.C.C. & Station. Capt. DARLING had constructed a circular drive which avoids the necessity of cars reversing in the yard.	
			The new collection of sick from Road Bullets by 142 F.A. commenced.	

M. C. Wilson
R. O. Purnell

1577 Wt.W10791/1773 500,000 1/15 D. D. & L. A.D.S.S./Forms/C. 2118.

Army Form C. 2118.

WAR DIARY
or
INTELLIGENCE SUMMARY.
(Erase heading not required.)

Instructions regarding War Diaries and Intelligence Summaries are contained in F. S. Regs., Part II. and the Staff Manual respectively. Title pages will be prepared in manuscript.

Place	Date	Hour	Summary of Events and Information	Remarks and references to Appendices
POPERINGHE	24/9/15		Rain fairly heavy all night. Men received their rations and cooked breakfast. Evacuation British MAPLE COPSE and Car Rendez-vous very much slower.	
		6 PM	Received Divn. Operation order No 8. Sent messages to O.S.C. 7th & 142nd F.Ambulances to arrange in accordance with heavy evacuation for collection on a large scale viewed to them on 21/9/15.	
		7 PM	Capt MAURICE established at Collecting Post LILLE GATE	
		6 PM	Capt BAZETT at Battle post on YPRES - MENIN road I 9 d	
		9 PM	Lt DOUGLAS & Lt FINDAY with all Bearers of A. Section & 7th F.A. with Bearers of 1st Battln 9th F.A. at Battle post MAPLE COPSE	
			Capt McDONALD and one Bearer and section 1st Battln post MAPLE COPSE	
		12 mid night	Lt WHITMAN and one Bearer and section at Battle post ZILLEBEKE village	
			Our officers and the Bearers but their all dug outs used each ZILLEBEKE Lake. Preparations complete by mid night 24/25 Sept for attack at dawn.	
B Station BRANDHOEK	25/9/15	8.30 am	Arrived at Advanced B Station in ambulance with battle arrangements. The attack commenced about 4 a.m. but received no messages from any battle posts.	
		9.30 am	Stretcher of Walking cases arrived from LILLE GATE. Message from Capt MAURICE wounded coming in fast. Sent from No 8. F.A. cars at once these cars to continue to circulate b'tween Adv. B Stn. and LILLE GATE as long as required.	
		11 am	Capt THOMPSON R.A.M.C. O/C 5 M.A. Convoy arrived the King and ready for ambulance. Capt MAURICE reports his post clear. 5 Officers and 50 Rank & file cleared by am 25 Nov 10 P. 17 C.C.Stations	
		12 noon	5 Officers and 72 Rank & file collected, dressed & evacuated.	
		4.10 PM	Priority message from Lt DOUGLAS. Have 3.30 P.M. "Have eighty stretcher cases MAPLE COPSE now, we shall have two hundred or more Stretcher cases altogether at MAPLE COPSE alone. Please send me any Bearers and ambulance cars possible."	
			Reply "My Ambulance wagon driven." Message received. I am sending all available help, including Infra cases from MAC. LILLE gate Posts 142 9.A. who formed you last night."	
			P. Whitcombe Lt.Col.R.amc	

1577 Wt W10791/1773 500,000 1/15 D. D. & L. A.D.S.S./Forms/C. 2118.

WAR DIARY or INTELLIGENCE SUMMARY

Army Form C. 2118.

Place	Date	Hour	Summary of Events and Information	Remarks and references to Appendices
Dressing Station BRANDHOEK	25/9/15		I saw the J.A.D.M.S. I Corps and asked him to obtain permission from D.M.S. 2nd Army to utilize 7 Cars of MAC Alleson D Station and our renderzvous ZILLEBEKE Road. He promised to telephone for permit.	
		6 PM	Message from Capt BAZETT. Seriously hurt in 10 SH. 7th Bn estimate hundred to hundred & fifty stretcher cases; probably have to carry from HOOGE. Can we have salvage men." To Capt BAZETT. Empty stretchers cased at MAPLE COPSE by 3.30 PM. Probable number two hundred. Am sending up tea & coffee as full as possible, and trying to borrow 7 MAC cars to work a convoy Capable of carrying 180 lying cases. Use every effort to clear MAPLE COPSE. You are 100-150 7th Bn Casualties received.	
			To O.C. 3rd Division Salvage Corps. At 25/9/15 sent work 7 MHC cars to Bn HQ at 6 PM. Please send forty salvage men to BRANDHOEK G.12.b.6.8. am Case knows very urgent.	
			By this hour in accordance with previous orders for battle collection the following heaves had arrived, and stood by use 6 large cars of 5 SHA, 6 of 142nd JA, and 3 of No7 JA:- Lt SCOTT and 36 bearers of 142 JA despatched at once in 6 cars of 142nd JA & report to Capt BAZETT. B. Lt Si French lad. division strength 30 NCOs & men despatched in cars of No8 JA to report to OC DOUGLAS at MAPLE COPSE	
		7.50 PM	2 officers and 26 men No7 JA. (This party should have been free 40 men but owing to a misunderstanding they were late.) Capt REID and 18 men, dispatched in the 3 remaining Cars of 7th JA to report to Capt BAZETT & order the remaining 22 bearers received in at 7 PM. These were sent up to assist at MAPLE COPSE under Lt DOUGLAS.	
		10.30 PM	2nd lord of stretcher cases arrived, sent from now on to 4.30 am only 18 lying cases were kept continually circulating.	
			3 NCOs and 30 men of Salvage Corps arrived. This arrival was much delayed enough by the fact that the first 40 had to wait for their kit	

M Mackenzie
N Collins

Army Form C. 2118

WAR DIARY
or
INTELLIGENCE SUMMARY.
(Erase heading not required.)

Instructions regarding War Diaries and Intelligence Summaries are contained in F. S. Regs., Part II. and the Staff Manual respectively. Title pages will be prepared in manuscript.

Place	Date	Hour	Summary of Events and Information	Remarks and references to Appendices
BRANDHOEK	25/9/15	10.30 pm	I sent to turn out medical party - L¹ MURPHY in C⁰ and 16 O/R's were sent off immediately to report to Capt¹ BAZETT, and the wounded were sent up as fast as available empty cars arrived.	
			Received message from L¹ DOUGLAS reporting his column to W/200-250 stretcher cases, and asking if I had received his + Capt¹ BAZETTS message (see attd). The R.A.M.C. applied to 68 G.H. for weoful G.S. waggons but managed to supply dump, there had been placed at his disposal, but he found that his personnel was not able to work up to M.A.D. Coys - & many farm back to be many to shell fire. He reports the track as a bog and that owing to the heavy rain which has fallen during the last 26 hours - The M.A.S. CAPS now shown this message, and in consultation with R.A.M.S. 3ʳᵈ Brigade, decided to ask for ambulance in Brigade and cars for 17th Division - 5294	
	26/9/15	12.5 am	Two officers and 32 O/Rs were sent in 3 large Daim's & a 2nd motor ambulance, no officers and three transports were despatched at once with a further report to C.M. BAZETT. (these known separately on the way in stored report) Three light cars and 2.2 Ford's with B⁰ Franco S¹ 19A also arrived at this time and were despatched to Capt¹ BAZETT.	
		1 am	Reported a car of No.7 D.A struck by shell when passing through M Square / YPRES. The driver killed. Four poilus in the Car are injured. They were picked up by the driver and waggon orderly of a No.5 Car and taken into the town occupied by M.O.A.	
			Message sent by cycle orderly to O.C. 3rᵈ Cdn D.A to remind L¹ HUBBARD came up with his lorry, and remind the Car to the workshops.	
		1.10 am	Message to M.O.H.S. 3rᵈ Brit Batta Corp. and Reserve of N¹¹ N² C.O officers arrived and alone were called up to proceed here 18 officers 232 other ranks.	
		2.30 am	I tried to give in with 20 more men arrived, had them helped across to armoury today	M¹ Hattie N.H Adjutant

1577 Wt. W10791/1773 500,000 1/15 D. D. & L. A.D.S.S./Forms/C. 2118.

WAR DIARY
or
INTELLIGENCE SUMMARY.
(Erase heading not required.)

Army Form C. 2118.

Hour, Date, Place	Summary of Events and Information	Remarks and references to Appendices
BRANDHOEK 2am 26/9/15	BRASHIER and 2nd car with 12 Bazus returned with verbal message no lamps required.	
	The loading and unloading party at the Dressing Station were relieved by some of those lately arrived French.	
5. 30 a.m.	The wounded continued to arrive with great regularity all through the night.	
	Subsequently heard from D DOUGLAS that the G.S. waggons [Horses] had disposal by the H.Q. 5th Inf Bde route of wounded resistance and saved the situation at a time when such to an extreme strain of the track from MAPLE COPSE to the Our Rundeg-road the horses were severely exhausted. This track it should be remembered is 2500 yards in length and not only were the 4 Army Horses carrying and wheeling stretchers over the same 10 times over this track, but others were carrying from Rd Dolls and trenches in Sanctuary Wood to MAPLE COPSE from about 8am on 25th to 8am on 26th Sept. The distances ranging from 1000 to 2000 yards, through Communication trenches and over tracks in the Wood. The same thing applied to the detachments under Capt BARRETT which worked between the trenches and posts.	
	5th Inf Bde to Ypres Headquarters at I 11 C.0.2. a distance of about 1000 - 1500 yards.	
	Third car received a message from D DOUGLAS stating that our total at MAPLE COPSE was clear by 3.40 a.m. and the only known of Scots Guards and 5 1st GORDONS who could not at present be evacuated from their front trenches.	
	Some T.R. Scots Guards and 5 1st GORDONS who could not at present be evacuated from their front trenches.	
	Loyd Casualties at my S. Station 23 Officers 396 O.Ranks	

M Middleton
Lt Col Ramc

Army Form C. 2118

WAR DIARY
or
INTELLIGENCE SUMMARY.
(Erase heading not required.)

Instructions regarding War Diaries and Intelligence Summaries are contained in F. S. Regs., Part II. and the Staff Manual respectively. Title pages will be prepared in manuscript.

Place	Date	Hour	Summary of Events and Information	Remarks and references to Appendices
BRANDHOEK	26/9/15	7.30 am	In our journey to MAE cars have returned from the CCS. I understand from Capt THOMPSON, that there is a bad block here and cases are being evacuated very slowly. We have received in my journey 97 stretcher cases and 25 sitting cases on my hands picked up that I have have been waiting for onward evacuation. The collection by the back route via DORMY HOUSE STREET - KINLEASNE VILLAGE - ZILLEBEKE HALT - KRUISSTRAAT was most successful and 836 cases were thus collected and evacuated by the 1H.2.PA. The arrangements being made tht O.C. MAJOR WIKEY who were responsible for working cases coming by this route after they reached him post in ZILLEBEKE village. The post for lightly wounded cases at LILLEGATE, under Capt MAURICE, was also a success. Cases were treated at this post and evacuated by the PA. Cars to tht D. Station. Message sent by N.O. O'Cg directly to Capt BAZETT to Ypres at BRANDHOEK with his orders; also to Capt MAURICE to Ypres with his detachment. The French who had been here lent and the salvage operators also "B" Section Reserve 81PA had gradually been brought back by MT.ln ambulances to join. OC 1H2.PA had also withdrawn his teams from all posts to KRUISSTRAAT.	
		7.45 pm	Thus were left at MAPLE COPSE, L.DOUGLAS, L.FINLAY and Reserve HQ Section 81PA. Wire to DOUGLAS - Please remain at Ypres post until your section area will relieve you tonight and please acknowledge.	W.Maclarty Lieutenant

1577 Wt.W10791/1773 500,000 1/15 D.D.&L. A.D.S.S./Forms/C. 2118.

Army Form C. 2118.

WAR DIARY
or
INTELLIGENCE SUMMARY.
(Erase heading not required.)

Instructions regarding War Diaries and Intelligence Summaries are contained in F. S. Regs., Part II. and the Staff Manual respectively. Title pages will be prepared in manuscript.

Place	Date	Hour	Summary of Events and Information	Remarks and references to Appendices
BRANDHOEK	20/9/15	10 a.m.	In anticipation of extra casualties tonight O.C. 1 & 2 Stand by to send Cars for our for the 7 P.H. collection tonight.	
			Wire to Lt DOUGLAS "The 7 P.H. collection will continue for our tonight arm. R.g. P.H. collection will be made with own Cars our Ypres should return by one if there are Lt FINLAY and run on our own nights.	
		8 P.M.	Wire to Lt DOUGLAS "O.R.H.S bring in casualties may return to normal conditions. Sgt STUART comes up to take over work of detached 8 men of C Section. Remainder of C Section return to Remy Siding tonight arm Lt FINLAY also to return.	
		7 P.M.	Capt BAZETT went up instead to take over at 7 P.H. collection, finding casualties there normal and C Section having experienced quiet and took Lt DOUGLAS for assistance. Seven of B Section went out and set up in Cars, also 16 Bearers from 7 P.A.	
	21/9/15	2 a.m.	All but 128 wounded collected & recovered Bearers & Supplementary 6 men. All but 33 of there were the result of a counter attack which took place about 10.30 p.m. last night.	
			Capt BAZETT left MAPLE COPSE, the advance post, and on August Sup. completely Alean? The Reserve detachment left at my post on the Capt Henry? N.C.O. & 12 men C. Section.	
		Q.R.	Cpl FERGUSON and 11 men of "B" Section were sent to Rev O'Halloran at BRANDHOEK to be utilized in relieving the detachment of "C" Section at MAPLE COPSE. Sgt STUART winning one was ought at this point returns to hand over and explain the duties to Cpl FERGUSON.	M.H. Sullivan
			Orders for Section Officers duly made up to 1st October to be shown at Orderly Room on that date. The section officers duly made up to 1st October to be shown at Orderly Room on that day.	R.V. Gallaudet

1577 Wt.W10791/1773 500,000 1/15 D. D. & L. A.D.S.S./Forms/C. 2118.

WAR DIARY
or
INTELLIGENCE SUMMARY

Army Form C. 2118.

Place	Date	Hour	Summary of Events and Information	Remarks and references to Appendices
POPERINGHE	28/9/15		A considerable number of the divisional reserve of stretchers and some of the wheeled carriers have not yet been collected since the attack on 25/26 night. Many stretchers were issued to regiments during tonight who were sent in looking up patients, every wounded being stretcher. Every effort is being made to recover these stretchers. The wheeled stretcher was destroyed by shell fire. Visited Aerodrome, and sent over for about 3rd Division and Reinforcements. M.O. & O.C. Med. Regt. taking all command to work in connection with the Reinf. attack.	
	29/9/15		A/Sgt STAINE returns of duty with 3rd Div.Train under arrangements made with O.C. 3rd Div. Train. Requisitioned 2000 bricks from ruins of brickyard in POPERINGHE - HAEGLE Road, this requisition was made at the request of Supply Officer Requisitioning Officer arrangement was not unreasonable. A permanent wrtd. land tenant of area occupied by myself from 1st Aug - 14 Sept and 15 K Sept concern, forwarded for approval to D.R. Rennes of one of the fields occupied at POPERINGHE Where O Coy having agreement, that my duty offered to Brig M. All available wagons, and a large fatigue working during tonight, the Brig had Heavy rain for past 24 hrs - Casualties very small during last two days. fine quiet again.	
	30/9/15		1st DOUGLAS was conducting last night and as the result of a mine explosion and a counter attack in the salient there were some 142 wounded evacuated 5'1 and 6 C.C.S. 1910 DRS for CCS HAZEBROUCK, the later bring accidents met unmanagement 1 Legally wounded case tried by Prelim Sorn. 1st DOUGLAS proceeded at HAZEBROUCK regd. to the wounded activities, and was unpt. to Bd. aware all the Commodities 11 Stretcher Cases Recommend. Drs. as not sufficient Fowers	M.C. Kindlati [signature]

1577   Wt.W10791/1773   500,000   1/15   D. D. & L.   A.D.S.S./Forms/C. 2118.

WAR DIARY or INTELLIGENCE SUMMARY

Army Form C. 2118

Place	Date	Hour	Summary of Events and Information	Remarks and references to Appendices
POPERINGHE	30/9/15	10 AM	Available owing to the non-delivery of two lorries which were not delivered. The first was from CPT FERGUSON my NCO at the Rail's post at MAPLE COPSE. Handed in S-26 PH 27/9/15. C/O 8th Field Ambulance 9/07th Bde BRANDHOEK. So would you arrange to send as many lorries as possible tonight". This lorry was delivered at my Dressing Station at BRANDHOEK at 10-15 am this morning. The other wire was sent by the 8th Inf Bde HQrs as has not yet been delivered. A further wire as follows: "N0 8 Dressing Station via 7th Bde Fullett - E47 30th Sept 90 wounded upheld by 8th Bde at MAPLE COPSE at 9 PH and 3 PM AMS DMH. There also reached my Dressing Station at BRANDHOEK at 10-15 am — The matter was reported by me to ADMS personally this morning.	
		11 am	Wire sent to Lt DOUGLAS RAMC C/O HQ 8th INF BDE X1 30th BAZETT MLZ you proceed in Motor Ambulance will reach rendez-vous at 6:30 PM tonight and I have sent with Motor Ambulance a written demand. 1 2 Schamed. OC 8th SM— Orders to CPT BAZETT RAMC "1) Please proceed to HQr 142 FA Bde 9th France by H-30 PM today. 2) You will proceed with this party & are provided by 142 FA now to reach the rendez-vous by 6-30PM. (3) Lt DOUGLAS has been instructed by wire to demand a 2nd journey & rendes-vous there and this is unnecessary in case. (4) You will take over command of a detachment 15 transmitted C.O. of B Section who will remain as a permanent detachment at MAPLE COPSE To O.C. "C" Section of no D Station BRANDHOEK. The following message has been wired to Lt DOUGLAS at 11 am, before his wire time? 9-50 arrived:- (text follows written) DOUGLAS — (add when to that lorries)	M. Nicholson V. Gilbert

1577 Wt. W10791/1773 500,000 1/15 D.D. & L. A.D.S.S./Forms/C. 2118.

WAR DIARY
or
INTELLIGENCE SUMMARY.
(Erase heading not required)

Army Form C. 2118

Place	Date	Hour	Summary of Events and Information	Remarks and references to Appendices
POPERINGHE	30/9/15		Up all morning. Traces of ATB Section in Camp from here at 7 PM, they will call at BRANDHOEK and at "FANCY FARM" and make them straight on to the Bandages and "C" Section leaves at BRANDHOEK to send up if required. Capt BAZETT will take up the Iodine and Candles, if you will send the Bandages and gauze."	
		3 PM	RAMC Operation orders received — No 9 by AOMS 3rd Division dated 30 Sept 1915 —	
		4.30 PM	Capt BAZETT and Barnes arranged left for MAPLE COPSE.	
		5 PM	Proceeded to Dressing Station to form Capt DARLING of final arrangements.	
		6.45	Arranged with OC 142 F Amb for one Bearer Sub div to be available at the Dump if required.	
		7 PM	Remainder of Bearers of ATB section left in Cars to BRANDHOEK and thence Mules & Finney	
		8 PM	to MAPLE COPSE. Ads to Stn Gas met Capt HAPGOOD— Proceeded to scene of engagement of my own to Lt DOUGLAS's Dispatched by him at 12.20 P.M. on relief. My present Maber at 7.30 P.M. —	
			The course of the Evening number of casualties last night now a mine explosion followed by a front attack. All day preparations have been made for a counter attack which after very several times postponed was delivered at 3 P.M. very heavy artillery first & not sustained by infantry for — 3 P.M. to 7.15 P.M. 2nd DOUGLAS was unable to estimate likely numbers of casualties — Capt BAZETT sent back message by orders of one of Capt of 142 Det for a trench out thru to hand up.	
		10-11	"C" Section Bearers sent down our F Amb in cars to assist.	
		12 mid night	Lt SCOTT and Bearer Sub div 142 F. pass up in Cars.	

3rd Division

121/7604

8th Field Ambulance

Dec 1915

Vol IX

WAR DIARY
or
INTELLIGENCE SUMMARY.
(Erase heading not required.)

Army Form C. 2118.

8th Fld Ambulance 3rd Division B E F

Place	Date	Hour	Summary of Events and Information	Remarks and references to Appendices
BRANDHOEK	1/7/15	2 AM	Lt DOUGLAS returned from MAPLE COPSE and upon clearing from our take, facility Capt BAZETT has taken over charge and remains with a permanent detachment of 12 men at MAPLE COPSE.	Belgium Pl 28 1/100000
		4 AM	Report all clear from MAPLE COPSE. 7 Fld wounded admitted since 8 AM yesterday 14-H.	
			Remnant of A.D.M.S. as body of an unknown officer brought to Dressing Station on night 28/29 Sept.	
		10 AM	No means of identifying him found after careful personal search. Buried after a brother during burial service of the CHESHIRE Regt. The 1st and 5th CHESHIRE Regts were units by O.C. D Stat.d and both being burying officers. Enquiries to be made if any CHESHIRE officers attached to a regt of 3rd or 14 Division.	
POPERINGHE			The 7th Fld Bty are taking over an extension of the front line to the right from the 138th Inf Bde 46th Division. This means to be completed by the morning of 3rd October, and may be subject of Orders No 9 - Am under this order my detachment at MAPLE COPSE as shown above. This morning Capt BAZETT received telegraphic orders to take one from a F.A. of 46th Div, 3 Lisgouls for medical personnel and stretchers situated in ARMAGH WOOD I 30 (a).	
		11.30 am		
		4 PM	Operation Order No 10 received. 1. R.f R.AM.C. OO No9 paras 2 to 3. All evacuation of sick from new line will be carried out through Advd Station in MAPLE COPSE. 2. The D.C of 8 Fld Amb will detail a MO and 8 men to take over 3 dugouts in ARMAGH WOOD and 1 Bn Orderlies occupied by sentry of St Cumb 4 B Am 1) they will be under the orders of H.Q of MAPLE COPSE and S.B who will equip the post with such medical material to act accordingly.	
		6 PM	Written report from Capt BAZETT received. The dug outs in ARMAGH WOOD have been officered in accordance with orders of ADMS. They are in good rep and well built. Capable of holding 20 stretcher cases and 16 Runners. We are evidently expected to undertake collection tonight. Have commenced cleaning up the lines. Am journey up to line tomorrow and night at night in order to prepare.	McMath Lt Col RAMC

WAR DIARY
or
INTELLIGENCE SUMMARY.
(Erase heading not required.)

Army Form C. 2118

Instructions regarding War Diaries and Intelligence Summaries are contained in F. S. Regs., Part II. and the Staff Manual respectively. Title pages will be prepared in manuscript.

Place	Date	Hour	Summary of Events and Information	Remarks and references to Appendices
Pt ROMBLI	1/10/15	6 PM	He was offered 2 NCOs and some 12 men as the strength of permanent detachment and an additional transit mess night. The following detachments was sent to MAPLE COPSE tonight. 1 NCO 5 men 13 Section permanent detachment for MONAGHWOOD, 2 Bearers for night collection, the whole under Capt HAGOOD. The permanent detachment under Capt BAZETT is now 2 NCOs 12 men of "B" Section. This detachment will be relieved every 4th day.	
		11.30 pm		
	2/10		Captain STEWART returned from leave.	
		12.45	Wire to ADMS 20th Div Sick 1 Slightly wounded of 9th Division on my FA at Sopenreghe. Am unable to accommodate anymore. Shall send instructions to disposal.	
		6 PM	Murphy to approve and 22 cases of 9th Division to RAPS 7th FA.	
	3/10	10 am	Recd of 9th Division still pouring in. Shall have 80 also of these on my hands to treat and feed at mid day. Still no reply as to disposal, am already full up with sick wounded of the Division alone.	
			Captain BAZETT wrote 9.30 PM 2/10. All quiet in salient. Wounded 1 Stretcher case 2 walking (RST), about 30 sick. Cases of badly swollen trench feet commencing 2 knight. Takes Hares cut down to 6-12 per night. Surrendered to his posts and huts in MAPLE COPSE. Young in fires. Cheshire 9 Coy R.E. will throw bags dug out and road by the day after tomorrow.	
		12.30	Notification from ADMS that there would be accommodation tonight to rec of 9th Div. Proceeded to interview Col of 9th Div. Col CREE and got arranged permission to send three cases of these to 26th FA. Sane O.C. 26th FA & Lt Col BUSWELL.	

1577 Wt.W10791/1773 500,000 1/15 D. D. & L. A.D.S.S./Forms/C. 2118.

WAR DIARY or INTELLIGENCE SUMMARY

Army Form C. 2118

Place	Date	Hour	Summary of Events and Information	Remarks and references to Appendices
POPERINGHE	3/10/15	10 Am	Ambulances arranged for those cases to be taken over this afternoon. Got Sgt Sick transferred to 28 F.A at 2.30 PM.	
		2 PM	Lt SIDNEY JOHN CULLUM RAMC TC reported for duty. This brings my personnel in Officers up to strength.	
		5.30 PM	Sgt STUART and 11 men relieve Cpl FERGUSON and 11 men at MAPLE COPSE dug outs.	
	4/10/15	9 AM	Hindu point from RAMC. LT DF FINLAY RAMC was detailed for duty with No 1 ROYAL SCOTS FUSRS in relief of Lt ROBERTS who proceeds to England on termination of his contract.	
		5 PM	Lt S J CULLUM relieves Lt DF FINLAY at dressing station BRANDHOEK.	
		6.45 PM	Capt J L STEWART relieved Capt BAZETT at Advanced D Station MAPLE COPSE. Between 5 45 and 7 PM Poperinghe was bombarded, 38 shells of which 17 were shrapnel fell in the town. The Italian & rear part of the Barracks were almost entirely knocked down to the bare lines, a small party of R AMC and the Officers fallen in and marched back to the Courtroom and as far as I can ascertain none among the troops in the town or the civilians. At HQ recurring at 7.30 PM. No casualties occurred among my personnel or details. Several houses were struck. Thirty four men each of the 9 Division were transferred to one of the Divisional Field Ambulances during the day. No new lines are being constituted as far as possible in accordance with 3 00/3 of specifications made the supervisor of Capt MAURICE CMG. General T O RMNZFC aided by Lieut J attaching at BRANDHOEK, and saw Capt STARLING who was apparently quite satisfied with the situation carried on 25/2/16.	MC Matthews Lt Col RAMC
	5/10/15		Heavy rain which had again rendered the use of wheeled stretchers between MAPLE COPSE & the Cry renders vans impossible. Intimacy of the Canadian to deal with the bad from day shows this light.	

WAR DIARY or INTELLIGENCE SUMMARY

Army Form C. 2118

Place	Date	Hour	Summary of Events and Information	Remarks and references to Appendices
PICKERING 3H.	6/10/15		Under orders from A.D.M.S. the O.C. and one O.R. have been sent for duty with the 4th MIDDX Regiment: Owing to casualties and furnishing of reliefs, my unit since 26/9/15 has been depleted of 4 NCO's + 6 Privates, the places of the NCO's having been filled by making acting Sergts + Cpls at the same time to supply of men suitable for each is rapidly diminishing. Division pointed out to the 2/2nd Londons when from A.D.M.S., the personnel of the 7/4 Field Ambulance so drawn out to these attached to motor cubic. The O.C. + O.R. despatched to me this morning and the following arrangements were made:— Party I: 1 Officer, 1 NCO (clerk), 1 NCO (nursing), 3 Pri (nursing) to be attached to my detachment at Dressing Station BRANDSHOEK, instructions issued at Main Dressing Station Chaiyecamp 3rd Day. Party II: 1 Officer, 1 NCO Rumsey and 6 Bearers to report each night at HQ at 5.30 P.M and proceed in 2 of the own cars to collecting area, and officer of 6 R.7.H. to accompany to instruct. Party III: 1 Officer, 1 NCO (clerk), 1 NCO Sackson to attend daily from 10 am to 12 noon at HQ for instruction in general routine and clerical duties. All were detailed to be on board by their own transit. Proceeded with OC 7H and 2 Duncan to Dressing Station BRANDSHOEK, as arranged for ambulance to be put in line as arranged above. Fifty Stretcher deficient, saw the Adjutant 7 B.R. and his ex Sergt, many of these were lent to infantry 27 June '15 & letter to A.D.M.S. requesting that these men to mind return all stretcher excess of authorized scale, also any Stretchers held by their Union of Caps to be sent either to A.D.M.S. Station or O Station.	
	7/10/15	7.30 am	The MO of WILTS Regt saying a man received at 9.30 P.M yesterday was still awaiting evacuation. This is the first notification we have received of this casualty. DOUGLAS went to the Regt and got and had the case removed, and explained arrangement to Capt LOVELL the M.D.—	W/o Hutton W/o Wallace
	7/10/15	1-5 am	Another run this time from 7th Battn R.R. about the same casualty, and asking for a Field Ambulance!! O/C to go to transport lines at once.	

Army Form C. 2118

WAR DIARY
or
INTELLIGENCE SUMMARY.
(Erase heading not required.)

Instructions regarding War Diaries and Intelligence Summaries are contained in F. S. Regs., Part II. and the Staff Manual respectively. Title pages will be prepared in manuscript.

Place	Date	Hour	Summary of Events and Information	Remarks and references to Appendices
POPERINGHE	7/10/15 8/10/15		The instruction of the personnel of the 74th F.A. is proceeding in accordance with the programme into abvs:— 1 N.C.O. 8 men of "C" Section relieve a similar party of "B" Section at PROVEN WOOD Capt BAZETT proceeds on collecting duty tonight, and will instruct officers & drivers of 74th F.A.	Belgium Sheet 28 2000
	9/10/15		Capt BAZETT proceeded last night to aid post of WILTS Regt. to remove a Stretcher suffering from Rheumatic Fever, and to deliver a note to M.O. re collecting personnel from this post. He brought back an acknowledgement from the M.O. of my Means explaining arrangement, and reports that the only way to clear this aid post is by sending a car through the LILLE GATE. Capt STEWART visited to investigate and report on certain dugouts near the cutting known on the road crossing I.24.C. These dug outs were supposed to be in course of construction for house of wounded track of Mile person al. when the 46th Division left this part of the line. The dug outs at present occupied by my detachment in POP.A.G.M. Hosp. are now reported to be battle dugouts and we could not avail able during active operations.—	
	10/10/15		The remainder of the tub. helmets were received yesterday morning. Issued to all men of 74th Section, and the N.C.O.s who are doing duty at H.Q. Each man landed in one respirator and one tube helmet, and signed for his tub. helmet. He printed instructions regarding the tub helmet were read out and explained, and the structure of the tube explained to the men.— The same procedure was carried out by O.C. 74th F.A. Secured from A.D.T.A.W.V. a list of equipment and outfit authorized for motor bicycles. Issued of difference found at 3rd Am. Officer. The wheels to travel from 3rd An'l T.A.M. allowed to overhaul all wagons, and print the new device on them —	N/S/Westicle A.W. Waue

WAR DIARY
or
INTELLIGENCE SUMMARY.
(Erase heading not required.)

Army Form C. 2118

Place	Date	Hour	Summary of Events and Information	Remarks and references to Appendices
POPERINGHE	10/10/15		Report by Capt STEWART RAMC on dug outs in neighbourhood of ARMAGH WOOD vicinity 9F3, received from 2nd & 3rd BATTS. "Capt STEWART reports as follows: There are no available dug outs in the cutting itself in wood crossing Square I34C, but 150 yards just East, just where the wood enters the wood is an unfinished dug out 18ft. x 20ft. There is room for it and it has evidently been abandoned, one end of it has been mentioned there is a river of slag and it can probably be observed from a ridge to the East. At the F of Fme Bryn mentioned there is a shelter of slag on 15 in a shelled spot surrounded by a trench. Covered with green canvas. These dug outs were quite safe from observation and one NCO and eight men could easily be housed in them. There would be no accommodation in them for wounded during an attack, but from this point it is only about a mile carry to the big dug out in MAPLE COPSE" The following message also sent to MOHS.- Capt STEWART reports that a working party of the 2/SUFFOLK regiment is occupying the large dug out for wounded in MAPLE COPSE. I should be glad if this party could be turned out and an order published stating that this dug out is reserved for wounded." Urgent message from MOHS, asking me to verify the report of occupation of wounded dug outs by 2nd SUFFOLKS. Message received from Capt STEWART RAMC 12-50 AM 11/10/15 "Large dug out occupied by eight men of 2nd SUFFOLKS, and this leaves no accommodation for wounded as there were toilets, 15 stretcher cases and twenty six sitting cases to-night. Am Have wire instructions. Copy forwarded to MOHS 3rd Division. The MAPLE COPSE detachment was relieved last night by C.Eccles.	
	11/10/15		Last night between 8-45 P.M.-9-15 P.M. The town was again shelled, fifteen shells were fired in all no damage done apparently. Type. T.M. 6303) 6 Pte. FURNEAUX. T. was killed whilst collecting wounded last night. He was buried in the Cemetery at BRANDHOEK. I attended his funeral and a party of 25 Officers & men.	W.J. Shuttock Lt. RAMC

Army Form C. 2118.

WAR DIARY
or
INTELLIGENCE SUMMARY.
(Erase heading not required.)

Instructions regarding War Diaries and Intelligence Summaries are contained in F.S. Regs., Part II. and the Staff Manual respectively. Title pages will be prepared in manuscript.

Place	Date	Hour	Summary of Events and Information	Remarks and references to Appendices
POPERINGHE	12/10/15		Captain HARGOOD relieved Capt STEWART at MAPLE COPSE. The former is ordered to report when twenty of 2/ SUFFOLK Regt have evacuated my dug out in MAPLE COPSE in same as with ADMS Bdg dated 11/10/15 stating that the OC 2/ Suffolk were annoying the walk. Captain STEWART reports that detachment of 2/ SUFFOLK Regt 2 evacuated the dug out in MAPLE COPSE	Belgium Sheet 28 1/40000
		6 PM	The town was again shelled, fifteen shells were fired of which 7 failed to burst. On this occasion known few cases were in the first hour. They went fired in rapid succession. The usual numbers arrived of patients and the greater part of the personnel was send out.	
	13/10/15	4 PM	MILLER - JACKS collected the stretchers, carrier, sent to MAPLE COPSE for trial. Report noted. O/Station BRANDHOEK, all correct. Capt BAZETT arrived there in relief of Captain DARLING proceeding on 8 days leave. Considerable activity on ST ELOI - KEMMEL front between 3.30 PM and 8 PM apparently a German offensive. The long range Gun shelled in neighbourhoods of the town from 6-45 PM to 9 PM at intervals. About 18 shells in all. The shells fell in a field about 3/4 mile outside town in BASSE-ROVILLE L/ DOUGLAS on 7 days leave.	
	14/10/15		Capt DARLING proceeds on 7 days leave. Arranged with 7 F.A. Unit for the road car of my unit which goes for 3 day overhaul on 15/10/15. Shall be fitted with 6 small electric lamps on the dynamo.	
	15/10/15		Agreement No 1 for land occupied from 1st August to 14 Sept sent to Claims Commission auto Sagmalier Raren - Payment made for reception of land from 1 August to 14 Sept is 7563/-. Receipt attached to impress accounts.	

M. Murdoch
L' Colonel
O.C. 8 F.A.

WAR DIARY
or
INTELLIGENCE SUMMARY

Army Form C. 2118

Place	Date	Hour	Summary of Events and Information	Remarks and references to Appendices
POPERINGHE	16/5		Under orders from A.D.M.S. the dug-outs in ARMAGH WOOD are to be handed over to the D.A.D of Division on the night 16/17 October. Arranged for Motor Lorries to pick up Officers & similar number (not CSM men) of "C" Section. Visited the A.D.M.S 9th Division and made all arrangements for handing over on the 29.9.24. Capt. in STEWART relieves Capt. HASGOOD at MAPLE COPSE tonight. The 20 M.O. of RIFLES reports some difficulty in evacuating Stretcher Cases from the HEDGE Trenches, owing to difficulty of carrying them through ZOUAVE wood. The M.O. has division at YEOMANRY POST. Attached him the following arrangement adopted:- 1 M.O. at YEOMANRY POST will arrange 3 and R M.O. at GORDON FARM. Z 16 & 8 to have all Stretcher Cases from the HEDGE Trenches (except C1). 2 Stretcher Cases from French C1, which can be carried through SANCTUARY WOOD, are sent to the M.O. at MAPLE COPSE. Walking Cases shall be sent to sub-post at M.O. at YEOMANRY POST; now the M.O. Yeomanry Sqn. These arrangements were sent in writing to M.O. at YEOMANRY POST and all appeared satisfied.	See Appendix 28 / hours
	17/10		Relieving L/Cpl LAWLEY who was wounded when collecting dead & wounded & died of wounds this evening. G.S.W. Chest and abdomen. Col LANKEY buried in English Cemetery ½ mile outside POPERINGHE on the REMINGHELST road.	
	19/10		Lt HS SUGARS Rouge 70 found on duty from leave. Sent accepted orders for hot baths and stores for Sams warning to 20 Som, to C.R.E. and permit refused of money. This amount was expended on material for hot showers and a hut for A.D. personnel.	
	20/10		Dvr MEREDITH died of P.B.C.W. for sleep out at his post when a party on the scene here. Orders for division to move to STEENVOORDE and district. Met at A.D.M.S. Office for conference of P.A. Commanders 9th Division week.	M. Mudduth R. Cochrane

1577 Wt. W10791/1773 500,000 1/15 D.D. & L. A.D.S.S./Forms/C. 2118.

Army Form C. 2118.

WAR DIARY
or
INTELLIGENCE SUMMARY.
(Erase heading not required.)

Instructions regarding War Diaries and Intelligence Summaries are contained in F.S. Regs., Part II. and the Staff Manual respectively. Title pages will be prepared in manuscript.

Place	Date	Hour	Summary of Events and Information	Remarks and references to Appendices
POPERINGHE	20/10		Went to BRANDHOEK and warned the Dressing Station to be in readiness to move on to O/C 51st FA, the 2nd Inf, and MARLCORPSE on 22 and info of 22/23 respectively. Arranged to meet the O/C 51st FA at BRANDHOEK at 11 am tomorrow.	Belgium Sheet 27
	21/10		Met O/C 51st FA, took him round Dressing station BRANDHOEK and HQrs POPERINGHE, arranged to hand over all surplus advance medical equipment and dressings. Operation Order No 12 received. One section of 8th FA to march with 8th Inf Bde proceeding to STEENVOORDE in evening 22 October. 8th Bde Motor ambulance received joining orders to march the 1st/3rd columns to meet starting point G/6 at 5.2 by 6.30 PM. FA Other A. section will accompany 8th Inf Bde on march from Rest billets to STEENVOORDE via OUDERDOM - POPERINGHE - ABEELE - STEENVOORDE. Captain HABGOOD will be at Starting point with 2 horse ambulance wagons at 7-15 PM. The remainder of the section will join the column at hour the function of the Rue de BOESCHEPE and the main road POPERINGHE-ABEELE tomorrow at 7-45 PM. Lt SUGARS will march with this detachment and report to Capt HABGOOD. Sick may be dumped at the Dressing points and will be picked up at the hour stated by Motor ambulance. E. Entrance to ABEELE 9.30 PM. Junction of main road ABEELE - STEENVOORDE with road to GODEWAERSVELDE 10.30 PM. E Entrance to STEENVOORDE at 11-30 PM. C. Section will hand over the Dressing station BRANDHOEK to detachment of 51st FA and will march to HQRS POPERINGHE during the night of 22nd on 22nd. By 12 noon n 22 nd.	Belgium Sheet Nieuve Wold 28

WAR DIARY
or
INTELLIGENCE SUMMARY.
(Erase heading not required.)

Army Form C. 2118.

Place	Date	Hour	Summary of Events and Information	Remarks and references to Appendices
POPERINGHE	21/10		Captain BAZETT will accompany the officers taking detachment of 51st J.A. who will proceed to MAPLE COPSE. Also D. Station, night of 21/22. He will fix any questions in replacing medical arrangements in this area. The detachment of 51st J.A. will remain at MAPLE COPSE. Lt. STEWART and detachment of 6 J.A. will be relieved on night 22/23 October & return H.Q.M.	
	22/10		BRANDHOEK Dressing Station handed over and "C" Section joined H.Q. at 1.30 p.m. A Section formed column of 8th Inf. Bde. at 6.30 p.m. in POPERINGHE in accordance with order abov. Quintets, arriving at new billets at 12.30 p.m. Joined H.Q. at STEENVOORDE and arranged to occupy a hutty completed house in Rue DEECKE as a Dressing Station for Sick H.Q.3rd and Divisional in neighbourhood.	
STEENVOORDE	23/10	11 am	Section head extension "C" Section and am in case to open D. Station in STEENVOORDE.	
		5.30 pm	Remainder of J.A. marching independently left POPERINGHE and reached new billets abt. K 25.d Sheet 27, by 9.30 P.M."	
	24/10		Capt. DARLING returned from leave and took over no. 3 Station in STEENVOORDE with 1 Curkum and Lt. SOGARS. The troops are housed in farms and barns in neighbourhood - The water supply in scanty and there are no arrangements in the STEENVOORDE area for bath, etc. Rewakin, bathing & laundry arrangements are badly needed in an area where troops are brought for rest and recuperation.	

W.Wyatt [?]
R.M. Newman [?]

WAR DIARY
or
INTELLIGENCE SUMMARY
(Erase heading not required.)

Army Form. C. 2118

Place	Date	Hour	Summary of Events and Information	Remarks and references to Appendices
STEENVOORDE	25/10/15		The D Station at STEENVOORDE is to be used also as a small DRS for cases which cannot be evacuated at 7 PM EECKE in turn. This morning am informed by His A.D.M.S. that the Oxfords have arrived on leave and now to such arrangements made for a party of 3 NCOs & men drawn from the 3rd Life Ambulance to proceed on 27th with other units of the 30 Division in wish placing by the King. Handed over command of FA to Capt BUCKLEY RAMS	
STEENVOORDE	26/10/15	10 am	Lieut. SU GARS. has gone to 1 & 2nd Brigade f Artillery to relieve M.O. who has gone on leave. Capt. STEWART relieved Lieut SUGARS at the Dressing Station at STEENVOORDE.	
STEENVOORDE	30/10/15	11 a.m.	Lieut DOUGLAS returned from leave —	
STEENVOORDE	1/11/15	10 am.	Capt. HABGOOD went on leave this morning — Capt BAGETT returned from leave —	
STEE				

3die/Nansen

Stig Sjöås Amundsen

1077/18
13
1 ex.
2 "

Army Form. C. 2118

6th Field Ambulance

WAR DIARY
or
INTELLIGENCE SUMMARY
(Erase heading not required.)

Instructions regarding War Diaries and Intelligence Summaries are contained in F. S. Regs., Part II. and the Staff Manual respectively. Title Pages will be prepared in manuscript.

Place	Date	Hour	Summary of Events and Information	Remarks and references to Appendices
STEENVOORDE	3/11/15	3 p.m.	Command of 7th Amb. taken over by Capt. A. R. WRIGHT. Reqce. made orders of D.M.S. 2nd Army. Lt. Col. HUDLESTON ordered to report to War Office.	
STEENVOORDE	4/11/15	10.30 a.m.	Captain G. K. MAURICE proceeded to ENGLAND on leave.	
STEENVOORDE	5/11/15	10.30 a.m.	Lieut. H. S. SUGARS rejoined on completion of Temp. Duty with R.A.	
STEENVOORDE	6/11/15	10.30 a.m.	Capt. H. C. BAZETT posted to Temp. Duty with 4th Middx. Regt.	
STEENVOORDE	7/11/15	10 a.m.	Capt. J. L. STEWART proceeded to Med. charge of 1st Gordon H'rs in relief of Lieut. E. L. M. HACKETT who has joined this unit.	
STEENVOORDE	13/11/15		Capt. BAZETT, rejoined from 4th Middx. Regt.	
STEENVOORDE	16/11/15		Capt. Lieut. CULLUM proceeded on leave.	
	20/11/15	10 a.m.	Capt. BUCKLEY proceeded on leave. I was instructed to proceed to BOESCHEPE to confer with O.C. No. 74. 7th Amb. with regard to taking over from Zion the Divisional Rest Station, Special Hospital (for left Infectious cases) + the Baths there.	
STEENVOORDE	24/11/15	9 a.m.	Capt. HABGOOD + Lt. SUGARS proceeded with 15 Tents Subdivision of "B" Section to BOESCHEPE as advance party to take on 1/c Special Hospital + Div. Rest station from No. 74. F'd Ambulance.	

5th Field Ambulance
Army Form C. 2118

WAR DIARY
or
INTELLIGENCE SUMMARY
(Erase heading not required.)

Instructions regarding War Diaries and Intelligence Summaries are contained in F. S. Regs., Part II. and the Staff Manual respectively. Title Pages will be prepared in manuscript.

Place	Date	Hour	Summary of Events and Information	Remarks and references to Appendices
STEENVOORDE	23/11/15	9.30 a.m.	Remainder of Fd Amb. with the exception of Capt. Darling & "C" Section proceeded to quarters at BOESCHEPE. "C" Section left at STEENVOORDE to clear up 15 Fd Section Hospital which they had been running for some weeks.	AOW
		5 p.m.	Capt. Darling & "C" Section reported their arrival at BOESCHEPE - thus completing the move of the Fd Ambulance to this place.	
BOESCHEPE	30/11/15	10.30 a.m.	Captain Buckley returned from leave -	

No 8. P. Cmd.

Dec / Vol. XI

3rd Div

F/1181

Dec 1915

Army Form. C. 2118

WAR DIARY
or
INTELLIGENCE SUMMARY
(Erase heading not required.)

Instructions regarding War Diaries and Intelligence Summaries are contained in F. S. Regs., Part II. and the Staff Manual respectively. Title Pages will be prepared in manuscript.

Place	Date	Hour	Summary of Events and Information	Remarks and references to Appendices
BOESCHEPE	3/12/15	10 a.m.	CAPTAIN. CULLUM returned from leave to-day.	
BOESCHEPE	11/12/15	10 a.m.	CAPTAIN. BAZETT evacuated with "appendicitis".	
BOESCHEPE	22/12/15	6 p.	CAPTAIN. CULLUM evacuated to No. 12. C.C.S. with Rheumatism.	
BOESCHEPE	24/12/15	6 p.	LIEUT. J.D. MARSHALL. R.A.M.C. joined this unit for duty from No. 17. C.C.S.	
BOESCHEPE	19/12/15	4 p.	LIEUT. SUGARS. R.A.M.C. proceeded to take on medical charge of 12th. W. York. Regt. in relief of LIEUT. L.S. SHOOSMITH. R.A.M.C. who on relief joined this unit for duty.	
BOESCHEPE	31/12/15	6 p.	This unit has remained in this place during the whole of this month performing the duties of Divisional Rest Station. There is nothing of special interest to note.	April? Leaver? Capt? J.? ? ? O.C. No 7. ? ?

3RD DIVISION
XXXXXXXXXX
MEDICAL

NO. 8 FIELD AMBULANCE.
JAN ₱ DEC 1916.

3

8 2d Amb.
Jan
Vol XII

F/118/2.

8 F.A

S/ Jan 1916.

Army Form C. 2118.

WAR DIARY
or
INTELLIGENCE SUMMARY.
(Erase heading not required.)

Instructions regarding War Diaries and Intelligence Summaries are contained in F. S. Regs., Part II. and the Staff Manual respectively. Title pages will be prepared in manuscript.

Place	Date	Hour	Summary of Events and Information	Remarks and references to Appendices
BOESCHEPE.	25-1-16	2 a.m.	Lieut. L.S. Stodsmith R.A.M.C. returned from leave.	
— ,, —	26-1-16	Noon	Capt. C.A. Dougall R.A.M.C. transferred to Special Bde R.E. G.H.Q. for duty.	
— ,, —	27-1-16	2 p.m.	Capt. E.L.M. Hickett R.A.M.C. proceeded to assume medical charge of 30th Bde R.F.A. for temporary duty.	
— ,, —	31-1-16	4 p.m.	Lieut. W.J.S. Smyth R.A.M.C. joined for duty from No. 26 General Hospital. During the whole of the month the Field Ambulance has been doing duty as Divisional Rest Station, one section acting as personnel for the Special Hospital for self inflicted cases.	A.L. Morton, Capt R.A.M.C. O.C. No. 8.

WAR DIARY
or
INTELLIGENCE SUMMARY.
(Erase heading not required.)

Army Form C. 2118.

Instructions regarding War Diaries and Intelligence Summaries are contained in F. S. Regs., Part II. and the Staff Manual respectively. Title pages will be prepared in manuscript.

Place	Date	Hour	Summary of Events and Information	Remarks and references to Appendices
BUSSEBOOM	3-1-16	1 p.m.	Nine R.A.M.C. personnel proceeded to No. 3 General Hospital for duty (Exchange of Billets).	
"	4-1-16	2 p.m.	Lieut. J.D. MARSHALL R.A.M.C. proceeded to take on permanent medical charge of 1/- 13th King's Liverpool Regt.	
"	5-1-16	9 a.m.	1 Cpl. 7 men R.A.M.C. joined for duty.	
"	5-2-16	6 p.m.	Lieut. H.M.D. TOWNSHEND joined this unit for duty from No. 3 General Hospital (Exchange of Billets).	
"	6-1-16	4 p.m.	Lieut. E.L.M. HACKETT, R.A.M.C. proceeded on leave.	
"	6-1-16	12 noon	1 N.C.O. 7 men R.A.M.C. proceeded to No. 3 General Hospital for duty (Exchange of Billets).	
"	7-1-16	5 a.m.	1 N.C.O. 7 men R.A.M.C. joined for duty from No. 3 General Hospital (Exchange of Billets)	
"	8-1-16	4 a.m.	Lieut. & D/M. E.J. TILBURY. proceeded on leave.	
"	9-1-16	9 a.m.	10 Reinforcements R.A.M.C. joined for duty.	
"	10-1-16	4 a.m.	Capt. W. DARLING proceeded on leave.	
"	16-1-16	10 a.m.	Capt. J. EMOYES R.A.M.C. taken on the strength of this unit - & proceeded on leave.	
"	16-1-16	2 a.m.	Capt. E.L.M. HACKETT R.A.M.C. returned from leave.	
"	14-1-16	2 a.m.	Lieut. & D/M. E.J. TILBURY, returned from leave.	
"	15-1-16	6 a.m.	Lieut. L.S. SHOOSMITH R.A.M.C. proceeded on leave.	
"	23-1-16	6 a.m.	Capt. W. DARLING R.A.M.C. returned from leave.	
"	26-1-16	4 a.m.	Capt. A.H. HARROD, R.A.M.C. proceeded on leave.	

S

Feb. 1916

No. 8. Field Ambulance.

COMMITTEE FOR THE
MEDICAL HISTORY OF THE WAR
Date 17 MAY 1917

140/1949

N 1574.

~~D.A.G.~~
~~at the Base~~
~~of Hayre Plante~~

Herewith War Diary of No 8
Field Ambulance for month of
February 1916. Please
acknowledge receipt.

M Anderson
Capt
A.D.M.S.
3rd Div

22/4/17

WAR DIARY or INTELLIGENCE SUMMARY.

Army Form C. 2118.

§ 3rd Aust

Place	Date	Hour	Summary of Events and Information	Remarks and references to Appendices
BOESCHEPE.	1.2.16	5 p.m.	CAPT. J.M. MOYES. R.A.M.C. joined for duty from 5th L.R.B.	
—	—	—	CAPT. W. DARLING. R.A.M.C. proceeded under orders from D.M.S. 2nd Army to assume command of No 28. 3rd Aust.	
—	2.2.16	8 p.m.	Lt. H.M.D. TOWNSHEND R.A.M.C. posted to M.I. charge of 3rd D.A.C.	
—	5.2.16	4 a.m.	Four Officers + 60 O.R. with G.S. Wagn proceeded by train from GODEVERSVELDE to take over new billets in NORDAUSQUES.	
—	6.2.16	7 a.m.	Remainder of Field Ambulance with transport proceeded by march route to OCAZEELE. Billeted in village for night.	
OCAZEELE	7.2.16	7 a.m.	Unit left village & proceeded by march route to NORDAUSQUES. Weather very wet.	
NORDAUSQUES	7.2.16	8 p.m.	Unit arrived + billeted in village - performing duties of D.R.S.	
—	9.2.16	6 a.m.	CAPT. G.K. MAURICE. proceeded on leave.	
—	11.2.16	11 a.m.	Lt. W.M.J. SMYTH. transferred sick to 20 C.C.S. ST. OMER.	
—	12.2.16	—	Lt. SHOOSMITH. posted to 4th R. Fus. 15th in temp.y Med. charge.	
—	18.2.16	—	CAPT. G.K. MAURICE. returned from leave.	
—	19.2.16	4 p.m.	R.A.M.C. under No 1/16 received — No 4889 Pte W.O. BROWNE + 269 Pte DEN	

WAR DIARY
or
INTELLIGENCE SUMMARY.
(Erase heading not required.)

Army Form C. 2118.

Place	Date	Hour	Summary of Events and Information	Remarks and references to Appendices
MARSEILLES	19-2-16	a.m.	O.C. of this unit mentioned in Despatches.	
—	20-2-16	—	10 O.R. R.A.M.C. joined unit for duty from No 5. Gen. Base Depot at ROUEN, as reinforcements.	
—	21-2-16	6 a.m.	CAPT. L. BUCKLEY proceeded on leave.	
—	23-2-16	3 p.m.	Lt. W. H. BLAKEMORE. R.A.M.C. joined for duty from No 2. Stat: Hosp.	
—	28-2-16	—	Lt. SMITHSMITH returned from Temp: duty.	

A.L. Wright
Maj. R.A.M.C.
O.C. No 6. F.A. Sand.

WAR DIARY
or
INTELLIGENCE SUMMARY
(Erase heading not required.)

Army Form C. 2118

8 3d Aus f

Place	Date	Hour	Summary of Events and Information	Remarks and references to Appendices
BOESCHEPE	2/2/16.		Capt. J. M. MOYES rejoined from leave. Capt. W. DARLING proceeded to No. 9D to Aust. to take over command.	This diary has been compiled from private records to replace the Diary of Feb. 1916 which was lost.
	3/2/16.		Lieut. H.M.D TOWNSEND R.A.M.C. proceeded to 3rd D.A.C. for duty.	
	4/2/16.		Lieut. W.J.J. SMYTH R.A.M.C. joined for duty from No. 26 General Hospital. CAPT. J. BUCKLEY in command 69th CAPT. J.M. MOYES left for leave 69th an advance party and one C.T. waggon to take over billets at NORDAUSQUES.	
	6/2/16. 7a.m.		Remainder of the unit 69th CAPT. A.R. WRIGHT in command, proceeded by march route to OEHTEZEELE, arriving at 6 p.m. and billeted for the night.	J.M.Maguire Lt Col R.A.M.C. Ireland
OEHTEZEELE	7/2/16. 7a.m.		The unit less advance party, proceeded by march route to NORDAUSQUES, arriving 4 p.m. and took over billets and accomodation for use from No 53 & No 2 Aub.	
NORDAUSQUES.	8/2/16.		Lieut. SMYTH R.A.M.C. was gazetted Brit to No 26 CCS.	
	10/2/16.		Lieut. SHOOSMITH R.A.M.C. proceeded to take over Medical charge of 4th Royal Fusiliers.	
	12/2/16.		Lieut. G.H. BLANEMORE joined for duty from No 2 Stationary Hospital.	
	21/2/16.			
	29/2/16.		During the period in which the unit was at NORDAUSQUES, they were all undergoing Divisional training. Squad, Company and Stretcher Drill. The whole unit was put through a fair test in resuscitation work. Bar-Bell Exercises, Heavy Marathons daily. There were also recreational training, football, boxing and running.	

J.M.Maguire
Lt Col R.A.M.C.
O.C. 8th F.A.

22/4/17.

3rd Div.

8th Fld. Ambulance

S
March 1916

3

8 7a Auch
  Vol XIV

8th Field Ambulance

WAR DIARY
or
INTELLIGENCE SUMMARY.
(Erase heading not required.)

Army Form C. 2118.

Place	Date	Hour	Summary of Events and Information	Remarks and references to Appendices
NORDAUSQUES	6.3.16		Captain J.G. Ingles R.A.M.C. proceeded to 13th Brigade R.A.M.C. for temporary duty	
-	7.3.16		Captain G.L.G. Hackol R.A.M.C. with an advanced party of twelve other ranks left NORDAUSQUES and arrived at RENINGHELST. The remainder of the unit left NORDAUSQUES by march route to RENINGHELST	
OCHTEZEELE	7.3.16		Unit billeted in Barn for the night	
-	8.3.16		Unit left at 10 a.m.	
RENINGHELST	8.3.16		Arrived and took over dressing station and billets from 9/51st Field Ambulance.	
-	10.3.16		Your R.A.M.C. Orderlies joined for duty from 8.5. General Base Dept - Rouen	
-	11.3.16		Your A.S.C.G.S. transferred to Rouen - Supplies to established.	
-	13.3.16		Lieut. L.S. Shoosmith R.A.M.C. reported for temporary duty from 4 Base Supplies	
-	14.3.16		Lieut. J.D. Marshal R.A.M.C. transferred to 2nd Suffolks for permanent duty	
-	20.3.16		Lieut. L.S. Shoosmith R.A.M.C. proceeded to 7th K.S.L.I. for temporary duty	
-	20.3.16		Lieut. W.H. Blakemore R.A.M.C. transferred to 13th Kings Liverpool to assume medical charge.	
-	21.3.16		Lieut. L.S. Shoosmith R.A.M.C. returned from temporary duty from 7th K.S.L.I.	
-	21.3.16		Captain A.H. Halgood R.A.M.C. admitted to hospital	
-	21.3.16		Captain L. Buckley R.A.M.C. admitted to hospital	

Army Form C. 2118.

8th Field Ambulance

WAR DIARY
or
INTELLIGENCE SUMMARY.
(Erase heading not required.)

Place	Date	Hour	Summary of Events and Information	Remarks and references to Appendices
RENINGHELST	26.3.16		Captain J. H. A. Pearson + Lieut A. G. Townsend and Lieut A. de L. Crayford joined for duty.	
" "	26.3.16		Captain A. H. Habgood Davis dismissed for hospital.	
" "	26.3.16		Captain G. K. Ironside, Captain E. L. Stackell with three sergeants and seventy bearers proceeded to VIERSTRAAT for collecting duty with 9° Field Ambulance.	
" "	26.3.16		Lieut A. G. Townsend one sergeant and twenty five men proceeded to VIERSTRAAT for collecting duty with 9° Field Ambulance. The party that left on the 26th returned.	
" "	29.3.16		Captain G. K. Ironside, Captain J. G. Inglis with two sergeants and fifty bearers proceeded to VOORMEZEELE for collecting duty with 9° Field Ambulance. The party which left on the 28th returned.	
" "	30.3.16		Captain L. Buckley, Lieut A. de L. Crayford, one sergeant and twenty five bearers proceeded to VOORMEZEELE for collecting duty with 9° Field Ambulance. The party which left on the 29th returned.	
" "	29.3.16		9° 10039 Pte Lee and 9° 48657 Pte Palmer David were wounded whilst collecting, the former being evacuated to 6 C.C.S. Pays and the latter man returned to duty.	

A.M. Cooper Lieut Colonel
A.M. Cooper No 22
O.C. No 8 F.A.

3rd. Div.

No. 8 F. Amb.

S/ April 1916.

COMMITTEE FOR THE
MEDICAL HISTORY OF THE WAR
Date 9 - JUN. 1915

3

8 Fd Amb
―――――
Vol XX

WAR DIARY
or
INTELLIGENCE SUMMARY.
(Erase heading not required.)

Army Form C. 2118.

Instructions regarding War Diaries and Intelligence Summaries are contained in F.S. Regs., Part II. and the Staff Manual respectively. Title pages will be prepared in manuscript.

Place	Date	Hour	Summary of Events and Information	Remarks and references to Appendices
RENINGHELST	1.4.16		Lieut. J.G. Hobbs proceeded to 2nd Bge. sick for permanent duty	
RENINGHELST	1.4.16		Lieut. H.G.D. Swinshed Smith proceeded to 40th Brigade Sect. as a for permanent duty	
"	2.4.16	5 am	Captain L. Buckley Smith bicycled from VOORMEZEELE. Lieuts. S. Bamford Smith and the bearers road out on 30.3.16 remained there.	
"	2.4.16	12 noon	Returned to move to METEREN on April 3rd 1916	
"	2.4.16	2 pm	Captain L. Buckley Smith, one Sergeant and nine men proceeded at 2 p.m. to METEREN to take over hospital from 9. 143 Field Ambulance	
"	2.4.16	9 pm	Lieut. L.S. Shoosmith and two Sergeants and forty stretcher bearers proceeded to return at VOORMEZEELE to be attached to 9.4 Field Ambulance for receiving duties	
"	3.4.15	7.30 am	Transport of Field Ambulance under Captain J.R. Lawrie and Captain J.R. Jagger Smith and Lieut. J.Q. Ro. C.J. Seeley left for METEREN- proceeding via LOCRE and BAILLEUL arriving there at 10 am	
"	3.4.16	9.30 am	After handing over the hospital at RENINGHELST to the advance party of 90. 6. Canadian Field Ambulance - the remainder of the unit proceeded over WESTOUTRE and MONT NOIR to METEREN arriving there at 12.30 p.m. Weather - Cloudless sunny warm day.	
"	3.4.16		Lieuts. S. Bamford Smith and bearers read out on 30.3.16 rejoined	

WAR DIARY
or
INTELLIGENCE SUMMARY

Army Form C. 2118.

Place	Date	Hour	Summary of Events and Information	Remarks and references to Appendices
METEREN	5.4.16		Captain A. B. Wright RAMC proceeded on leave to United Kingdom.	
"	8.4.16		Captain E. J. McHackett RAMC proceeded to 5th East Yorks for temporary duty.	
"	13.4.16		Captain J. Buckley RAMC proceeded to A.D.M.S. 3rd Division for temporary duty in office.	
"	16.4.16		Captain E. J. McHackett RAMC returned from temporary duty.	
"	17.4.16		Captain A. B. Wright RAMC returned from leave.	
"	19.4.16		Captain J. Buckley RAMC returned from temporary duty with A.D.M.S. 3rd Division.	
"	"		Captain A. B. Wright RAMC appointed temporary Major from 3.12.15	
"	"		Lieut. C.W. Thomson RAMC joined for duty from No. 15 General Hospital.	
"	20.4.16		Captain A.H. Holgood RAMC 6 to C section left METEREN and took over hospital and Billets from 1st Northumbrian Field Ambulance at WESTOUTRE.	
"	21.4.16		Captain E.K. Lawrie and Lieut. L.W. Thomson with thirty one other ranks left METEREN and took over Advanced Dressing Station LA-CLYTTE from 1st Northumbrian Field Ambulance	
"	22.4.16		Major A.B. Wright RAMC in command left METEREN with remainder of B.H.Unit Ambulance personnel and transport and arrived at WESTOUTRE.	
WESTOUTRE	24.4.16		Lieut. L.W. Thomson proceeded to 1st Cheshire Battalion for reserve duty.	

3rd Division

No 8. Field Ambulance.

January 1916

S

COMMITTEE FOR THE
MEDICAL HISTORY OF THE WAR
Date 31 AUG 1916

Army Form C. 2118.

WAR DIARY
or
INTELLIGENCE SUMMARY.
(Erase heading not required.)

8th Field Ambulance

Vol 16

Instructions regarding War Diaries and Intelligence Summaries are contained in F. S. Regs., Part II. and the Staff Manual respectively. Title pages will be prepared in manuscript.

Place	Date	Hour	Summary of Events and Information	Remarks and references to Appendices
WEST-OUTRE	15.5.16		Lieut. H. de L. Crawford transferred to No. 10 C.C.C. Station for personal duty	
"	13.5.16		Lieut. L.S. Shoosmith said proceeded on leave to United Kingdom	
"	21.5.16		Captain L.J. Steward said joined for personal duty from No. 10 Stationary Hospital	
"	21.5.16		Lieut. C.M. Gettleson said joined for personal duty from No. 10 Stationary Hospital	
"	22.5.16		Lieut. L.S. Shoosmith said returned from leave.	
"	26.5.16		Captain L. Buckley said and seven other ranks left WEST-OUTRE by march route and took over hospital and billets at METEREN from 2nd Northumbrian Field Ambulance.	
"	29.5.16		Major A.L. Wright said in command left WEST-OUTRE with remainder of 8th Field Ambulance personnel and transport and arrived at METEREN.	

A.L. Wright
Maj. R.A.M.C.
O.C. No 8 F.A.

3rd Div.

No. 2 F Amb.

S/
5 Aug 1916

Army Form C. 2118.

WAR DIARY
or
INTELLIGENCE SUMMARY.
(Erase heading not required.)

8 yth Amb
Vol 17

Instructions regarding War Diaries and Intelligence Summaries are contained in F. S. Regs., Part II. and the Staff Manual respectively. Title pages will be prepared in manuscript.

Place	Date	Hour	Summary of Events and Information	Remarks and references to Appendices
METEREN	1.6.16		CAPTAIN L.T. STEWART R.A.M.C proceeded to the 2ND ROYAL SCOTS for temporary duty.	
—	3.6.16		CAPTAIN A.H. HABGOOD R.A.M.C proceeded on leave to UNITED KINGDOM.	
—	4.6.16		CAPTAIN E.L.M. HACKETT R.A.M.C proceeded to 33RD BRIGADE R.F.A for temporary duty.	
—	4.6.16		CAPTAINS G.K. MAURICE, J.M. MOYES AND LIEUT. L.S. SHOOSMITH R.A.M.C with 119 other ranks, 3 ambulance wagons, 1 S.A. wagon and 12 horses proceeded to the CANADIAN CORPS for temporary duty.	
—	6.6.16		CAPTAIN L. BUCKLEY R.A.M.C returned from leave.	
—	10.6.16		CAPTAIN L.T. STEWART R.A.M.C returned from temporary duty from 2ND ROYAL SCOTS.	
—	13.6.16		CAPTAIN A.H. HABGOOD R.A.M.C returned from leave.	
—	15.6.16		CAPTAIN E.L.M. HACKETT R.A.M.C returned from temporary duty from 33RD BRIGADE R.F.A.	
—	17.6.16		the personnel and transport attached to CANADIAN CORPS rejoined	
—	18.6.16	4:30 a.m	MAJOR A.R. WRIGHT R.A.M.C in command of Unit left METEREN by Canal Route to WEMMARS CAPPEL	
WEMMARS CAPPEL	19.6.16	4:30 a.m	Left WEMMARS CAPPEL by Canal Route to BROXELLE.	
BROXELLE	20.6.16	4:30 a.m	Left BROXELLE by Canal Route arriving at CORMETTE at 2 p.m. and occupied hospital and billets	
CORMETTE	21.6.16		CAPTAIN L.T. STEWART R.A.M.C transferred sick to No 10 STATIONARY HOSPITAL.	

3rd Division

No. 8. Field Ambulance

July 1916

51

COMMITTEE FOR THE
MEDICAL HISTORY OF THE WAR
Date 13 SEP 1915

Army Form C. 2118.

WAR DIARY
or
INTELLIGENCE SUMMARY.
(Erase heading not required.)

8 F Amb

Place	Date	Hour	Summary of Events and Information	Remarks and references to Appendices
CORMETTE.	1-7-16	9.30 p.m.	MAJOR A.T. WRIGHT, Opr. with unit transport, proceeded by road en route to WIZERNES Station, arriving there about midnight.	
WIZERNES	2-7-16	1. a.m.	Unit entrained with transport - less Motor Ambulances - to proceeded to PRENVILLERS CANDAS, arriving there at 11 a.m. Train route :- Via CALAIS, BOULOGNE, ABBEVILLE.	
" "	" "	6 a.m.	All Motor Ambulances proceeded under CAPT. E.L.M. HACKETT, R.A.M.C. by road from CORMETTE to CANDAS. Unit detrained.	
CANDAS.	" "	12 noon		
" "	" "	3 p.m.	Unit transport proceeded by march route to ST. HILAIRE. Billeted in ST. HILAIRE. Motor Ambulances rejoined from CANDAS.	
ST HILAIRE	3-7-16	1 a.m.	4 Motor Ambulances under CAPT. E.L.M. HACKETT, R.A.M.C. proceeded to report to No. 25 M.A.C. CAPT. E.L.M. HACKETT, proceeded from Unit to report for duty to D.R.S. ALLONVILLE.	
" "	" "	8 a.m.	Orders received to march off forthwith with 8th Buffs Bgde.	
" "	" "	9 a.m.	Marched off after collecting evacuating sick from units.	

2353 Wt. W2544/1454 700,000 5/15 D.D.&L. A.D.S.S./Forms/C. 2118.

Army Form C. 2118.

WAR DIARY
or
INTELLIGENCE SUMMARY.
(Erase heading not required.)

Instructions regarding War Diaries and Intelligence Summaries are contained in F.S. Regs., Part II. and the Staff Manual respectively. Title pages will be prepared in manuscript.

Place	Date	Hour	Summary of Events and Information	Remarks and references to Appendices
ST HILAIRE	3-7-16.	9.a.m.	LIEUT. G.M. BETTLESON. R.A.M.C. transferred sick to Cas. Cl. Sta.	
FLESSELLES	—	2 p.m.	Arrived at OLINCOURT CHATEAU near FLESSELLES. Billeted in CHATEAU.	
—	4-7-16.	2 p.m.	CAPT. L.T. STEWART. R.A.M.C. rejoined unit for duty from No. 10. Stationary Hosp.	
—	—	4.30 p.m.	Unit paraded with transport & proceeded by march route to CARDONETTE.	
CARDONETTE	5-7-16.	12.30 a.m.	Arrived in CARDONETTE. Billeted for the night.	
—	—	9.30 p.m.	Unit paraded with transport & proceeded by march route to CORBIE.	
CORBIE	6-7-16	3 a.m.	Arrived at a meadow on the NORTH Bank of the SOMME about 3 kilometres along the CORBIE - VAUX road. Billeted for the night in tents.	
—	—	4 p.m.	LIEUT. F. KINNEAR. R.A.M.C. joined for duty from No. 14. General Hosp.	
—	—	8.30 p.m.	Unit proceeded by march route to BOIS LES CELESTINS, - S. West of BRAY. Billeted in woods under Bivouacs in Huts for the night. Weather - Very cloudy & raining.	

WAR DIARY
or
INTELLIGENCE SUMMARY.
(Erase heading not required.)

Army Form C. 2118.

Instructions regarding War Diaries and Intelligence Summaries are contained in F. S. Regs., Part II. and the Staff Manual respectively. Title pages will be prepared in manuscript.

Place	Date	Hour	Summary of Events and Information	Remarks and references to Appendices
BOIS LES CELESTINS	7-7-16	11 a.m.	The whole of Bearer Sub-divisions under CAPT. G.K. MAURICE, with CAPT. MOYES & LIEUT. SHOESMITH proceeded to work with 8th Infy. Brigade to be affiliated to them for collecting duties. Tent sub-divisions remained in BOIS LES CELESTINS.	
" "	8-7-16 Morn.		Tent sub-divisions with Transport proceeded & marched to Cross-roads on main CORBIE-BRAY road, S. west of MORLANCOURT. Bivouacked in field at Cross Roads. Tent sub-divisions of No. 7 Field Ambulance bivouacked in same field. All Horsed Transport parked in field at cross-roads, about 1 kilometre west of where personnel are bivouacked. All Motor Ambulances proceeded to be attached to call under orders of the O.C. XIII Corps Main Dressing Station.	
N. of MORLANCOURT	9-7-16	10 a.m.	Three Horsed Ambulances with horses & personnel proceeded to report for duty to D.C. 142 7th Arml. at SAPPER CORNER at BRAY. Weather much finer after 2 wet days.	

Army Form C. 2118.

WAR DIARY
or
INTELLIGENCE SUMMARY.
(Erase heading not required.)

Instructions regarding War Diaries and Intelligence Summaries are contained in F. S. Regs., Part II. and the Staff Manual respectively. Title pages will be prepared in manuscript.

Place	Date	Hour	Summary of Events and Information	Remarks and references to Appendices
Naw				
MORLANCOURT	9-7-16	3 p.m.	LIEUT. Y. DRMR. LE POIDEVIN. R.AMC. from 3rd Cav. Fd. Ambulance, 1st Cav. Div. joined for duty, as Dr. But in relief of Lt. D. TILBURY. F.S.I. who departed to report for duty under D.M.S. 1st Army.	
"	15-7-16 6.a.m.		LIEUT. F. KINNEAR. left to report for temporary duty at 16th C.C.S. R.P Walking Wounded Post.	
"	16-7-16		Tent- Subdivisions remaining in Reserve in same bivouac. 10 men of Tent sub-division attached to Bearers for one day. reported.	
"	20-7-16 noon		Orders received to proceed from Reserve. Report with Tent division and personnel, others transport for duty at XIIIth Corps Main Dressing Station.	
XIIIth R. Corps Main Dressing S.S.	"	2 p.m.	Reported for duty to Lt. Col. ELSINOR R.AMC. (Commanding No 27 Fd Amb.) O.C. M.D.S. Brewing Station XIIIth Corps.	
"	"	10 p.m.	Tent Sub division opened up receiving wounded	
"	21-7-16 5 p.m.		CAPT E.L.M. HACKETT. RAMC. rejoined from one day's duty at Stretcher Post.	

Army Form C. 2118.

WAR DIARY
or
INTELLIGENCE SUMMARY.
(Erase heading not required.)

Instructions regarding War Diaries and Intelligence Summaries are contained in F. S. Regs., Part II. and the Staff Manual respectively. Title pages will be prepared in manuscript.

Place	Date	Hour	Summary of Events and Information	Remarks and references to Appendices
XIII Corps Train Dressing Stn	21-7-16	6 p.m.	Orders received to fr. Maj. A.R. WRIGHT. R.A.M.C. to assume command of Main Dressing Station XIII Corps Fr. in relief of Lt. Col. ELSMIE. R.A.M.C.	
—	22-7-16	6 a.m.	Assumed command of Main Dressing Station. CAPT. L.T. STEWART. R.A.M.C. proceeded to take on temp. med. charge of 3rd Div. D.A.C.	
—	23-7-16	8 p.m.	CAPT. H.Q. WILLIS. R.A.M.C. (T.C) posted for temp duty.	
—	24-7-16	9 a.m.	CAPT. E.L.M. HACKETT. proceeded to take on temp. med. charge of 3rd Div. D.A.C. in relief of CAPT. L.T. STEWART. who proceeded on temp. med. charge of 1st Northbay Fac. Transfusion Stat. on temp. duty at Main Dressing Station. Train Sub-division of Nos 5. 6. 7. 700 Ft. Amb. of 2nd Division.	
—	—	3 p.m.	Opened for duty at Main Dressing Station. Surg. Gen. Sir. A.T. SLOGGETT. Dir. Gen. Army Med. Service visited the Main Dressing Station.	
—	26-7-16	2 p.m.	No. 142 Ft. Amb. (3rd Division) joined Main Dressing Station. No 5. Ft Amb. (2nd Division) left Main Dressing Station.	

WAR DIARY
or
INTELLIGENCE SUMMARY.

(Erase heading not required.)

Army Form C. 2118.

Place	Date	Hour	Summary of Events and Information	Remarks and references to Appendices
XIII Corps Main Dressing Stn.	26-7-16	6 p.m.	The 1st/3rd West Lancs Ft. Amb. (55th Division) joined Menin Dressing Station.	
—	27-7-16	11 a.m.	The 2/1st West Lancs Ft. Amb. (55th Div.) relieved the 2/1st Wessex Ft. Amb. (55th Div.) joined this Main Dressing Station.	
—	31-7-16	2 p.m.	The 2/1st N. Lancs Ft. Amb. left this Dressing Station.	
—	—	10 p.m.	The 72nd Ft. Amb. (24th Division) joined this Dressing Station.	

Casualties in No 8. Ft. Amb. during the month of July:—

	Killed	Wounded
9th	1	—
11th	2	—
14th	1	—
15th	1	3
22nd	1	4
23rd	—	4
24th	4	3
	8 killed	**18 wounded**

All these were Casualties in action.

A.V. Lorgué
Major, R.A.M.C.
O.C. No 8. Ft. Amb.

Vol 19

Aug. 1916.

WAR DIARY.
of
O.b. 8. Field Ambulance.

for the month of August 1916.

COMMITTEE FOR THE
MEDICAL HISTORY OF THE WAR
Date -5 OCT. 1916

Army Form C. 2118.

WAR DIARY
or
INTELLIGENCE SUMMARY.
(Erase heading not required.)

Instructions regarding War Diaries and Intelligence Summaries are contained in F. S. Regs., Part II and the Staff Manual respectively. Title pages will be prepared in manuscript.

H.Q. No 8 FIELD AMBULANCE
3rd DIVISION

Place	Date	Hour	Summary of Events and Information	Remarks and references to Appendices
XIII Corps Main Dressing Stn.	1-8-16	2 pm	The 1/3rd N. Lancs. F.Amb. left here this afternoon.	
"	"	10 pm	The 106th & 707th Fd Amb. (35th Div.) joined this Dressing Station.	
"	3-8-16	2 pm	The 105th & 706th Fd. Amb. left this Dressing Station.	
"	4-8-16	—	The 102nd Fd. Amb. left this Dressing Station.	
"	"	—	They 9 2nd Fd (24th Div) left here.	
"	10-8-16	4 pm	The 105th - 106th - 107th Fd. Amb. joined here.	
"	11-8-16	5 pm	The 6th & 700th Fd. Ambs. left here.	
"	14-8-16	5 pm	The 1/3 West Lancs. Fd. Amb. (55th Div) joined here. RAMC O.O. No 27 received. The 8th Fd. Amb. Bearer Division with 8th Fd. Suffks Regt be trained in reserve at Bronfay Farm. Capt. Buckley R.A.M.C. detailed to take over charge of the XIII Corps Walking Wounded Post at Bronfay Farm.	
"	"	5 pm	The 2/1 West Lancs. Fd. Amb. (55th Div) joined here.	
"	19-8-16	10 am	The 1/3 W. Lancs, 2/1 W.Lancs, 2/1 Wessex Fd.Amb. left here.	
"	"	4 pm	The 8th Fd. Amb. Bearers moved into action in relief of Bearers of No 7. Fd. Ambulance.	[signature]

Army Form C. 2118.

WAR DIARY
or
INTELLIGENCE SUMMARY.
(Erase heading not required.)

Place	Date	Hour	Summary of Events and Information	Remarks and references to Appendices
MAIN DRESSING STATION	19-8-16	10 p.m.	No 105 Fd Amb. left for rest.	
"	20-8-16	8 p.m.	R.A.M.C. O.O. No 28 received.	
"	"	10 a.m.	8/15 Fd Amb. bearers relieved from the line & went with 8/15 Staff Bde into reserve.	
"	"	2 p.m.	142 Fd Amb. joined here.	
"	21-8-16	4 p.m.	Handed over command of Main Dressing Station to Lt. Col. HARVEY R.A.M.C. O/C. No 61. Fd Amb. (20th Div).	
"	22-8-16	10 a.m.	CAPT. G.K. NADRIES left with all Horse Transport to proceed by march route to POULAINVILLE.	
"	23-8-16	6 a.m.	CAPT. A.H. HABGOOD left with Tent sub-division personnel, to entrain at MERICOURT. CAPT. MOYES, CAPT. SHOESMITH & bearer sub-division left MEAULTE by CAPT. HABGOOD + Tent Sub-division at MERICOURT. All entrained at 10 a.m. & detrained at CANDAS at 2 p.m. Proceeded by march route to Billet at VACQUERIES at 4 p.m. CAPT MAURICE arrived at VACQUERIES with Horse Transport at 4.30 p.m.	
"	"	10 a.m.	CAPT. HACKETT, proceeded with all units Ambulances to VACQUERIES.	

G.H. Long Lt.
Maj R.A.M.C.
O.C. N of F.A.

WAR DIARY
or
INTELLIGENCE SUMMARY.
(Erase heading not required.)

Army Form C. 2118.

Place	Date	Hour	Summary of Events and Information	Remarks and references to Appendices
MARTIN BUSSART Sector VII	24-8-16	2 p.m.	MAJOR A.R. WRIGHT & Lt. R.M. LE POIDEVIN Capt. Bejean 7L Ambulance. Sergt. Major Watts also left Bejean 7L Amb. All arrived at VACQUERIE	
VACQUERIE	25-8-16	10 a.m.	Left by march route to BEAUVOIR RIVIERE, arriving at 2 p.m.	
BEAUVOIR	26-8-16	10 a.m.	Left by march route to BLANGERVAL arriving at 2 p.m.	
BLANGERVAL	27-8-16	10 a.m.	Left by march route to HUCLIER arriving at 4 p.m.	
HUCLIER	28-8-16	10 a.m.	Left by march route to RUITZ arriving at 4 p.m.	
RUITZ	29-8-16	3 p.m.	Left by march route to NOEUX-LES-MINES arriving at 4 p.m. Took over Allabs. & Hospital from No 111 7L Amb.	
NOEUX	30-8-16	10 a.m.	Proceeded with Capt. Maurice & Capt. Moher & 2 Sgts Knesmotz the advanced dressing station at PHILOSOPHE & Capt. Maurice collecting post at St GEORGE'S DUGOUTS. General procedure of collecting wounded from the HULLUCH SECTOR.	
	31-8-16	2 p.m.	Personnel proceeded to take over the Cast. incidents station from the 25th 7L Amb. (8th Div.)	

A.R. Wright
Major R.A.M.C.
O.C. No 8 Fd Amb.

SECRET
Oct 19/16

War Diary.
N° 8 Field J. Ambulance.

From 1ˢᵗ Sept '16 to 30ᵗʰ Sept '16

To H.Q.
H.Q's Office
Vol 20

COMMITTEE FOR THE
MEDICAL HISTORY OF THE WAR
Date 26 OCT 1916

Army Form C. 2118.

WAR DIARY
or
INTELLIGENCE SUMMARY.
(Erase heading not required.)

Instructions regarding War Diaries and Intelligence Summaries are contained in F.S. Regs., Part II. and the Staff Manual respectively. Title pages will be prepared in manuscript.

Place	Date	Hour	Summary of Events and Information	Remarks and references to Appendices
NOEUX LES MINES	1-9-16	10 a.m.	Visited PHILOSOPHE. Reconnoitred ground between new place & the advanced collecting post at St GEORGES, with a view to providing station for Relay bearers Aug. no 6. Site selected.	
—	2-9-16	10 a.m.	Bearers of A. Section – 10 in number proceeded to PHILOSOPHE for the purpose of digging the new dug outs – Work to commence to-night.	
—	3-9-16	—	Visited PHILOSOPHE – inspected site & progress of previous night's digging.	
—	—	6 p.m.	Visited dugouts at rear post with A.D.M.S. 3rd Division	
—	4-9-16	3/-	Lt. D.J. FOLEY R.A.M.C. joined for permanent duty from No 25 General Hospital.	
—	—	—	Further party of 10 bearers & one N.C.O. from A section proceeded to PHILOSOPHE for digging duties. Ward Orderly for Eying cases in Nummer at PHILOSOPHE.	
—	5-9-16	3 p.m.	CAPT. E.C.M. HACKETT proceeded to PHILOSOPHE to relieve [illegible signature]	

Army Form C. 2118.

WAR DIARY
or
INTELLIGENCE SUMMARY.
(Erase heading not required.)

Instructions regarding War Diaries and Intelligence Summaries are contained in F. S. Regs., Part II. and the Staff Manual respectively. Title pages will be prepared in manuscript.

Place	Date	Hour	Summary of Events and Information	Remarks and references to Appendices
NOEUX LES MINES	5-9-16	3 p.m.	Capt. Maurice, Capt. Shoesmith, proceeded to St. Georges Aug 6 to relieve Capt. Moyes.	
—	6-9-16	1 p.m.	Capt. Maurice & Capt. Moyes rejoined offs Hd Qrs. offrs Reveilly are to Capt. Machinist & Capt. Smoesmith respectively.	
—	7-9-16	9 a.m.	Proceeded with A.D.M.S. & Philosophe – inspected relay bearer dugouts & advanced collecting posts in Tenth Avenue.	
—	—	6 p.m.	C. Section bearers proceeded to relieve bearers of B. Section in advanced collecting posts in Tenth Avenue.	
—	8-9-16	10 a.m.	B. Section bearers rejoined Hd Qrs offrs Reveilly en route C. Section bearers.	
—	—	4 p.m.	Proceeded to Philosophe which was visited respectively by the Director-General Army Medical Services in company with D.M.S. 1st Army, D.D.M.S. 1st Corps, A.D.M.S. 3rd Division.	
—	10-9-16	10 a.m.	Visited Philosophe – & bearer relay dug outs.	
—	—	4 p.m.	Visited Advanced Bearer posts in Tenth Avenue with A.D.M.S.	

WAR DIARY or INTELLIGENCE SUMMARY

Army Form C. 2118.

Place	Date	Hour	Summary of Events and Information	Remarks and references to Appendices
NOEUX LES MINES	11/9/16	2 pm	CAPT. L. BUCKLEY R.A.M.C. left 16 Ambulance & took over 15 in relief of DARLING, 5th Div.	
"	12/5/16	10 am	Visited A.D.S. at PHILOSOPHE.	
"	"	2 pm	CAPT. PIERIAN R.A.M.C. left 15 AMC on had charge of 45th Fld. Amb. in relief of CAPT. WILLIS, who rejoined 14 Bde.	
"	13/9/16	10 am	Visited Relay Bearer Post & A.D.S. in Tenth Avenue.	
"	14/5/16	"	Lt. FOLEY R.A.M.C. proceeded to St. Georges A.D.S. in Tenth Avenue in relief of CAPT. LADYSMITH, who rejoined 14 Bde.	
"	15/9/16	2 pm	DDMS. I corps visited RAPS in Tenth Avenue.	
"	16/5/16	6 am	CAPT. LADYSMITH proceeded to A.D.S. Tenth Avenue in relief of Lt. FOZIEY, who proceeded to report for duty 15 ADMS 47 Div.	
"	"	2 pm	CAPT. WILLIS, proceeded to A.D.S. PHILOSOPHE in relief of CAPT. HACKETT, who rejoined 14 Bde.	
"	17/5/16	10 am	Visited A.D.S. PHILOSOPHE.	
"	18/5/16	10 am	CAPT. MOYES proceeded to A.D.S. PHILOSOPHE in relief of CAPT. WILLIS, who rejoined 14 Bde.	
"	19/5/16	10 am	CAPT. WILLIS proceeded to A.D.S. Tenth Avenue in relief of	

WAR DIARY
or
INTELLIGENCE SUMMARY.

(Erase heading not required.)

Army Form C. 2118.

Place	Date	Hour	Summary of Events and Information	Remarks and references to Appendices
NOEUX LES MINES.	19-4-16		Cont. Capt. Ayresmith who rejoined H.Q. etc.	
	20-5-16	2pm	Lt. Muir Rattie joined for duty from No 136 Fd. Amb. Visited Dis. ons in Relay Posts with A.D.M.S. 3rd Div.	
	21-5-16	10 am	Divs. First Army hill. G.O.C. 3rd Div Staff, 3rd Div - visited Inspected PHILOSPHE, Relay Bearer Post - also in Toule Avenue.	
		2pm	Div S First Army visited Inspected Hospital in Noeux L. Mines.	
	22-5-16	9am	Ft. amb. paraded with all transport - inspected by March past. with G.O.C. 3rd Div. Supp'd Later.	
ALLOUAGNE			ALLOUAGNE area. Billeted for it night in Trucks at ALLOUAGNE.	
	23-5-16	10am	Ft. Amb. proceeded by march in M. with 9th Inf. Bde. Group to RADINGHEM where it joined 15.8th Inf. group. Billeted & found up Hospital in CHATEAU at RADINGHEM.	
RADINGHEM	24-5-16		Visited by A.D.M.S. 3rd Div.	

WAR DIARY
or
INTELLIGENCE SUMMARY.

(Erase heading not required.)

Army Form C. 2118.

Place	Date	Hour	Summary of Events and Information	Remarks and references to Appendices
RADINGHEM AGN	25.9.16	3 p.m.	CAPT. T.N. CRAWFORD R.A.M.C. joined for duty from No 1. C.C.S. on Liaising at RADINGHEM.	
" "	26.5.16			
" "	29.9.16	6 p.m.	Lt. MUIR proceeded to take over medical charge of 13th King's Liverpool Regt.	
" "	30.9.16		Still in Training Area.	
			During the month the following Honours have been awarded to their units:-	
			— Distinguished Conduct Medal — No 15-803 Sergt. H.B. STUART R.A.M.C.	
			— Military Medal — No 5664. Cpl (A/Sgt) J. ROGERS. R.A.M.C.	

Wel Wrake
Maj. R.A.M.C.
O.C. No 6. T. Amb.

140/1788

A.D.M.S.
3rd Division

Oct. 1916.

COMMITTEE FOR THE
MEDICAL HISTORY OF THE WAR
Date -2 DEC. 1916

Secret

Vol 21

War Diary
No 8 Field Ambulance
From 1/10/16 to 31 Oct 16

Army Form C. 2118.

WAR DIARY
or
INTELLIGENCE SUMMARY.
(Erase heading not required.)

Instructions regarding War Diaries and Intelligence Summaries are contained in F. S. Regs., Part II. and the Staff Manual respectively. Title pages will be prepared in manuscript.

Place	Date	Hour	Summary of Events and Information	Remarks and references to Appendices
RADINGHEM	1-10-16.	9 a.m.	The Field Ambulance in training in 1st Army Training Area.	
— " —		After	Capt. L. S. SHOOSMITH. proceeded to take over Camp? incl. charge of the 8th E. Yorks.	
— " —	3-10-16	10 a.m.	Fd. Amb. with transport proceeded by march route to AMBRICOURT. Billeted for night in village	
AMBRICOURT	4-10-16	8 a.m.	Hired Transport needed Capt. G. K. MAVIES & Capt. WILLIS left AMBRICOURT by march route for LEALVILLERS.	
— " —	7-10-16	3 p.m.	Remainder of unit proceeded by march route for ST. POL.	
ST. POL.	7-10-16	11 p.m.	Entrained at ST. POL.	
EGLISE EGLISE	8-10-16	7:30 a.m.	Detrained at BELLE EGLISE & proceeded by march route to LEALVILLERS where the Horse Transport had arrived the previous night.	
LEALVILLERS	— " —	2 p.m.	Fd. Amb. with transport proceeded by march route to MAILLY MAILLET WOOD arriving at 5 p.m. Billeted in huts.	[signature]

2353 Wt. W2514/1454 700,000 5/15 D.D.&L. A.D.S.S./Forms/C. 2118.

Army Form C. 2118.

WAR DIARY
or
INTELLIGENCE SUMMARY.
(Erase heading not required.)

Instructions regarding War Diaries and Intelligence Summaries are contained in F.S. Regs., Part II. and the Staff Manual respectively. Title pages will be prepared in manuscript.

Place	Date	Hour	Summary of Events and Information	Remarks and references to Appendices
MAILLY MAILLET	10-10-16	6 am	Fd. Amb. "billeted" in huts in wood behind MAILLY MAILLET. Collecting tech from Regts in rest area attained.	
"	11-10-16	10 am	Visited site of A.D.S. Walking Wounded Collecting Post at COLIN CAMP & COURCELLES hill. A.D.M.S. Fd. Amb. with transport - less Bearer Sub-division - proceeded by secret route to FOREEVILLE.	
"	13-10-16	10 am	Bearer sub-divisions remained in huts in MAILLY MAILLET WOOD under CAPT. H.G. WILLS & CAPT. T.M. CRAWFORD. Fd. Amb. - less Bearer Subdivisions - arrived at FOREEVILLE. Billeted in village.	
FOREEVILLE	14-10-16	9 am	Resumed command of V.Corps. Main dressing Station which consists of 2 Tent-Subdivisions of No 8 Fd. Amb. & 3 Tent-Subdivisions of 1/1, 1st & 9th Amb. Royal Naval Division.	
"	"	2 pm	Commenced attuninances for 30/10/16 of 3rd Div. Walking Wounded Post at COURCELLES	
"	15-10-16	10 am	"B" Section Tent-Sub-division proceeded to COURCELLES & Spare	

Army Form C. 2118.

WAR DIARY
or
INTELLIGENCE SUMMARY.
(Erase heading not required.)

Place	Date	Hour	Summary of Events and Information	Remarks and references to Appendices
	Continued			
POPERINGHE	15-10-16	10 p.m.	Walking Wounded Collecting Post :- CAPT J.M. MOYES in charge.	
"	17-10-16	10 a.m.	Lt. L. KILROE R.A.M.C. joined for duty from No. 100 F'd Amb.	
"	18-10-16	2 p.m.	1st F'd Amb. Royal Naval (63rd) Division was relieved in Divisional Dressing Station by the 101/3rd Highland F'd Amb. (51st Div).	
"	20-10-16	3 p.m.	Lt. MUIR rejoined for duty from 13th King's Liverpool Regt.	
"	21-10-16	"	Lt. LADDSMITH rejoined from 8th Bn. Y & L. Regt.	
"	23-10-16	"	Capt. R.C. MACLACHLAN R.A.M.C. joined for duty from the 20th K.R.R.C. on being relieved by Lt. A.H. MUIR.	
"	28-10-16	9 a.m.	Capt. WILLIS & Capt CRAWFORD with draft rejoined H.Q. & Dressing Station Staff.	
"	31-10-16	"	Last 6 days has been extremely rainy weather. Still in occupation of Divisional Dressing Station. Staff.	

A.W. Longridge
D.A.D.M.S.
R.N.D.
No. 8.

Nov. 1916

3rd Div. 140/1849

No. 8. Field Ambulance.

COMMITTEE FOR THE
MEDICAL HISTORY OF THE WAR
Date -3 JAN. 1917

Confidential

War Diary   Vol 22

O.C. 8 Field Amb.

November 1916

WAR DIARY
or
INTELLIGENCE SUMMARY.
(Erase heading not required.)

Army Form C. 2118.

Place	Date	Hour	Summary of Events and Information	Remarks and references to Appendices
FORCEVILLE	4/11/16		B. Section tent sub division left behind complete collecting post for Lesqueilles - 18 Bearers and 9 men were left in charge of stores.	
	6/11/16	2 a.m.	One of the 2nd cars of the unit caught fire about 2 a.m. - A board investigation into the case was under RAMC	
	6/11/16	11 a.m.	Capt. G.K. MAURICE RAMC assumed command of this unit vice Temp. Lt Col. A. R. Wright, transferred to V Corps as D.A.D.M.S.	
	7/11/16		Divisional Baring station at FORCEVILLE was taken over by 15 Ashland 7th Bucks, 51st Division. RAMC	
	7/11/16	10.30 p.m	Lieut L. KILROE was transferred to 8th East Yorks for duty as M.O. i/c.	
	7/11/16	8 p.m	Capt. J. DAVIS RAMC joined this unit for duty from 3rd 79nd-de Royal Naval Division.	
	9/11/16	11 a.m	Surgeon General SKINNER inspected the main Dressing Station.	
	9/11/16	2 p.m	Capt J. DAVIS RAMC was transferred to No 4 Battery R.H.A. for duty as M.O. i/c.	
	9/11/16	8 p.m	Capt. L. BUCKLEY RAMC joined for duty from 56th Division.	
	10/11/16	10 a.m	Bearer sub division of A + B sections with CAPT WILLIS and CAPT CRAWFORD, CAPT WILLIS in command, proceeded to COLINCAMP and EUSTON. B section proceeded to Walking Wounded Collecting post near COURCELLES.	
	11/11/16		Tent sub division of B section under CAPT. SHOOSMITH moved to EUSTON.	
	11/11/16	11 a.m	C Section bearers under CAPT SHOOSMITH moved up to EUSTON.	
	12/11/16		CAPT MOYES joined tent sub division of B section and carried all preparations for Wounded.	

WAR DIARY
or
INTELLIGENCE SUMMARY.
(Erase heading not required.)

Army Form C. 2118.

Place	Date	Hour	Summary of Events and Information	Remarks and references to Appendices
FORCEVILLE	14/11/16	6.54 am	Thirty 3rd Division Ambulances began to arrive at Main Bearing Station at Pam.	
	15/11/16	10 a.m.	Bearer Subdivision of A+B Sections with CAPT WILLIS RAMC & CAPT CRAWFORD RAMC returning Headquarters.	
	15/11/16	3.30 pm	Bearer Subdivision of A+B Sections with CAPT WILLIS RAMC and CAPT CRAWFORD RAMC proceeded to walking wounded Collecting post near COURCELLES & immature.	
	15/11/16		B.A. Subdivision with CAPT MORES arriving from walking wounded Collecting post, leaving 1 N.C.O. & 4 men in charge of Stores.	
	16/11/16 17/11/16		9 reinforcements arrived. Bearer Subdivisions of A B C sections with CAPT GILLIS, CAPT CRAWFORD + CAPT SHOOSMITH joined Headquarters 10.a.m.	
	18/11/16 3.p.m.		CAPT J. BUCKLEY RAMC departed to assume command of No 31 M.A.C.	
	20/11/16		Lieut R.G.GORDON RAMC arrived and was posted to No.7. 7th Amb. on 6 July, 7.9 Amb. with transport marched to VAUCHELLES and look over 51st Divisional Rest Station. 228 Patients were taken over. An advanced party with CAPT MORES RAMC and their Subordinates POIDEVIN proceeded by car at 2am to commence Our work.	

Signed
OC Field Amb
O.C. No 8 F.A.

Army Form C. 2118.

WAR DIARY
or
INTELLIGENCE SUMMARY.
(Erase heading not required.)

Instructions regarding War Diaries and Intelligence Summaries are contained in F. S. Regs., Part II. and the Staff Manual respectively. Title pages will be prepared in manuscript.

Place	Date	Hour	Summary of Events and Information	Remarks and references to Appendices
VAUCHELLES	25/4/16	1 pm	CAPT CRAWFORD RAMC with 4 NCOs and 40 bearers proceeded to EUSTON A.D.S. in relief of No 7 F.A. bearers.	
	26/4/16		CAPT SHOOSMITH RAMC. proceeded to take over Veterinary Medical charge of the 1st Northumberland Fusiliers RAMC	
			CAPT. LAMBERTON joined this unit for temporary duty.	
	27/4/16		CAPT SHOOSMITH rejoining this unit and proceeded on leave to the United K'ingdom. CAPT. HACKET RAMC. proceeded to take over Veterinary Medical charge of the 1st Northumberland Fusiliers.	
	29/4/16		CAPT WILLIS RAMC proceeded to EUSTON in relief of CAPT CRAWFORD shortening to Headquarters.	

G Murison Col RAMC
Lieut Col. to Count.
O.C.

SECRET

140/1900

Vol 23

3rd Qrt

War Diary
3a Ambulance

8
f from 1 Oct 16 to 31 Dec 16

Dec 1916

51

COMMITTEE FOR THE
MEDICAL HISTORY OF THE WAR
Date 31 JAN. 1917

WAR DIARY or INTELLIGENCE SUMMARY

Army Form C. 2118.

8 Field Ambulance

Place	Date	Hour	Summary of Events and Information	Remarks and references to Appendices
VAUCHELLES	1/12/16	7 p.m.	CAPT. WILLIS R.A.M.C. returned to Headquarters with the Bearers, after being relieved by bearers of 142 F.A.	
		9 p.m.	CAPT. H.H. CLARKE R.A.M.C. joined this unit for duty.	
	3/12/16	10 a.m.	CAPT. R.C. MACLACHLAN R.A.M.C. proceeded on leave to the South of France.	
			CAPT. LAMBERT on R.A.M.C. was evacuated to C.C.S. on account of inguinal strain.	
	4/12/16		CAPT. J.R. MOREJ proceeded on leave to the United Kingdom.	
	5/12/16		One N.C.O. & five men of Pavilion proceeded to COLINCAMPS as a digging party for constructing Hospital Dug-out near "Hour Trench".	
	6/12/16		The above were relieved by 1 N.C.O. & 10 men of B section.	
			20.20326 Dr BONNER J. A.S.C. died suddenly whilst on duty. A Post-mortem examination was held on ground cause of death was found to be rupture of Thoracic Aneurysm.	
	8/12/16		Digging party of B Section relieved by 10 men of C section. These parties are relieved every three days.	
	9/12/16		CAPT. CLARKE R.A.M.C. proceeded to take over medical charge of 11th Northumberland Fusiliers in relief of CAPT. HACKETT. Lieut Smith LE POIDEVIN proceeded on leave to the United Kingdom.	

Army Form C. 2118.

6 Field Ambulance

WAR DIARY
or
INTELLIGENCE SUMMARY.
(Erase heading not required.)

Instructions regarding War Diaries and Intelligence Summaries are contained in F. S. Regs., Part II. and the Staff Manual respectively. Title pages will be prepared in manuscript.

Place	Date	Hour	Summary of Events and Information	Remarks and references to Appendices
MUCHELUES	10/12/16		CAPT. HACKETT R.A.M.C. rejoined this unit on being relieved.	
	12/12/16		CAPT. HACKETT R.A.M.C. proceeded on leave to the United Kingdom.	
	13/12/16.		52 bearers under Capt. Wills proceeded to Euston to become Collecting Station from the line in relief of bearers of 142nd & 143rd Bgds.	
	14/12/16.		Capt. CLARKE R.A.M.C. rejoined from 1st Northumberland Fusiliers for duty with this unit.	
	15/12/16 3am		Capt. SHOOSMITH returned from leave.	
	16/12/16		Capt. Lieut. T. FRANKLIN R.A.M.C. who joined this unit for duty on 13/12/16 proceeded to Euston for duty with his Regiment.	
	17/12/16.		CAPT. R.C. MACLACHLAN rejoined from leave to the South of France.	
			CAPT. CLARKE R.A.M.C. proceeded by train to report to A.D.M.S. CALAIS for duty.	
	18/12/16		CAPT. A.H. CLARKE R.A.M.C. proceeded to Calais to report to A.D.M.S.	
			CAPT. T.M. CRAWFORD R.A.M.C. transferred to 12th West Yorks for temporary duty.	
			CAPT. J.M. MOYES R.A.M.C. returned from leave.	
	20/12/16		CAPT. H.G. WILLIS R.A.M.C. proceeded on leave.	
	24/12/16		Lt. Col. G.K. MAURICE R.A.M.C. proceeded on leave.	
	26/12/16			

Army Form C. 2118.

E Field Ambulance

WAR DIARY
or
INTELLIGENCE SUMMARY.
(Erase heading not required.)

Instructions regarding War Diaries and Intelligence Summaries are contained in F. S. Regs, Part II. and the Staff Manual respectively. Title pages will be prepared in manuscript.

Place	Date	Hour	Summary of Events and Information	Remarks and references to Appendices
VERSAILLES	24/12/16		Capt & Capt. E.I.M. HACKETT R.A.M.C. returned from leave.	
	27/12/16		Capt. E.I.M. HACKETT. R.A.M.C. with 2 N.C.Os and 14 men took over the Advanced Dressing Station, Éincamps today.	
	29/12/16		Capt. R.C. MacLACHLAN R.A.M.C. evacuated to C.C.S. sick.	
	31/12/16		Capt. T.M. CRAWFORD R.A.M.C., rejoins from temporary duty with 12th West Yorks	

M Mingo Capt R.A.M.C.
for O.C. E F.A.

3RD DIVISION
MEDICAL

NO. 8 FIELD AMBULANCE
1917.

January 1917

140/94 Vol 24

SECRET

3rd Division

War Diary

of No 8 Field Ambulance

for month of January 1917.

COMMITTEE FOR THE
MEDICAL HISTORY OF THE WAR
Date 13 MAR. 1917

Army Form C. 2118

S____ Ambulance

WAR DIARY
or
INTELLIGENCE SUMMARY
(Erase heading not required.)

Instructions regarding War Diaries and Intelligence Summaries are contained in F.S. Regs., Part II. and the Staff Manual respectively. Title Pages will be prepared in manuscript.

Place	Date	Hour	Summary of Events and Information	Remarks and references to Appendices
VAUCHELLES	3/11/17		Capt. T.M. Crawford R.A.M.C. proceeded on leave to the United Kingdom.	
"	6/11/17		Capt. H.G. Willis returned off leave.	
"	7/11/17		Lt-Col. G.K. Maurice R.A.M.C. returned off leave.	
"	7/11/17	7.30 a.m.	The Ambulance proceeded by route march to Beuval.	
BEUVAL	8/11/17		Lieut. R. Franklin R.A.M.C. proceeded to 10th R.B. Fusiliers for temporary duty.	
"	9/11/17		The Ambulance proceeded by route march to Canaples.	
CANAPLES	10/11/17		Capt. H.G. Willis proceeded to the 2nd Suffolk Regt. for temporary duty.	
"	12/11/17		The Ambulance proceeded by route march to St. Ouen.	
ST. OUEN	13/11/17		Lieut. C. Hilman-Smith R.A.M.C. joined for duty from No. 14 R.A.M.C. reinforcements proceeded to 47 C.C.S. for temporary duty.	
"	14/11/17		Capt. T.M. Crawford R.A.M.C. returned from leave.	
"	16/11/17		Lieut. C. Hilman-Smith proceeded to 1st East Yorks Battalion for temporary duty.	
"	17/11/17		Lieut. J.P. Pegum joined for duty from No. 81 M.A.C. Capt. L.S. Shoosmith proceeded to No. 81 M.A.C. for duty.	
"	19/11/17		Lieut. P. Black R.A.M.C. joined for duty from 7th R.B. 2nd Battalion and relieved by Lieut. J.R. Pegum.	
"	23/11/17		Lieut. R. Franklin rejoined this unit for duty.	
"	27/11/17		Capt. H.G. Willis R.A.M.C. rejoins this unit for duty.	

5 Field Ambulance

WAR DIARY
or
INTELLIGENCE SUMMARY
(Erase heading not required.)

Army Form C. 2118

Instructions regarding War Diaries and Intelligence Summaries are contained in F.S. Regs., Part II. and the Staff Manual respectively. Title Pages will be prepared in manuscript.

Place	Date	Hour	Summary of Events and Information	Remarks and references to Appendices
ST. OUEN	27/1/17		At ST. OUEN, horse standings were built & roofed in. Men were busy completing a week. Training & lectures were commencing. The weather has been very cold for the last week.	
	28/1/17		The Ambulance proceeded by route march to BEUVAL. There was a very severe frost making the roads very difficult & treacherous. The men arrived late in foot in BEUVAL.	
BEUVAL	29/1/17		The Ambulance proceeded by route march to BEUVOIR.	
BEUVOIR	30/1/17		The Ambulance proceeded by route march to BLANGERVAL.	
BLANGERVAL	31/1/17		The Ambulance proceeded by route march to MARQUAY. The weather on entering intensely cold. The state of the roads made travelling very difficult. Horses. The temporary shortage of forage together with the cold and working hrs caused a serious loss of condition in the horses. During the march from ST. OUEN the Ambulance marched in the 8th Inf 7 Brde Group.	

M Munro?
Lt Col R.A.M.C
O.C. 5th Fd Amb

Medical
140/1994   Vol 25

3rd Divn.
Feby 1917

SECRET

War Diary
of
O.C. No 8 Field Ambulance.

From Feby 1st 1917.
To Feby 28th 1917.

COMMITTEE FOR
...DICAL HISTORY O...
Date 4 APR 1917

Army Form C. 2118

WAR DIARY
or
INTELLIGENCE SUMMARY
(Erase heading not required.)

Instructions regarding War Diaries and Intelligence Summaries are contained in F.S. Regs., Part II. and the Staff Manual respectively. Title Pages will be prepared in manuscript.

Place	Date	Hour	Summary of Events and Information	Remarks and references to Appendices
MAR QUAR.	1/2/17		LIEUT. L. KILROE R.A.M.C. joined for duty from D.R.E. YORKS.	
	3/2/17		LIEUT L. KILROE R.A.M.C. proceeded to D.R.E. YORKS for temporary duty.	
	4/2/17		LIEUT. R. BLACK R.A.M.C. proceeded to 56th Company A.S.C. for temporary duty.	
	6/2/17			
	7/2/17		Lt-Col. G.R. MAURICE in command proceeded to the Field Ambulance and transferred by march route	
	8/2/17		to WANQUETIN and billeted for the night. Personnel were billeted in Bruno barns, the Officers in an	
WANQUETIN	9/2/17	10 a.m.	hut. The weather continues intensely cold	
			Lt.Col. G.R. MAURICE in command proceeded with the unit by march route to HAUTEVILLE and opened Hospital. Personnel were billeted in barns. There were no officers billets. Two Armstrong huts were put up for sleeping accommodation for Officers and the pack store was temporarily as a mess.	
HAUTEVILLE	12/2/17		LIEUT. L. KILROE R.A.M.C. rejoins from temporary duty with D.R.E. YORKS.	
	13/2/17		CAPT. H.G. WILLIS R.A.M.C. was transferred sick to No. 37 C.C.S.	
	16/2/17		52 O.R.S. proceeded to ARRAS as digging party attached to New Zealand Tunnelling Company.	
	17/2/17		CAPT. H.G. WILLIS R.A.M.C. rejoined from 37 C.C.S.	
			The weather has turned much warmer and a thaw commenced.	
			2 Nissen huts have been erected as billets for Officers of this unit.	
	20/2/17		CAPT. E.W. ADCOCK R.A.M.C. joined for duty.	
	21/2/17		LIEUT. L. KILROE proceeded to 1st R.S. Fusiliers for temporary duty.	
	23/2/17		LIEUT. L. KILROE rejoined from temporary duty.	

Army Form C. 2118

WAR DIARY
or
INTELLIGENCE SUMMARY
(Erase heading not required.)

Instructions regarding War Diaries and Intelligence Summaries are contained in F.S. Regs., Part II. and the Staff Manual respectively. Title Pages will be prepared in manuscript.

Place	Date	Hour	Summary of Events and Information	Remarks and references to Appendices
HAUTEVILLE	26/2/17		Pte DAVIES R.A.M.C. was wounded whilst employed in Dressing at ARRAS.	
	27/2/17		CAPT. E.M. HACKETT R.A.M.C. proceeded on Special leave to the United Kingdom on renewal of Contract.	
	27/2/17		Pte CURTIS. R.A.M.C. was wounded whilst employed in Dressing at ARRAS.	
	28/2/17		The weather continues fine and warm and the country is beginning to dry.	

Maurice
J.A.J. A.M.C.
O.C. 8th Fd Amb.

1875 Wt. W5193/826 1,000,000 4/15 J.B.C. & A. A.D.S.S./Forms/C. 2118.

140/2042

3rd Field Ambulance

No 8. Field Ambulance

May 1917

COMMITTEE FOR THE
MEDICAL HISTORY OF THE WAR
Date 11 MAY 1917

Army Form C. 2118.

WAR DIARY
or
INTELLIGENCE SUMMARY.
(Erase heading not required.)

Medical

Vol 26

War Diary of
H.S. "Asturias"
March 1917

WAR DIARY or INTELLIGENCE SUMMARY

Army Form C. 2118

Place	Date	Hour	Summary of Events and Information	Remarks and references to Appendices
HAUTEVILLE	1/3/17		Lieut. FRANKLIN R.A.M.C. proceeded on special leave (important affairs) to the United Kingdom.	
"	2/3/17		D.D.V.S. VII Corps inspected the horse part of this unit.	
"	6/3/17		A.D.M.S. 3rd Div. with Capt. Adcock withdrawn from supervising the B section in ARRAS and proceeded to take over temporary medical charge of 8th E. Yorks Battalion.	
"	7/3/17		Capt. ADCOCK R.A.M.C. was withdrawn from supervising the B section in ARRAS and proceeded to take over temporary medical charge of 8th E. Yorks Battalion. A lecture was given at this Hospital by Lieut. WALKER, surgical Specialist, on the use of the Thomas's splint for fractured thigh. Over twenty M.O.s of the Division were present. All were convinced of the advantage & practicability of using this splint in the most advanced positions. Lieut. WALKER states that he has had great difficulty in convincing other Divisions.	
"	13/3/17		Pte. ELLIOT and Pte. DENIS R.A.M.C. of this unit were wounded whilst employed in digging at ARRAS.	
"	15/3/17		Capt. HACKETT & Lieut. FRANKLIN R.A.M.C. rejoined from leave.	
"	18/3/17		Lieut. FRANKLIN R.A.M.C. assumed temporary medical charge of the 2nd Suffolk Regt.	
"	21/3/17		Capt. CRAWFORD with B Section proceeded by march north to GANQUESTIN and took over the hospital and wounded patients from No 7 F.A. Aubz.	

WAR DIARY or INTELLIGENCE SUMMARY

Army Form C. 2118

(Erase heading not required.)

Place	Date	Hour	Summary of Events and Information	Remarks and references to Appendices
HAUTEVILLE	20/3/17		The Dressing Party, having completed work in ARRAS, proceeded by march route to WANQUETIN. This party did most excellent work in the Caves at ARRAS. Four Casualties were sustained.	
	22/3/17		Capt. ADCOCK R.A.M.C. assumed permanent Medical charge of 8th EAST YORKS Regiment.	
	22/3/17		The Field Ambulance less B Section proceeded by march route, under Capt MOYES, in command, to WANQUETIN. Owing to the congestion of troops at WANQUETIN part of the hospital accommodation had to be used as billets. – The horses have stood in the open. The weather has been hot, cold winds, snow, & rain most days.	
	31/3/17		Owing to the hot weather and the congestion of horses and the road to this hospital, the road became impassable and horses became wounded Cases have died. There has been nothing else of importance to report.	

J. Maurice
Lt Col R.A.M.C.
O.C. 8th F.A.

140/2086

No. 8. Y.A.

COMMITTEE FOR THE
MEDICAL HISTORY OF THE WAR
Date — 6 JUN. 1917

MEDICAL

Army Form C. 2118

WAR DIARY
or
INTELLIGENCE SUMMARY
(Erase heading not required.)

Place	Date	Hour	Summary of Events and Information	Remarks and references to Appendices
GANGUVETIN	1/4/17		29 N.C.Os and men proceeded to No 19 C.C.S. for temporary duty.	
"	2/4/17		LIEUT. S. ASPINALL arrived for duty. The weather is extremely bad with heavy snowstorms.	
"	3/4/17		CAPT. T.M. CRAWFORD and LIEUT. MUNROE with all available personnel proceeded to the RONVILLE Caves in ARRAS to make preparations for accommodating the Bearers and Lt Infantrymen.	
"	4/4/17	5.30pm	Lt Col G. R. MAURICE in command with CAPT HOKES, CAPT HACKETT, and CAPT WILLIS, the whole Horse Division and C Section but Motorization proceeded by march route to the RONVILLE Caves, arriving about 9.30 p.m., where they remained till morning of 9/4/17. Rooms, one Closet and Greatcoats were carried. The Caves were very hot and the air bad. Total personnel of the Unit accommodated in the Caves were Six Officers and 123 Other Ranks. The Ambulances, Personal Baggage, Stores, many Rooms and the transport, remaining at GANGUVETIN. The necessary equipment for opening a A.D.S. had been previously forwarded on Lorries, and was placed in the RONVILLE Caves.	
"	5/4/17		LIEUT FRANKLIN Rame reporting from temporary duty with 2nd Battalion and 9 remaining with LIEUT ASPINALL at Headquarters, GANGUVETIN.	
"	6/4/17		LIEUT FRANKLIN proceeded to report to A.D.M.S. 12th Division for duty.	
"	9/4/17		76th Infantry Bde attacked at 5.30 a.m. Bright clear frosty morning, with occasional	

Army Form C. 2118

WAR DIARY
or
INTELLIGENCE SUMMARY
(Erase heading not required.)

Instructions regarding War Diaries and Intelligence Summaries are contained in F. S. Regs., Part II. and the Staff Manual respectively. Title Pages will be prepared in manuscript.

Place	Date	Hour	Summary of Events and Information	Remarks and references to Appendices
WANCOURT.	8/4/17	8 p.m.	Transport and H.Qrs. wagons of the Batt. moved to ARRAS and billeted. Lieut. ASPINALL R.A.M.C. proceeded to take over medical charge of 10th Royal Welsh Fusiliers to relieve Lieut. EVANS R.A.M.C. who was killed.	
		9 p.m.	The village of TILLOY having been reported captured, C. Coln. Batt. moved forward into it. Lt. Col. G.R. MAURICE in command, and 2nd in Command Capt. T.N. CRAWFORD brought up the CAMBRAI Road towards TILLOY. CAPT. T.M. MOYES in command of the leading Coy. with CAPT. DILLIN & LIEUT. HEIROE accompanying C. Coln. Batt. advancing as far as DEVIL's WOOD. At this point left the leading Coy. was and last advance was left in shell holes while 2nd Lt. PW Maurice & Capt. T.M. MOYES went forward & reconnoitred. At 4.30 p.m. an advanced dressing station was opened for receiving wounded and the leading Division was cleaning the Regimental and First. The necessary equipment was carried up by the first Battalion in Road Shops. Both Lieut. Information and leading Battalion remained in action till 8.30 a.m. 14/4/17.	
	10/4/17		Lt. Col. R.H. MAURICE assumed command of the Advanced medical arrangements under instructions from ADMS 3rd Corps.	
	11/4/17		The weather remains extremely bad with snow and hail storms. Advance matters and blankets in the NONVILLE Caves were sent for, drawn and by the leaving Division. Very bad from C.C.S. The men's Great Coats which had been left with their Packs and blankets in the NONVILLE Caves were sent for, drawn and by the leaving Division.	

WAR DIARY or INTELLIGENCE SUMMARY

Army Form C. 2118

Place	Date	Hour	Summary of Events and Information	Remarks and references to Appendices
ARRAS	13/4/17		Short period of rest.	
	14/4/17	8.30 a.m.	Maj. G.D. MAURICE recommenced the Advt. Information and hence Officers proceeded by march route to ARRAS, heavy loads and over the A.D.S. and seen into a unit of the 9th Division. The unit was billeted in the Girls School Dressing Station in ARRAS for the night.	
ARRAS			The chief difficulties in the cleaning of wounded Transport. The Hygiene area in (i) The congestion on the roads making it difficult to get Cars & transit waggons beyond TILLOY. (2) The bad weather making heavy work for the bearers carrying in the mud. (3) The extreme darkness at night, causing the bearers to lose their way in the open country. Throughout the whole of operations between the R.A.P. and Hitchen.	
	15/4/17		C. Galo. Advt. Information was billeted in the BOULEVARD CARNOT, ARRAS. C. Section Bearers in the Girl School. The remainder of the unit was billeted in the FAUBOURG AMIENS, ARRAS. been transport. The weather continues very cold.	
	20/4/17		There is a marked improvement in the weather. The total casualties in the unit during the recent operations are five wounded.	
	22/4/17		LIEUT. W. LAOE proceeded to take over temporary Medical Charge of the 1st Northumberland Fusiliers.	

WAR DIARY
or
INTELLIGENCE SUMMARY.
(Erase heading not required.)

Army Form C. 2118.

Hour, Date, Place	Summary of Events and Information	Remarks and references to Appendices
ARRAS 23/4/17	The Reserve Division has marched up to trenches known as the Brown line North of the CAMBRAI-ARRAS road and about halfway between TILLOY & MONCHY-LE-PREUX. They left ARRAS about 3 p.m. CAPT. MOFFE[?] D.S.O. is in command. CAPT. WILLIS to assist him. At the Brown line Capt. MOFES established Head with the Regimental Aid Posts Officers of the 8th Bde.	
24/4/17	8th Infantry Bde moved to the MONCHY defences. The Reserve Division moved to dugouts about half a mile S.W. of MONCHY, and in conjunction with the Reserve of No. 7 & No. 6 AusBns took over the clearing of ground from MOYCHY and east of MONCHY. About a hundred dead and forty shellshock cases of other Divisions were cleared by the two Irisa Divisions in the course of the last 40 yards in addition to the togh 29th of the Bde Brigades in the line. The shelling was very heavy throughout.	
27/4/17.	CAPT. T. M. CRAWFORD R.A.M.C. proceeded to report to the War Office on expiration of contract.	

Army Form C. 2118.

WAR DIARY
or
INTELLIGENCE SUMMARY.
(Erase heading not required.)

Instructions regarding War Diaries and Intelligence Summaries are contained in F. S. Regs., Part II. and the Staff Manual respectively. Title pages will be prepared in manuscript.

Hour, Date, Place	Summary of Events and Information	Remarks and references to Appendices
ARRAS. 28/4/17.	The Bearer Division was relieved by the Bearer Division of 142 F.A. Relief completed at 6 p.m. The Bearers returned to Billets in the BOULEVARD CARNOT. The Transport and Quartermaster Office moved to the BOULEVARD CARNOT from the FAUBOURG DAMIENS. LIEUT. 12/L ROE rejoining from duty with the 1st Northumberland Fusiliers. The weather of the past week has been exceptionally fine.	
30/4/17.	There is nothing further to report.	

G. Maurice
J.P. Clarke
O.C. 8th F.A.

B.E.F.

Summary of Medical War Diaries of No. 8. F.A. 3rd Div. 6th Corps

3rd ARMY.

18th Corps from 19th May.

OPERATIONS ON WESTERN FRONT - 1917 April - May.

Officer Commanding - Lt.Col. G. Maurice.

Summarised under the following headings :-

Phase "B" - Battle of Arras - April - May 1917.

1st Period - Attack on Vimy Ridge - April.

2nd Period - Capture of Siegfried Line - May.

B.E.F.

8th F.A. 3rd Div. 6th Corps. 3rd ARMY.   Western Front.
O.C. = Lt. Col. G. Maurice.   April 1917.

PHASE "B" - Battle of Arras - April - May 1917.
   1st Period - Attack on Vimy Ridge-April.

Headquarters at Wanquetin.

April 1st.   Moves. Detachment. O & 29 to 19th C.C.S. for duty.
4th.   2 & Advance Party to Ronville Caves, Arras. 5.30 p.m. B.D. and C. Section, T.S.D. to Ronville Caves, Arras.
9th.   Operations. 7th Inf. Bde attacked at 5.30 a.m.
             Moves. To Arras.
             Medical Arrangements. On capture of Tilloy C. Section T.S.D. proceeded up Cambrai Road towards Tilloy. At 4.30 p.m. A.D.S. opened at Tilloy and Br. D. cleared R.A.P.s. Equipment carried in sandbags.
10th.   Lt.Col. Maurice assumed command of forward Med. Arr.
             Moves. Detachment. Bearers returned to Arras on relief at A.D.S. by 29th Div.
             Casualties. R.A.M.C. 9-10th O & 5 wounded.
                Lt. Evans M.O. 10th R. Welsh Fus. killed.
15th-22nd.   Operations R.A.M.C. Nothing of note.
23rd.   Moves. Detachment. B.D. to Brown Line North of Cambrai-Arras Road.
24th.   B.D. to dugouts ½ mile S.W. of Monchy behind 8th Inf. Bde and in conjunction with Brs of 7th F.A. cleared wounded from Monchy and S.E. of Monchy.
24th-28th.   Casualties. About 140 L.D.W. of other Divisions cleared in the period 24th-28th in addition to W... of 2 Bdes.
28th.   Operations Enemy. Shelling very heavy throughout.
             Moves. Detachment. B.D. to Arras on relief by B.D. 142nd Field Ambulance.

SECRET

3rd Div.

War Diary
of
No 8 Field Ambulance

Vol 28

From 1-5-17 To 31-5-17

Medical

COMMITTEE FOR THE
MEDICAL HISTORY OF THE WAR
Date 10 JUL. 1917

B.E.F.

8th F.A. 3rd Div. 6th Corps. 3rd ARMY.   Western Front.
O.C. = Lt. Col. G. Maurice.   April 1917.

1.

PHASE "B" - Battle of Arras - April - May 1917.
   1st Period - Attack on Vimy Ridge - April.

Headquarters at Wanquetin.

April 1st.	Moves. Detachment. O & 29 to 19th C.C.S. for duty.
4th.	2 & Advance Party to Ronville Caves Arras. 5.30 p.m. B.D. and C. Section, T.S.D. to Ronville Caves Arras.
9th.	Operations. 7th Inf. Bde attacked at 5.30 a.m.
	Moves. To Arras.
	Medical Arrangements. On capture of Tilloy C. Section T.S.D. proceeded up Cambrai Road towards Tilloy. At 4.30 p.m. A.D.S. opened at Tilloy and Br. D. cleared R.A.P.s. Equipment carried in sandbags.
10th.	Lt.Col. Maurice assumed command of forward Med. Arr.
	Moves. Detachment. Bearers returned to Arras on relief at A.D.S. by 29th Div.
	Casualties. R.A.M.C. 9-10th O & 5 wounded. Lt. Evans M.O. 10th R. Welsh Fus. killed.
15th-22nd.	Operations R.A.M.C. Nothing of note.
23rd.	Moves. Detachment. B.D. to Brown Line North of Cambrai-Arras Road.
24th.	B.D. to dugouts ½ mile S.W. of Monchy behind 8th Inf. Bde and in conjunction with Brs of 7th F.A. cleared wounded from Monchy and S.E. of Monchy.
24th-28th.	Casualties. About 140 L.D.W. of other Divisions cleared in the period 24th-28th in addition to W. of 2 Bdes.
28th.	Operations Enemy. Shelling very heavy throughout. Moves. Detachment. B.D. to Arras on relief by B.D. 142nd Field Ambulance.

WAR DIARY or INTELLIGENCE SUMMARY

Army Form C. 2118

Place	Date	Hour	Summary of Events and Information	Remarks and references to Appendices
ARRAS.	2/5/17	2 p.m.	CAPT. MOYES in Command with Capt. Willis proceeded with the Bearer Division to take over the clearing of the wounded of the 8th Infantry Bde., which is to attack at 3.45 a.m. on 3/5/17. Whilst marching into position the bearers encountered a very heavy barrage of gas shells. Box respirators had to be worn. Two men were killed by direct hit from a gas shell. CAPT. MOYES was wounded in the right leg by a splinter of shell. Capt. Willis was fatally gassed but remained with the bearers until relieved. Revd. Klose wounded in shoulder whilst attending to Padre Burchell who was severely wounded in the leg & bleeding profusely from the popliteal artery. Casualties in the first 24 hours. Killed. O.R. four. Wounded. Officers two. O.R. fiveteen. Gassed. O.R. ten. Gassed & remaining at duty. Officers one. O.R. twelve.	
"	3/5/17			
"	4/5/17	6 am.	A.B. + C Sections Bearers returned to H.Q.	
"	"	7.30 pm	Capt. E.L.M. Hackett with one Sergeant & fifteen Bearers left for the line.	
"	5/5/17	2.20 a.m.	The above Officer & bearers returned to H.Q. having with a similar party from W.7.F.Amb. cleared all the R.A.P's. Injured returned of Cpl. Dewing & bearer of 142 F.Amb. Capt. S. Mc NAUGHTON arrived for duty.	
"	6/5/17	7.30 p.m.	Five bearer squads under Capt. Willis left to relieve 142 & bearer posts & A.D.S.	

WAR DIARY or INTELLIGENCE SUMMARY

Army Form C. 2118

Place	Date	Hour	Summary of Events and Information	Remarks and references to Appendices
Arras	7/5/17		Capt. McNaughton proceeded to 12th West Yorks for permanent duty.	
	8/5/17		Capt. R.A. LEEMBRUGGEN + Capt. E.T.C. MILLIGAN arrived for duty. One Sergt., one Corporal + 20 O.R. proceeded to line to relieve tramway party. Capt. Newlands left for temporary duty to 14th Gordon Highlanders to relieve Capt. Stewart who was gassed whilst trying to dig out his orderlies who were buried by a shell. ※ Signed J. AYLEN	
	9/5/17		J. AYLEN arrived for duty.	
	10/5/17		Lieut. Aylen proceeded to Somptis francopet for instruction under Capt. Willis. Shells struck H.Q. at Boulevard Const. severely wounding Cpl. Cameron who died shortly afterwards + wounding Cpl. Relay, A.S.C. M.T.	
	11/5/17		Reeves + Capt. Willes + Lieut. Aylen returned to H.Q.	
	12/5/17		Capt. S.G. O'GRADY arrived for duty.	
	13/5/17		Capt. O'Grady proceeded for temporary duty with R.S. Fus.	
	15/5/17		Capt. C.H. LLOYD arrived for duty. Unit. left ARRAS 7.15 AM by march route to BERNEVILLE arriving there 10 A.M.	

WAR DIARY or INTELLIGENCE SUMMARY

Army Form C. 2118

Place	Date	Hour	Summary of Events and Information	Remarks and references to Appendices
BERNEVILLE	16/5/17		All available motor Ambulances & horse spare left for WANQUETIN with Capt Mulligan to assist in recent work at dump which was on fire. N. Col. Maurice left for two later. Casualties few.	
	19/5/17		Left Berneville at 11.45 A.M. by march route arriving at GOUY-EN-ARTOIS at 2.30 P.M.	
GOUY-EN-ARTOIS	19/5/17	11.15AM	Capt. H.S. Willis proceeded on special leave to United Kingdom on termination of contract. Capt. C.H. Stoyel proceeded to 37th Durham Temporary duty. Left GOUY-EN-ARTOIS by march route arriving at the LIGNEREUIL H.Q. area. Horse transport in rear of front to H.Q. area in Lillers. Officers in buses except C.O. who marched with...	
LIGNEREUIL	20/5/17		Lt. Col. G.K. Maurice accompanied the Brigadier to Boulogne proceeding from there on leave to the United Kingdom on 22.5 inst. Capt. E.L.M. Hockett was left in command of the unit during his absence.	

WAR DIARY or INTELLIGENCE SUMMARY

Army Form C. 2118

Place	Date	Hour	Summary of Events and Information	Remarks and references to Appendices
LIGNEREUIL	28/4/17		Revd: J. Ayken proceeded to 40th Brigade R.F.A. for temporary duty	
			Capt. R.A. Greenway proceeded to 2nd Suffolks to relieve Capt. J.D. Marshall D.S.O. who proceed this Unit for duty on being relieved.	
	21/5/17		The North hole the Savannan. The village & commenced work of leveling	
	22/5/17		Capt. J.D. Marshall proceeded to spend leave to United Kingdom on completion of leaving.	
	26/5/17		Fourteen Reserve reinforcements arrived for duty with this unit.	
	28/5/17 11.30am		Capt. C.H. Lloyd reported this unit from A.D.M.S. 37th Div.	
	31/5/17		Capt. C.H. Lloyd proceeded to 8th K.O.R.L. Regt. for temporary duty in stead of Capt. Wallace.	
			During the past the Unit was engaged in general & R.A. Hackett. internal interior work. Ordered housing hygiene, sanitary Capt. Rowe. defective lines & other efforts. Also the necessary work has been dis- Re. O.C. 103 Field Ambce, attended on watering, sanitation & drawn for Wyke & du Ordnance Battlers on which we also form.	

B.E.F.

Summary of Medical War Diaries of No. 8. F.A. 3rd Div. 6th Corps

3rd ARMY.

18th Corps from 19th May.

OPERATIONS ON WESTERN FRONT - 1917 April - May.

Officer Commanding - Lt.Col. G. Maurice.

Summarised under the following headings :-

Phase "B" - Battle of Arras - April - May 1917.

1st Period - Attack on Vimy Ridge - April.

2nd Period - Capture of Siegfried Line - May.

B.E.F.   1.

8th F.A. 3rd Div. 6th Corps. 3rd ARMY.   Western Front.
O.C.= Lt.Col. G. Maurice.   May 1917.

PHASE "B" - Battle of Arras - April - May 1917.
  2nd Period - Capture of Siegfried Line - May.

May 2nd.   Moves. Detachment.) B.D. to front to clear wounded
            Operations Enemy Gas)
                                  of 8th Infantry Bde.
                     Bearers encountered very heavy
            barrage of gas shells.
            Casualties R.A.M.C. O & 2 killed.
                     Capt. Mayes wounded.
                     Lt. Kilroe wounded.

3rd.   Operations. 8th Infantry Bde attacked at 3.45.
            Casualties R.A.M.C.) O & 4 wounded.
            Cas. Gas R.A.M.C.   )
                                   O & 2 killed.
                                   O & 10 wounded Gas.
                                   1 & 12 wounded Gas remained at duty.

4th.   Moves. Detachment. Brs rejoined Headquarters.
4th-5th.   1 & 17 Bearers with 1 & 17 Brs 7th F.A.
            cleared all R.A.P.s and rejoined Headquarters on relief
            by 142nd Field Ambulance.

6th.   1 & 5 Bearer Squads relieved 142nd
            F.A. Bearers at Br. P's and A.D.S.

8th.   O & 22 relieved previous party.
            Ops. R.A.M.C.   ) Capt. Stewart M.O. 1st Gordon Hrs.
            Cas. R.A.M.C.Gas.)
                               gassed while trying to dig out his
            orderlies who were buried by shell.

10th.   Ops. Enemy.   ) Shell struck Headquarters of Unit.
            Casualties. R.A.M.C.)
                                 O & 1 wounded. (D. of W.)
                                 O & 1   "   A.S.C. attd.

11th.   Moves. Detachment. Bearers rejoined Headquarters.

8th F.A.   3rd Div.   6th Corps.   3rd ARMY.   Western Front.
O.C. = Lt. Col. G. Maurice.   May 1917.

18th Corps from 19th May.

PHASE "B" - Battle of Arras - April - May 1917.
   2nd Period - Capture of Siegfried Line - May.

May 15th.   Moves. To Berneville.

16th.   Ops. R.A.M.C. All avilable Motor Ambulances and Br. Squads to Wanquetin to assist in rescue work at dump which was on fire.

18th.   (Moves. To Gouy-en-Artois.

19th.   (Transfer. To 18th Corps.

           To Lignereuil.

B.E.F.

8th F.A.   3rd Div.   18th Corps.   3rd ARMY.   Western Front.
O.C. - Lt. Col. G. Maurice.   May 1917.

PHASE "B" - Battle of Arras - April - May 1917.
    2nd Period - Capture of Siegfried Line - May.

May 19th.   Moves. and Transfer. To 18th Corps. To Lignereuil.
20th-31st.   Ops. R.A.M.C. Nothing of note.

B.E.F.

1.

8th F.A. 3rd Div. 6th Corps. 3rd ARMY.   Western Front.
O.C.= Lt.Col. G. Maurice.   May 1917.

PHASE "B" - Battle of Arras - April - May 1917.
  2nd Period - Capture of Siegfried Line - May.

May 2nd.   Moves. Detachment.) B.D. to front to clear wounded
           Operations Enemy Gas.   of 8th Infantry Bde.

           Bearers encountered very heavy barrage of gas shells.

           Casualties R.A.M.C. O & 2 killed.
                               Capt. Mayes wounded.
                               Lt. Kilroe wounded.

3rd.   Operations. 8th Infantry Bde attacked at 3.45.
           Casualties R.A.M.C.) O & 4 wounded.
           Cas. Gas R.A.M.C.   )
                                  O & 2 killed.
                                  O & 10 wounded Gas.
                                  1 & 12 wounded Gas remained at duty.

4th.   Moves. Detachment. Brs rejoined Headquarters.

4th-5th.   1 & 17 Bearers with 1 & 17 Brs 7th F.A. cleared all R.A.P.s and rejoined Headquarters on relief by 142nd Field Ambulance.

6th.   1 & 5 Bearer Squads relieved b42nd F.A. Bearers at Br. P's and A.D.S.

8th.   O & 22 relieved previous party.

           Ops. R.A.M.C.   ) Capt. Stewart M.O. 1st Gordon Hrs.
           Cas. R.A.M.C.Gas.) gassed while trying to dig out his orderlies who were buried by shell.

10th.   Ops. Enemy.   ) Shell struck Headquarters of Unit.
           Casualties. R.A.M.C.)
                                 O & 1 wounded. (D. of W.)
                                 O & 1   "   A.S.C. attd.

11th.   Moves. Detachment. Bearers rejoined Headquarters.

1.

B.E.F.

8th F.A.   3rd Div.   6th Corps.   3rd ARMY.   Western Front.
O.C. = Lt. Col. G. Maurice.   May 1917.

18th Corps from 19th May.

PHASE "B" - Battle of Arras - April - May 1917.
　　2nd Period - Capture of Siegfried Line - May.

May 15th.   Moves. To Berneville.
16th.   Ops. R.A.M.C. All avilable Motor Ambulances and Br. Squads to Wanquetin to assist in rescue work at dump which was on fire.
18th.   (Moves. To Gouy-en-Artois.
19th.   (Transfer. To 18th Corps.
　　　　　　To Lignereuil.

B.E.F.

8th F.A. 3rd Div. 18th Corps. 3rd ARMY.   Western Front.
O.C. - Lt. Col. G. Maurice.   May 1917.

PHASE "B" - Battle of Arras - April - May 1917.
    2nd Period - Capture of Siegfried Line - May.

May 19th.   Moves. and Transfer. To 18th Corps. To Lignereuil.
20th-31st.   Ops. R.A.M.C. Nothing of note.

Vol 29

14/2230

June 1917

SECRET.

War Diary

of

No 8 Field Ambulance.

From 1/6/17 to: To ~~30/6/17~~ 1/6/17.

COMMITTEE FOR THE
MEDICAL HISTORY OF THE WAR
Date −7 AUG.1917

WAR DIARY or INTELLIGENCE SUMMARY

Army Form C. 2118

Place	Date	Hour	Summary of Events and Information	Remarks and references to Appendices
LIGNEREUIL	1/6/17		The Unit with Transport proceeded to ARRAS and billeted in the ECOLE NORMALE. CAPT. LLOYD proceeded to 8th KORL on temporary duty.	
ADDAS	2/6/17		J/RIGH. MAURICE returned off leave.	
			Two Sergeants, 1 Corporal and 40 other ranks took over the A.D.S. and the clearing of the Right sector of the Divisional front.	
			LIEUT AYLEN rejoined from temporary duty with the 40 Bde R.F.A.	
	5/6/17		CAPT. MARSHALL D.S.O returned off leave.	
	8/6/17		CAPT. LLOYD rejoined from duty with 8th KORL.	
	10/6/17		Recruiting learners proceeded up the line. Tent Registration in ADS was reinforced. CAPT. MILLIGAN in charge of ADS. CAPT. WILLIS in charge of Squires.	
	13/6/17		Seventeen squads of bearers in the line, and Suffolk battalion and 1st Gordon captured Infantry Hill at 7.30 a.m. Bearers of 8th & 9th Ambs cleared 2nd Suffolk battalion. Those wounded continued clearing the line through Tom Candle & Rocket until relieved on night of 18th/19th at 7p.m. Som was incredibly by the enemy. There was one gas case, no shell and 5 wounded. Their work was extremely good.	

WAR DIARY
or
INTELLIGENCE SUMMARY

Army Form C. 2118

Place	Date	Hour	Summary of Events and Information	Remarks and references to Appendices
ARRAS.	17/6/17		LIEUT & QM. LE POIDEVIN proceeded on leave.	
			The unit less 2 Officers CAPT Willis & CAPT Lloyd and the bearer Division proceeded by march route to NOYELETTE and billets for the night, the bearer Division being attached to the 7th Aubris.	
NOYELETTE	18/6/17		The unit less bearer Division proceeded to LIENCOURT, & billets.	
LIENCOURT	20/6/17		CAPT WILLIS & CAPT LLOYD with the bearer Division rejoined.	
	26/6/17		CAPT HACHETT proceeded on leave.	
	28/6/17		The unit proceeded by march route to BEUREPAIRE with 8th Infantry Bde Group.	
BEUREPAIRE	29/6/17		The unit less Transport marched to DOULLENS and entrained. It then proceeded by train to ACHIET-LE-GRAND, detrained and marched to GOMIECOURT. Transport proceeded by road.	
GOMIECOURT	30/6/17		The unit proceeded by march route to BEUGNY and billets.	

J M Maurice
Lt Col RAMC
O.C. 8 F.A.

MEDICAL
Vol 30

140/2298

SECRET

WAR DIARY

OF

No 8 FIELD AMBULANCE.

From 1st July 1917

To 31st July 1917.

COMMITTEE FOR THE
MEDICAL HISTORY OF THE WAR
Date 10 SEP. 1917

Army Form C. 2118.

WAR DIARY
or
INTELLIGENCE SUMMARY.
(Erase heading not required.)

H.Q. No. 8 FIELD AMBULANCE
3rd DIVISION

Hour, Date, Place	Summary of Events and Information	Remarks and references to Appendices
BEUGNY 1/4/17.	C.B. ALLAN takes bath & wearing ordered under CAPT GILLIS & CAPT LLOYD took over the ADS and the clearing of the left sector of the Divisional front.	
2/4/17.	Lieut G.H. MAURICE with the remainder of the unit took over charge of the wounded in Station at BEUGNY at about 11 am. LIEUT 6.9 M. LE POIDEVIN returns from leave yesterday.	
3/4/17.	The 29 N.C.Os and men reporting from 19 C.Cs. The charge of these men and the Casualties caused by the Battle of ARRAS has caused considerable disorganisation. The work of reorganising the unit commenced.	

WAR DIARY
or
INTELLIGENCE SUMMARY.
(Erase heading not required.)

Army Form C. 2118.

Hour, Date, Place	Summary of Events and Information	Remarks and references to Appendices
4/7/17. BEUGNY.	CAPT. J.D. MARSHALL and one Lieut. Aut. Anderson proceeded to 39 C.C.S. on temporary duty. The effective reorganisation of the unit has accordingly been stopped. S.O.C. IV Corps visits this Hospital.	
6/7/17. "	CAPT. F. HENDERSON R.A.M.C. (attd) returned to duty from the 1st N.P.H.	
7/7/17. "	1 N.C.O. and 12 O.R.s proceeded to dig a new A.D.S. in a more advanced position than the one taken over. CAPT. BAKER R.A.M.C. whereas posted to this unit on temporary duty, on 2/7/17, was honorary to 142 F.A. CAPT. CUTLER R.A.M.C. at present in here to the U.K. reported to this unit for duty.	
9/7/17. "	1 Sergeant and 9 O.R.s were despatched to pull down Nissen Huts which will be transported into this area for the use of this unit.	

WAR DIARY
or
INTELLIGENCE SUMMARY.

(Erase heading not required.)

Army Form C. 2118.

Hour, Date, Place	Summary of Events and Information	Remarks and references to Appendices
10/7/17. BEUGNY.	CAPT. GILL & CAPT. LLOYD and the bearers gathering in the line been relieved by CAPT. HACKETT, CAPT. HENDERSON and another party of bearers. The pack ponies were ADS were not relieved. 1 NCO and 40 ORs proceed 9.9. to take over charge of the Baths at BEUGNY.	
13/7/17.	LIEUT. T. O'KEEN RAMC proceeded to report to the Base Officer on relinquishing his commission.	
15/7/17.	G.O.C. 3rd Division inspected this Hospital.	
17/7/17.	1 O.R. was Detailed for water duties with the 1st R.S.Fs	
18/7/17.	20 ORs were Detailed for water duties with the 40 Bde R.F.A. CAPT. CUTLER RAMC returning off leave and forwarded to report to ADMS 69th Div for duty. CAPT. HACHETT relieving CAPT. GILL at the ADS. C. Section bearers relieved B. section bearers in the line.	
21/7/17.	The Bigging for B. Section lengthened owing to Shortage of lines.	

WAR DIARY
or
INTELLIGENCE SUMMARY.
(Erase heading not required.)

Army Form C. 2118/

[Stamp: H.Q. No. 8 FIELD AMBULANCE * 3rd DIVISION *]

Hour, Date, Place	Summary of Events and Information	Remarks and references to Appendices
23/7/17. BEUGNY	The party that was detailed for the purpose of pulling down Nissen Huts returned. The two Nissen huts have been transported here and are in pieces of encirclure.	
25/7/17.	CAPT. CARR-HARRIS DAMC was posted for duty with this unit. SGT FRYER R.A.M.C. proceeded from temporary duty with the 17th Corps Rest Station.	
27/7/17. 31/7/17. 31/7/17.	CAPT. MILLIGAN R.A.M.C. was posted to No. 45 C.C.S. for temporary duty. IV Corps instructed this hospital. S.O.C. IV Corps inspected the Line under CAPT. B. Leslie, hears on proceeded to C. Leslie-bearers. The ADS is HACKETT in relief of C. Leslie-bearers. The ADS is being transferred from CHAUFFORS No.9 to 7.7.6.9.0. where the 9/88/g bcly have been at work. The work is not yet complete and has necessarily been done very leisurely because. The weather this month has been hot for the most part with thunderstorms at times. A great deal of	

WAR DIARY or INTELLIGENCE SUMMARY

Army Form C. 2118.

H.Q. No 8 FIELD AMBULANCE 3rd DIVISION

Hour, Date, Place	Summary of Events and Information	Remarks and references to Appendices
3/7/17	Work has been done. Several Nissen huts have been erected. Have started in process of construction and general large dug-out 17 in process of construction and general improvements have been started in the camp. It has been necessary to keep a complete leaves subdivision in the line for clearing wounded at night. A main dressing station and an advanced dressing station have been open by this unit. A party of 12 men has been kept continuously digging a new A.D.S. In front of the Bothies at REVENIR in support of this unit. A few salvations and stores officers have been supplied. To CCS and in addition the unit is 13 O.R's deficient. Can orderlies and officers servants have been utilized to the utmost in the work in hand. In erecting NISSEN huts and in the standing, the General, The health of however has been very good on the whole and Circul and other amusements have been arranged for them in the evenings.	

J.F. Marre
O.C. Fn |

SECRET.

Aug. 1917

War Diary. 140364

No. 8. Field Ambulance

From 1 August — to 31 August 1917.

Vol 31

COMMITTEE FOR THE
MEDICAL HISTORY OF THE WAR
Date −1 OCT. 1917

WAR DIARY or INTELLIGENCE SUMMARY

Army Form C. 2118

(Erase heading not required.)

Place	Date	Hour	Summary of Events and Information	Remarks and references to Appendices
Beaupre	Aug 3rd		Capt. H.H. Carr Harris proceeded to 20th K.R.R. for duty.	
"	Aug 4th		Capt. J.D. Purcell D.S.O. (+ party) 11 O.R.s rejoined from Divisional duty with 29. C.C.S.	
"	Aug 6th		Capt. R.E.L. Hackett with horses & ordinary party consisting of H.Q. n. Section on A.D.S. s. in Eastern road & Chauffer's work to 142 Field Amb.	
"	Aug 7th		Capt. H.S. Willis A.C. + Bearer Party (provided to take over advanced command from A.D.S. + line at O.29.a.5.4	
"	Aug 9th		6. Pack Reserve from 142 F.A. Amb + 1 A.C.S (5 off Ranking) + 11 O.R.s Rejoined from this unit. Proceeded to A.D.M.S. 142nd Bde for duty.	
"	Aug 13th		Capt. P. Henderson + (party) 23 bearers rejoined (Capt. H.S. Willis A.C. Rejoined, proceed for duty from) unit in the line. 97th Bde. group	
"	Aug 14th		Corp. H.C. Knight proceeded to Divisional Gas School to commence instruction in Anti-gas measures	

WAR DIARY
or
INTELLIGENCE SUMMARY
(Erase heading not required.)

Army Form C. 2118

Instructions regarding War Diaries and Intelligence Summaries are contained in F.S. Regs, Part II. and the Staff Manual respectively. Title Pages will be prepared in manuscript.

Place	Date	Hour	Summary of Events and Information	Remarks and references to Appendices
Beaupré	Aug 17th		Capt. J. Cathcart - Barne, joined for duty from 27th M.A.C.	
"	Aug 20th		Capt. C.H. Rhoyd with horse party struck Capt. J. Henderson + party in the lines.	
"	Aug 23rd		Capt. H.S. Willis proceeded 15.40 to R.T.A. for temporary duty. 6'5 8" taken group for ditto ditto. Capt. J. Cathcart " " " " " " ditto ditto. Lt. Col. E.K. Maurice M.C. proceeded to England on 1 months leave. Period 24-8-17 to 23-9-17. Capt. E.L.M. Hackett taking over temporary command of the Ambulance during his absence.	
"	Aug 24th		The G.O.C. to Cotes inspected the Dressing Station + expressed himself well pleased with the arrangements + the water arms, + the neatness + cleanliness of the place in general.	
"	Aug 28th		Capt. H.S. Willis + E. Cpl. Barnes returned. Capt. C.H. Rhoyd + B. Sect: leaves in the line.	

WAR DIARY
or
INTELLIGENCE SUMMARY
(Erase heading not required.)

Army Form C. 2118

Instructions regarding War Diaries and Intelligence Summaries are contained in F. S. Regs., Part II. and the Staff Manual respectively. Title Pages will be prepared in manuscript.

[Stamp: H.Q. No 8 FIELD AMBULANCE 3rd DIVISION]

Place	Date	Hour	Summary of Events and Information	Remarks and references to Appendices
Bourgon	August 29th		Capt. H. Henderson + 5 squads of bearers proceeded to the lines to reinforce bearers with Capt. H.S. Willis. A.D.M.S. + Capt. Hackett visited R.A.P. also R. tire 42...	
		3.50	Capt. C.H. Floyd proceeded with 4 cars + sgt. wheelwrights to evacuate sick + wounded.	
		2.A.M.	from R.A.P. to C.C.S. 4.	
		7.A.M.	Capts Hackett, Henderson + Floyd + 6 squads of bearers returned to # 9.	
"	Aug 30th		A medical board consisting of Lt-Col Halgard, Ramer, Capt. Willis	
		5.P.M.	+ Capt. Marshall met at S. P.M. there to examine into the mental condition	
			Pte B. ott 45R Fus. Capt. Henderson relieving Capt. Willis in the line	
		6.30 P.M.	Capt. Willis + Capt. Floyd returned to A.D.S.	
		7.30 P.M.	Nine squads of bearers proceeded up the line to reinforce bearers under with Capts Willis, Floyd, Henderson, very few casualties either night	

WAR DIARY or INTELLIGENCE SUMMARY

Army Form C. 2118.

Place	Date	Hour	Summary of Events and Information	Remarks and references to Appendices
Peronne	August 1/17		Walk down by the Ambulance during the forenoon. The work of construction has been continued, & both entrances & the embankment between Stablings at Farmwood, has proceeded steadily during the month & with the fittings & three Stablings, the Dressing Stations & nursing quarters. In all 20 huts has been erected. Fires & flues & a complete system of water's ducts. The Drainage plans has been fairly satisfactory - small & fitted with 2 autoplain [?] humps, has rather [?] & gratings hole etc. A Cat-walk [?] of [?] & raised Ambulance loopers has been constructed [?] & curved drain under the three Stablings & have been channeled. By the R.O.C. as the best in his division. A gale on the night of the 27th 28th interfered in the 3 tents forming the gas ward, which is now out of use, & accommodating 16" in place of 25 cases. It has been fitted with a portable Hutchinson Oxygen Apparatus (4 patients) in action. A [?] [?] [?] always there. By [?] chief in common & construction, an average of 50 men per diem was employed on work at M.D.S. The weather through the month has been alternately wet, stormy & [?] with bright & fine intervals. Wind strong & mostly between W.S.W. & S.		

R. M. Hackett.
Capt RAMC
31/6/17

MEDICAL. SECRET. Vol 32

WAR DIARY.
OF
No. 8 FIELD AMBULANCE.

From 1·9·17. To 30·9·17.

COMMITTEE FOR THE
MEDICAL HISTORY OF THE WAR
Date 5 NOV. 1917

Army Form C. 2118.

WAR DIARY
or
INTELLIGENCE SUMMARY.
(Erase heading not required.)

Instructions regarding War Diaries and Intelligence Summaries are contained in F.S. Regs., Part II. and the Staff Manual respectively. Title pages will be prepared in manuscript.

Place	Date	Hour	Summary of Events and Information	Remarks and references to Appendices
BEUGNY	4/9/18		The Hospital was handed over to 2/1 London Field Ambulance and the unit proceed by march route to BARASTRE. C. Bolton leaves with Capt Willis in charge rejoined H.Q.	
BARASTRE	8/9/18		The men are billed daily, instructed in special work and are living after 9 and reorganizing.	
	16/9/18		Capt. E.L.H. HACKETT with an advance party proceed to the GATOU area by car. Lieut. Wilson, U.S. Army joined for duty from No 9 CCS. Personal and transport proceed by train to GODEWAERSVELDE and detraining and proceed No 2 area GATOU and billets for the night.	
GATOU	19/9/18		Lt. Col. G.N. MAURICE rejoined from leave, having been received by A.D.M.S. and Director of the following of evacuation.	

T2134. Wt. W708—776. 500000. 4/15. Sir J. C. & S.

WAR DIARY
or
INTELLIGENCE SUMMARY.
(Erase heading not required.)

Army Form C. 2118.

Place	Date	Hour	Summary of Events and Information	Remarks and references to Appendices
POPERINGHE	28/9/17		CAPT. HACKETT proceeded to No 6 M.A.C. for duty.	
	20/9/17		The Unit proceeded by march route to a Camp on the Poperinghe-Ypres road, at G.4.c.4.8. LIEUT. WILSON and 25 Other ranks proceeded to the C.W.C.P. for duty. CAPT. MILLAR RETURE proceeded to No 32 CCS for duty.	
	23/9/17		Unit proceeded by march route to BRANDHOEK and took over the T/Capt Gas Centre at the Collecting Station. All motor Ambulances of the Unit joining No 6 M.F.C. for duty.	
	25/9/17		CAPT WILD is also reported from leave, having been recalled by A.D.M.S. 2nd Division, on 22nd inst. proceeded to 97 CAPT. HENDERSON and 100 Lunars R.A.M.C. reinforced by 30 infantry to take over in charge of the 8th Inft. Bde.	
	26/9/17		CAPT MARSHALL D.so. proceeded to 12th W. Yorks for duty.	

WAR DIARY
or
INTELLIGENCE SUMMARY

(Erase heading not required.)

Army Form C. 2118

Place	Date	Hour	Summary of Events and Information	Remarks and references to Appendices
	30/9/16		CAPT. WILLIS and CAPT. HENDERSON with the bearers rejoined H.Q. Advanced party of No 11 Ambulance F.A. arrived to take over the Bar Cenba and Bur Collecting Station. The weather has been very fine for the operations. Enemy aircraft have been active, an average of about 40 casualties a night occurring in close proximity to the Bar Cenba. There was a smithing and limited 776 Bar Cases were admitted. Since their arrival on the Som. On average of about 400 sitt upcarts daily. L/Cpl. MORRIS Cenba. and CAPT. LLOYD are the only available officers in this work, the remainder being detailed by M.DMS to take on Corps Duties, i. Sent up the line to relieve Casualties. Only 2 3 other ranks were available to staff the Bar Collecting Station and Bar Cenba. The clearing of the line was carried out very satisfactorily.	

J. Shannon
Lt Col RAMC
O.C. 8 F.A.

No. 8. F.A.

COMMITTEE FOR THE
MEDICAL HISTORY OF THE WAR
Date -8 DEC. 1917

WAR DIARY or INTELLIGENCE SUMMARY

Army Form C. 2118

Place	Date	Hour	Summary of Events and Information	Remarks and references to Appendices
BRANDHOEK	1/10/17		Handed over for treatment centre & main Collecting Station to No 11 Australian F.A.	
	2/10/17		Transport proceeded by road route to WINNEZEELE, personnel by busses. Arrived WINNEZEELE 4 p.m. and billeted.	
WINNEZEELE	3/10/17		Field Ambulance less transport, Lt.Col G. H. MAURICE in command, 2n/Lt CAPTS. HENDERSON, HACKETT, MARSHALL, WILLIS, LLOYD & DOLLING, paraded at 9.80 a.m. 2n/L 8th 9th B.de. & took in a.Brevens by G.O.C. 3rd Div.	
RENESCURE	4/10/17		The unit entrained by road route to RENESCURE, arriving about 4 p.m. Billeted.	
BERLENCOURT	5/10/17	10 p.m.	The unit marched to STOMER on the way. Train left STOMER on train.	
	6/10/17		Detraining at BAPAUME about 3 p.m. & marched to BERLENCOURT. The camp at BERLENCOURT was very indifferent.	
	10/10/17		The war diaries for last 4 days have consisted of pulling softer sites of the 8th Bde. & in offering after the horses at DONNEREUSE.	
	11/10/17		An advance party proceeded to ACHIET LE GRAND to commence taking over VI C.C.S.	
BIHUCOURT	12/10/17		Remainder of unit marched to BIHUCOURT & took over VI C.C.S. at 2 p.m. from 2/2 West Riding F.A.	
	13/10/17		CAPT. MARSHALL D.O. proceeded to U.K. on 1 weeks furlough. Australians have transferred from Camp at ACHIET LE GRAND to Civil Camp at BIHUCOURT.	
	14/10/17		A.D.M.S. 3rd Corps inspected C.C.S.	

WAR DIARY or INTELLIGENCE SUMMARY

Army Form C. 2118

Place	Date	Hour	Summary of Events and Information	Remarks and references to Appendices
Bittercourt	16/10/17		A great deal of work has been done in this Camp. Six Armion huts have been made with light & rough material has been drawn in lorries, loading etc.	
	19/10/17		There is nothing to report except that a great deal of work is being done in the Camp. Six Armion huts, 5-pub huts have been drawn and are in process of erection.	
	20/10/17		Dressing Dt "C" Coy & Rooms Dt "B" Coys inspected C.R.S.	
	26/10/17		Six Armion huts have been completed and two Pub huts nearly completed.	
	27/10/17		Rooms & C Coys inspected C.R.S.	
	28/10/17		Capt. Henderson proceeded to 4th Field Ambulance for temporary duty.	
	29/10/17		Capt. Lloyd proceeded to England on termination of contract.	
	31/10/17		There is nothing further to report. The progress in building has been somewhat retarded by the difficulty of obtaining material & transport. But there has been so much work that every available man has been employed from early morning till dusk.	

J Whannia
Lt Col RAMC
O.C. 8th F.A.

140/678

No. 8. 7. a.

COMMITTEE FOR THE
MEDICAL HISTORY OF THE WAR
Date   17 JAN. 1918

WAR DIARY
or
INTELLIGENCE SUMMARY
(Erase heading not required.)

Army Form C. 2118

8 Fd Amb
J.L. 34

Place	Date	Hour	Summary of Events and Information	Remarks and references to Appendices
Bihucourt	4/11/17		C.O.C. 3rd Div. presented military medals ganed in the battles of Arras on Maj's Trae.	
	6/11/17		D Ons & Corps Inspected C.R.S. The process of how being the confirmation Delays through leave & gradual thawing.	
	14/11/17		All the huts have been erected & felled, There is still much work to be done.	
	18/11/17		27 Ons proceeded to No 45 CCS to Duty. 7 bearers proceeded to VAULX as Divisional reserve of bearers. B. Section lent substitution increasing the Bryan Relay of MAUCOURT to attend to walking wounded collecting post after dark.	
	19/11/17		The Battalions of the 8 & Terr. attacked. Casualties slight.	
	24/11/17		The bearers at VAULX relieved No 7 bearers in the NOREUIL Sector.	
	28/11/17		B. Section lent substitution rejoining the Q'ualres.	
	29/11/17		Bearers were relieved from the NOREUIL Sector by No 7 F.A. bearers & proceeding to Gave to billets over the A.D.S. & clearing in the LAGNICOURT Sector.	
	30/11/17		29 bearers were returning to the Q'ualres of the Head quarters of the unit, for further...	

WAR DIARY
or
INTELLIGENCE SUMMARY

Army Form C. 2118

Place	Date	Hour	Summary of Events and Information	Remarks and references to Appendices
Billocourt	30/11/15		The weather for the month has been exceptionally mild & dry. It has been very difficult to keep the cars going owing to having eleven men left to work it and a great number of organization work. The personnel that have rejoined the last few days has made things easier. But there is still a great shortage.	

J McManus
J. Col. RAMC
O.C. 8th F.A.
30/11/15

140/2618

COMMITTEE FOR THE
MEDICAL HISTORY OF THE WAR
Date -1 FEB. 1918

Army Form C. 2118

INTELLIGENCE SUMMARY
or
(Erase heading not required.)

Instructions regarding War Diaries and Intelligence Summaries are contained in F.S. Regs., Part II. and the Staff Manual respectively. Title Pages will be prepared in manuscript.

Place	Date	Hour	Summary of Events and Information	Remarks and references to Appendices
BEHAGNIES	16/12/17		Lt. Col. G.K. Maurice M.C. in Command of the unit proceeded to Behagnies, & took over the Camp H.1.d central (Sheet 57 c.), aerre!	
	17/12/17.		The weather is intensely cold.	
	20/12/17.		Capt. J.D. Marshall D.S.O. proceeded to take over temporary medical charge of the 2nd Suffolk battalion. Capt. J. Ferguson proceeded on leave to the U.K. Capt. 2. Lt. M. Hackett proceeded to A.D.S. Vaulx.	
	25/12/17.		The weather still remains very cold. No festivities could take place owing to the Scenes being in the Line.	
	29/12/17		Lt. Col. G.H. Maurice O.C. in command the unit proceeded by march route to Boiseleux-au-Mont, & billets in huts. Accommodation good.	
	30/12/17.		The leaves on the Capt. Willis R.C. incoming reporting the Devoulis. Capt. Hackett rejoined yesterday.	
	31/12/17.		The weather continues very severe.	

J. Maurice
Lt. Col. R.A.M.C.
O.C. 8th F.A.

Army Form C. 2118

WAR DIARY
or
INTELLIGENCE SUMMARY
(Erase heading not required.)

Vol 35

Place	Date	Hour	Summary of Events and Information	Remarks and references to Appendices
BIHUCOURT.	Dec 6/17		All missen huts occupied by the personnel have been tarred, and painted.	
VI Corps R.S. South.			New soakage pits & grease traps constructed for the baths, & all cook houses & the messes.	
	7/12/17		D.D.M.S. VI Corps inspected the C.R.S.	
	10/12/17		The bearers from the A.D.S. at C.29.a.54 (Sheet 57°↓ horse) returned to BIHUCOURT, being relieved by the 75 Field Amber.	
			The new incinerator which heats the drying room completed, & is very satisfactory. —	
			CAPTAIN FLEMING R.J. RAMC. assumed medical charge of the 1st Royal Scots Fusiliers.	
	12/12/17		CAPT H.G. WILLIS. M.C., and CAPT F. HENDERSON with bearers proceeded to the A.D.S. at VAULX, relieving the 7 Field Amber.	
	14/12/17		The VI Corps Rest St. (South) was closed. Slight cases of sickness being transferred to C.R.S. (North), more severe cases of sickness to C.C.S.	

3RD DIVISION
MEDICAL

NO. 8 FIELD AMBULANCE.
1918.

Mar 8. F.A.

WAR DIARY
or
INTELLIGENCE SUMMARY
(Erase heading not required.)

Army Form C. 2118

8 Fd Amb

Camp Boislieu au Mont { S 10 Central } Sheet 57c

Vol 39

Place	Date	Hour	Summary of Events and Information	Remarks and references to Appendices
Boislieu au Mont	1918			
	Jan 4/18		Capt. H.G. WILLIS. M.C. proceeded on leave to the United Kingdom.	J.M.
	Jan 7/18		Capt. J.D. MARSHALL. D.S.O. rejoined from temporary duty with the 2nd Bn The Suffolk Regt.	J.M.
	Jan 10/18		Lieut S.A. MURRAY. U.S.A. Medical Reserve, & Lieut. R.E. CONN. U.S. Army Medical Reserve joined this unit for duty from England.	
			Lieut-Col G.K. MAURICE M.C. RAMC. proceeded on leave to the United Kingdom.	J.M.
	Jan 19/18		Lieut R.E. CONN. U.S.A proceeded to the King's Shop. L.Iy. for temporary duty.	J.M.
	Jan 21/18		Capt H.G. Willis M.C. RAMC. returned from leave.	J.M.
	26/1/18		Capt. F. HENDERSON and Capt. H.G. WILLIS M.C. RAMC. with 80 NCOs & OR. proceeded to the A.D.S. at HENIN N.32 d.2.0. Sheet 51.2 1/40000, and took over the A.D.S. + various posts in the line.	J.D.M
	27/1/18		Lt. Col. G.K. MAURICE M.C. R.A.M.C. returned from leave.	J.D.M.
	31/1/18		Since arrival in the Boisleux-au-Mont area the billets have all been painted as far as possible against enemy aircraft. Cushelture standings, harness room, Nose-bar de lous - been erected. A Divisional bathhouse for 500 men, Cinquets, and a Dry't, room is under construction. A Hospital for 60 convalescent patients is being carried on.	G.K. Maurice Lt Col RAMC O.C 8 FA

Secret

War Diary of
No. 8 Field Ambulance.

From 1/8/18 to 28/8/18.

Vol 37

WAR DIARY
or
INTELLIGENCE SUMMARY

(Erase heading not required.)

Army Form C₂ 2118

Place	Date	Hour	Summary of Events and Information	Remarks and references to Appendices
PEOTILLEUX	4/2/18	am Apr IV.	A" section. Bearers proceeded to the lines to evacuate those brought to required to a new line of evacuation of the wounded.	
	5/2/18		The weather is exceptionally mild & fine.	
	7/2/18		Lt. R.E. CONN R.A.M.C. rejoins from temporary duty with the 7th W.S.A.B. Accommodation for 46 patients has been made available.	ffeh
	9/2/18		CAPT. J.D. MARSHALL D.S.O. R.A.M.C. proceeded to No. 8 General Hospital sick. Lt. R.E. CONN proceeded to 8th East Yorks for temporary duty.	
	10/2/18		CAPT. W. HENDERSON R.A.M.C. has taken on the strength of this unit.	
	14/2/18		The accommodation for patients in this camp has been increased and 60 patients can now be accommodated.	fff
	18/2/18		The weather continues fine & the had frost at night. A great deal of work has been done up the line, there large dugouts being practically completed.	ffh
	19/2/18		The A.D.M.S. 3rd Division & Lieut. Col. C.H. Kerrin M.C. have a been prilected.	ffh
	20/2/18		I ford him and A.D.S. Weather changed. Thaw set in with wind & rain.	ffh

WAR DIARY
or
INTELLIGENCE SUMMARY

(Erase heading not required.)

Army Form C. 2118

Place	Date	Hour	Summary of Events and Information	Remarks and references to Appendices
Belisario Redoubt	21/9/16		Considerable progress made in the cultivation of wadi gardens in the camp. Day fine but windy.	
	28/9/16		Day fine but weather broke down in the evening with bad rain. Revd. Col. G. H. Maurice Capt. Michell, Capt. Willcocks, Capt. Y. Henderson attended a lecture at 142 Field Ambulance - given by A.D.M.S. "Revision on infusion operations".	
	29/9/16		Lieut. C. A. Murray, U.S.A. proceeded to the 147 Corps Medical School for ten days course of instruction. Hospital visited & inspected by Col Beier R. Moore a/ A.D.M.S. v/ Corps. Weather storing wind & rain still prevailing. Although the weather on the whole has been very favourable for air raids, owing to the moon being at its height the enemy has shown no signs of bombing activity. During the night about 9 P.M. enemy attempted attack on this recently VNRFR southward, freezer. Immediately repelled.	
			Hospital cleared & patients to trade accommodation for 147 Field Ambulance's Still in/frens-	
			All the evacuated patients returned today to 142 Field ambulance for further treatment. Healthy	

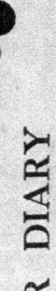

Army Form C. 2118

WAR DIARY
or
INTELLIGENCE SUMMARY

(Erase heading not required.)

Instructions regarding War Diaries and Intelligence Summaries are contained in F. S. Regs., Part II. and the Staff Manual respectively. Title Pages will be prepared in manuscript.

Place	Date	Hour	Summary of Events and Information	Remarks and references to Appendices
Boulogne a/Mer	24/9/18		Accommodation for the 7 Field Ambulance handed over to Major W.H. Pitt, todays. The billets occupied by them	[signature]

[signature]
B Maurice
Lt Col AMC
O.C. 8 F.A.

No. 8. F. A.

COMMITTEE FOR THE
MEDICAL HISTORY OF THE WAR
Date — 12 MAY 1918

Army Form C.2

WAR DIARY
or
INTELLIGENCE SUMMARY
(Erase heading not required.)

No 8 Field Ambulance

JC 38

Place	Date	Hour	Summary of Events and Information	Remarks and references to Appendices
Boulogne a.m.nt	1/3/18		The A.D.M.S. 6" Corps accompanied by the A.D.M.S. 3rd Div. inspected the A.D.S. Henin N 32 d. 2.0. about 51.B. 1/40000. Lieut & O C M' le Poidevin proceeded on leave to the Channel Islands.	Mr
	2/3/18		Lieut S.A. Murray M.O.R.C., U.S.A. reported from the 6" Corps Medical School	Mr
	3/3/18		Capt. H. Henderson RAMC evacuated sick to C.C.S. Lieut S.A. Murray M.O.R.C., U.S.A proceeded to the 2nd Bn. Royal Scots for temporary duty.	Mr
	6/3/18		Lieut C.A. Bardsley M.O.R.C., U.S.A. joined the unit from 1st Gordon Highlanders.	Mr
	10/3/18		Lieut R.C. Conn M.O.R.C., U.S.A. struck off the strength of the unit on 10.3.18. on being evacuated sick to C.C.S.	Mr
	18/3/18		Lieut C.A. Bardsley M.O.R.C., U.S.A proceeded to the 46th Brigade R.F.A. for duty	Mr

WAR DIARY
or
INTELLIGENCE SUMMARY
(Erase heading not required.)

Army Form C. 2

Instructions regarding War Diaries and Intelligence Summaries are contained in F. S. Regs., Part II. and the Staff Manual respectively. Title Pages will be prepared in manuscript.

Place	Date	Hour	Summary of Events and Information	Remarks and references to Appendices
Boisleux au Mont	22/3/18		The 6th F.A. + M.C. Post at Henin evacuated + reopened at Boyn-Beaurelle. The field ambulance Horse transport evacuated Boisleux au Mont + moved to Wailly.	Ahr
	23/3/18		Lieut. Col. F.K. Maurice, C.O. 8th Field Ambulance evacuated Boisleux au Mont at 2 pm + proceeded to M.27.d.4.9. Sheet 51.15 1/40,000 (near Mercatel)	Ahr
near Mercatel	27/3/18		The M.C. Post established here was removed. Foley as this place began to be rather heavily shelled. It was reopened on the Arras-Mercatel-Boisleux Road above the H in Inthorne Street Leno 11	Ahr
	28/3/18		Left Mercatel Arras-Road + proceeded to Wailly arriving at 9 pm.	Ahr
Wailly	30/3/18		The 4th Field Ambulance of the 2nd Canadian Division relieved the O. Field ambulance at Wailly, the relief being completed by 2 am	Ahr

Army Form C. 2118.

WAR DIARY
or
INTELLIGENCE SUMMARY.
(Erase heading not required.)

Place	Date	Hour	Summary of Events and Information	Remarks and references to Appendices
Hailly	30/3/18		Left Hailly at 2 am & proceeded to Bellancourt arriving at 4 am. At 2 p.m. the unit left Bellancourt & proceeded to Sus St Leger arriving at 7.30 pm.	Appx. Appx.

JJMaurice
Lt Col RA ac
Cmdg 8th Bde R.F.A.

140/2902.

8 A. Field Ambulance.

SECRET.

WAR DIARY.

of

O.C., No. 8 Field Ambulance.

From 1st APRIL To 30th APRIL, 1918.

=*=*=*=*=*=*=*=*=*=*=*=*=

Army Form C. 2118.

WAR DIARY
or
INTELLIGENCE SUMMARY.
(Erase heading not required.)

No 8 Field Ambulance

April 1918.

Instructions regarding War Diaries and Intelligence Summaries are contained in F. S. Regs., Part II. and the Staff Manual respectively. Title pages will be prepared in manuscript.

Place	Date	Hour	Summary of Events and Information	Remarks and references to Appendices
Sec. 5 Logen	1/4/18		Unit proceeded by march route to the Trevent Avenue to Crupts Road embussed & proceeded to Auchel (C. 27b Sheet 36 B 1/40,000) arriving about 3 pm	Apr.
Auchel	4/4/18		The unit left Auchel by march route at 9 am arriving at Annequin at 2.15 p.m. Billeted in the boys school at Annequin (F.9.a.7.5 Bethune combined sheet 1/40,000)	Apr.
Annequin	5/4/18		Lieut F. H. Boone R.A.M.C. T.C. joined for duty from 14 General Hospital on 4.4.18	Apr.
Annequin	10/4/18		The hospital & billets at Annequin handed over to 1st Field Ambulance - This unit proceeded by march route & arrived at 4 p.m. at M. 20.6.8.8. Bethune combined sheet 1/40,000	Apr.
M.20.6.8.8.	12/8/18		Owing to enemy shelling, the unit evacuated the hospital at M. 20.6.8.8. & moved to M. 20.6.5.5. The enemy heavily attacked the line held by the 8th Brigade at noon & after very severe fighting the 1st Royal Scots Fusiliers & the 2nd the Royal Scots were forced back to about 400 yards.	Apr.

(A8004) D. D. & L., London, E.C. Wt. W1771/M231 750,000 5/17 Sch. 93 Forms/C2118/14

WAR DIARY
or
INTELLIGENCE SUMMARY.
(Erase heading not required.)

Army Form C. 2118.

Instructions regarding War Diaries and Intelligence Summaries are contained in F. S. Regs., Part II. and the Staff Manual respectively. Title pages will be prepared in manuscript.

Place	Date	Hour	Summary of Events and Information	Remarks and references to Appendices
M.20.b.8.5 Bethune sheet 1/40,000	14/4/18		The unit moved into the Barn recently occupied by the 3rd Sin. Headquarters (M.20.a Bethune combined sheet 1/40,000) Lieut A.S. Westmorland RAMC S.R. assumed temporary medical charge of the 3rd Machine Gun Battalion based at Annezin.	WM
M.20.a	15/4/18		The unit left the barn at M.20.a.3 at 2 p.m. & proceeded to Annezin arriving there at 3 p.m., taking over hospital & billets from the 1st Field Ambulance. This hospital was used as A.D.S., M.I.R. & Post, & for cases of casualties from enemy shelling, all wounded being treated & then sent to the M.D. Station at L'Ambouyes near Chocques.	WM
Annezin	18/4/18		The Bearer division J.M.S. unit relieved the Bearer division of 142 Field Ambulance in the line by 4 p.m.	WM
Annezin	21/4/18		The following were awarded the Military Medal for gallantry in the field :- M2/018473 Pte H.J. Spratt, M.2.01568 Pte F.A. Gleand 96186 Sergt. J. Mackenzie, 58908 Sergt. J.D. Hart, 16,820 Pte H. Yeo 93724 Pte S. Walker, 63357 Pte A.M. Bennett, 31242 Pte W.H. Harris 35496 Pte H.J.S. Fabb, 12,712 S. Sergt M. Hutchinson, 1967 Pte H. Sayer	WM

WAR DIARY
or
INTELLIGENCE SUMMARY.
(Erase heading not required.)

Army Form C. 2118.

Place	Date	Hour	Summary of Events and Information	Remarks and references to Appendices
Annezin	22/4/18		The unit left Annezin at 2 P.M. & proceeded to L'Abbaye men Choques where the M.D. Station was being run by 142 Field Ambulance. Capt. E. L. M. Hackett & Capt. H. C. Millin were gazetted acting Majors while in command of sections of the ambulance.	AM.
L'Abbaye	25/4/18		Lieut. J. H. Roome R.A.M.C. took over temporarily the charge of the 13th Kings Liverpool Regt.	AM.
L'Abbaye	26/4/18		Capt. H. S. Mullan R.A.M.C. joined for duty.	AM.
L'Abbaye	29/4/18	3 P.M.	Owing to an outbreak of illness — influenza in type, among the crew, the Unit proceeded to Lozinghem & arrived there at 3 P.M. Nº 52,818 Sergt. A. Jones R.A.M. was awarded a bar to the military medal. The following were awarded the military medal — Nº 2/226364 Pte S. F. Harding, Nº 79004 Pte H. Murhead, Nº 26096 Pte A. Sprunjett.	AM.
Lozinghem	30/4/18		Capt. H. S. Mullan took over temporarily the medical charge of the 7th Bde R. F. A.	AM.

B. Munnis
Lieut R.A.M.C. O.C. 85 F.A.

14 d/2983.

No. 8 Field Amb.

May 1918

War Diary
of
66.8 Field Ambce
From 1/5/18 to 31/5/18

WAR DIARY
or
INTELLIGENCE SUMMARY.

Army Form C. 2118.

Place	Date	Hour	Summary of Events and Information	Remarks and references to Appendices
Bois des DAMES	1/5/18		The unit is in huts & bivouacs in the Bois des Dames close to LABEUVRIERE.	
"	2/5/18		Lieut JOHNSON M.O.R.C. U.S.A. joined for duty from No. 113 F. Amb. The right section of the line was taken over by this unit. A.D.S. BOURNELLE DIMCH in charge.	
	3/5/18		The weather fine & warm.	
Bois des Dames	4/5/18		CAPT. F. HENDERSON R.A.M.C. was ordered to the Military Gov.	
	5/5/18		Elephant Shelters are being erected in the school at AUVERIN and on the Canal Bank at the car post to protect against hostile Shelling.	
	7/5/18		Major H.G. WILLS M.C. was awarded the D.S.O.	
	8/5/18		The bearers in the line & the A.D.S. Party on being relieved by No. 7. F.A. rejoined Headquarters	
	10/5/18		The period at my the line is being occupied by cleaning, inspection, refitting etc. The present arrangement of working one unit in the line with a Res. of Infantry is very satisfactory. It provides opportunity for inspections, cleaning of horses, and for General supervision of the unit, also is better than helping with Carrying Shells in the line; in addition it provides change of scene & ground for the men, the two sections being taken over alternately.	

WAR DIARY
or
INTELLIGENCE SUMMARY.
(Erase heading not required.)

Army Form C. 2118.

Place	Date	Hour	Summary of Events and Information	Remarks and references to Appendices
Boris aux DIAms.	12/5/18		The unit took over the A.D.S. at D'ARRAYE, (post-acti-) from 149 F.A. Bearers number 52 O.Rs. Nursing personnel 20 Rs. There is war in the form of exciting Splinters most nights in this sector of the line also, but the casualties were than half number.	
	13/5/18		Number of Officers in the A.D.S. are turned from two to three.	
	16/6/18		Not many casualties have occurred on this front in the last few days, in spite of fairly heavy shelling. The weather continues intensely hot.	
	18/5/18		A very heavy yellow Cross Gas bombardment on front occurred about Dawn. At 10.30 a.m. a report reached us at 8 P. F.A. that motor cars were required in order to clear Gas cases. At 11 A.M. two car of the 8 P. F.A. were pressed & the A.D.S. having sent the remainder of the P. F.A. cars to help in the forward area. At 11.30 about 100 cases were still at the Car post in ST NIZIER. Great numbers of Gas Cases reported at all the 8 Bn A.D. and Regt to throughout the Day. The last cases were cleaned at 7.30 p.m. In all about 1010 cases were cleared. All available cars from all the S.A.'s of the Division were employed, also two heavy Ambulance Wagons, and Errands carrying two or three lacies, of the S-2 hours	

WAR DIARY or INTELLIGENCE SUMMARY

Army Form C. 2118.

Place	Date	Hour	Summary of Events and Information	Remarks and references to Appendices
Corps Rec	Donnes 26/5/18		employed in the lines. 28 were gassed. They were gassed through prolonged exposure to a mild concentration of gas in MINE E, & are unavoidable, as respirators cannot be worn for long while stretchers are being carried. Only 28 were evacuated. The remainder being treated at O.P.F.A. stationed. Capt Fleming & Lieut Murray (M.Os. i/c of 1st F.A.s 70 & 9th Royal Field artillery) were both slightly severely gassed. They were relieved during the afternoon by Officers from No.8 F.A. & were taken on the strength of this unit. The unit was relieved in the line at 7.30 p.m. by No.7 F.A.	
	27/5/18 I.P.		Major E.L.M. HACKETT. proceeded on one months Special leave to the U.K.	
	28/5/18 I.P.		The men who were gassed 26th in Flopital here are progressing satisfactorily. Lieut MURRAY M.O.R.C. USA. has in pieces, we all are unusually fine for May last.	
			CAPT. FLEMING. is not in hurry at all & is being evacuated this day.	

Army Form C. 2118.

WAR DIARY
or
INTELLIGENCE SUMMARY.
(Erase heading not required.)

Instructions regarding War Diaries and Intelligence Summaries are contained in F. S. Regs., Part II. and the Staff Manual respectively. Title pages will be prepared in manuscript.

Place	Date	Hour	Summary of Events and Information	Remarks and references to Appendices
Bois DES DAMES	29/5/18.		There is considerable shelling of back areas. It has become necessary to shift the horses as shells falling near the standings.	
	30/5/18.		Major H.E. Willis DSO M.C. & Capt. Henderson M.C. proceed with a party of stretcher bearers, and tent personnel to Aunezin, to take over the ADS at Aunezin and the clearing of the right sector from 142 F.A.	
	31/5/18.		There is nothing to report.	

R M Maurice
Lt Col RAMC
O.C. 8th F.A.

War Diary
of
O.C. 8 Field Ambulance

June 1918.

WAR DIARY
or
INTELLIGENCE SUMMARY.
(Erase heading not required.)

Army Form C. 2118.

Vol 4

Place	Date	Hour	Summary of Events and Information	Remarks and references to Appendices
Bois des Dames	2/6/18		The night such continues fairly quiet. The enemy the previous area is nearly complete.	
	4/6/18		Two H.D. bones H.E. & high bombs from enemy aircraft. Capt. A.C. Lambert joined for duty.	
	8/6/18		There is nothing to report. The units in the line are being worked by two Sergeants — any Strings with Relieve.	
	10/6/18		Lieut. Ornitage Au.O.R.C. U.S.A. joined for course of instruction.	
	13/6/18		In view of pending offensive, the 9th & 76th Infantry Brigades Sections have been sent up the line. Also the night R.A.P. of Curlu & Ce has been taken over by this unit.	
	14/6/18		The H.Q. of the unit moved to Aurrezin as a Battle H.Q. All officers of the unit visited there for the night.	
	15/6/18		Attack commenced 12.15 a.m. H.Col. Nuzum to begin bulbs worked the car post at 3 a.m. There were no difficulties in evacuating wounded.	
	17/6/18		At 9 a.m. moved H.Q. back to Bois des Dames. Lieut. Bo. N.E. Au.O.A.C. U.S.A. rejoined from temporary duty into 8th R.O.R.s.	
	20/6/18		Capt. Lambert took over temporary medical charge of 8th R.O.R.s. Capt. Milles took over temporary medical charge of 2nd the Royal Scots.	

WAR DIARY or INTELLIGENCE SUMMARY

Place	Date	Hour	Summary of Events and Information	Remarks and references to Appendices
Bois des Dames	22/6/18		Major St G Willis. DSO M.C. proceed on leave to U.K.	
	25/6/18		Capt. H.S. Millar rejoined for duty. Lieut Ambrose MORC. USA. rejoined his unit after completing course of Instruction.	
			Lieut. Murray. G.O.R.C. O.S.a. assumed medical charge of 3rd Div. R.E.	
	26/6/18		Major Hackett returned from leave.	
	29/6/18		Major Hackett & Capt: Henderson M.C. relieved Lieut Bostwu & Capt. Millar at Aurrezin. Both the latter officers are suffering from P.U.O.	
	30/6/18		The most marked feature of the month is the prevalence of P.U.O. in all units. The Base of officers of this unit have been complaining free of ill-health & Capt H.S.M.T. have been both affected.	

JM Maurice
Lt Col R.A.M.C.
O.C. 8th FA

140/3131.

No. 8 T.A.

COMMITTEE FOR THE
MEDICAL HISTORY OF THE WAR
Date -6 SEP 30

6

SECRET.

War Diary
of
No 8 Field Ambce

From 1/7/18   To 31/7/18

WAR DIARY
or
INTELLIGENCE SUMMARY.
(Erase heading not required.)

Army Form C. 2118.

Place	Date	Hour	Summary of Events and Information	Remarks and references to Appendices
Bois des Tailles	4/7/16		Lieut. F.S. Perdue M.R.C. U.S.A. proceeded to 7½ K.S.L.I. on temporary duty. Lieut. Shurrock who was attached to this unit for few days returned from R.v.O.	
"	7/7/16		Captain H.S. Mulle Rame arrived from service medical charge of 40" Troops R.F.A. in chief to Lieut-Bradley Lieut. U.S.A. who joined this unit for duty. Lieut. C.A. Bradley M.R.S. U.S.A. proceeded to w 3d.C.C.S. for temporary duty. Major H.G. Willis D.S.O. Rame returned from leave.	Herbert Major Rame Ambulance to O.b.E. 9th field Ambulance

Army Form C. 2118.

WAR DIARY
or
INTELLIGENCE SUMMARY.
(Erase heading not required.)

Instructions regarding War Diaries and Intelligence Summaries are contained in F. S. Regs., Part II. and the Staff Manual respectively. Title pages will be prepared in manuscript.

Place	Date	Hour	Summary of Events and Information	Remarks and references to Appendices
Rine Sin Camp	9/7/16		The G.O.C. XIII Corps inspected the 3rd Div from transport 21-2-15 P.M.	
	11/7/16		Captain A.S. Glynn R.A.M.C. joined this unit for duty from the Base.	
			Lieut. Shucksmith R.A.M.C. rejoined 7th R.S.F. for duty & relieved Lieut. F.S. Perdue who returned to this unit.	
	21/4/21		Major H.S. Willis D.S.O. + Lieut. G. Perdue returned to Capt. A.S. Glynn + Lieut. G. Perdue returned to Hackett + Capt. Henderson with A.D.S. Convoyeur	
	18/7/16		Capt. A.S. Glynn assumed temporary medical charge of 46th R.F.A. R.F.A.	Hackett visited father for O.C. Sixteen Ambulance

Army Form C. 2118.

WAR DIARY
or
INTELLIGENCE SUMMARY.
(Erase heading not required.)

Instructions regarding War Diaries and Intelligence Summaries are contained in F. S. Regs., Part II. and the Staff Manual respectively. Title pages will be prepared in manuscript.

Place	Date	Hour	Summary of Events and Information	Remarks and references to Appendices
Paris des Dames	16/7/16		Lieut. F.S. Protheir relieved Captain A.S. Chapman at A.D.S. Annoyeur.	
"	27/7/16		Capt. F. Hudson A.C. proceeded on special leave to United Kingdom: 27/7/16 — 6/8/16. Major J.S. Hackett relieved Major H.S. Willis & Lieut. F.S. Protheir Major R.M. Hackett at A.D.S. Annoyeur at A.D.S. Annoyeur	
"	31/7/16		Lieut. F.S. Protheir relieved Major Hackett at A.D.S. Annoyeur	Stephen T Major at O.C. 3rd Field Ambulance

Confidential
WO 43
160/2900

War Diary
of
8th Field Ambulance.

August 1918.

Army Form C. 2118.

WAR DIARY
or
INTELLIGENCE SUMMARY.
(Erase heading not required.)

Instructions regarding War Diaries and Intelligence Summaries are contained in F. S. Regs, Part II. and the Staff Manual respectively. Title pages will be prepared in manuscript.

Place	Date	Hour	Summary of Events and Information	Remarks and references to Appendices
Bois des Dames	1/8/18		Weekly relief of drivers in the line took place.	
"	5/8/18		Capt. Quinn Rowe rejoined from leave any duty of 69th 46th 158 R.F.A.	
"	6/8/18		The A.D.S. at ANNEZIN & drivers posts in the line were handed over to 58th F.A. 59 Amb. 19th Div. at 5 p.m. Attacks of 8th F.A. relieving H.Q. from the line.	
"	7/8/18		The unit marched over the 11th to the Bois des Dames & the Officers Hospital Name to 58th F.A.	
GRICOURT.	8/8/18		It Cal. R.A. Menzies in charge the unit proceeded by march route to GRICOURT arriving at 3.45 p.m. & billeted for the night. A field hospital was opened for the use of the 8th & 9th Bdes. Mr. C.A. BARDSLEY LIORC. USA. was attd. off. the strength of this unit. Recruit training commenced	
GARLUZEL	13/8/18		The Field Ambulance, Mus mechanical & Horse transport arrived at RAFYS Station & detrained at MONDICOURT. Proceeded by march route to GARLUZEL & billet. 9 Major G.W.LS R.C. D.S.O. was in charge. The Horse transport under Capt. HENDERSON proceeded by road & defended arriving at GARLUZEL 5/8/18 at 3 a.m.	
SAULTY.	15/8/18		The unit proceeded by march route to SAULTY at 2 a.m. & opened a Divisional rest station	

WAR DIARY
or
INTELLIGENCE SUMMARY.

Army Form C. 2118.

Place	Date	Hour	Summary of Events and Information	Remarks and references to Appendices
SAULTY	16/8/18		Autumn Training Commenced.	
	19/8/18		The unit proceeded by march route to BIENVILLERS, having after dark & arriving at 2 a.m. Major HACKETT took over Charge.	
	20/8/18		Lt. Col. Churrie D.C., Major Willis DSO M.C. & Capt HENDERSON M.C. reconnoitred the line from MONCHY au BOIS F.E. of AYETTE. Major HACKETT in charge the unit, less Lines transport proceeded by march route to MONCHY au BOIS arriving at 10.25 p.m.	
	21/8/18		At 2.20 a.m. The heavier Division tire took up position S.E. of ADINFER Wood, with M.G.1 proceeded by tanks rendezvous to amplify positions. The Barrage Com menced, Major Willis, Capt Henderson & Capt Glynn & M.G.1 Churnies & Major Cottle's proceeded Zern at 4.55 a.m. At 5.15 a.m. heads to the old British Front line in AYETTE Churrie & Major Anderson & two Coys to push there, at Lewes, Lieut Anderson & cars to push there, at Serre wear for Servais, Lewes. 6 by 6.30 a.m. Cars were heavily 5.45 a.m. a A.D.S. was established Nere & by 6.30 a.m. Cars were heavily engaged between Ayette & Courcelles. The Division advanced & the Cleaning Churrie ments conformed to the Pile line temporarily over the went to the Division advanced & The ADINFER DOUCHY	
	22/8/18			
	23/8/18			

WAR DIARY
or
INTELLIGENCE SUMMARY.

Army Form C.2118.

(Erase heading not required.)

Place	Date	Hour	Summary of Events and Information	Remarks and references to Appendices
HAMELINCOURT	28/8/18		A billeting party took over half completed M.D.S. of Guards Divn. at AYETTE.	
	29/8/18		Tiring above Att. to M.D.S. Inevitable The Camp was struck & a M.D.S. opened at 1 p.m. at S.28.c.7.3. in HAMELINCOURT — Bon Levee — on west Road. In the course of the day the whole unit moved this site including Horse transport.	
	31/8/18		The 76th & 9 th light B'ds have been in action. The 8th Infy Bde is in support. The heaviers have not yet been called upon since arrival at this M.D.S. site.	

[signature]
J R Dacre
O.C. 8th F.A.

Appendix IV

SECRET.

3rd DIVISION R.A.M.C. OPERATION ORDER No. 111.

30th August, 1918.

Map Reference Sheet 57C, 1/40,000.

1. The 3rd Division has been ordered to capture ECOUST and LONGATTE tomorrow 31st inst.
   In conjunction with this operation the 62nd Division on the right and 56th Division on the left will take part in the attack.

2. The 9th Infantry Brigade will carry out the attack together with one Battalion of the 76th Infantry Brigade which will be under orders of the G.O.C., 9th Infantry Brigade.

3. Zero hour will be 5-15 a.m.

4. O.C., No. 142 Field Ambulance will be responsible for the evacuation of wounded from the 9th Infantry Brigade.

5. O.C., No. 7 Field Ambulance will be responsible for the evacuation of wounded from the Battalion of the 76th Infantry Brigade taking part in the attack.

6. O.C., No. 8 Field Ambulance will detail two Ford Cars to report forthwith for duty to O.C., No. 142 Field Ambulance at T.25.c.2.8.

7. The pool of horsed ambulance wagons will be broken up forthwith and Os.C., Nos. 7 and 142 Field Ambulances will make as much use as possible of their horsed ambulance wagons and Ford cars for evacuations from the forward area.

8. Evacuation from the Main Dressing Station and W.W.C.Post will be as detailed in 3rd Division R.A.M.C. Operation Order No.110.

9. Field Ambulances to acknowledge.

Lieut-Colonel,
A.D.M.S., 3rd Division.

Copies to:-
All recipients of O.C. No.

Acknowledged

14/3259

No. 8 Field Amb.

Feb. 1918

COMMITTEE FOR THE
MEDICAL HISTORY OF THE WAR
Date 9 NOV 30

Nº 8. Zecco Ambler.

Army Form C. 2118.

WAR DIARY
or
INTELLIGENCE SUMMARY.
(Erase heading not required.)

Place	Date	Hour	Summary of Events and Information	Remarks and references to Appendices
HAMELINCOURT	1/9/18		The Division HQ moved into Major Willis' old Quarters and to a position in the Vraucourt - St Leger road, close to Vraucourt, taking on O.P.S. 8th & 9th Bdes. relieving 14th Michigan Pt. Bde. of 8th Inf. Bde. came under orders.	
	2/9/18		Hq this unit. There was no reversal of events. Lt Bedina A.R.C. U.S.A. evacuated sick Rees.	
	3/9/18			
RANSART	6/9/18		The Division was withdrawn. Reliefs. 8th J.A. proceeded by march route to RANSART. Billets.	
	7/9/18		Major H. S. Willis bombarded to No. 7 J.A. for false casualties Bertrix 9 hr No. 7 J.A.	
	8/9/18		Capt. D.M. WALTER joining for duty.	
	9/9/18		The unit trained & manoeuvred in area Gomiecourt & contra.	
ADINFER	10/9/18		Lt Col Wanni & Capt Sheldon remounted the line.	
	11/9/18		The unit proceeded by march route to BEAUMETZ. & found a train ready thereon.	
	15/9/18			
	16/9/18			

WAR DIARY
or
INTELLIGENCE SUMMARY.
(Erase heading not required.)

Army Form C. 2118.

Place	Date	Hour	Summary of Events and Information	Remarks and references to Appendices
BEUVRY.	16/9/18.		Seven seniors of teams proceeded up the line to clear the wounded of 8r Inf. Bde.	
	18/9/18.		Captain C. H. Floyd joined for duty. Casualties in from 2 areas present no difficulties. No enemy shelling.	
	20/9/18.		The M.D.S. established a bit. The unit satisfying up the place.	
	26/9/18. 8.7pm		The whole Lucas Division, the nursing orderlies hung up the line. Lt-Col. 8th Durham, 10th Argyll Highrs, 1/1 Argyll Inders. A.D.M.S. 9 S.E. Marines. Through the night the cars being loaded with Donts & Clients, Stretchers undefined from during the night. Before sun rise was going through.	
	27/9/18		The Division attacked at 5.30 a.m. The clearing of wounded sent away. Transport from M.D.S. was the chief difficulty. Heavy ambulance wagons were largely employed.	
	28/9/18 30/9/18		Italian Division was in the front of the line. During the 9th, the 10th A.D. Divisional Boundary about 9 miles 9 cases through the A.D.S. The units standing by to move at short notice. M. Ulverson yx1. None	O.C. 8th 74

WAR DIARY
or
INTELLIGENCE SUMMARY.

(Erase heading not required.)

Army Form C. 2118.

Place	Date	Hour	Summary of Events and Information	Remarks and references to Appendices
Pilocourt	1/8/16	1 AM	Unit arrived at Pilcourt at 1 AM leaving Left Beaumetz at 9.45 P.m on 30/7/16. Unit opens A.D.S. at 5. A.M. which became M.D.S. by middle of day. Major J. Henderson I/C D.92 bearers proceeded up the line & Capt. H.G. Floyd & party to A.D.S. (advance) at Hamelincourt.	L.2.5. & 2.6. Shut.57.C. 1/40300
	2/8/16		Pte. Walker. S. was killed in action on 1/8/16.	
	8/8/16		Major Henderson & Capt. Floyd with bearers & A.D.S's party opened Unit at Ribeaucourt. (Humantown)	
	9/8/16		Unit proceeded by march route to Beaumetz arriving there at 2 P.m. + took on D.R.S. from F.A. 9/lm 62nd Divn. Brohon. 1.13.&.2.14.	
Beaumetz	11/8/16		Capt. K.M. Walker proceeded on leave to the U.K.	
	12/8/16		Unit proceeded by march route to Ribemont. L.25.A.9.5	L.25.A.9.5

E.M. Haskell
Major R.M.

WAR DIARY
or
INTELLIGENCE SUMMARY.

Army Form C. 2118.

(Erase heading not required.)

Instructions regarding War Diaries and Intelligence Summaries are contained in F. S. Regs., Part II. and the Staff Manual respectively. Title pages will be prepared in manuscript.

Place	Date	Hour	Summary of Events and Information	Remarks and references to Appendices
Abscon	15/9/16		T/Major F. Hudson R.C. is to be Adding Major from 23/9/16 whilst commanding Section of 6 Muse. Islands. Authority VI Corps.	L.25.A.M. G.S. 57.C./10003
	18/9/16		The G.O.C. 8th Inf. Brigade & Brig. Genl. Indus formed hidden Mules. Rode a Model Boundarism Pomon this week.	L.25-A.G.S. 57/C./10003
	21/9/16		Unit proceeded by Church Roué to CATTENIERS. H.12.	57.B.
	22/9/16		Unit proceeded by Church Roué to QUIÉVY. D.19. Major Hudson + Capt. Lloyd proceeded to leave with Prisoners.	57.B.
			9/- 4/g: a. P. B. Rodeson proceeded on leave on A.D.S. at. El. Major Hackett joined to SOLESMES & found an A.D.S. at. El. of the Royal O.B. proceeded by Steamers which became a Running hospital thereafter transport proceeded	Phil. 57.B. Adj. 090
	23/9/16		M.D.S. at 12 Noon. 23/9/16 Major F. Hudson was transfered in chain + adopted to duty 22/9/16 rose 23/9/16	

M. Hackett
Major RAMC

WAR DIARY
or
INTELLIGENCE SUMMARY.

(Erase heading not required.)

Army Form C. 2118.

Instructions regarding War Diaries and Intelligence Summaries are contained in F. S. Regs., Part II. and the Staff Manual respectively. Title pages will be prepared in manuscript.

Place	Date	Hour	Summary of Events and Information	Remarks and references to Appendices
Salonika	23/10/16		Pr. + L.A., L.L. Wilkinson joined unit for duty from 30.C.C.S. Capt. C.H. Lloyd posted to 77 Regt 3 Bde for temp. duty.	57, B. 40.350
"	24/10/16		Capt. K.M. Walker returned from leave.	
			Remounts, Mule & Horse transport. left Quarry & found unit at Salonica.	
"	25/10/16		Arrived at Salonica cast & function as M.D.S. Unit was inspected by Surgeon General Sloggett. Sharing centre established under Capt. Crowp & Capt. Clegg. Review. 1 N.C.O. & 11 O.R. rank & file attached to his group. Major Henderson awarded bar to his M.C.	"
			Capt. C.H. Lloyd awarded M.C.	"
"	29/10/16		Capt. Walker proceeded to A.D.S. at Sembuzus & Guvezne.	"

R.H. Hartnell
Major R.A.M.C.

Army Form C. 2118.

WAR DIARY
or
INTELLIGENCE SUMMARY.
(Erase heading not required.)

Instructions regarding War Diaries and Intelligence Summaries are contained in F. S. Regs., Part II. and the Staff Manual respectively. Title pages will be prepared in manuscript.

Place	Date	Hour	Summary of Events and Information	Remarks and references to Appendices
Flexures	29/10/16		Lt-Col G.K. Keane proceeded on leave to the U.K.	
	29/10/16		Major Hudson & Capt. Walker with Bison's started from the line to H.Q. at Gézaincourt	57.B. 1/10/16
	31/10/16		Hair-lines 1 R.C.O & M.O.2. who remained at Corps Speedway Coll. proceeded by Armed Roads to Bavillers	

John Hackett
Major R.A.M.C.

116/3401

No. 8 T.O.

Nov. 1918.

14

Army Form C. 2118.

WAR DIARY
or
INTELLIGENCE SUMMARY.
(Erase heading not required.)

N° 8 2td Arm

WB46

Place	Date	Hour	Summary of Events and Information	Remarks and references to Appendices
BEVILLERS	1/11/18		Opened Hospital to mix of 8th Infy. Bde. Lt. MURRAY U.S.A. rejoined from temporary duty with 9th Royal Fus.	
	2/11/18		Lt. MURRAY U.S.A. posted to 8 July with 3rd Div. R.E. Capt. ad. GLYNN posted to 89 Bty R.F.A. for duty as M.O. Capt. LLOYD rejoined from temporary duty as M.O. 10th R.S.	
SOLESMES	4/11/18		Unit proceeded by march route at 9 a.m. to SOLESMES & billeted.	
	8/11/18		There is nothing to report.	
ROMERIES	10/11/18		Unit proceeded by march route to ROMERIES.	
	11/11/18		Hostilities ceased at 11.00 hours. Wide 3rd Div. G.Rs.	
	12/11/18		2nd Lt. P. Le POIDEVIN returned from leave.	
	13/11/18		2nd Lt. P. Le POIDEVIN proceeded to No 3 C.C.S. for duty. Lt. MURRAY U.S.A. O.S. Corps. 10th Fus. for duty from 3rd Div. R.E.	
FRASNOY	17/11/18		The unit proceeded by march route to FRASNOY & billeted.	
	18/11/18		The unit proceeded by march route to NEUF-MESNIL	
NEUF MESNIL FERRIÈRE LE GRAND	20/11/18		The unit left NEUF-MESNIL at 8 a.m. and proceeded by march route to FERRIÈRE LE GRAND. Lt. Col. G. H. MAURICE O.C. returned from leave at this U.L.	
BOUSIGNIES	23/11/18		The unit proceeded by march route to BOUSIGNIES.	
THUIN	25/11/18		The unit moved to THUIN.	
SOMZÉE	26/11/18		The unit moved to SOMZÉE.	

Army Form C. 2118.

WAR DIARY
or
INTELLIGENCE SUMMARY.
(Erase heading not required.)

Place	Date	Hour	Summary of Events and Information	Remarks and references to Appendices
FURNAUX.	28/11/18		The unit moved to FURNAUX.	
YVOIR.	29/11/18		Moved to YVOIR, & crossed the MEUSE. The infant this month. The unit has moved in C: Fonts, (8 Sept 13th Prof) & has collected the sick of 8th Inf & 13th Prof & "D" Pont (artillery front). The sick on the cases has been very heavy. The 9nfluenza to evacuate to O.C.s being very great. In addition two cases have been taken for chronic retained purposes & sick civilians from in front of the leading 13th Pont. The unit has been 24 h. march onto each way. The band at Stan-Ste The men are well but the cases will inevitably break down when the pressure of work is relieved.	

30.11.18.

J. M. Smith
LIEUT. COLONEL R.A.M.C.
O.C. 8TH FIELD AMBULANCE

COMMITTEE FOR THE
MEDICAL HISTORY OF THE WAR
-6 MAR 1919
Date

WAR DIARY
or
INTELLIGENCE SUMMARY.
(Erase heading not required.)

Army Form C. 2118.

Place	Date	Hour	Summary of Events and Information	Remarks and references to Appendices
AWAGNE. GIRBELSRATH.	1/12/18.		MARCH 9 to AWAGNE Wed. 9.ay. Lt Hubbard 9 mile U.S.A. join us for Bul:	
	31/12/18.		The following moves took place by march route during month of December 1918:- 4TH MALLOY. 5TH HEDRE. 6TH NV. 7TH FRENNE. 8TH VAUX CHAVANNE. Major Shercott & CAPT WALNER proceed to report to Casual Base de Jonjon on 20/7. 9TH OUDIGNE. 11TH VERLEMONT. LIEUT HUBBARD proceed to 8 JTH'S DIV. In 12TH BEHO. 13TH Crones German frontier to LEISTER. 14TH SCHÖNBERG. 15TH KRONENBURG. 16TH BLANKENHEIMERDORF. 17TH MUNSTEREIFEL. 18TH ENZEN. 19TH HUDDERSHEIM. 20TH GIRBELSRATH. Billets varied, but on the whole part were not good. Weather indifferent on the march, but only periodically bad. Since arrival here bother has been much keener, now practically every day. The village troops be confortable for the men if it was possible to obtain a Lib. building material for comp. houses etc., but this appears impossible. Work on the central office is very keen with demobilization. The civil population & the new conditions to Geol with.	

G.K. Lumsden
Lt.Col. Comm'g 7th No 8.
8.Fd Amb
18547

No. 7. A.

WAR DIARY or INTELLIGENCE SUMMARY

Army Form C. 211

No P. Ja Amban

Vol 48

Jan 1919.

Place	Date	Hour	Summary of Events and Information	Remarks and references to Appendices
GIRBELRATH	2/1/19.		Bn OC & Adjutants. from looking the Square in the way of Coordinates of Police.	
	3/1/19.		1 Sept & Seven proceeded on a low allocating POWs from camps in the vicinity of MANORIA.	
	7/1/19.		Major E Mr Hewett devised the military Gov., Cap T. Green numbered in detaches.	
	9/1/19.		Lieut. & 9 Lt. J. Wilkinson proceeded on leave to U.K.	
	16/1/19.		Major H. Givier F.T.C. proceeded on leave to U.H.	
	20/1/19.		The another has become more & more fairly occupied.	
	25/1/19		1st & 6 men returned, having completed their allocation of POWs.	
	30/1/19.		The evening had by continues its has been used delays through everywhere out interval.	

M. Lemming
Lt 21 more
Cmag No 8 P P Amban

140/3524

No. 8 F.A.

Feb. 1919

Army Form C. 2118.

WAR DIARY
or
INTELLIGENCE SUMMARY.
(Erase heading not required.)

8 Fd Amb

Instructions regarding War Diaries and Intelligence Summaries are contained in F. S. Regs., Part II. and the Staff Manual respectively. Title pages will be prepared in manuscript.

Hour, Date, Place	Summary of Events and Information	Remarks and references to Appendices
GIRBELSRATH. 3/2/19.	CAPT. LLOYD R.C. proceeded on leave to U.K.	
4/2/19.	No 1 San. Sec. arrived & billeted in this village.	
7/2/19.	The unit was inspected by the Major General Comdg 3rd Divn.	
10/2/19.	The weather exceedingly cold.	
17/2/19.	Lt. J. Ilee Williams rejoined from leave.	
19/2/19.	Unit moved to DÜREN & took over Marie College as C.C.R.S.	
21/2/19.	The weather has turned quite mild. Lieut. & Q.M. Wilkinson proceeded to No. 7 F.A. for kit & eqpt.	
28/2/19.	CAPT. LLOYD R.C. returned off leave. Very little training or evacn as unit has been trouble during the month owing to shortage of personnel.	

J. Mahanine
Lt Col RAMC Comdg No 8 F.A

116/3507.

17 JUL 1919

No. 8 4. O

No. 1418

Army Form C. 2118.

WAR DIARY
or
INTELLIGENCE SUMMARY.

(Erase heading not required.)

March 1919

Army Form C. 2118.

O.C. 8th F. Amer.

Instructions regarding War Diaries and Intelligence Summaries are contained in F. S. Regs., Part II. and the Staff Manual respectively. Title pages will be prepared in manuscript.

Hour, Date, Place	Summary of Events and Information	Remarks and references to Appendices
GIRBELSRATH A.3.19	One Serjeant & 16 men sent for temporary duty at N°17 C.C.S.	
" 5.3.15	The Transport of N°5 F.A. proceeded by road to KERPEN and completes the move to EFFEREN on the 6th instant.	
EFFEREN 6.3.19	Remainder of unit landed on Vi Corps Rail Station at DUREN and proceeded by main road to EFFEREN	
" 16.3.19	Lt Colonel S. K. MAURICE M.C. proceeded on leave. The move of the 3rd Division to change to the Northern Division. List of Wilkinson completely & the Strength and A.R. Bentham taken on.	
" 25.3.15	The unit was inspected by the G.O.C. Northern Division.	
" 28.3.15	Capt. a/Major F. Henderson M.C. R.A.M.C. proceeded to N° 1 Convalescent Camp Cologne for acclimatisation	

Alban Capt RAMC
LIEUT. COLONEL R.A.M.C.
O.C. 8TH FIELD AMBULANCE.

160/35-Pr

No. 847.0.

13 AUG 1915

Army Form C. 2118.

WAR DIARY
or
INTELLIGENCE SUMMARY.

(Erase heading not required.) O.C. No. 8 Field Ambulance April 1919

Place	Date	Hour	Summary of Events and Information	Remarks and references to Appendices
EFFEREN	4/4/19		Capt Owens. U.S.A. Amc. proceed to 1st Replacement Depot- St Aignon, France.	
	5/4/19		Lieut. S.M. Meenin returned from leave.	
	2/4/19		Lt. Col. Benham proceeded on leave to U.K.	
	17/4/19		Lt Col Benham returned from leave.	
	19/4/19		CAPT. LLOYD Amc. proceeded on seven days Special leave to Belgium.	
	26/4/19		Capt Lloyd a.c. returned from leave.	
	30/4/19		There have been no features of interest during the month. Demobilisation continues very slow. The weather throughout the month has been cold to the time of year.	

30/4/19

J M Meenin
Lieut Col
Comdg No 8 F.A.

Army Form C. 2118.

WAR DIARY
or
INTELLIGENCE SUMMARY.

8th F.A.

Nov 1919

Place	Date	Hour	Summary of Events and Information	Remarks and references to Appendices
EFFEREN	11/5/19		Capt N Stewart, D.O. R.C. + Capt C.H. Lloyd, M.B. proceeded to England independently for demobilisation.	
	24/5/19		Capt a.d. Westmorland proceeded to 74th Bde R.F.A for duty.	
	28/5/19		Lieut Col G.R. Maurice, M.B. proceeded to England independently for demobilisation. All equipment + stores being packed + rendered to for handing in.	

3/5/19

R.R. Benham
Capt RM R.M.C
8th Fd Ambce

23 MAR 1920

L. Robinson's Narrative of experiences when

with No. 8 Field Ambulance during the

Retreat and subsequent months

No. 8 Field Ambulance.

Narrative of Lt. H. Robinson, R.A.M.C.

On August 7th. 1914 I was medically examined at the War Office for a Temporary Commission in the R.A.M.C. On August 8th. I signed the Contract, and was directed to report myself to the A.D.M.S. at Devonport next day. I got to Devonport on the afternoon of August 9th., and reported to the A.D.M.S. Colonel Mc.Leod, first thing next morning. Five other Temporarily Commissioned Officers went down to Devonport at the same time as I did. The six of us were detailed for Medical Charge of troops in forts round Plymouth. I was directed by Major Wade to proceed to the fort at Dunstone's Plantation. He could not tell me where this fort was as it was not shewn on the map, but advised me to take a cab to Plymstock and then ask the way. I went to Plymstock in a taxi, and asked half a dozen people in the village for Dunstone's Plantation. None of them had ever heard of it. At last I found an aged inhabitant who replied to my question:

"O yes! You mean Bunny's ears."

It turned out that a wood on the top of a hill near Plymstock had originally been known as Dunstone's Plantation, but that some wanderer returned from South America had re-christened it Buenos Ayres, and this had been corrupted by local usage into "Bunny's ears". The original name was almost completely forgotten. The taxi drove up the hill as far as it could, and then I got out and walked. At the top I found a party of Territorial Engineers very busy with tapes and pegs. The Officer in charge told me that he was then engaged in laying out the lines for the projected fort, which had been planned three years before, but never commenced, because the Government would not give any money. With the possibility of German warships in the Channel, the plans of the Fort had been got out of their pigeon-hole, and the Engineers were just starting to make it. He advised me to return to Plymstock and find the Captain in command of a company of Sherwood Foresters, which was billeted there.

I found this Officer, Captain Phelan, and he was very glad to get a Doctor as he had no one to see his sick men. He was a regular Officer, and was very much annoyed at being posted to a Battalion of Special Reserve. He and his subalterns were billeted in the largest house in the Village, and he told me to billet myself at the vicarage. Here I was received with open arms by the Vicar - Mr. Wreford - and his wife. I spent a very pleasant week with them at Plymstock, seeing a few sick every morning at Plymstock, both from Captain Phelan's Company and from another Company which was stationed at Oreston. I ate a great deal of fruit out of the Vicar's garden, and I took his two boys, Roger and Martin, out bathing. My duties were very light. I went once over to Plympton to see Lieutenant Fraser, who was one of the six who had travelled together from London to Devonport; the others were out of my reach.

17th. August 1914

On the 17th. August I was ordered by Telephone to report at once to the A.D.M.S. Devonport. As soon as I did so I was detailed to No. 8 Field Ambulance, then at St. Dunstan's Abbey Schools. I reported myself to the Commanding Officer - Lt. Colonel Stone, and discovered that I was required to complete Establishment owing to one of the Officers, Major Steele, having been passed as medically unfit for service. The Adjutant of No. 8 F.A. I found to be Captain Connell, whom I had met years before when returning from East Africa. I was posted to "C" Section, commanded by Major Foster.

The Mess of No. 8 Field Ambulance consisted of the following Officers: Lt. Colonel Stone, of whom I shall have more to say later. Major A.G. THompson was the second in command: at that time he had seen twenty-two year's service in the Army and was of standing for Lt. Colonel, only waiting a vacancy for his promotion. He was a man for whom I formed a profound admiration. Major Foster, to whose section I was posted, was considerably his junior in the Service, having only just been promoted from Captain. With him, too, I always had the most cordial relations. Besides these there was a Major of the Special Reserve, by name Dalby. He was a small wizened man, with a single eye-glass, and had been called up from practice at Torquay. He never had the physique for active service, and was of very little use to the Unit as he was soon completely knocked up. Capt. Connell was Adjutant. The remaining Officer of the Regular R.A.M.C. was Denyer, a very nice chap, but not possessed of much initiative. Besides these there was Capt. Darling of the Special Reserve, a rotund Scotsman of philosophic temperament, and a very good fellow. The Quartermaster, Tilbury, had just been promoted from Sergeant-Major, and was a very pleasant, quiet fellow. He took incessant chaff with great good nature, and got in an effective repartee about once a month. There was one other Temp. Commissioned Officer beside myself - Lt. Greenfield. We had two Padres attached to the Unit - the Rev. E.G. Macpherson, First Class Chaplain, and the Rev. H.C. Meeke. The former was Church of England, and had been born and brought up in the Army, he wasthrough the Siege of Ladysmith, and was senior C,of E. Chaplain in the whole of the original Expeditionary Force. He was a real good chap, but had trouble with his eye-sight, which eventually led to his return to England. Meeke was a Fourth Class Chaplain, Presbyterian, and about as unlike one's conception of a Presbyterian Chaplain as could possibly be imagined. He was a very witty Irishman, most excellent company, and one of the best.

We must have been the most middle-aged Mess that ever went on a European Campaign. Both Macpherson and Stone must have been over 50, and only four out of the twelve were under 40, and not a single one of us was less than 30. Ten out of the twelve were married, and seven of us were wearing Campaign medals. The Sergt.- Major of No.8 F.A. was called Lee, and had just been promoted from Staff-Sergeant. He was an excellent clerk, but not quite strong enough and hard-of-heart enough for/a Sergt.Major of recently mobilised Unit. Of the other N.C.O's. I shall speak in due time. Few of them knew each other by sight, or their Officers, nor did they know the men under them. The latter were a motley collection - some Regulars and some Special Reserve.

The attached Army Service Corps Drivers for our vehicles were an even more ill-assorted collection. They were mostly "crocks", and but a few of them knew anything about driving. This was an inevitable consequence of the system by which mobile Medical/Units of the Expeditionary Force depended for their transport/drivers upon men supplied by the Army Service Corps. Naturally the A.S.C. Officer whose business it was to detail men for this detached duty, took care to send all those who were useless to himself. The system in force in the Territorial Army was a much better one. In the Field Ambulances of that Force the transport men did not belong to the A.S.C. but were properly enlisted in the R.A.M.C. They were therefore trained by the Officers under whom they would have to serve when mobilised. Further, admission to the transport section was regarded as a privilege because it carried with it a penny a day extra pay and the right of wearing spurs. It was thus possible to punish a man for slackness by making him return to ordinary duty, and to reward a keen man by placing him in the transport section. This system was far preferable to the Regular Army system, and it is to be hoped that the latter will be abandoned.

A Field Ambulance is organised in three sections, each of which is complete in itself, with its own Ambulance wagons, General Service wagons, forage cart, water cart, operating equipment, Officers, N.C.O's. and men. It is thus possible to split a Field Ambulance into three parts, any one of which can be sent off at once on detached duty and is absolutely self-contained.

The Ambulance wagons allotted to No. 8 F.A. were of MarkVI type. This type was a very distinct improvement on all previous types. The wagons were full-lock, and could thus be turned within a very narrow space; they were provided with solid rubber tyres, and were the last word in horsed ambulance construction.

Almost as soon as I joined No. 8 F.A. I was absolutely horrified at the way in which everybody ignored the Commanding Officer, from the second in command down to the temporary Commissioned Lieutenant. But I soon found that this was inevitable, as otherwise nothing would ever have been done. Colonel Stone refused to sanction the formation of a Mess; he said that the Officers of each Section were to mess separately, and that they were to live on such rations as might be issued. As he commanded "A" Section in person, the Officers in that section could do nothing in the matter; but Major Thompson who commanded

"B" Section, decided that in the "B " Section Mess there should be something else besides bully beef and biscuits. The Officers of "B" Section accordingly subscribed a pound or so each, and they laid in a large stock of various delicacies.from the Army and Navy Stores in Plymouth. As soon as Foster heard of this he thought the example worth following, and I was sent into Plymouth to do the same.

On the 18th. August the Unit was due to leave Devonport by rail according to the Mobilization plans. Col. Stone would make no arrangements for getting away as he said he expected orders from the Railway Staff Officer. Major Thompson asserted that according to Mobilization Orders it was the Commanding Officer's business to find out when his train started, not the Railway Staff Officer's business to send him word about it. As Col. Stone refused to do anything, Major Thompson went first to the Station and found out the time at which our two trains started, and then to the A.D.M.S. to whom he stated the situation. The result was that Orders were eventually issued for the Unit to entrain. The greater part of the entrainment of the transport was done under the supervision of Greenfield and myself. We were considerably hampered by not knowing the names of the N.C.O's., but as we both had had experience in entraining mounted units of the Territorial Force we got through all right.

18th. August 1914.
19th. August 1914.

About midnight on August 18th. the trains started for Southampton, and we arrived at that port on the morning of the 19th. and proceeded to embark our transport and ourselves on the S.S. "Almerian" which sailed at 8 p.m. No. 9 F.A. was also on board the S.S. "Almerian". I soon discovered that the Adjutant Captain Roberts R.A.M.C. was an old student friend of mine. No. 9 F.A. had the old Mark V* wagons, and there was considerable debate between the two Units as to the respective merits of their wagons. Lt. Colonel Mc.Loughlin, who commanded No.9, was perfectly certain that the solid rubber tyres of ours would never stand the wear and tear of active service. On this point he turned out to be quite wrong, for at the end of six months we had not required to renew a single tyre. I imagine that No. 9

F.A. soon got heartily sick of their Mark V* wagons in France, as these have only a three-quarter lock, and it is practically impossible to turn them on a narrow or medium width road.

Padre Macpherson, being an old Campaigner, immediately took steps to promote the comfort of our Mess; he arranged with the Steward to provide dinner for No. 8 F.A., and he prevailed upon the Captain to lend us the Saloon for this purpose.   When No. 9 F.A. heard of this they copied our example, but had to wait until we had finished as there was barely room for our Mess in the Saloon. The only incident of the voyage across the Channel was a mild row between Mc.Loughlin and Thompson: McLoughlin gave an order to a man of No. 8 F.A. to do something which Thompson thought a man of No. 9 should have done.   Thompson objected, but was promptly squashed by McLoughlin, who reminded him very pointedly, that he, McLoughlin, was Thompson's senior in rank.   Stone of course ought to have taken the matter up, but as usual could not be persuaded to do anything.   The night was fine, and our passage across the Channel was very smooth, most of us slept on deck.

20th. AUGUST, 1914.

Next morning we found ourselves entering the estuary of the Seine, and we steamed all day up the River to Rouen.   The river turns and twists about in a broad flat valley enclosed by low hills, at one moment it is close to the northern row of hills, at another close to the Southern.   There were many steamers ahead of us on the river and many behind us, but owing to the rather serpentine course it was difficult to make sure sometimes whether any given ship was ahead of us or behind us.   At every ferry and hamlet there were crowds of women and children, all shouting at the top of their voices, Vive L'Angleterre; the Troops replied with "Tipperary", and "Are we down-hearted?"

We got to Rouen at tea-time and commenced to dis-embark. As at Southampton, the greater part of the work was done by Corporal Snape of the A.S.C.   But for this man I doubt if the job would ever have been done, as the A.S.C. Sergeant was absolutely useless. Snape worked like a nigger himself and managed to infuse a little energy into a few of his men.   He understood handling horses, and practically dis-embarked our seventy horses single-handed.   We did not complete dis-embarkation that evening, but finished it next

21st.,
August,
1914.

morning, the 21st. August, early. During disembarkation a rubber tyre came off one of our wagons. The only man who knew how to replace it was Tilbury the Quadrille.

Before leaving Rouen I went to a chemist's shop and purchased a glass hypodermic syringe with a bottle of morphia solution. This proved invaluable and the best investment I ever made in my life.

We marched through Rouen to a Rest Camp at Mont St. Aignan, where we found tents already pitched. This Camp was outside the town at the top of a steep hill, and our transport stuck for sometime half way up it. Probably the horses were somewhat stiff from the voyage, and they were in any case a scratch collection, hastily commandeered in England, and driven by men very few of whom knew anything about driving. My own horse was a grey pony, which I had to take because I was the last to join and that was the only horse left. He had been starved by his civilian owner, and brutally illtreated. He was a small pony, and I thought that if I rode him much he would very probably break down. The consequence was that I marched on foot practically the whole of the Retreat from Mons, and the pony later on turned out very well and carried me easily.

22nd.
August,
1914.

On the 22nd August we entrained at Rouen. We found the French trucks exceedingly ill-adapted for/our wagons. Their system is to load vehicles by means of/ramps leaned up against the side of the open truck. This system means frightfully hard work when the vehicles are heavy, and leads to great delay in loading. Furthermore, the system by means of which the wagons are fixed to the truck in France is a very bad one, and causes much unnecessary damage to the wheels of the vehicles. As we were all strange to these abominable French trucks our entrainment was naturally slow. We got off about noon, and travelled via Amiens. At one station through which we passed we saw a French Hospital train being fitted up. We had one stop to water the horses, but apart from this went straight through to Valenciennes, which we reached at 1 a.m. on August 23rd.

23rd.
August
1914.

Here we found the only French Railway Staff Officer I have ever met who knew anything about his job. He was very keen and useful, and helped us greatly in detraining. Probably all the good ones they kept for their own Army.

8.

We left Valenciennes by road about sun-rise. We were to have marched direct from Valenciennes to Mons along a straight road, but before we started news came that Uhlan patrols had cut this road, so we were despatched along the road leading E.S.E. from Valenciennes to Bavai. To the best of my recollection we turned off this road through Wargnies Le Grand. At one of the villages before we reached this point - which must have been either Curgies or Jenlain - I was leading my horse along the side of the road when I suddenly came across an Officer whose face I knew. He was standing by a car watching our Unit as it went past. I was so astonished at recognising Sir John French, under whom I served for a long time in South Africa, that I entirely forgot to salute him. After passing through Wargnies our route was roughly N.E., but I cannot remember through what villages we passed. I know we went through a small forest, and I know we arrived eventually in the afternoon within sight of Mons. My impression is that we probably passed through Wasmes and Paturages, but I am not certain of this. I know we passed close to several mine-dumps, and can remember that some of our Ambulance wagons were sent off to bring in wounded from a small house. I did not go on this duty, and after that I can remember passing through Frameries. During the earlier part of this long march we experienced enthusiastic hospitality from the Belgians, who gave us fruit, cigars and other presents as we passed through their villages. In one street I was walking with Greenfield when two pretty girls passed us; one of them made a dash at Greenfield and insisted on giving him a handkerchief, which he accepted. Later on he found inside the handkerchief a note informing him of the donor's name and address, and asking him to write to her. They made no attempt to give me any handkerchiefs.

When we left Frameries, I believe we must have gone N.E. and then S.E.; at any rate I am pretty sure we made a considerable detour before we reached Noirchain, where we found the Headquarters of the 3rd. Division. It was now late in the evening, and both men and animals were pretty tired. We had two or three wagons full of wounded, and we all bivouacked in the open on some piles of hay and straw. There was some discussion in the Mess as to how many miles we had travelled from Valenciennes; some said as much as 40, but I do not think myself it was more than 32 or 34 miles.

24th. August. 1914.

We left Noirchain at 5 a.m. on August 24th. and took the main road leading S.S.W. towards the Belgian frontier. Soon after passing the boundary we marched across the battle field of Malplaquet, where we saw a monument to commemorate that Battle. We trekked all morning and arrived at Bavai about noon. The last three or four miles of the road was W.S.W.; the road was fairly free from traffic and therefore marching was comparatively easy. Just outside Bavai we parked the wagons in a large field, and not realising that we had any further to go, I had my bath unpacked and had a cold bath. As most of the Officers had foolishly left their canvas baths in England, they were very envious of my having a bath, and three or four of them borrowed it and had baths themselves. Then we got some firstclass omelettes in a little pub, and were very disgusted to get an order to march again at 2 p.m.. Just as the Ambulance was marching through Bavai, an order came that two of the Officers were to proceed to a Convent in the town, and were to dress all the British wounded in the Convent. Connell and myself were selected for this job, and we were ordered to follow the Ambulance as soon as we had dressed all the wounded we could find. We spent the whole afternoon in the Convent dressing the wounded, most of whom were light cases; about six o'clock all the wounds were dressed. I should say here that an Officer of No. 7 F.A. was there as well as Connell and myself.

Not Lt. Hamilton as he was captured at Mons.

Having carried out our orders, Connell and I left the Convent; I afterwards found out that the Officer of No. 7, whose name was Hamilton, did not leave the Convent, but stayed there all night, and was captured by the Germans next morning. Whether his orders were different from ours, or whether a fresh lot of wounded, which detained him, came in directly we had left, I do not know. As I was crossing the street outside the Convent, a tall Officer with a Staff Cap came up to me and said:

"Oh! You're a doctor! Come along with me."

He took me into the principal Hotel in Bavai, and shewed me a Major of the Gordon Highlanders lying in an easy chair. He was shot through the shoulder, and the Colonel who had accosted me said:

"I want to know if this Officer can be taken thirty miles in a motor car?"

The Gordon Major's wounds had been dressed, so this was rather a difficult question. However, he was a big, powerful man, and after feeling his pulse and taking stock of him I said:

"It is most undesirable that this Officer should be moved; you must give me an idea how great the urgency is."

This was an artful attempt to extract a little information from the Staff on the Military situation, but the tall Officer was quite equal to the occasion.

He smiled, and said;

"You must take it from me that I want to send him, and I want to know whether he will survive the journey; I cannot tell you more than that."

I said:

"I think he will survive the journey, but I do not think he ought to try it unless the need is very great."

The Staff Colonel replied:

"That will do, you can go."

As I was leaving the Hotel I asked a subaltern who the Staff Colonel was.

"Oh," he said, "that's Colonel Seeley, the late Minister for War."

I may add here that the wounded Major, whose name was Allan, evidently got safely through his journey, because I saw the announcement of his marriage early in 1916. He was one of the patients whom our wagons had picked up at Mons the day before.

Just as I left the hotel a Frenchwoman asked me to see a wounded English officer in her house. I went with her into a house close by, and found a young artillery subaltern who had been wounded just on one side of the bridge of his nose. He was coughing up blood, and I could feel the bullet which had wounded him under the skin of his neck not far above the collar bone. He had lost a good deal of blood, and was in a state of great nervous excitement: all the poor boy could think of was his two guns which he had got safely away from Mons. He had not been able to rejoin his battery or to report the saving of his guns, and his one anxiety was to let his Major know that he had got the guns away. It was obviously impossible to let the poor boy travel except upon an Ambulance wagon - of which there were none available at that time - so I gave him a dose of morphia, reassured his anxiety about the guns, and did my best to cheer him up before I left him. Whether he was left in Bavai, or whether, later on, any one was able to take him away, I never found out.

It was now sunset, and I proceeded to follow No. 8 Field Ambulance down the main road towards Le Quesnoy. The road was absolutely jammed with transport of every description - guns, ambulances, transport wagons, Infantry, and troops of all kinds. The block was so great that the transport could only move a few yards at a time before halting. By sticking to the ditch most of the time I managed to get along fairly well, although it was not easy when darkness fell. I arrived at the village of Bermeries about having no notion until then where No. 8 F.A. was.. Fortunately I ran across one of the privates belonging to the Ambulance, and he directed me to the bivouack, which was in a field. On the way I reconnoitred the village fairly thoroughly as I had some difficulty in finding the bivouack. Connell had rejoined the Ambulance some time before I did, because he had not been stopped by Colonel Seeley. I had something to eat, and went to sleep in the grass about mid-night, but was very disgusted when at 1 a.m. on August 25th. an orderly came into the field with a message for Colonel Stone to resume the march at once. As I was lying next to Col. Stone of course this wakened me up, and we had to turn to to get the men out and the wagons in-spanned. We left Bermeries by the road to Le Quesnoy. Soon after leaving the village the road happened to run due W. and the Colonel got very worried as he thought he was on the wrong road. He and I were together at the head of the column, and he expressed his doubts about the road to me. As I had reconnoitred the village in the darkness before, I was quite sure we were on the right road, and told him so. However, he would not believe it, and asked me to get my compass out to find the direction we were going in. As it was a fine night and every star was shining in the sky, I told him that there was no need for a compass. The Pole Star was high in the heavens on our right hand. I pointed it out. He looked at it, and said:

"I do not think that is the Pole Star, are you quite sure?"

I managed to reassure him, and we kept along the road. This Officer was completely incapable of reading a map or of finding his way anywhere; he always got lost if left to himself, and one of the Sergeants who was a bit of a wag, by the name of Hurst, christened him " The Pathfinder."

We left the main road some time during the morning, branching off it to the East of Le Quesnoy. I fancy that we passed through Potelle and Ghissignies and Witerlant, but am not quite sure. At any rate we out-spanned for the mid-day halt at Vendegies.

It was on this march that another curious incident occurred. I had been sent forward, mounted, to find a suitable place for one of our hourly halts. I found a small farm where there was a well, and in a field alongside there was a milk-maid milking a herd of cows; I told her I would buy the whole of the milk, and then went back to the Field Ambulance. Thompson was at the head of it, and I told him what I had done. He was very pleased, and as soon as we arrived at the farm, he and others of the Officers bought the milk and distributed it to the men, each of whom had three-quarters of a pint. As they were very done with the incessant marching they were very glad of this drink of milk; but, when the distribution was about half way through, Colonel Stone, who had been behind, came up and found out what was going on. He immediately made a great fuss, and said it was most imprudent of Thompson and myself to let the men drink the milk because of the danger of typhoid fever. As we had seen the milk drawn fresh from the udders of the cows we did not think the risk was so great as Colonel Stone imagined. At Vendegies we out-spanned in an orchard which I had selected when sent forward for this purpose. As soon as we got into the orchard both Officers and men began to eat the ripe fruit - plums, and apples and pears - off the trees. Hardly had we begun to do this when Colonel Caton Jones, the A.D.M.S., came into the orchard. He did not see that the Officers were eating the fruit but he saw some of the men doing so, and he immediately made a great fuss, rated the men unmercifully, and shouted at the top of his voice:

"Don't you know that the Duke of Wellington had men shot in the Peninsula War for less than this!"

Just at this point one of the Officers, I forget which, came forward and told the A.D.M.S. that the owner of the orchard had given free permission for the Troops to take his fruit. Whether this statement was true, or was a happy improvisation, I do not know, but it entirely spiked the guns of the A.D.M.S.. While we were in this orchard we saw one of the earliest aeroplane battles of the War; a French and English German aeroplane were circling round each other high above our heads, and we could hear the faint pop of their shots at each other. After a while the German machine, which was a Taube monoplane, had his radiator pierced by the Frenchman. He had to come down, and landed in a field near an English Battalion, / the Lincolns. We heard afterwards that he managed to escape into a wood, but his machine of course was captured.

In the afternoon we left Vendegies and travelled S.W. through Ovillers, Amerval and Neuvilly. Whilst on this march we got a view in the distance of the town of Le Cateau. We also passed some French Dragoons who were going in the opposite direction; this was quite enough to start the rumour that the French Army was coming up to help us, but it is now a matter of history that nothing of the kind took place. Neuvilly lies in a valley through which runs a pretty little stream. After passing through the village we made for Troisville, arriving about sunset. We passed over a fairly high hill, on the way and bivouacked in a farm near the Southern end of Troisvilles. After dark a Section of No.7 Field Ambulance also bivoucked on the same farm. They were separated from us by a barbed wire fence, and it was too dark to see their faces, but I can remember that Major Maurice of No. 7 F.A. was one of the Officers of that Section.

The junior Officers of No. 8 F.A. made themselves a comfortable doss in a workshop. Late in the evening there was a conference in the farmhouse, and for some reason or other the Greenfield and myself and one or two other junior Officers of No. 8 F.A. arrived at the conference before the Majors of either No.7 or No.8 F.A's. We found the A.D.M.S., Col. Stone and Col. Kennedy - the Commander of No.7.F.A. - with a large map spread out on the farmer's table. The three of them decided to set the map, and to my dismay their notion of setting a map was to put a compass on it and turn the compass round until the North point of the Compass - not the needle - corresponded with the North axis of the map. In the upshot, Greenfield and I had to show these very senior Officers of the R.A.M.C. how a map should be set. Nor did any of the three know whereabouts on the map our farmhouse was. As I had watched the village as we came through it and compared it with the map, I was pretty confident that I knew where we were. I pointed out to the A.D.M.S. a spot on the map which I believed to be our position, and I said to him:

"If I am right, we shall find on leaving the front door of this house a road to Bertry about fifty yards to the left, and another road, leading to Bertry also, about the same distance to the right. If we find these two roads then we know where we are on the map."

They were so uncertain of their own position, that they actually took the trouble to go out into the street in accordance with this suggestion. Both the roads I had predicted were found, so that settled the question of where we were. After the conference, in which only the senior Officers took part, we resorted to our doss in the work-shop, and prepared for a comfortable night. Just as we were snuggling down, the Colonel sent an order that all Officers were to sleep alongside the wagons. As a matter of fact, I, personally, slept in a wagon - on a seat.

26th. August, 1916.

We had an early turn-out on the morning of the 26th. August. The A.D.M.S. sat on the seat of one of the wagons and addressed the crowd of Officers in the dawn, explaining the plan of operations for the day. I cannot remember whether Colonel Kennedy or Major Maurice attended this conference or not; but at any rate, No 8 Field Ambulance left Troisvilles very early in the morning and passed through Bertry, where the Ambulance wagons of one or two sections were despatched towards Audencourt, and the rest continued to the village of Montigny. When we got near Montigny I was sent on ahead to pick out a suitable field for the transport. The only instruction I got was that in case of a Retreat our road was that leading towards Clary. Acting on this hint, I picked out a nice field with a good water supply just at the edge of the village on the /Clary road, and here the wagons, other than the remaining ambulance wagons, were outspanned. The horses were not unharnessed though they were allowed to graze.

We all set to work to prepare accommodation for the reception of many wounded. We took the Parish Church, two schools, and a small Protestant Chapel for this purpose, and filled them all with mattresses lent us by the villagers. We also collected eggs and milk, and made a lot of boiling water for beef tea and surgical purposes. We also set some of the men to work to make improvised splints out of pieces of wood, and I think some 30 or 40 odd splints were thus prepared. The remaining Ambulance wagons went out towards Caudry. I stayed in the village, and after a time the wounded began to arrive. We spent all the morning in dressing them, and my syringe and morphia were in constant request. I had the satisfaction of seeing a man with a badly shattered arm go fast asleep within a quarter of an hour of having his arm put on one of our improvised splints and a dose of morphia. We took turns to go to the Inn for lunch; and in the afternoon, as many wounded were arriving, we unpacked our operating equipment and began to do operations. I had completed an amputation of the thigh for a horrible shell wound, and was just about to tackle a similar one of the foot, when the A.D.M.S. came into the School at 4 p.m. and said:

"You must all leave here in five minutes, the Germans are coming in."

This was rather a "facer." My patient was already under chloroform, and I had already got the knife in my hand. I said to the A.D.M.S.:

"What about this poor chap on the table?"

He said:

"Put him back on his mattress, we can't take him away."

The orderlies threw all the equipment, sterilisers, instruments, dressings, etc. into the G.S. wagons, as there was no time to pack things. I washed my hands, put on my coat, and was just leaving the School when I met Major Thompson entering it. He said:

"Good-bye, old chap, I've got to stop here."

I forget what I answered: I was totally flabbergasted by the news. I shook hands with him, and I have never seen him since. It turned out that the A.D.M.S. had given Colonel Stone instructions that one Officer and six orderlies were to be left in Montigny in charge of the wounded. We could remove only a very few of the latter as all, or nearly all, our ambelance wagons were out on the field collecting there. Colonel Stone on receipt of this order should, of course, have left behind either the junior Officer of the Ambulance, or the one who was of least use to him. As a matter of fact the junior Officer was Greenfield, to whom I was only three days senior; but instead of leaving one of the juniors he actually left his own Second in Command, and easily the best Officer in the whole Ambulance. Why the A.D.M.S. permitted this to be done I have never understood. His own account of the whole affair, which I heard from him long afterwards does not throw much light on the mystery. One of the six orderlies who remained behind was my servant - a man called Greenlees, who had served in S. Africa, and had been a very useful servant to me during the four or five days the Campaign had lasted. He volunteered for the duty of remaining behind, which does not say much for his opinion of his master.

We put a few of the lightly wounded men on top of the baggage in the General Service wagons, but the great majority of them (about 120 I fancy) had to be left behind, as I have said before. If we had known that the Staff contemplated a retirement that day, we could have sent some of the wounded to the railway station at Bertry, but we were all given to understand until four P.M. that there was no chance of a Retreat. Had we been equipped with motor ambulances instead of horsed ambulances we could of course have saved practically the whole of our patients. We left Montigny within the five minutes allotted by the A.D.M.S. My groom, who was an awful ass, brought me my horse not properly girthed up. I did not notice this in my hurry, and at once mounted the horse. The saddle twisted round, and I took a very nasty toss. I split the right knee of my riding breeches, and barked about two inches of skin off my right elbow. I felt very queer for about half an hour, and got on to a wagon alongside Padre Macpherson. However, the fresh air soon revived me, and I was none the worse for the tumble.

We retreated up the hill towards Clary, and when we had got halfway to that village somebody said:
"Look at Montigny!"

When we looked round we saw the village was on fire in about six or seven places. It had been shelled by the Germans the moment after we left. We heard eventually that Thompson was taken prisoner by the Germans, and was detained by them for ten months in violation of the Geneva Convention. What happened to the six orderlies I do not know, probably they were released at the same time as Major Thompson. Altogether we lost that day over 40 men - killed, wounded and prisoners - out of a total strength of 240 odd. We had no Officer casualties except Thompson.

After leaving Clary we turned off the high road and went across some fields. I am uncertain of our exact route, all I can remember is seeing some of our own guns taking the same line as we did. We passed to Westward of the Bois de Pinon, and regained a good road at Elincourt. Thence we turned due West to Malincourt and then due South again to Beaurevoir. When nearing this latter village, the Colonel missed the proper turning and took us about two miles out of our way. I happened to be near him at the head of the Column, and went up to him to tell him that we had missed the proper road. It was, however, too late then to rectify the error, because there was a great mass of transport on the road behind us. I ran back as hard as I could to the turning we had missed in order to stop the next Unit from committing the same mistake as we had done. Fortunately I got to the turning just as the leading vehicles of the next Unit arrived there, and told the Officer in charge that our Ambulance was on the wrong road. We got to Beaurevoir about 11 p.m. after marching hard since 4. It was pouring with rain, and pitch dark. This little village was absolutely packed with a miscellaneous collection of many Units of the 3rd. Division. It was impossible to drive through the village as the whole road was completely blocked. Col. Stone had only orders to proceed to Beaurevoir, so he left the Unit to try to find the Staff and get further orders. Luckily we had come to rest just outside a small Inn. Three or four of the Officers went into the Inn, and asked what they had to eat. They produced one or two eggs and three or four of the enormous French loaves about four or five feet long; they had also got some beer. We called the men in one by one, and every man was given a mug of beer and a crust of bread. I presided at the bread counter, breaking off lumps of bread as nearly as possible of an equal size, and distributing them as the men filed in. A good number of the men were too tired to want anything to eat; all they wanted was to go to sleep - which they did, under the wagons and on the pavement in the pouring rain. It was perhaps lucky that many of them did not come for these rations, because the supply only just lasted out for those who did come.

27th. August 1914.

I see in my pocket diary that we left Beaurevoir at midnight; my recollection is that it was 1 a.m., but probably the diary is more likely to be right, at any rate we left the village after stopping one or two hours in it. Our orders were to follow the Unit in front of us, which happened to be No. 9 Field Ambulance or a part of it. As we left the village we discovered that some of our missing ambulance wagons were in the village, but the congestion of traffic was so great that it was impossible for us to pick them up. We left Beaurevoir by a road leading South, and after slow progress owing to the accumulation of traffic, we went up a steep hill and arrived on what was called the Roman Road, the general direction of which is N.E. and S.W. Here, the wagon just in front of us turned to the left - i.e. N.E.. Our only instructions were to follow the Unit in front, but we knew perfectly well that our proper line of retreat was to the right. It was pitch dark, and a hasty confabulation was held over the map by the light of matches. With some difficulty we persuaded Col. Stone to disobey his orders and go to the right. It turned out afterwards that No. 9 F.A., which we were following, had also gone to the right, but that two or three of the wagons at the tail end of No. 9 had been specially detailed to convey some wounded to a small railway station, which was reached by turning to the left, so that if we had obeyed our instructions and turned to the left we should have been wrong. The wagons which made this turn to the left, and so nearly misled us, were, I believe, under the command of Lieut. Tulloch.

We kept on down the main road as far as Estrees. There we came across a Staff Officer who turned us off the Roman Road. He provided us with a peasant lad to act as a guide, and we took

a round-about route through country roads all night until the
morning. I believe we passed through Levergies during this -
the early morning of August 27th. - but what other villages we
traversed I do not know. It was on this morning that we came
across an extraordinary collection of jettisoned stores by the
road-side. For at least a mile, probably more than that, there
were piles every ten yards of British shells, ammunition, horse-
shoes, saddlery and many other articles of equipment for mounted
troops. We could not understand what this meant, but thought
that an artillery position must have been selected beforehand/somewhere near
to this place, and that these munitions had been left behind for
the guns. Much later on we heard from the gunners that this
supposition was not correct. What had happened was that the
Commander of an ammunition Column had lost his nerve and his head,
and had ordered every blessed thing he had got to be thrown down
by the wayside and abandoned. We also heard that he was court-
martialled for this, and severely punished, but I do not know
whether this is true.

We arrived about breakfast time on August 27 th. at the
outskirts of the large town of St. Quentin. Here we were blocked
by traffic in front of us, and halted for more than an hour. We
seized the opportunity to get some breakfast. Whilst I was
standing in the road at this point, a car came along and got
blocked like the rest of us. The man inside put his head out
of the window and got into conversation with me. He had a Staff
cap on, but was wearing a Coat Warm British with no badges of
rank, and I had no idea who he was. I found out afterwards that
he was Brig. General Wing, who was commanding the artillery
of the 3rd. Division. He was long afterwards promoted Major
General in command of a Division, and was killed at the Battle of
Loos. General Wing asked me a few questions about our experiences, and ended by asking me what I thought of the show? I said
"I hope to God I shall never see the British Army run away as fast
as this again."

He laughed, and said:

"I hope so too."

Considering that he had just lost twenty guns at the

battle of Le Cateau - of which I was unaware at the time - he was remarkably cheerful, and I may add that he was exceedingly popular throughout the Division. After breakfast we went on into the town where a number of Staff Officers were controlling the traffic like the policemen at Piccadilly Circus. There were several roads leading into the town, and each road was one mass of transport of all descriptions. The Staff were sorting out the different Divisions, and directing them by which road they were to leave St. Quentin. As many of the Units had got badly mixed it was a very slow job getting through the congested streets of the town. The first part of No. 8 Field Ambulance got through a gap in the traffic and proceeded to a rendezvous on the main road towards Ham, overlooking the village of Dallon. The rear wagons with which I was, had to wait their opportunity to get through. As we approached the exit of the town the Colonel decided to take three ambulance wagons full of wounded to the station and deposit them on a train there of which we had heard news. He accordingly ordered me to follow the main body of the Ambulance in charge of the other wagons we had with us, whilst he turned off to the left towards the Station, taking Greenfield with him. Hardly had I parted from him when he sent a message after me to tell me to halt where I was till his return. I knew that this might mean half an hour or half a day, so I just halted my wagons till he was out of sight, and then went on. As it happened, the Colonel on returning from the railway Station lost his way altogether, as usual, and in spite of Greenfield's protests he insisted on leaving St. Quentin by a road which took him towards the Germans. He was completely lost as far as we were concerned for about three days, and everybody hoped he was lost for good; but Greenfield found the way for him, and eventually he turned up again.

Greenfield had a great story when he came back about Colonel Stone's sleep-walking. He said that one night, whilst away on this jaunt, the Colonel must have started to walk in his sleep. At any rate, he left the bivouack, wearing nothing but his shirt and a pair of socks, and then, having presumably wakened up, he could not find the wagons again, so he lay down in the ditch, just as he was, and went to sleep. The night was dark; and in the morning he was found asleep in the ditch about twenty yards from the wagons.

When we arrived at the rendezvous near Dallon we were provided by the Staff with stencilled copies of the areas allotted to each of the Units of the 3rd. Division, excluding the Infantry. The ground thus parcelled out was a huge stubble field with very heavy soil. The only patch of grass was a small field adjoining it, which according to the plans belonged to No.8 Field Ambulance and the Divisional Engineers. On arriving, we discovered a Battery of Artillery in possession of our half of the field. We pointed out to them that they had got our ground, but as they had out-spanned their guns, they declined to move. We therefore appropriated the other half of the field which by rights belonged to the Engineers. Fortunately the latter did not turn up to claim it.

After lunch we took the road once more, but our heavy wagons had great difficulty in negotiating the loamy soil of the stubble field across which we had to pass. Two of the heaviest got hopelessly stuck, and Major Foster, who was now commanding the Ambulance in the absence of Col. Stone and of Major Thompson, left me behind to get them out. He also left Corporal Snape, and after a lot of manhandling/ the wheels and flogging the horses, we got the first wagon out on to the road; but the second one could not be moved for love or money, so we had to unload it, push it out, and reload it again. I found a French peasant, who, for a few coppers, gave us a hand at this job and worked very well. We then followed on and caught up the Ambulance a few miles down the road.

We continued on the main road S.W. towards Ham, passing through Roupy and near to Fluquieres, and /Aubigny. The road was fairly full of wheeled transport, but we did not have many checks until we reached Ham in the early evening. We crossed the Somme on the N. edge of the town, whereas the Canal which takes most of its waters passes on the S. side. In the town there was a considerable block in the traffic, and in the market place there was a large pile of rations which were being distributed by an A.S.C. Officer to every soldier who asked for them, irrespective of his Unit or any other consideration. I secured a tin of bully beef and some biscuits. Just past the market place we got blocked again, and whilst waiting to go on a soldier came out of a side street, and asked me for some dressings for a wounded Officer. I thought I had better go and investigate this case myself, so I took a satchel of dressings off the nearest wagon, and went with the soldier. We went a little way down a side street and then turned into a court-yard at the back of a fair sized house. Here I found Major Fielding of No. 7 Field Ambulance, in attendance upon an Officer who was lying upon the ground with his brains blown out. It was he who had sent out for the dressings, and he told me that the Officer was Colonel Boileau chief Staff Officer of the 3rd Division, and that he had just committed suicide. We dressed his wounds together, and Major Fielding took charge of all his papers and belongings. As there was nothing more we could do for him I left the court-yard, with Major Fielding still in charge of the case. I heard afterwards that Colonel Boileau died the same night in the convent at Ham. *(Major Fielding was an old friend, as he had been adjutant of the School of Instruction in London when I passed for Captain in my Territorial days.)*

When I came out the Ambulance was still blocked in the street but we soon moved on, and turned off S.E. through the town and across the canal. This, as it turned out, was not the right direction, but we had no orders except to find ourselves a billet in the town. Shortly after crossing the canal we came to a large beet sugar factory, and Major Foster and I explored it. We thought it a good enough billet for the Ambulance, so we took the whole Commando inside. The wagons were parked in the large yard, the men established themselves in the work-shops, and the Officers took possession of the Manager's house. Here, the two women who had been left in charge looked after us very well, and we had a good rest. Soon after we had got into the sugar factory, a Section of one of the Cavalry Field Ambulances turned up and asked if they might share the billet. As there was plenty of room we of course agreed, and the three Officers of that Ambulance spent the night there with us. Major Foster and

I shared a bed together, as there were not enough beds for every man to have one to himself.

28th. August 1914.

In the morning we were still without orders as to the day's march, but one of the Sergeants, by name Hurst, happening to go into the town, found the bridge over the canal being mined by the Engineers. He immediately got it into his head that the Germans were upon us, and he ran back to the factory shouting out that the Bridge was being mined, and we must leave at once if we did not want to be captured. As a matter of fact this was quite a false alarm. We were already on the opposite side of the Canal to the enemy, and there was no occasion for panic. However, we could not tell exactly what the situation was, so Major Foster took the prudent course of ordering an immediate march. As my servant had been left behind at Montigny, I had to do up my own valise, and this made me a little bit late in the hasty scramble. The result was that as I ran out into the yard with my valise on my shoulder, the last wagon was in the act of leaving the factory, and the whole of the men had already left. I threw my valise on to the wagon, and then walked round the yard to see that nothing had been left behind. I could not see any of our gear anywhere about, so followed the Ambulance towards the Canal. When I got to the Canal I found they had turned off Westward on the towing path on the Southern side of the Canal, and following the same path, I presently came to one of our wagons in the Canal with the horses almost up to their withers. The transport Sergeant whose name was Blake, was standing on the bank holding my horse, and the wagon drivers were making very half-hearted attempts to get the horses out. Sergeant Blake, as usual, was doing very little. By gingering up the men, and ordering the traces to be cut, I soon got the two horses loose, and after a struggle we got them on to the Bank; but meanwhile the wagon had been sinking deeper and deeper into the thick mud of the Canal, and by this time it was nearly out of sight. This wagon was one which usually carried the Officers' valises, and many of the mens' kits, also some of the C.O's. official property, such as the Stationery Box. As it happened that morning several of the Officers' kits had been put on other wagons - my own included - so the whole mess was not bereft of its valises. A few of the mens' kits were salved, but most of them were lost. It was obvious that without all sorts of appliances which we had not got and a great many men, it was impossible to rescue the wagon, so I left it where it was and sent the horses on to follow the Ambulance. I then turned to Sergeant Blake, who was still holding my grey pony, which had neither saddle nor bridle, and I asked him what he was doing with it, and why it was not saddled? He said that in the hurry of departure he had not been able to find a man to saddle it, but he also told me that he knew where the saddlery was. He had left it in an empty sugar-vat in the factory. I gave Sergeant Blake the rough side of my tongue for his laziness and folly; and knowing what a fool he was, I took the horse myself and went back to the factory instead of sending him. I found my saddle and bridle in the place he had described, minus the two saddle wallets, which I never saw again. Fortunately the pony stood quite quietly to be bridled and saddled - which was contrary to his usual custom.

I then retraced my steps and followed the Ambulance along the main road leading due S. from Ham. The road was not very full of transport, so I soon caught it up. The Colonel was very much upset by the loss of this wagon, when he found out about it later on. What chiefly weighed on his mind was the loss of his Official Diary of the Unit, of which he had at that time already filled in 80 pages. He used to put down the name of every Unit that passed us on the road, or that we passed, and generally had his Diary out of the Wagon three or four times a day to fill it up. He also lost his kit and a 40 guinea gold watch, which he had been foolish enough to bring from England.

At the first village we came to which must have been Muille Villette, the D.A.D.M.S. - Major Chopping - sent me back to Ham to find out how many empty beds there were in the Hospital attached to the Convent there. I went back on foot as I thought the road was so congested that I should not be able to get along on horse-back. As it turned out there was not such a block as I had thought, and I should have done better to have taken my horse. I went back into the town, crossing the bridge over the Canal, which the Engineers were then mining - not the same bridge as that over which we had crossed on the previous evening - and found the Convent Hospital. It was here that Colonel Boileau had died the night before. They told me the number of empty beds they had; and I returned along the road I had come.

When I caught up the Ambulance and Major Chopping I was rather disappointed to find that my errand had been useless, as the D.A.D.M.S. had changed his mind, and no longer thought of leaving any wounded in that Hospital.

We kept on down the main road to Noyon, bearing a little to the West of South through the village of Guiscard. Before reaching Noyon we turned off to the West to the village of Genvry and camped on a farm just South of that hamlet. All along this march the road was very much congested with guns and other traffic. It was a typical pavé road, such as are all the main roads (over) which we passed. The stone-sets down the middle of the road stand heavy traffic very well, though they bump a good deal and make an awful noise; but the weak point of these pavé roads is that the macadam on the two sides of the central pavé is badly laid, and is very soon cut to pieces when a large army passes over it. On this road, as on many others of the high roads in the Ile de France, there is a constant succession of apple and pear trees on both sides of the road. These were in full bearing, and a good deal of the fruit was fairly ripe, though the quality of it was nothing to boast of; but at any rate it helped the men to bear the fatigues of marching in the broiling August weather which prevailed, and was a welcome addition to our rations.

The next village North of Genvry is Crisolles, whither I was sent with a message for somebody - I think it was the A.D.M.S., but I am not sure. Crisolles was full of artillery.

Most of our missing ambulance wagons had by this time rejoined excepting those still away with Colonel Stone. At this camp we learned that the rumour of the latter's capture by the Germans, which we had heard, was not true. There was considerable disappointment in the camp. Here, both men and horses got a very decent rest, which they all badly needed.

29th. August 1914.

On the next day, August 29th., we did a morning march through Noyon to Cuts. We skirted the Northern edge of Noyon, and left by Route Nationale No. 38 instead of by the direct route to Cuts through Pontoise. The direct road was required for the Infantry, etc., and after marching due East a little way from Noyon we struck on to a country road at a railway crossing and passed through Morlaincourt, Varesnes and RueMillon. At Varesnes we crossed the Oise. Here, as everywhere else, sappers were preparing the bridge for blowing it up. We got to Cuts early in the afternoon, and parked the wagons in a field just North of the village, with Nos. 7 and 9 Field Ambulances. I was sent to the 2nd. Army Corps Headquarters which were at the Chateau of Cuts, to see Captain Wroughton, and give my account of Colonel Boileau's death. As I was leaving I met Colonel - now Surgeon-General - Porter, the D.D.M.S. 2nd. Corps. He stopped and spoke to me - asked me who I was, and what I belonged to. I cannot remember whether I told him that I was Temp. Commissioned, but in any case he could easily have guessed it from my age and rank and medal ribbons. At any rate he asked me a question which he certainly would not have asked had I been a regular R.A.M.C. Officer. He said:

"What do you think of Colonel Stone?"

This question in itself showed that the higher authorities were aware of some of the latter's shortcomings. I am afraid my reply was somewhat theatrical; I said:

"I have served sixteen years in the Regulars and auxiliary forces, under many Commanding Officers, but I have never yet seen the equal of this man for incompetence."

Colonel Porter asked me for some instances; I told him the incident of the Pole Star and one or two other cases, and we then parted.

We left Cuts at 10 p.m. and had a very long and tiring night-march to Vic-sur-Aisne. I cannot even remember by what road we left Cuts, the whole march is nothing but a nightmare in my recollection. This night a trouble, which had been increasing steadily ever since we left Mons reached its maximum. This was

the unauthorised riding of the R.A.M.C. orderlies upon the
ambulance wagons and other transport. The men were naturally
tired by the incessant marching and fatigues of the Retreat;
but the horses were just as exhausted or even more so, and it
was common prudence to spare them in every conceivable
way, as no one could foresee how long the retreat would last.
According to the usual custom of the Service the wagon orderly
of each vehicle is allowed to travel on the vehicle instead of
having to march, but no one else, excepting the driver, may
escape marching. In War time peace conventions ought to be
disregarded if they interfere with military efficiency, and I
tried to persuade the Colonel that no wagon orderlies ought
to be allowed to ride on the wagons. The matter was discussed amongst the Officers, and for a short time the Colonel
did forbid this practice. But he afterwards rescinded his
order, and allowed the orderlies on the wagons. If the practice had stopped at that the matter would have been trivial,
but a large number of men who had no right whatever to be on
the wagons would take every opportunity of getting on them when
they thought they would not be detected, and during night marches
detection was exceedingly difficult. It was the work of two
Officers to travel up and down the line of transport during the
night, turning the men off the wagons. On one occasion I hauled
six men off a G.S. wagon, and five off the one behind it. These
wagons were very heavily loaded and were an even greater strain
upon the horses than the ambulance wagons. If we had known the
N.C.O's better, we should of course have held them responsible
for checking this practice, but our hasty mobilisation prevented
us from knowing the N.C.O's., just as it prevented the N.C.O's
from knowing the men. My impression is that Greenfield and I
did more in the way of husbanding the horses' strength, by turning
men off the wagons, than the rest of the Officers put together -
but I may be wrong about this. It was of course a simple matter
to take the names of all the men found violating the order about
riding upon the wagons, but unfortunately we got practically no
support from the C.O. when we brought the men up. I believe I

am right in saying that not a single man ever received anything more than a mild reprimand for this offence during the Retreat.

If the C.O. had thought fit to order us to turn a blind eye to this practice, one might have disagreed with his policy, but one would have known where one stood; as it was, he would neither rescind the order against the men stealing rides, nor enforce it; with the result that the men naturally got out of hand.

29th - 30th. August 1914.

I cannot recollect, even with the aid of the map, what route we took on this march. We passed through a village, which I cannot identify, where there was rather a tricky in and out turning. I was with the first half of the Ambulance which had got ahead of the second half owing to a wagon or wagons having broken down temporarily. Knowing that the rest of the Ambulance was some little way behind, I left a sentry at each of the two corners in the village so that they should not miss the way; but by some means or other they missed the road we had taken, and actually got to Vic. before we did. I think it is quite possible that they picked up a local guide who knew a better road than the one we took. I can remember coming out on a cross-road on to the side of a hill which was crammed with artillery, into the middle of which we had to insinuate ourselves; but all else is a blank until we got to Vic-sur-Aisne about 7 or 8 o'clock in the morning. We got stuck going through the town, and halted about a mile further on near the railway station. This was about 10 or 11o'clock on Sunday, August 30th. It was here I fancy that Colonel Stone rejoined us, or else at Cuts the previous day.

We discharged on to a train such patients as we had on the wagons, and then went up a long, stiff hill further South still. We camped on the top of a plateau in a stubble field near La Bargaine Farm on the road to Coeuvres at 3 p.m. There was no water within three-quarters of a mile, and the selection of this camping place by the Colonel was the kind of thing one had come to expect of him.

The Retreat from Mons had now lasted just on a week, and although it was to continue for another week, the worst of it was over. By this time, indeed from the time we left St. Quentin,

the different Units had recovered a fair degree of order; and
the Army, though retreating, was not in the least demoralised.
Indeed on the Retreat from Mons, and on that from Le Cateau,
the amount of cohesion that was retained, at any rate in the
3rd. Division, was really remarkable considering the hammering
they had taken from vastly superior forces. I can remember on
the afternoon of Mons, being somewhat upset by the state in
which the Royal Scots Fusiliers seemed to be. We met first
a party of this Battalion consisting of a sergeant and six or
seven men. They assured us that they were the sole survivors
of the Regiment. But two or three miles further on we picked
up another party of a dozen or more, who were likewise under
the impression that they were the sole survivors of the Regiment.
Both these parties marched with us towards Noirchain, and before
we had got very far we came across a whole company or even more
of the Battalion on the march, so we handed over to them our
stragglers, and were relieved to find that their pessimistic forebodings were not exactly accurate.

In the same way we frequently saw stragglers, often
in small bodies of two or three or four, making their way Southwards on their own account; and sometimes I am sorry to say they
had thrown away their great-coats, and even occasionally their
rifles. But these detachments were comparatively uncommon,
and most of them had been rounded up by the time we left St.
Quentin.

Fortunately the country through which we passed was
naturally fertile, and the inhabitants were friendly, so that
all these bodies of stragglers were fed by the peasantry. Indeed I believe that some of these wanderers actually kept away
from main roads, for fear they would be rounded up by the Provost
Marshal, and made to rejoin their Units.

It is difficult for me to reconstruct my own sensations
and opinions as I conceived them at that time. I have found
out since that the 1st. and 2nd Divisions saw no serious fighting
at all during this time; and that the 3rd. the and 5th bore the main
brunt of the German onset / both at Mons and Le Cateau. This of course
was not known to me at the time; and when I heard that our Division

alone had lost twenty guns at Le Cateau, I naturally imagined that similar losses had been sustained by the rest of the Army; which in fact was not the case.

It will have been gathered from what has gone before that I, personally, was not under ~~shell~~ fire either at Mons or Le Cateau. Our bearer parties and the Officers with them were under very heavy fire at Le Cateau, and had many casualties. At Mons we passed close to some of our own artillery in action, and saw enemy shells bursting about three-quarters of a mile away; but to the best of my recollection we had no casualties in the Ambulance at Mons. I think, in spite of what I have said about my erroneous deductions concerning the First Corps, that on the whole I did not realise quite how serious the peril of the British Expeditionary Force was during this week. Our old Padre Macpherson used to visit the Staff every day. He knew them all intimately, and I believe they made use of him to disseminate optimistic views of the situation. At any rate he always used to return from his visits to the Staff full of favourable forecasts; we were always coming next day to an impregnable position, already entrenched, which could be held against the Germans for ever. We never came to it, but every day the Padre assured us that we should reach it to-morrow. These rumours spread amongst the men like wild-fire, and I have no doubt they did a great deal of good in keeping up the spirits of the troops. Personally, I very soon lost faith in the Padre's prophesies; but an optimist is always a preferable comrade to a pessimist, and I used to listen to the old man's yarns even when I did not believe a word of them.

He also used to talk a great deal to the peasantry in the villages through which we passed. They could see he was a Curé, and they used to ask his advice as to whether they should stay at home or flee Southward. He always strongly advised them to stay where they were, assuring them that no harm would come to them, and that the German advance would not reach them. Probably he took this line at the desire of the Staff, whose object would be to keep the roads clear of refugees in order that the troops might not be hampered. It was not often that the many refugees whom we did pass actually caused any serious inconvenience to the Ambulance, but they must have contributed to the congestion of the roads which was often intense. The most pathetic sights were to be seen throughout the Retreat - old men and old women, young women and children, driving in farm carts or trudging on foot, with the whole of their belongings packed on to an ancient wheelbarrow or perambulator. Certainly there would have been far more of them had it not been for Padre Macpherson.

At La Bargaine we had a decent rest, the horses were taken off to water at the nearest available source, the cooks made a hot meal for the men and for us, and by sunset everyone was ready to turn in. I may say here that the Colonel's scheme for the Officers of each Section to mess ~~together~~ by themselves had of course broken down. When all three Sections were together as was usually the case one mess was inevitable. "B" and "C" Sections who had provided themselves with the Mess boxes as already described used to open the aforesaid boxes on alternate days, and it was of course impossible not to offer the Officers of "A" Section a share of what was going, nor did we desire to be so selfish. But it went rather against the grain to have to offer the Colonel his share of the contents of our Mess boxes, especially as his appetite was so voracious that he ate three times his proper share. He never made any allusion to the contents of these boxes, or to the boxes themselves, though they had been bought and stocked to all intents and purposes in contravention of his orders.

31st. August, 1914.

We were ordered to march at 3 a.m. from La Bargaine, and owing to the need of everybody for sleep, and to the distance we were from our water supply, it was thought best not to have any breakfast before starting but to have Reveille at 2.30. Accordingly we took the road in the early hours of the morning without the horses having been watered, and without the men having been fed. It turned out that we were not on the right road for our next destination and we had to retrace our foot-steps for a little way. I was sent ahead to see if a country road could be found which would bring us on to our proper road to the South. I found a very good unmetalled country road, and rode along it until it joined the high road we were making for. I considered this country road was quite practicable for our wagons, and rode back to the Colonel to tell him so. However, he did not like the look of it and would not allow the Ambulance to go along it; the result was we went a more round-about way, and were late for the rendezvous, which had been prescribed for us, at (I think) Point 157. Thence we trekked through Depouy, Mortefontaine, Taillefontaine, Feigneux, and so toward Crepy-en-Valois. I believe we passed through Bonneuil-en-Valois, between Taillefontaine and Feigneux. On this march we passed through the forest of Villers Cotteretts, also known as the Foret Dominale de Retz, and it was on this march that two incidents occurred which illustrate the character of our C.O.

We had been on the road three hours, and the horses, which had started off without having had a drink, were getting very thirsty and done up - the country was rather hilly. At 6 o'clock we had our hourly halt close to a small farm where there was a well. The farmer's people supplied us with fruit, and the men took the opportunity to fill their water-bottles. We asked the Colonel if we might halt for twenty minutes to water the horses; he refused on the grounds that we might block the road for some Unit behind us - for which he, of course would get into trouble. As a matter of fact there was no Unit in sight behind us on the road at that time. We then asked him if we might halt at the first stream we came to in order to water the horses; he said this was impossible for the same reason. We then asked him what was to happen, as the horses would break down unless they could get some water. The Colonel, who always admitted that he did not know one end of a horse from the other, said that if there was water handy when we halted at 7 o'clock he would allow the horses to be watered. Then we said supposing there is no water when we halt at 7 o'clock, what is to happen? He replied that they would have to go on till 8 o'clock. As luck would have it we came to a very nice stream at the edge of the forest at 7 o'clock; so the horses all got watered, and we proceeded.

At 9 o'clock we were in the middle of the forest, and when we halted at the hour the Officers approached the C.O. with the request that the men might be given some rations, which had not been distributed owing to our early start; he declined to issue the rations on the ground that there was no time, and said that the men ought to have saved something from the previous day's rations. They had not been told to do so, and had naturally eaten them all. There was an additional reason for issuing the rations, namely to lighten the loads of the wagons which contained them. The Colonel was still obsessed by the fear that we might block the road for the people behind. The French forests have roads cut through them which are as straight as arrows, and we could see our back track for the best part of a mile; there was not a single person on it, so there would have been ample time to give out rations without any chance of blocking those behind us. The men had been grousing to the Sergeants, who had approached the Subalterns, who had passed on the word to the senior Officers, and the whole Mess stood round Colonel Stone whilst our argument with him was proceeding. Fortunately Padre Macpherson was equal to the occasion; he was of senior rank to the Colonel, so of course he could say what he liked; what he said was: "Colonel Stone, if you don't issue rations to your men I am going now to report you to the General."

The rations were then issued.

When we got near Crepy, late in the afternoon, after a long march, we found ourselves blocked and had to halt. It turned out, or it was rumoured, that German Cavalry had entered some villages on the far side - that is the West side - of Crepy, which is a fair sized town, so instead of halting in Crepy as had been intended, we turned Eastward again, and bivouacked after dark at Vaumoise. Here we found the 8th. Brigade and camped alongside it.

Sept. 1st. 1914.

The next day, September 1st., we started off South from Vaumoise through the South-Western edge of the same forest that we had travelled through the day before. I was left behind at Vaumoise on some errand, which I cannot remember, with orders to follow on directly I had carried it out. The Ambulance thus got half an hour or an hour's start of me, and when I followed on, I found myself on the road with the 2nd. Battalion Royal Scots which was in the 8th. Brigade. I got into conversation with Major - now Brigadier-General - J.F. Duncan, of whom I afterwards saw a great deal. He had then just been appointed to command the Battalion in the place of Lieut.Colonel Mc. Micking, who had been left wounded and a prisoner at Le. Cateau. When the Campaign began, a week before, he was junior Major of the Battalion but the senior Major was not considered quite equal to taking the command, so Major Duncan got his chance.

He is a very able, as well as exceedingly pleasant Officer, and when we got to know him later on, we all liked him very much. We had a long march through Levignen and Fresnoy to a farm at Chevreville. This too was a very hot march over a high, dusty plateau, through interminable fields containing mostly beets. At Chevreville we camped in a farm which was in charge of a very capable French woman whose husband had gone to the War. She exerted herself to the utmost to make us comfortable, with results which were satisfactory to her for the time being, though ultimately, I expect, disastrous. Our wagon horses, which we had brought from England, were on the whole a very fine set, but the incessant strain upon them was beginning to wear out all except the strongest, and we had by this time a great many which were not up to their work. Many of the drivers were very inexperienced, not to say incapable, the harness was new, and many of our beasts were badly galled. The result was that by this time, September 1st., it had become necessary to replace some of them. if we were to get along properly; and this meant commandeering from the French people. The Frenchwoman at our farm had twelve fine horses in her stables, and before going to bed in the evening we discussed among ourselves how many of these we should take in the morning. I was in favour of taking seven or eight, but some of the others thought this was rather too hard upon the woman. However, when morning came and we broached to the lady the question of commandeering her horses, for which she would have been well paid by our Army authorities, she was very distressed, and made piteous appeals to us not to take them. She had been so kind to us, possibly with a view to this very emergency, that her appeals naturally carried weight; but War is War, and I was in favour of taking what we needed. However, I was over-ruled by the others, and we left the farm without taking a single animal. I suppose that unless some of the Units behind us took some of these horses, the whole dozen of them fell into the hands of the Germans. The woman in that case is not likely to / have got any compensation.

2nd. Sept. 1914.

On September 2nd. we left Chevreville, and after a comparatively short trek of six hours, we out-spanned in the middle of the day between Monthyon and Ivernay, passing Forfry on the way. About 6.30 p.m. we left this bivouac and marched until 11 p.m. We crossed the Marne in the darkness at Trilbardou, and camped at Lesches alongside No. 7 Field Ambulance.

Marne crossed

3rd. Sept. 1914.

On September 3rd. we left Lesches early in the morning and made our way through Crecy and Sancy to Vaucourtois, which is nearly due East from Lesches; We found the 8th. Brigade at Vaucourtois. We had a long halt outside Crecy, as it was doubtful where we had to camp, and we had to send out scouts to find out where the 8th. Brigade had got to.

4th. Sept. 1914

Rest day

On September 4th. we were told that we were to have a whole day's rest in camp, and we did have the greater part of a day's rest; but at 6 p.m. we had to start off South through La-Chapelle-sur-Crecy, and thence all night through the Forest of Crecy to a hamlet called Retal, South of Liverdy. This was another horrible night march, or rather night-mare, and I remember very little of it, except that whenever we stopped for five or ten minutes on the road we all went to sleep in the dry ditches. By this time we were commandeering horses freely from the French peasants, and leaving behind our own broken down or galled animals instead.

Night march

horses commandeered

At Retal we stopped the whole of Saturday the 5th., and the 8th Brigade stopped there too. This was the furthest point South that we reached, though some of the Cavalry and First Corps Ambulances appear to have travelled further South still.

F.a's furthest point South — Retal

5th. Sept. 1914.

The end of the Retreat

The great Retreat was now over, having lasted thirteen days all but a few hours. Many of the men were very much done up, and many of them had worn out their boots. In the Mess we all showed signs of wear; I, personally lost nearly a stone in weight, and I suppose the others all did the same. But the only one who was seriously knocked up was Major Dalby; he got gaunter and more tired every day, and was quite useless from an early stage in the Retreat. Beyond sitting on his horse, looking like death itself, I really think he took no part in the work of the Ambulance. The marches had been very long, and during the first week almost incessant; we had sometimes been on the road twenty-two hours out of the twenty-four. The men

[margin note: Rations]

[margin note: Comparison of conditions with those in S. African War. & R.A.M.C. with infantry men]

were soft in condition, as were the Officers too, when we left England; but there had been no lack of rations on the Retreat, and even if there had been we did pretty well out of the farmers. Bearing in mind that the R.A.M.C. rank and file have no rifles, or ammunition, or entrenching tools to carry, and that they were frequently allowed to put their great-coats and water-bottles on the wagons, and that they had no out-post sentry duty to perform, no trenches to dig, and very few of the heavy fatigues that fall to the lot of the infantry-man, there was no excuse for them breaking down. Having served as an Infantry soldier in South Africa, where the marches were just as long, and where there were no roads, almost no rations, and nothing to get off the country, I was not disposed to regard our fellows as hardly used. The consequence was I was very hard-hearted about the question of riding on the wagons, and of dropping on malingerers and crocks in general. I expect the men thought I was a bit of a slave driver, but I do not think they bore me any permanent ill-will for it; certainly some of them were miserable specimens physically, and I daresay they did feel pretty bad on the long marches. But their hardships were nothing at all compared with those of the Infantry whose performances during the great Retreat, were equal to any ever accomplished by the British Army.

The Advance to the Marne, and
The Battle of the Aisne.

6th. Sept. 1914.

On Sunday, September 6th. we got our orders to march Northward from Retal.. We had a long, slow march through Liverdy to Crevecoeur, and thence through the Forest of Crecy to Hautefeuille. Hautefeuille is on the edge of the Forest of Malvoisine, and at the shooting box where we bivouacked there was a large collection of iron plates which in former days were used at the back of fireplaces in good French houses; these large iron plates had on them in relief the Coats of Arms of the proprietors, and apparently it is a craze with wealthy Frenchmen nowadays to collect them. Certainly the owner of this house who, we were told, was a wealthy chocolate manufacturer, had a large collection of them.

7th. Sept 1914.

The next day, September 7th., we loafed about doing nothing until the evening when we started off via Faremoutiers and Coulommiers to Chauffry. We did not get to Chauffry until after mid-night, and we were guided to our bivouac by the loud snores of Captain Darling, who had been detached with three wagons a day or two before to accompany the 8th. Brigade; Darling was a notorious snorer, and when in the darkness we heard his music proceeding from a field alongside the road, we felt sure that we had reached the right camping ground. Coulommiers had been the scene of horrible German brutalities; we did not of course know this at the time, and in our passage through the town in darkness we naturally had no chance of coming across evidences of them.

8th. Sept. 1914.

The next day, September 8th. we started off early from Chauffry to Rebais, via St. Denis. At Rebais, also, horrible atrocities had been committed. I think it was in this village or else at St. Denis that I was sent off on an expedition to commandeer horses; I was often picked out for this job, and on this particular occasion Snape, who was with me, insisted on taking a big black stallion; rather against my will I let him do it, and the brute gave us awful trouble afterwards. I made up my mind never to take a stallion again.

After leaving Rebais we found the road very much blocked, and had long halts in the middle of the day doing nothing.

Early in the afternoon I was told that Darling, who had gone on ahead with the three wagons as he had done the previous day, had got a lot of wounded at a village called Boisbaudry. It was somewhat vague where Boisbaudry was, but I was given the general direction across country, and told to find it. By good fortune I managed to hit the right direction, and found Darling at Boisbaudry in a School-room, with a good many wounded, and more constantly pouring in. I set to work with him to deal with the cases, and the place was very soon more like a shambles than anything else. Darling and I, with our coats off, were covered in blood up to the elbows when General Smith-Dorrien came in. We stood to attention as best we could, but our Corps Commander said:

"You get on with your work and don't take any notice of me."

He went round the School-room talking to the wounded, and left after a few minutes. This was the first time I had seen Sir Horace since I had served in his Brigade in South Africa, when I was in the ranks of the 1st. Suffolks.

After a while the rest of the ambulance turned up, and all hands set to work to make a dressing station in the village. We had about 100 wounded casualties from an action fought on the Petit Morin, a short distance to the North; this was a rear-guard action by the Germans to delay our advance. We were pretty busy most of the night attending to these wounded; and next morning, September 9th., Foster, Darling and I were left behind at Boisbaudry to look after them while the rest of the Ambulance followed on towards the Marne. We had with us no Ambulance wagons, only a G.S. wagon, a water cart and a forage cart, with a tent sub-division and a few drivers. Orders were to evacuate the wounded by any means we could at the very first opportunity, and then to follow on after our Unit. We put a sentry out on the high road, which was only a mile away, with orders to stop the first empty convoy going South. During the day a motor lorry convoy, heavily laden, passed going Northwards, and our sentry stopped the Officer in charge who promised to call in at Boisbaudry on his return journey. This sentry was posted at a cross-road where there was a public house called the Gibraltar; I was rather astonished to find an

Inn sign of this description in Northern France. During the day two of our wounded died, one of whom was a German, and a party of fifty-one unwounded German prisoners passed through the village under escort. After mid-night the motor lorries turned up; they were thirteen in number, and we made them as comfortable for the wounded as possible by bedding them with straw, still even then the lorries must have been horribly uncomfortable for the unfortunate wounded, and I fear their sufferings that night were terrible. There were, of course, no motor ambulances available to remove them, and our own horsed wagons had gone on after the Army in order to deal with fresh casualties. We loaded the wagons by the light of lanterns; and Darling was sent with them in charge of the wounded to Coulommiers, whither the convoy was bound. At Coulommiers he handed them over to either a Hospital or an Ambulance train, and travelled North again with the lorries when they went forward with fresh supplies. The result was that he caught up No. 8 Field Ambulance before we did, as our progress was much slower.

10th.
Sept.
1914.

Early on the 10th September, Foster and I and the men took the road Northward; we crossed the Petit Morin where it ran through a deep gorge, and continued on through Orly and Bussieres to the Marne at Nanteuil. At Nanteuil we saw enormous quantities of empty wine bottles - the results of German occupation. The bridge at this town over the Marne was intact, and the story we heard was that the party of German Engineers told off to mine it had got so completely intoxicated that they had failed to carry out their mission; the result was, that when the German rear-guard withdrew across the river, the bridge could not be destroyed, and the 3rd Division which had expected to be obliged to construct pontoon bridges was relieved of that necessity, and crossed without difficulty. On the North side of the town the road goes up a perfectly wicked hill, and there were ample evidences that a good many vehicles, both of our own and of the enemy, had had grave difficulties in getting up it. Our own horses made pretty heavy going at this hill, and we had to rest them, when we did get to the top, for some time.

We then kept on Northwards and arrived, about dark, at the village of Bezu. Here we billeted ourselves in a very fine old chateau, which had been converted, evidently a very long time before, into a farm, and had thus no doubt escaped destruction at the Revolution. It consisted of two square court-yards connected by a portcullised-arch passing under a grand old square tower, furnished with a spiral stone staircase, vaulted crypts, and enormous Salons - now converted into granaries. We made ourselves very comfortable under the archway, and the farmer's wife showed us over her lovely house, which must have dated from the 15th. or 14th. century. The iron back of the fireplace of her huge kitchen was still in place, with a Coat of Arms surmounted by a coronet; she could not tell us whose Coat of Arms it was, or anything about the history of the Chateau. In the crypt were enormous numbers of empty bottles whose contents had been consumed by the Germans two or three days before. The pigs had also turned on the taps of her cider casks, so we could not get any to drink; the smell of cider was very strong and very tantalising.

11th, Sept. 1914.
After spending the night very comfortably at Bezu, we set off early in the morning, and it was at the Northern end of this village that we came across an Officer of No. 9 Field Ambulance - Lient. Carberry. He had been left there in charge of 7 or 8 cases of abdominal wounds, and his orders were similar to those which Major Foster had had at Boisbaudry; but this sportsman had decided not to allow his wounded to be moved until they were in his opinion fit for removal, and this, in the case of abdominal wounds, meant several days or weeks. As Foster and I rode through about a hundred yards ahead of our company, he came out of the house which he was using for his Dressing Station, and went up to Foster and said:

"I advise you, sir, to keep close to your men, for there are Germans lurking in the woods all round."

I believe that this statement was to some extent true; parties of Germans were wandering about in the woods looking for an Englishman to surrender to - they were terrified to surrender to the French peasants for fear of having their throats cut. This Officer was taking no risks from the German stragglers he had heard about; he had about seven or eight improvised Red Cross flags hanging out of the windows of the house, and adorning the

Church which was alongside. He also displayed on chairs in the streets a row of khaki coats, belonging to himself and his orderlies, with the Red Cross brassards very much in evidence. We found out long afterwards that he had stayed in this village some two or three weeks, and had saved one out of the abdominal cases left in his charge, the others had all died as indeed abdominal wound cases generally did in the early days of this Campaign.

We travelled on via Marigny, Neuilly, Vinly, and Chezy-en-Orxois where there is a fine old church and a beautiful fountain. Thence we went on in pouring rain via Dammard to Neuilly-St.-Front, which is a small town, The rain this afternoon was of great violence, and by the time we got to Neuilly everybody was soaked to the skin. It was about 4 o'clock in the afternoon, and we quartered ourselves in a snug little farm just on the Northern edge of Neuilly. Here we got news that No. 8 F.A. was at Oulchy-la-Ville, a few miles further on. Foster, who was very conscientious, said that we should have to start again to catch them up, but as we had already done a very long march, and got drenched, I thought the next day would be quite time enough. However, Foster would have it that we must push on, but we stayed an hour or two at the farm in order that we and the men might dry our clothes. During this process, Foster felt symptoms of soreness of the throat and mentioned the fact to me; I looked at his throat and couldn't see very much the matter with it, but I had sense enough to diagnose a severe tonsillitis, and to forbid him, on medical grounds, to go any further. I ordered him to bed, and went out and told the men that we were not going on. This news was received with great joy, as they were thoroughly comfortable in a large barn, and there was ample accommodation under cover for the horses. The old lady at the farm, who was the mother of the proprietor, treated us very well; we slept on a thick carpet of straw in one of her rooms, which had been put down for the benefit of some German Officers two or three days before. In this part of France the inhabitants could not do too much for us, as they had suffered a good deal during the six or seven days that the Germans had been there. During the day's march we had passed not only several bunches of German prisoners, but also abandoned German artillery limbers, motor buses, cars, lorries, and other transport. It was said that at the Marne a private soldier found a German military car abandoned by the side of the road; the only piece of portable property was a small locked case, which he appropriated and afterwards broke open. It contained about half a dozen medals and decorations, which had evidently belonged to a German Officer of high rank, and were intended to be worn at the triumphal entry into Paris.

12th. Sept. 1914.

On September 12th. Foster's throat was quite recovered, and we left our comfortable quarters early in the morning. Outside Neuilly we came to a fork in the road with a placard showing the 3rd. Division as having passed along the left-hand fork; this turned out to be an error, and someone must have moved the placard so as to point along the wrong road. We naturally followed the sign and passed through Billy-sur-Ourcq and St. Remy, where there is a lovely 13th. century church, and through Le Plessier Huleu and Hartennes to Neuville St. Jean. Here we halted for lunch at a fine old convent, now converted into a farm. We then continued on through of these places (St. Remy I fancy) Droizy, Muret and Nampteuil; at one we found that we were following the 5th. Division instead of the 3rd, so we branched off Eastward. Eventually after passing along a pretty valley through Violaine. We presently came to a high road packed with Units of the 3rd. Division, and No. 7 F.A. was passing along this road just as we reached it, we fell into a gap immediately behind them, and continued on Northward in the pouring rain.

After a little while the road got hopelessly blocked, and I persuaded Foster that since we were not under definite orders as the other Units were to go to definite places, we had better shift for ourselves, and billet at a little village just off the main road called Cuiry Housse. This excellent advice Foster followed, and to the disgust of our friends in No. 7 F.A., who would have liked to have done the same, we branched off from the road towards this village. Here we invaded a very nice farm belonging to a very decent chap called Charles Hacard, who treated us exceedingly well. When the German invasion swept over Cuiry Housse, he buried all his drinkables under a layer of clay in his barn, and the Germans had not found them. By this time he had dug them up again, and he gave us some of the most wonderful cognac I have ever tasted in my life. We slept in beds here, and the men were thoroughly comfortable in the out-buildings.

13th.
Sept.
1914.

The next day, September 13th., we moved on very early to Braine, where we found No. 8 Field Ambulance in the Market Square. No. 8 F.A. was now under the command of Major Maurice, whom we had met at Troisvilles the night before Le Cateau; he was at that time Senior Major of No. 7 F.A., and had superseded Colonel Stone by order of the General a day or two before we reached Braine. Colonel Stone had been placed under arrest, and was still with the Ambulance, looking like a lost sheep, and with no duties to perform. No charge was ever brought against him to the best of my knowledge, and he was given an appointment of some sort in Paris a few days afterwards. As I never saw him again after he left No 8, I may as well sum up here my opinions about this Officer.

Colonel Stone possessed, as far as I can see, every possible disqualification for a Commanding Officer. He was absolutely careless about the welfare of his Officers, his men and his horses; he took no interest whatever in looking after the individual members of his command in any way. He was incapable of preserving discipline amongst the men, and yet by his perpetual worrying he had even the best of them in a state bordering on chronic mutiny. None of the Officers, as I have already said, ever took the slightest notice of anything he ordered - to have done so would in most cases have been to invite disaster. He was quite incompetent from the professional medical aspect, as well as militarily; he was terrified of the Staff, and would not even choose a bivouac or establish himself in a billet without their permission. On the night that we bivouacked at Vaumoise he arrived there about sunset, and found the 8th. Brigade camped in a very nice field. He knew that this was our destination, and that there was another field bordering the road and exactly alongside the Brigade; but in spite of all our persuasions, he could not be induced to march his Ambulance into this field, but kept us waiting on the road alongside it for an hour, until he had interviewed the Brigade Staff. As soon as the latter became acquainted with our arrival, and the state of affairs, they of course immediately ordered us to bivouac on this empty field; but if Colonel Stone had had sense enough to do what we all urged him to do, the horses would have been out-spanned, and the men

44.

would have got their evening meal/an hour and their sleep sooner than was actually the case.

It is possible that his inordinate terror of the Staff was due to events which had happened before the War; for according to what Officers of the R.A.M.C. told me afterwards, he had made a conspicuous muddle of some manoeuvres a year or two before the War.

Although he was no horseman,/while on the march he was practically never seen off his horse; his shrill plaintive voice, and an extraordinarily thin whistle on which he used to produce a feeble piping note when he wished to command attention, were constantly to be heard, although he seldom had anything to say worth listening to. Indecision and vacillation were two of his principal characteristics. Another was his greed; he was exceedingly tall /and most emaciated, and yet he ate more than any one else in the Mess. As I have said, "B" and "C" Sections had provided themselves, at their own expense, with Mess boxes, more or less in contravention of his expressed wishes; he did not possess back-bone enough to raise any objection to this, nor had he self-respect enough to refrain from sharing in the contents. We did not grudge him a fair share of what was going, but we did rather object to his wolfing down about three times his proper proportion. But unamiable as these traits of his character were, there were two sins which were totally unforgiveable. One was his cowardice - the mere sound of guns in the distance invariably set him shivering like a leaf. During the whole of the Retreat he was incapable of writing an order, (or his preposterous diary) without resting both his fore-arms on his knees, and this same tremor of his hands was painfully obvious when he took a cup of tea. The other sin which I shall never forgive him was his abandoning Major Thompson at Montigny. I cannot conceive that any other motive than jealousy can possibly have accounted for this act. Thompson was the exact antithesis of Colonel Stone: he was a good soldier, a good disciplinarian, and popular with both Officers and men; he worked untiringly, and he did a lot towards improving the deficiencies of the Ambulance by playing off his Section ~~of the Ambulance~~ against the others. He used to address them as the Busy Bees, and to exhort them to show "A" and "C" Section how things should be done. He was only a year or two junior in the R.A.M.C. to Colonel Stone; and he was a married man with four children. Colonel Stone's insane folly in leaving poor Thompson at Montigny deprived the latter for many months of his chances of distinction: incidentally it led to Colonel Stone's disappearance from the 3rd Division. He was sent down to Paris and given some unimportant post there in connection with the Red Cross. Long afterwards I met a nurse who had worked under him in Paris, and I found that her opinion of him was very much the same as mine. He should, in the first place, never have been promoted to the rank which he had reached; and in the second place the proper course to have taken would have been to place him on the retired list as soon as his measure was taken in the Retreat.

Before we reached Braine we had also lost, beside Thompson and Stone, our little Major Dalby. It was on either the first or the second day of our march Northward, after the Retreat, that an opportunity occurred of sending two or three wagon loads of sick Infantry to a town where they could be evacuated. Major Dalby was sent off on this job in charge of the wagons, with instructions similar to those which Foster had had at Boisbaudry, namely to rejoin as soon as possible. Several members of the Mess entrusted Dalby with small amounts of money to invest for them in various commodities, such as soap, razors, candles and the like; but Dalby never reappeared. The wagons came back and we learned that he had fallen sick himself, and had been admitted to Hospital with the patients of whom he was in charge. He was apparently invalided thence to England, and none of the people who had given him the money ever heard from him, or ever got the money or the things which they had asked him to purchase. How he came to forget his commissions entirely like this was a problem we never solved; he must have been taken pretty seedy I suppose, and unimportant matters like that must have slipped his memory. He was a pitiable sight at the end of the Retreat, and I really think it was all he could do to sit on his horse; he hardly ever spoke, he never took any part in the work of the Ambulance, and though he was a decent little chap we were all glad to get rid of him.

After this time I never again saw, until many months afterwards, Colonel Caton Jones, the A.D.M.S. of the 3rd. Division. I do not know exactly when it was that he was sent to the base, but it was somewhere about this time. As we saw him on the Retreat he was nothing but a puling old woman; but the R.A.M.C. regulars assured us that in his day he had been reckoned a good Officer. Whether that was so or not his day was long since past; he was terribly crippled by rheumatism, and after the first two or three days of the Retreat he could not get on his horse, but used to ride mostly in one of our Ambulance wagons, and thus we saw more of him than we should otherwise have done. He was sent down to the A.D.M.S. at Havre, where I met him several times long afterwards. He was still distinctly an old woman, but not a bad old sort, and I think he meant well. In his place we got a scowling, saturnine fellow, named Reilly; he never impressed us as being any good, and only stayed with the Division a short time; he was then sent home to England and had some gall stones removed. Doubtless he was in considerable pain from this cause whilst with us, so it is perhaps not fair to judge him by his performances at this time.

As I am being personal I will jot down a few notes about some of the other members of the Ambulance. The invaluable Snape I have already mentioned, and also the egregious Blake; the third N.C.O, of the attached A.S.C. was a very decent man called L/Cpl. Meade. He ~~was a very simple fellow who~~ worked well, and he knew something about horses. Of the R.A.M.C, proper there was Sergt. Hurst - the man who christened Col. Stone,"The Pathfinder". He was not a bad fellow, and had a certain amount of education, a little bit inclined to lose his head, and he had a dreadful stoop which would have driven a Sergeant-major of a smart Regiment into an apoplectic fit. Then there was Sergt. Joyce, a jolly, fat, smiling fellow, with ferocious moustaches; he could sing a good song, and was a very good N.C.O. in every way. Sergt. Mercer was also by no means a bad fellow, and quite a good N.C.O.

Staff Sergt. Cole was a man who had some ~~received a great~~ education, but he had not got much in the way of heart. He kept the men up to the mark fairly well, but did not by any means always set a good example. Corporal Stewart, afterwards promoted Sergt., was a funny little thick-headed fellow who had not got much control over the men, but he had one crowning virtue - he was steady as a rock under fire. Corporal Barton, was a long,

47.

lanky chap of whom the same, unfortunately, could not be said. L/Cpl. Richards was a man who was very useful indeed, a good worker and not a bad carpenter. We used to put him on to making splints out of old boards and other pieces of wood; and I liked him very much. The best driver in the A.S.C. Section was a youngster named Ross. He unfortunately could be trusted to get drunk if there was liquor within ten miles. The first time he did this was at Lesches, the day after we crossed the Marne: the second time was at Braine, and he was then warned by Major Maurice, that the next offence would mean a General Court Martial, and quite likely the death penalty. Nothing however could cure Ross's unfortunate failing; and twice after that I had him hidden away when drunk, as I did not want him to get into the serious trouble which would have ensued had Major Maurice found out about it. He was a splendidly plucky fellow, and quite one of the best workers in the Ambulance; I expect by this time he has come to a bad end. Then there was a funny old chap called Campbell, whose story was rather pathetic. He was cook of "C" Section, and I first heard his story when I was left behind with Foster and Darling at Boisbaudry. He told me then that he had served already in four Campaigns and had five medals. I wondered how it was that he never wore his khaki coat, but always went about in a brown sweater; Tilbury enlightened me as to the reason. It appeared that Campbell belonged to an Infantry Battalion which was left in South Africa in Garrison after the end of the War. Campbell was very "fed up" with the Veldt, and deserted. He was, of course, captured and court martialled, with the result that his five medals were confiscated. When this War began he immediately volunteered for service again, in the hope that a good record would result in his decorations being restored to him. He was about 45 years of age, and a regular old Army bird. I trust that he will get his medals back again some day.

We had with us also an ex-medical student named Doherty. He had finished two or three years of his Medical Course, when he had a row with his people, and enlisted in the Army. After serving his time he had gone on to the Reserve, and been called up at the outbreak of the War. For a long time he was employed as cycle Orderly; Major Maurice got him first one stripe, and then two, and, months later I met him at No. 9 Stationary Hospital near Havre, as a full Sergeant. Corporal Voisy was another quite efficient N.C.O.; he got the medal for Distinguished Conduct in the Field later on in recognition of gallant service rendered at Vailly.

As soon as we returned to No. 8 Field Ambulance in the morning of September 13th. at Braine, I was informed that I had been transferred from "C" to "A" Section; I also learned that Connell had been deposed from the position of Adjutant and that Darling had been appointed instead. This was a change for the better, as Connell was exceedingly lazy, and never did any work of any sort. As a matter of fact there is no provision in the R.A.M.C. Establishment for an Adjutant in a Field Ambulance; the appointment is purely unofficial, and there is really no need to have an Adjutant at all. Some Commanding Officer appoint Adjutants, others do not - Major Fielding, for instance, who commanded No 7 Field Ambulance for many months did without an Adjutant, but Nos. 8 and 9 always had one.

Major Maurice, who was now commanding No. 8 F.A., was a vast improvement on Colonel Stone. He took a great interest in his horses, and was a very capable woods-man - the advantage of which we were soon to perceive. Before very long we were ordered out of Braine along the road N.W. to Chassemy. After going a mile or two we came to a standstill, with Infantry in Artillery formation in the fields alongside the road. An Artillery duel of some violence was going on just ahead of us, and I spent most of the day loafing about doing nothing; Major Maurice and one or two of the other Officers, went on ahead with bearer parties, but I was left with the main body. Captain Connell was one of those who had gone forward, and he was standing talking to three of / combatant Officers a mile or so ahead of the Ambulance, when a shell burst right amongst them; two of them were killed instantly, Connell and the fourth officer were not touched. Later in the afternoon we went on to Chassemy itself, and bivouacked in a field just South of that village. The Staff had ordered Major Maurice to park the Ambulance in the Market Square of Chassemy, but the Major, who had spied out the land for himself, told them that he did not regard the Market place as suitable for the purpose as it was under direct observation by the enemy from the hills on the North side of the Aisne; he asked to be allowed to camp in this field, which was sheltered from observation by a large wood surrounding two sides of it. The Staff said he could do as he liked provided they knew where to find him when wanted. Similar orders had been given to Lt. Colonel Kennedy, who was commanding No. 7., but instead of raising an objection as Major Maurice did, Colonel Kennedy meekly did what the Staff told him. The result was that when the village was violently bombarded next morning, No. 7 F.A. had 6 killed and 9 wounded, two wagons blown to smithereenes, and several horses killed as well; whereas, No.8, cunningly hidden at Major Maurice's instance, had no casualties at all except a mere skin wound of one Officer.

We heard a story of incidents which happened at Chassemy at this time, but it sounded so incredible that I was half inclined to disbelieve it. However, on the day we left Braine, I had an opportunity of asking one of the principal actors in the story whether it was true, and he assured me that it was, so I will put it down here. Lieutenant Colonel Kennedy, who was commanding No. 7 F.A., was standing in the doorway of a small house in Chassemy when the shelling began; a shell came in through the roof of the house and burst inside, the force of the explosion blew old Kennedy out into the street where he fell on his face. He picked himself up with some difficulty, being old and fat, and had hardly finished feeling himself to see whether he was wounded, when another shell burst in the street right in front of him and blew him back into the house, without touching him in the slightest.

A Staff Officer of the 3rd Division - Major Farmer - was sitting on his horse close by and laughing heartily at the misadventures of poor old Kennedy; however, he did not laugh long, for a few moments after another shell came and blew his horse's head off. He extricated himself from the horse's body, and mounted his orderly's horse. He had hardly got on it when another shell burst in Chassemy, and this time it blew his horse's rump off. After that Major Farmer went about on foot for the rest of that day; neither he nor Colonel Kennedy were so much as touched by a splinter. It was Major Farmer who told me that the details of this story were quite accurate.

14th.
Sept.
1914.

On the morning of September 14th. Foster and I were sent forward towards the river with a bearer party. We were ordered to go to the edge of the wood facing the river, to establish ourselves behind some hay-stacks, to remain there, and look out for such casualties between us and the river as might take place. We found the hay-stacks easily enough, and planted ourselves behind them. We were away about 200 yards to the West of the road leading North from Chassemy towards the River at Vailly, and we were separated from the river by a level meadow through which the road ran. Just as we got there the Cavalry, who had been across the river, came streaming back into the shelter of the wood. The road from the bridge was being violently shelled by the Germans, and the Cavalry came along it in small parties of one or two, galloping at full speed across the open stretch which may have been about a quarter of a mile in length. It was very exciting watching the troopers riding for their lives across this shell-swept road. From where we were we could see them just before they started gathering up speed for the gallop; the Germans could not see them until they had come out on to the open road, by which time they were at top speed. Every party was received with two or three or more shells, and there must have been many narrow/escapes that day. We stayed behind the hay-stacks the whole morning watching the Cavalry run the gauntlet, and two or three Regiments must have got back before the first casualty occurred. A cloud of smoke from a shell hid one of the gallopers altogether, and we thought he must be killed; but as the smoke cleared off we could see the horse stretched on the road, and the man crawling on hands and knees into the ditch. I went round through the wood with a stretcher party to fetch him in, but by the time I got to the part of the wood which was nearest to the wounded man, Major Fielding, who was also out with a bearer party on a similar mission to ours, had got the man under cover. If we had known where Major Fielding was posted, I might have saved myself the trouble of going after this man. I then returned to the hay-stacks, and the shelling continued; many of these shells burst quite close to the stacks, but of course as long as we kept behind our cover we were perfectly safe. One of the men was holding my horse, and being rather an idiot he held the reins much too long; a shell burst near and frightened the horse, the man lost his head and let go, and I saw my horse trotting over the meadow which was being swept by shrapnel. I cursed the man for being such a fool, and went after the horse myself as the best way of recovering him. Fortunately the horse escaped injury, and took the road back towards Chassemy. Before he reached the village he was rounded up by some Cavalrymen who were off-saddled in the grounds of the Chateau, and I recovered him from them. I then went back to the hay-stacks, and after a while we got a message from Major Maurice recalling us. As we approached Chassemy in obedience to this order, we found the village was being very heavily shelled, so we decided not to go through it, and made a long detour through the woods along bridle paths. By watching the compass very carefully we hit off our direction correctly, and came out of the wood right into the field where No. 8 F.A. was camping. We found them all crouched in the shelter of the wood at the edge of the field, as a good many shells had been coming over; but as I have already said we had only one casualty, and that was a wound so slight that it did not incapacitate the victim. This was Lt. Bazett who had joined the Ambulance at Braine to fill up our establishment. Bazett was a very nice young chap, completely indifferent to shells and similar missiles, and very well up in his professional work. He was a Fellow of his College at Oxford, and a great acquisition to the Ambulance. Another Officer also joined

at Braine - a youngster named Davidson. He was much too delicate f
for the sort of life we were living, and did not last for long.
But he was a nice young chap; we were sorry when he had to go down
to the Base.

After dark I went with Major Maurice northward towards
the river once more, because we heard that Capt. McQueen of No. 7
F.A. had a lot of casualties which required removal. McQueen
was on the Eastern side of the road from Chassemy to Vailly, where
he had been posted in a similar position to Foster and myself.
The night was pitch-dark and we had some difficulty in finding him;
we took several wagons down and relieved him of his cases. Long
afterwards he told me an anecdote of his difficulties that day at
the edge of the wood facing the river. He received an order to
take his Bearer Party from the edge of the wood across the open to
some houses on the river-bank, where a number of wounded had been
collected. The open stretch which he had to cross was still being
shelled by the Germans, and before starting out from the shelter of
the wood he addressed his men, telling them that they had better get
across as quickly as they could lay their legs to the ground, he told
them not to bother about keeping line, but to "hook it" across the
open, when he gave them the word, as hard as they could go. He then
gave the order to advance, and ran across the meadow to the house by
the river as fast as possible. When he got to the river, very
pleased at not having been killed on the way, he was horrified to
find that only two out of his 36 Orderlies had made the journey;
the others were nowhere to be seen; later on, when the shelling had
stopped, he went round to the edge of the wood to round up the skulk-
ers, he found 23 of them still there, but the other 11 had actually
retreated through the wood instead of following him to the river.

While Major Maurice and I were trying to find Mc.Queen,
we met a very dishevelled figure on the road, dripping wet, minus
hat and coat;- this was the attached Medical Officer of the 4th.
Battn. Middlesex Regiment. It appeared that he had swum both the
river and the canal, and was making his way Southward when we met
him. Major Maurice stopped him, and discovered what he had been
doing. The Major asked him if he had had any orders to retire,
he said, he had not, but had heard a rumour that a general
retirement was taking place. Major Maurice talked to him pretty

straight, told him to go back at once to his Battalion, and not to think of doing such a mad thing again.

Somewhere about mid-night, Foster, Greenfield and myself were sent across the river into Vailly. The Aisne at this point runs parallel to a canal; the bridge over the river had been blown up, but that over the canal was still intact. We crossed the river by a pontoon bridge and made our way into Vailly - a small town on the North bank of the Aisne, which just comes down to the river but only just. We went through the main street of Vailly, Northwards in which many of the houses were burning, and up to the Brigadier's Office at the North end of the town. Here we found an empty house which we broke into, and after establishing the men in the shelter of a very high bank, we went to sleep in the house. This would be about 2 or 3 a.m. on September 15th. Soon after dawn we were aroused by firing, and found that bullets were coming through the walls of the house we were in, so we beat a hasty retreat, and took over a Dressing Station in the Church at Vailly, and in some neighbouring buildings: these consisted of a School, a Doctor's house, which was constructed for the purpose of a Nursing Home; and the Curé's house alongside the Church.

15th.
Sept.
1914.

The Church at Vailly was a beautiful 12th. Century building, very large and very solidly built. Joan of Arc had met some monarch or other at this town, and one of the chapels in the Church was dedicated to her. We soon had large numbers of wounded on our hands; the whole floor of the Church was speedily covered with mattresses which we commandeered from the houses in the town, and the other three buildings were also fitted up for the reception of wounded. At the School there were some five or six young French women who had had some First Aid training, and made themselves very useful under the direction of a middle aged woman, who afterwards got the Royal Red Cross on Major Foster's recommendation; in the Church, in the Curé's house, and in the Doctor's house we had only our own Orderlies, and we were soon very busy attending to the wounded.

The Brigades of our Division were up the hill about half a mile outside the town, struggling to reach the top, but unable or less to do so as the Germans were very strongly entrenched there.

The influx of wounded was incessant, and we had to handle 500 of them in the first 48 hours. The Germans had a lot of guns at Fort Conde on the hills West of Vailly and North of the river, and they shelled the town all day incessantly, and also at intervals during the night. The lower end of the town near the river was more easily visible to them than the upper end, where the Church was, and they very soon had all the lower end of the town in blazing ruins; they also shelled the pontoon bridge with great pertinacity, but although they hit it once or twice they never succeeded in breaking it, and the damage was always easily repaired. The Engineer Officer who was in charge of this bridge had to live in the smallest of small houses just at the bridge head, and could be seen for most of the day smoking a cigarette, and urging troops crossing the bridge to hurry up, as it was unhealthy. He must have had hundreds of narrow escapes, but I believe he was never hit. After a day or two the Engineers managed to put a plank gang-way across the gap of the proper bridge, and foot-passengers could then use this bridge instead of crossing by the pontoons, but of course all transport had to cross by the latter.

One room in the Curé's house was appropriated for the Officers' Mess. The Curé himself lived in a deep underground cellar, down a flight of about twenty stone steps, he thought it was safer down there, and he was most certainly right. I, more or less, took charge of the Church, though the others used to come and assist whenever they had a spare moment; Foster and Greenfield devoted themselves mainly to the School, to Dr. Lancry's House, and to the Curé's house.

The scene inside that Church was one which defies all description. It was a large Church for the size of the town, and the whole of the floor space was covered with mattresses: we even had to put them on the altar steps. Wounded men, covered in mud and blood, were everywhere; and space was so precious that we could not even keep gang-ways through the rows of mattresses: to get to our patients we had to step over others. Many of the wounds were very serious, and my bottle of morphia was in constant request;- in fact, it was very soon empty and I got a fresh stock from a chemist in the town. After dark the difficulty was to get the place lighted, but the Curé - who was a charming old fellow, and intensely anxious to be helpful - himself gave us the thick wax candles off the Altar. I

I managed to find in a shop also some pastilles which gave off a pleasant odour when burned, and I used to keep a dozen or so burning all round the Church in order to counteract the horrible odour - as of a shambles - which otherwise pervaded it.

During the three nights that I spent in Vailly I slept altogether about five hours. Fresh batches of wounded kept coming in at all hours of the day and night, and the work was absolutely incessant. Nevertheless there were occasional diversions, even in Vailly. One day I was asked to go and see two children in the town who had been wounded by the bombardment. I was taken along a street, and down into the underground cellars with which most of the houses were provided. Here I found two children, one of them slightly and the other seriously wounded. I dressed their wounds, and the parents, who had a large assortment of live stock with them in the cellars, gave me four eggs as a fee. I took these eggs back to the Church and offered them to a good many of the wounded, both officers and men, but I could not get a single man to accept one; every man said he was quite sure there must be some who wanted it worse than he did. Eventually I gave them to some French civilians who had been wounded in the bombardment and admitted into our Dressing Station.

On another occasion a French woman came to the Church and asked for someone to go with her to the assistance of a wounded English soldier who was in a house at the South end of the town near the bridge. This was the part which was always the most heavily shelled. I took a couple of stretcher bearers and a stretcher, and went with her to rescue the soldier. As we went down the street a high explosive shell burst about twenty yards in front of us, but the Frenchwoman took absolutely no notice of it, so we could hardly do less. She then turned into a side street in which all the houses except three had been totally shattered by the bombardment; in one of the houses that still stood we found a Frenchman suffering from two not very severe wounds. She had told us a deliberate lie about the case, no doubt because she thought that we were more likely to come to the rescue of a British soldier than of a French civilian. Of course we were rather annoyed at being "had", but were bound to make the best of it. What happened to the Frenchman eventually I never heard, because immediately on getting back to the Church I was taken to Dr. Lancry's house to do an amputation, and I do not know what the bearers did with the Frenchman.

A good many of our wounded died in the Dressing Station, and we generally had them buried in the garden of the Dr.'s house. One day when a grave was being dug for this purpose the diggers unearthed a collection of silver plate and other treasures, which the Doctor had evidently hidden there before he fled from his house; we immediately had the hoard covered up, and the graves were dug after that in another part of the garden.

I can remember another case which raised a somewhat disputable point. A soldier was taken into Dr. Lancry's house suffering from a horrible shell wound of the abdomen. A piece of his abdominal wall about as big as a pudding plate had been shot clean away, and one could see two or three broken ribs, a large piece of his liver, large intestine, small intestine, and omentum in the cavity. Although men have recovered many times in this War from wounds which apparently must have been fatal, in this case it was indisputable that recovery was totally out of the question. I advised that the man should be given a poisonous dose of morphia at once; but I was overruled, and the man lingered on for two or three days occupying a bed which had better have been given to somebody less seriously wounded. It is of course a very large question whether any doctor is ever justified in deliberately killing a patient; but I think if ever that course is humane and defensible, it was so in this case. The man was unconscious from the shock of his injuries, so there was no question of his being able to send any messages to his relatives, to make a will, or anything of that sort; he was of course, given small doses of morphia - enough to prevent his feeling pain - but if I had had charge of him I should have given him two grains straight off.

Another case I can remember is that of a man who was in the Church suffering from a compound fracture of the femur. He was in great pain, so I anæsthetised him with chloroform whilst I put him on a long splint. Having thus set his fracture, I passed on to other cases, and about half an hour later whilst engaged with

one of them, an orderly came up and asked me to go at once to the
patient with the fractured femur; I thought something must have
gone wrong with him, so I crossed the Church to where he lay. When
I got there he seized my hand and kissed it, explaining to me
that he had sent for me to thank me for the comfort in which he
now found himself on recovering from the anaesthetic. I was
slightly annoyed at having been called away from a serious case
merely to receive this expression of thanks, but I had not the
heart to rebuke him.

On one occasion a soldier was taken into the Church
with a nasty shell wound which exposed his collar bone, and a
moderate sized artery was bleeding under the bone. There was
some difficulty in stopping the haemorrhage but at last I managed
to do it by some tight plugging and firm bandaging, and left the
man lying on his mattress with instructions that he was on no
account to allow anybody to touch his bandages except myself, and
that if the pain caused by the constriction of the shoulder became
unbearable, he was to send word to me about it. About an hour
or two later, as I was making my round of the Church, I was horrified to see a French V.A.D. lady unbandaging my patient. I
went up to find out what was going on, and asked the man why he
had not obeyed my instructions, and why he had let the French girl
attempt to dress his wounds. He told me that he had had very
severe pain, and that the French lady was so kind that he had not
told her of my orders.- also probably the soldier could not speak
French. The French V.A.D. lady was not sufficiently trained to
know that she was doing anything wrong, and possibly it was the
discovery that her energy had been misdirected that prevented
these girls from doing as much work in the Church as they did in
the School and the doctor's house. They were always very willing
and obliging, and nothing was too much trouble for them. The
same was true of the old Curé, who frequently used to undertake
odd jobs like fetching buckets of water, and other household
drudgery.

Every night after dark the Ambulance Wagons of Nos. 7,
8 or 9 Field Ambulance, came up from/Chasemy to the edge of the
Braine via
wood on the South side of the river, where Fielding was stationed
on the day Foster and I had a stretcher party behind the haystacks.

There they halted, and bearer parties with stretchers were sent across the pontoon bridge into the town. All the patients who were fit to be moved were then carried on stretchers or assisted to walk down through the town and across the river to where the Ambulances were waiting, and were driven back to Braine. Many of the cases, however, were much too bad to be moved in this way, but on the last day that I was there, September 17th., an order was received that all cases were to be evacuated no matter how serious they might be. This looked rather ominous, and I took it to mean that the military authorities were not by any means sure they could maintain their foothold on the North bank of the Aisne. Although I did evacuate a great many cases in obedience to this order which were really not fit to travel, I did keep back a handful of the worst of all. This evacuation of the wounded from Vailly after dark was quite an exciting affair at times. The enemy used to send a shell or two at the pontoon bridge every twenty minutes during the night, so once a shell had burst there one felt reasonably safe for the next quarter of an hour or so; but if one happened to be going down with wounded to the bridge and no shell had come for a good many minutes, there was always a good chance of catching one just as the bearers got to the bridge.

After the first 48 hours in Vailly our troops got themselves fairly well dug in, and the number of casualties steadily diminished. At the same time the enemy's shells began falling more and more thickly in the upper part of the town, as the lower part was by this time pretty well demolished. On the last night that I was there three houses in the little square in front of the Church were demolished by artillery during the night, and a large lump of shell was found on the doorstep of the main entrance to the Church. Bullets used to sing down the streets of the town pretty well all day; fortunately the walls of the Church - which was made of stone - were several feet in thickness and no bullet could do them any harm. Occasionally they would come in through the windows, all of which were high up from the ground. So far as I know we had only one orderly wounded during these three days.

After I left Vailly on the night of September 17th. the shelling got nearer and nearer to the Church, and it was thought advisable to clear all the western end of the Church of wounded. Not many hours after this had been done a shell came through the walls of the Church, and burst inside. Fortunately not a single one of the wounded was touched, but the incident throws a curious light upon the psychology of War and the veracity of the British soldier. It so happened that a private of the Northumber^{land}/ Fusiliers, a battalion of /which Regiment formed part of our Division, was lying wounded that night on a mattress on the altar steps of the East end of the Church. After he had been taken to England he gave a description which was published in the "Daily Mail" of his adventures and experiences in France. He described how he had been wounded, how his pals had taken him away from the trenches and handed him over to stretcher bearers, how he had been admitted to the Church ^{and}/placed on a mattress on the altar steps, and how a shell came into the other end of the Church. So far his story was absolutely accurate in every detail; but he ended up by saying that fifty of the wounded lying in the Church were killed. No doubt he was too far away to be able to see actually what occurred, and quite possibly he believed what he stated in the "DailyMail"; at the same time his account of the fifty deaths was totally unfounded, and I mention the incident to show how a man can ^{give}/get a perfectly truthful account of experiences in War, and yet end it up with a gross and culpable inaccuracy.

On the same night that we went into Vailly Major Fielding took a party of No. 7. Field Ambulance across the river. He established himself in a barn somewhere outside the town; I never succeeded in discovering where it was, but I fancy it was on the East side somewhere. When his barn got full of wounded, he used to send them on to us, and we heard many stories of Major Fielding's intrepidity. This very able and very gallant officer had a complete contempt for fire of all kinds; his men said that his favourite amusement was catching shells in his hat. One of the stories we heard about him at this time was that he had driven an Ambulance wagon out between the German trenches and our own. It was certainly true that he had an Ambulance wagon with him, whereas we had none with us, but I fancy this story was an exaggeration. Anyhow Major Fielding's reputation throughout the 3rd. Division for daring and gallantry was second to none, and he was in all respects the beau ideal of a R.A.M.C. Officer. I shall have more to say of him later on.

The old Curé, who was so very helpful to us, was a fine fellow. More than once he expressed to me his profound admiration for the stoicism of the British wounded. It is absolutely true that in that Church, crammed with wounded men, many of them with broken limbs and horrible shell wounds, it was a rare thing to hear the slightest sound indicative of pain; the half dozen or more of the wounded French civilians whom we had there made more noise than five hundred wounded English soldiers. I can never think of Vailly without thinking also of the wonderful hardihood of our fellows. In such circumstances British soldiers are seen at their best; their wonderful restraint and mutual sympathy with one another, excited my perpetual admiration. I can remember a young Officer coming into the Church with two boxes of cigarettes which he had just received by post from England; he gave me the two boxes for distribution to the wounded, so I proceeded to give them out. I heard one of the wounded say:

"'Aint he a toff to bring us these; they didn't cost less than ten bob a hundred."

The Brigadier of the 8th. Brigade, Brig. General B.J.C. Doran, used to come down and inspect our arrangements from time to time: although nothing very wonderful intellectually, he was a fine old soldier, and he was credited with the statement that "He would be damned if the Germans should push him back across the Aisne, as long as one English soldier could stand upon his legs." This was rather poor comfort for us at the Dressing Station, for if the Brigadier had carried out his intention, it would have meant that we should all have been captured by the Germans instead of being able to make our escape. However, the story may not have been true, though we believed it at the time.

During our stay in Vailly there was so much work for the Medical Officers to do in the Dressing Station, that it was impossible to spare one to go out with the Bearer Parties; the result was that our Bearer Parties had to go out under the N.C.O's., and so far as I know they did their work very well. On one occasion a soldier of the 4th. Middlesex came in to conduct a Bearer Party up to a trench where there were a lot of wounded. It was broad daylight at the time, but the guide managed to lose his way and led the whole party straight into a German trench. The corporal in this bit of trench made them all prisoners, but on conducting them to the nearest officer, that worthy - who cannot have been quite so Hunnish as the rest of his countrymen are - reprimanded the Corporal for taking Red Cross Orderlies prisoners, and released the whole lot at once. They arrived back in Vailly a good deal scared, but none the worse for their adventure. Nearly two years after this time Corporal Voysey, who had become a Sergeant in the meanwhile, received the medal for Distinguished Conduct in the Field for his good work at Vailly, but I do not know whether he was with this particular party.

On the night of September 17th. Major Maurice sent up two or three Officers of No. 8 F.A. to relieve us Greenfield and myself; Major Foster was not relieved as there was no Officer in No. 8 F.A. of his standing who could relieve him. Greenfield and I were rather annoyed at having to go, and I think we both felt that we would have preferred to see it out with Foster; however, the orders were definite, and the relief had arrived, so there was nothing for it but to return.with the evening evacuation of wounded across the river, and so via Chassemy to Braine.

By the time we got to Braine it was after mid-night, and the only direction I had as to where No. 8 F.A. was established was to keep along the road leading S.E. out of the town till I got to the Railway Station. However, as it was pitch dark, and I did not know how far the Railway Station was, I went into a large building which I passed, and discovered that it was being used by Captain Mc. Queen of No. 7. F.A. as a temporary clearing station. Mc.Queen was asleep on three chairs and was wrapped up in a blanket, so I seized three more chairs, wrapped myself up in some curtains which were handy, and went to sleep too. Early next morning I went along to the Railway Station, and found No. 8.F.A. camped in a field, with the Officers' Mess established in a small pub just opposite the station.

This day, September 18th. I had a good rest at Braine and

61.

wrote out for Major Maurice an account of the adventures of Foster, Greenfield and myself since we had been detached from the Ambulance. That evening I was sent off to Vailly again in charge of the convoy for evacuating the wounded. It was now my turn to go across the bridge in the dark with a lot of stretcher bearers, and up to the Church to evacuate wounded. I had some food with Foster and the others there, heard the story of the shell which had come into the Church, and found that things were settling down and casualties becoming rapidly fewer; I got back to Braine somewhere about midnight. And now began a very pleasant interlude after our weary Retreat, and the subsequent labours of the Advance and of Vailly.

There was very little work to do in Braine, and we led a comparatively civilized life in our little pub - I even had a bedroom, and a bed to sleep on -with plenty of spare time in which to explore the country round about. Braine is a little market town through which meanders the river Vesle (a tributary of the Aisne) which rises close to Rheims; and there is quite a fine church there. On this river, and within 100 yards of the pub where we were living opposite the railway station, there was a bathing shed which was quite useful.

On September 20th. I spent a good many hours helping to load three Hospital Trains which arrived to take away the wounded; over a thousand wounded from Vailly and other parts of the Front were evacuated from Braine that day.

On September 21st. I was again sent to Vailly at night in charge of a Convoy; and it was on this night also that No. 9 F.A. relieved Major Foster and our fellows at Vailly. When No. 9 F.A. took over charge at Vailly they decided to live in the Curé's cellars - a precaution for which we were inclined to jeer at them, though on looking back I certainly think it was a wise one. They did not have nearly so arduous a time in Vailly as we had had because the daily casualties had fallen to very small dimensions by this time. Major Foster had borne the principal burden of the work at Vailly, for he had been there a week when he was relieved. The experience had told upon him very greatly, and for months afterwards his nerves were not at all good; he had a horrible hunted look in his eyes, which took a long time to wear off: but he had the satisfaction of being mentioned in Despatches, as was also Major Fielding of No. 7 F.A.

In a large building within the Station precincts was established a part of No. 2. Casualty Clearing Station in charge of Major Leake, R.A.M.C. - now Lieut. Colonel Leake, C.M.G. Leake was a very good fellow, and he was badly understaffed, so I frequently used to go and give him a hand at dressing his cases. As he was alone, we made him a temporary member of our Mess, and we all got on very well with him.

During the day many of us devoted ourselves to riding and walking about the country round Braine. Most of our expeditions had material objects - such as the purchase of eggs, chickens and other additions to our menu, and we also had parties to collect blackberries and apples.

On September 23rd. I rode out to Cuiry Housse to see my old friend Charles Hacard, also to buy some eggs off him if possible. He received me with open arms, but had no eggs, as unfortunately an Army Service Corps crowd were camped not far away and they bought all his eggs about 5 a.m. every morning. On this day I met an old South African friend, Captain Lloyd Jones, R.A.M.C, on the Station at Braine. I took him into our Mess to have a meal, and found out that he had been through the Retreat as Medical Officer to the King's Liverpool Regiment, in which another old South African friend - Percy Hudson - was Adjutant. Lloyd Jones had been transferred from the Liverpools to take charge of No. 4 Field Ambulance, which had suffered very serious casualties in Officers and materiel in the Retreat from Mons. When I met him he was just going down to Paris to get new wagons and new supplies. He afterwards made a great success of this Field Ambulance, which corresponded with the Guards Brigade: he ultimately got the D.S.O. for his work in this connection.

It was on one of these days at Braine that I came across that very gallant fellow Captain Rankin, R.A.M.C. When I saw him he was lying on a stretcher on Braine Station platform; he was smoking a cigarette and talking with animation. He had recently had his leg amputated somewhere above the knee, but said he was in no pain and was quite comfortable and well. We were horribly shocked to hear a day or two later that he had died suddenly of Embolism; but he had already received the award of the V.C. for his work at the time when he received his injuries.

On September 24th. I rode over to Mont Notre Dame a few miles from Braine, where a Company of the London Scottish was employed at the Railway Station. As luck would have it I found in this Company my cousin, Sergt. Harry Kerr, and also another friend, Corporal St. John Young. I stayed with them some little time, went up the hill to see the beautiful ruined Abbey of Mont Notre Dame, and then went back to Braine.

By this time Major Maurice had got fairly settled in the saddle, and had already brought about several much needed improvements in No. 8 F.A. for one thing he had sacked Sergt. Blake, and obtained from the Divisional Train a much better N.C.O. in his place. This was Sergt. Vaughan, who was quite a good man, though not the equal of the wonderful Snape. Vaughan always pulled very well with Major Maurice, and the transport section worked infinitely better than it had done in Sergt. Blake's time. The Major had also effected a change for the better in our messing arrangements. Col. Stone's restriction on the formation of a Mess was of course broken down immediately Major Maurice took command; and the Mess cook, whose name was James, having been caught by the Major in the act of using dirty dishes for our food, was promptly sacked, and somebody else whose name I can't remember was put in his place. James was a decent old thing, but had no idea of cooking and no idea of cleanliness; he did much better as a bearer than as a cook, and was always very steady under fire. Meeke always used to speak of James as "the "food-spoiler."

In the cellars of the public house in which we were established we found two casks of wine, one red and the other white; it was pretty poor stuff certainly, but better than drinking water of whose antecedents we were dubious, so for some days we subsisted upon the wine. One night, however, burglars broke into the cellars, and in the morning the casks were practically empty. There is no doubt that some of our own men did this, but all our efforts failed to discover who the culprits were. Although some of the officers were very indignant, I did not feel that the men were so very much to blame, as the wine belonged to them just as much or as little as it did to us. I may mention here that during the first

few weeks of the Campaign we had a lot of trouble with ~~thieves~~ thefts by the men; no property was secure, and the Mess cups and plates disappeared almost as soon as they were bought. By the time we got to Braine almost every man in the Ambulance had an enamelled cup and plate; as our mess stock had required to be replenished/during this period there is no doubt that many
two or three times over
of these cups and plates were really Mess property, but one enamelled cup is very like another, so that it was impossible ever to prove that thefts had occurred. The reason for this making free with our property was no doubt that the hastily mobilized men of the Unit neither knew nor cared two-pence about their officers; as we got to know them and they got to know us, we gradually had less and less trouble of this sort.

Major Maurice was a good disciplinarian, by which I mean that he kept discipline reasonably tight without being a martinet, and without hazing the men. He dropped on several offenders pretty heavily the first week or two as an example to the rest; and it was part of his policy to insist on all the junior Officers attending at the orderly room when he was "telling off" the prisoners.

One of the cases which were tried by Major Maurice at this time was that of an orderly who disappeared from Braine under circumstances which at the time were mysterious. No one knew where he had gone and he was regarded as a deserter. It appeared afterwards, that he had accompanied a wounded Officer to the platform of Braine Station where a hospital train was being loaded. He helped put the Officer's baggage on to the train and was also very officious in giving a hand at some work for the nursing sister on the train. Having thus carried favour with her he then offered to accompany the Officer to the Base and look after him on the way down. Probably the Officer had no idea that the orderly did not belong to the Ambulance Train for he accepted this offer, and the man accordingly travelled down on the train. The Officer Commanding the train knew nothing about his presence, and he made himself so useful to the sister that she asked no questions. Unfortunately for this young rascal the Railhead for most of the Ambulance Trains at this time was Braine, so that it was only 4 or 5 days before the same train turned up again at that town. When this happened somebody spotted our friend the orderly at the station, although he kept himself in the back ground as far as possible. Before an escort could be sent to arrest him the train had gone again, but now that we knew what had become of him it was a simple matter to meet that train the next time it arrived at Braine. The man was arrested and tried. The Staff gave permission for his offence to be treated as "absence without leave" instead of "desertion", and he escaped with 28 days Confined to Barracks, which is/the maximum penalty that could be imposed without a Court Martial.

It was on one of these days, I think on September 22nd or 23rd, that a very sad death occurred at Braine. We had established a sort of temporary off-shoot of Major Leake's Clearing Station in the principal room of our pub, where we could take in a dozen or so patients; a young Officer of the Northumberland Fusiliers was brought down from Vailly with a very serious wound of the Pelvic Viscera. He was in a bad state of collapse, and though he revived for a short time after transfusion - which I performed - he soon after collapsed again and died. His name was Lieut. Tottie; and his brother was drowned the same day that he died in the disaster to H.M.S. Cressy. He was buried in the Station-master's garden at Braine, along with a few other soldiers who died in Major Leake's Clearing Station: I made a sketch of his grave and sent it to his people at home.

On September 25th. I see in my diary that the only event of importance was the purchase of a goose, and the procuring of a large stock of apples and blackberries. Although about this time we had plenty of leisure and very few duties to perform, we generally made ourselves useful to somebody - either to the Hospital Train people or to Major Leake, or in some other way. There was always plenty going on on the Railway Station; new drafts were constantly arriving, and the station was a great scene of bustle and traffic all day. MacPherson and Meeke were always very busy on the Station distributing post-cards to the wounded men and collecting them again when the men had filled them in and addressed them; and their work was so much appreciated by both Officers and men who were passing through wounded that they both got mentioned in Dispatches.

About this time Motor Ambulances put in their appearance for the first time during the Campaign, and although they were at first very few in number, their speed compensated for this and made them exceedingly useful. They were not sent to Vailly on the nocturnal expeditions to evacuate the wounded, but were kept for transferring wounded from the main Casualty Clearing Station in Braine to the Railway Station, which is about three-quarters of a mile outside the town. The visits to Vailly to evacuate the wounded became less strenuous as the number of casualties diminished. Word was sent every evening to the A.D.M.S. as to the approximate number of cases, and the requisite number of wagons were then detailed from Nos. 7, 8 and 9 F.A's.. There was another bracing stunt of the same kind which fell to our lot, and that was the removal after dark of wounded from Brenelle, where most of the Divisional Artillery were stationed on the top of a ridge overlooking the river. They bombarded the Germans on the heights opposite, and the Germans bombarded them. They lived in some large caves, but had a fair number of casualties, and wagons had to be sent there nearly every night. The road was described very hilly and very bad, but I never happened to be allocated to this particular job.

My boots had got pretty well worn through by this time, so I took the opportunity of having them soled at a bootmakers in Braine; I also bought there a pair of French civilian boots of fantastic design. The man assured me that they were real Balmorals; I do not ever remember buying Balmoral boots before, and I have no intention of ever buying them again. Nevertheless they were fairly comfortable, if rather eccentric in pattern. Another useful individual whom we encountered at Braine for the first time was the Field Cashier, a Major Beamish. A Regulation was introduced to the effect that Officers might draw from the Field Cashier not more than £5 at a time, and not more than £15 in any one month. The difficulty was to find the Field Cashier, who was a most elusive personage; but, having spent most of one day in following him about, I at last ran him to earth and got my £5, which was very useful as the money I had brought from England was all spent. The official regulation laid down that Officers of the Special Reserve were not entitled to this privilege but only those of the Regular Army. When Major Beamish asked me whether I was Regular or Special Reserve, I replied quite truthfully that I was Regular, not Special Reserve, and drew my £5; but those Temporarily Commissioned Officers who were foolish enough to tell Beamish that they were Temporarily Commissioned were told that this placed them on the same footing as the Special Reserve, and they got no money. This stupid restriction was afterwards removed, but it would have been far better if it had never been enacted.

On September 26th I went over to Mont Notre Dame again and saw my cousin, who was afterwards very badly wounded at Messines and had to be invalided out of the Army as his wounds took eighteen months to heal. At Mont Notre Dame the most excellent pears and apples could be purchased, and I took a small sack-full of them back to Braine for the Mess.

On September 30th. I went out with Major Maurice and one or two other officers on an Expedition to Courcelles and the heights above it in the direction of Dhuizcel and Vieild'Arcy. From the top of this ridge, which is the same as that on which Brenelle is, we could see across the valley of the Aisne on to the hills where the 1st Corps were fighting. The previous day I had been for a tour round through Courcelles, Bazoches, and home via Mont Notre Dame. On this latter expedition I called at a very large farm on the high road towards Rheims with the idea of getting some provisions. The farm buildings consisted of two very large square court-yards adjoining each other. All the front doors were locked; on going round to the back I managed to find my way in through a small postern door, and found myself in a large yard where twenty or thirty geese, about forty or fifty ducks, and over a hundred hens were disporting themselves. I found an aged farmer and offered to buy some eggs, but he said he hadn't got any; so I then offered to buy either a fowl or a duck or a goose, and was told there were none for sale. In the room where he sat were several sacks full to the top of walnuts; so I offered to buy some walnuts, but these also he declined to sell. I told him what I thought of him as far as my limited French vocabulary would allow, and went out. Outside the building there was a very nice orchard, so I proceeded to fill my pockets with apples. The old man came waddling out whilst I was doing this and wanted to stop me. I told him that I had offered to buy his things, and he had refused to sell them; that but for the English he would have had the Germans in his farm who would have taken everything he had got in the world, and that I intended to take a few apples and also some blackberries of which there was a large crop growing on some bushes. He abused me, saying that the English were far worse thieves than the Germans; but I took no notice of him at all, and rode off with my pockets and haversack bursting.

It was on either September 30th or October 1st, I rather think the morning of the latter, that one of our Non-Commissioned Officers reported to the Major that he had seen a pile of Medical Stores reposing in a ditch alongside the road from Braine to Courcelles. Some of these stores were reported to be labelled "No.8 Field Ambulance", and as we were decidedly deficient in this part of our equipment, a wagon was harnessed up and I was sent off in charge of it to bring in the loot. When I got nearly to Courcelles I found a heap of cases which were covered with a tarpaulin but otherwise quite abandoned. On looking them over I found that several cases were labelled with the names of Battalions in the 3rd Division. About half of these were for the 8th Brigade and the rest for Battalions in the other two Brigades. I had also passed on the road a good many soldiers belonging to the 8th Brigade and had found out from them that the Brigade was in billets at Courcelles, having just been withdrawn from the trenches at Vailly. I therefore loaded up the wagon with all the cases that were labelled for the Battalions of our Brigade, took them into Courcelles, distributed them to the Regimental Medical Officers, who were exceedingly glad to get them as they were practically out of supplies, and then drove back to pick up the rest of the stores. Those for Battalions not in our Brigade I left at the A.D.M.S's. Office in Braine, and those for our Field Ambulance I took back to camp. I gave no receipt to anybody for these medical stores nor did I take receipts from the Officers to whom I distributed them. So possibly someone or other was deficient in his amount of a quantity of valuable R.A.M.C. equipment. Whoever he was he had left them unguarded at the side of a high-way so it was his own fault entirely if he did not know what happened to them.

www.ingramcontent.com/pod-product-compliance
Lightning Source LLC
Chambersburg PA
CBHW080821010526
44111CB00015B/2589

9781474504348